Playing the Globe

Playing the Globe

Genre and Geography
in English Renaissance Drama

Edited by
John Gillies
and Virginia Mason Vaughan

Madison • Teaneck
Fairleigh Dickinson University Press
London: Associated University Presses

© 1998 by Associated University Presses, Inc.

All rights reserved. Authorization to photocopy items for internal or personal use, or the internal or personal use of specific clients, is granted by the copyright owner, provided that a base fee of $10.00, plus eight cents per page, per copy is paid directly to the Copyright Clearance Center, 222 Rosewood Drive, Danvers, Massachusetts 01923. [0-8386-3739-6/98 $10.00+8¢ pp, pc.]

Associated University Presses
440 Forsgate Drive
Cranbury, NJ 08512

Associated University Presses
16 Barter Street
London WC1A 2AH, England

Associated University Presses
P.O. Box 338, Port Credit
Mississauga, Ontario
Canada L5G 4L8

The paper used in this publication meets the requirements of the American National Standard for Permanence of Paper for Printed Library Materials Z39.48–1984.

Library of Congress Cataloging-in-Publication Data

Playing the globe : genre and geography in English Renaissance drama / edited by John Gillies and Virginia Mason Vaughan.
   p.   cm.
Includes bibliographical references and index.
Contents: The mental maps of English Renaissance drama / Virginia Mason Vaughan — Elizabethan drama and the cartographizations of space / John Gillies — Gelded continents and plenteous rivers / Bruce Avery — A room not one's own / Rhonda Lemke Sanford — Genre and geography / Linda McJannet — Shakespeare's Greek world / Sara Hanna — Britain and the great beyond / Richmond Barbour — Slave-born Muscovites / John Michael Archer — Strange outlandish wealth / Barbara Sebek — Marlowe, the Timur myth, and the motives of geography / John Gillies — The "strange" geographies of Cymbeline / Glenn Clark — Domains of victory / Anthony Miller.
  ISBN 0-8386-3739-6 (alk. paper)
  1. English drama—Early modern and Elizabethan, 1500–1600—History and criticism. 2. Geography in literature. 3. English drama—17th century—History and criticism. 4. Geographical discoveries in literature. 5. English drama—Foreign influences. 6. Geographical myths in literature. 7. Space and time in literature. 8. Renaissance—England. 9. Literary form. I. Gillies, John, 1947– . II. Vaughan, Virginia Mason.
PR678.G46P57 1998
822'.30932—dc21   97-34945
                                                                              CIP

PRINTED IN THE UNITED STATES OF AMERICA

Contents

Preface: The Mental Maps of English Renaissance Drama VIRGINIA MASON VAUGHAN	7
Introduction: Elizabethan Drama and the Cartographizations of Space JOHN GILLIES	19
Gelded Continents and Plenteous Rivers: Cartography as Rhetoric in Shakespeare BRUCE AVERY	46
A Room Not One's Own: Feminine Geography in *Cymbeline* RHONDA LEMKE SANFORD	63
Genre and Geography: The Eastern Mediterranean in *Pericles* and *The Comedy of Errors* LINDA MCJANNET	86
Shakespeare's Greek World: The Temptations of the Sea SARA HANNA	107
Britain and the Great Beyond: *The Masque of Blackness* at Whitehall RICHMOND BARBOUR	129
Slave-Born Muscovites: Racial Difference and the Geography of Servitude in *Astrophil and Stella* and *Love's Labor's Lost* JOHN MICHAEL ARCHER	154
"Strange Outlandish Wealth": Transglobal Commerce in *The Merchant's Mappe of Commerce* and *The Fair Maid of the West, Parts I and II* BARBARA SEBEK	176
Marlowe, the *Timur* Myth, and the Motives of Geography JOHN GILLIES	203
The "Strange" Geographies of *Cymbeline* GLENN CLARK	230

Domains of Victory: Staging and Contesting the Roman
Triumph in Renaissance England 260
  ANTHONY MILLER

Contributors 288
Index 290

Preface: The Mental Maps of English Renaissance Drama

VIRGINIA MASON VAUGHAN

OUR world has become increasingly fragmented. Torn apart by religious, political, linguistic, racial, and cultural differences, the human race now seems more prone to think and act locally than globally. The map of Europe changes almost daily, as ethnic groups assert their independence in Russia, Georgia, and, most violently, in Bosnia. In Rwanda and Burundi, warring tribes seek to exterminate each other. In the Western Hemisphere, even the seemingly stolid state of Canada may be dissolved because French-speaking Quebeçois want their own country.

A characteristic of all these struggles is a need to live in social groupings that share comfortable commonalties—kinship, language, education, customs, dress, religion, and so forth. Inside the group, whether it be the Greek *polis*, the Roman *civitas*, the European nation-state, or the American Indian tribe, shared customs and values foster a sense of common heritage and collective identity. Ever since the ancient Greeks labeled people outside the city as "barbarians," human communities have measured themselves, even defined themselves, in contrast to outsiders. The resulting anxieties about the other have often prompted conquest, colonization, or efforts at amalgamation.

Exposure to people from radically different backgrounds evokes a variety of responses. Sometimes we emphasize the perceived differences, even to the point of demonizing the other. An example might be the monsters in the popular American film *Aliens*: ferocious, carnivorous, horrifying, the filmmakers created them to look and act in opposition to all the qualities we think of as human. Filmmakers also can evoke the opposite response, emphasizing characteristics that make alien creatures seem amazingly human—"like us." The extraterrestrial in Stephen Spielberg's *ET*, for example, looked strange but cuddly, and movie audiences were moved by his "human" qualities, especially the conflict he felt between longing to go home and love for his adopted human family.

In their approaches to interplanetary life, contemporary filmmakers are practicing what John Gillies describes (in a term borrowed from the eighteenth-century philosopher Giambattista Vico) as "poetic geography": "'the property of human nature that in describing unknown or distant things, in respect of which they ... have not had the true idea themselves ... men make use of the semblances of things known or near at hand.'"[1] In the Renaissance, when reports from Africa and the New World struck their readers as fabulous as science fiction strikes us today, the writers sought to describe what they saw in terms of what they knew. Tribal chieftains were described as "kings," and clothing (or the lack thereof) was compared to European dress.

Explorers' accounts were greeted with wonder and anxiety. Portuguese navigation around the Cape of Good Hope and the exploration of the New World brought not only new knowledge to England but new questions. The topography, flora, fauna, and most importantly, the human inhabitants of these territories were drastically different. Somehow the burgeoning new information, whether fact or fancy, had to be assimilated. New spaces were mapped and new peoples categorized according to their similarity to, or difference from, the familiar inhabitants of the Old World. Wonder itself became commodified: "wonder cabinets" of artifacts from Africa and the New World proliferated in Europe during the early modern period, and Trinculo claims that in England "they will lay out ten to see a dead Indian."[2]

By the late sixteenth century, literate English people could explore this world of wonder from the comfort of their own homes through books. For cartographic knowledge, they could turn to the Latin text of Abraham Ortelius's *Theatrum Orbis Terrarum* (1570), the first systematic atlas ever published. There readers found the world delineated spatially: they could begin with a map of the entire known world, follow with maps of each of the four continents, and proceed to individual countries. According to Robert W. Karrow, "the importance of the *Theatrum Orbis Terrarum* for geographical knowledge in the last quarter of the sixteenth century is difficult to overemphasize."[3] Unsurpassed until Mercator's atlas appeared twenty-five years later, Ortelius's *Theatrum* went through twenty-four editions during his lifetime. It circulated widely in Europe and remained in print until 1612. More to the point, because Ortelius's maps are the focal point of several discussions in the essays that follow, it is important to understand their impact on western European thought in the late sixteenth century.

Born in Antwerp in 1527, Abraham Ortelius began his career as an illuminator of maps. After developing a successful business as a dealer in antiques, old coins, and maps, he traveled through Europe, collecting maps as he went. During the 1550s, he met the leading cartographers of Europe and became close friends with Gerhard Mercator. Trips to England introduced him to John Dee, Richard Hakluyt, and William Camden. In the 1560s, he launched a scheme to produce a new kind of atlas. Until then, collections of maps could be bought, but they were custom-designed for the individual buyer and included uneven sheets and incompatible designs. Ortelius's innovation was to have the maps engraved in a uniform shape and design and to add a geographical description of each major location.

The first *Theatrum* consisted of seventy maps and fifty-three sheets and included a list of the eighty-seven cartographers who had been used as sources. It sold out immediately. In response to his invitation for suggestions from his readers, Ortelius received many requests for additional maps, and some readers even sent him some of their own. Every five years he issued an "Additamenta" of new maps that could be bound with the previous volume, and the next full edition included the additional maps. The *Theatrum* grew from 53 sheets in 1570 to 119 in 1598, the year of Ortelius's death. After the first Latin editions, the atlas was translated and published in the vernacular languages of Europe, including a handsome English folio in 1606.

This anthology embodies the implied link between spectacle, drama, and geographic space assumed in Ortelius's title. *Orbis terrarum* reflects the Roman view of the world as a circular disk; *theatrum* poses the world as a stage, a setting for human action.[4] The monumentalizing frontispiece represents the four continents as female figures whose costumes and body language—like the actor's—convey an elaborate semiotic code. Europe, the regnant figure at the top, bears the cross and scepter. Her destiny is hegemony over the rest of the world; her duty is to Christianize and civilize the earth. Asia, to the left, is the exotic bearer of spices and perfumes. Africa, nearly naked (and colored black in illuminated copies of the atlas) is haloed by the hot rays of the sun. Below these known regions lies the young figure of America, totally naked, demurely holding the severed head of one of her conquests. The female bust beside her represents Magellanica, the terra incognita below the straits of Magellan.

The Frontispiece to Abraham Ortelius's *Theatrum Orbis Terrarum* (London, 1606). By permission of the Folger Shakespeare Library.

Like a magnificent classical portal, the frontispiece invites the reader to enter the entire world. Ortelius's maps and descriptions, culled from classical and contemporary cosmography, enabled the Renaissance viewer to visualize the great events of history, to understand the power relations of ancient cultures, and to understand the peoples and heroic characters of the past. Like the dramatist's poetry, the maps were intended to teach and delight through a wonderful combination of written text and visual spectacle.

As John Gillies's introduction to this volume makes clear, the sudden availability of geographic knowledge in the late sixteenth century from Ortelius's *Theatrum* and other sources, including Richard Hakluyt's compendium of travel narratives, *The Principal Navigations* (1589), created a revolution in ways of thinking about cartographic space. Such texts provided readers with a range of ways to be *mapminded* (to use Gillies's term): geographic, military, economic, classical, and romantic. The essays collected here explore these different ways of thinking and make what heretofore was unknown palpable and comprehensible. They cover a variety of spatial relations, cultures, and ethnic identities and discuss a wide range of literary texts, including works by Sidney, Marlowe, Jonson, Heywood, and not least, Shakespeare.

This book germinated in the seminar, "Playing Across the Globe: The Geography of English Renaissance Drama" at the Shakespeare Association of America's annual meeting in 1995. Since then, each essay has been carefully revised in light of the seminar's common themes. Many of the essays refer to a text that influenced much of the discussion, John Gillies's *Shakespeare and the Geography of Difference*, which was published shortly before the 1995 SAA and provided the most extensive analysis of Shakespearean geography since J. D. Rogers's chapter, "Voyages and Exploration: Geography; Maps," in *Shakespeare's England* (1932).[5] Linked with Gillies's other work, this anthology initiates a new period in the analysis of English Renaissance drama's conception of the world beyond English shores and of the others who inhabited those spaces.

Ever since ancient Babylonians and Egyptians drew the first maps, cultures have relied on pictorial images to chart the unknown. A map, according to the OED, is "A representation of the earth's surface or a part of it, its physical and political features, etc., or of the heavens, delineated on a flat surface of paper or other material, each point in the drawing corresponding to a geographical or celestial position according to a definite scale or projection." In this definition, the map is a material object that stands for a particular space. In contrast to a written itinerary that uses words to provide the reader with directions and a verbal picture of landmarks, the map is a visual representation that relies on shape, pattern, and sometimes color.

In the early modern period, a map could also be "a circumstantial account of a state of things" (OED 2a), or "the very picture or image of" (OED 2b), or "the mental conception of the arrangement of something" (OED 1b). Just as the topography of England's counties could be represented by lines on a sheet of paper,[6] a lover might map the contours of a woman's face, studying the visual image or, as a Petrarchan sonneteer might say, "drawing" it in the "table" of his heart.

Shakespeare is typical of his time in using the term *map* in both literal and figurative senses. In *King Lear* and *1 Henry IV*, Lear and Hotspur call for the display on stage of what seems to be a literal map. As Bruce Avery indicates in his analysis of these scenes, even with the material object at hand, its powers of accurate representation are subject to political manipulation. Thus, in the aftermath of Cordelia's refusal to comply with his wishes, Lear divides his kingdom into two portions instead of three, and Hotspur insists that the course of the Trent River be changed to enhance his portion.

Shakespeare also uses the word *map* in its second, more metaphorical sense. In *2 Henry VI*, for example, the saintly king pleads for his uncle Gloucester's life, arguing that in his face lies "the map of honor, truth, and loyalty" (3.1.203). To Queen Isabella, her husband Richard's face is "The map of honor" (*Richard II*, 5.1.12), while Lucrece's face is "a map which deep impression bears / Of hard misfortune, carv'd ... with tears" (*Rape of Lucrece*, 1712–13).

In Petrarchan love poetry, the face of the woman is an erotic space to be mapped. This gendered language of many English Renaissance sonnets parallels cartographic discourse, which like Ortelius's frontispiece, frequently personified the four continents as female figures. The metaphor of rape for the invasion and plundering of distant territories appears in Sir Walter Ralegh's famous claim that Guyana, as yet unexplored, "hath still her maydenhead." As Rhonda Sanford's discussion of *Cymbeline* demonstrates, Iachimo's inventory of Imogen's body, the act of mapping itself, implies penetration. Faced with Iachimo's knowledge of Imogen's most intimate feature, the mole beneath her breast, Posthumus assumes the worst, reading the visual image for the act of conquest itself.

As Lear and Hotspur no doubt realize, mapping is often "an instrument of national policy, partly conscious and officially controlled, partly spontaneous and inspired by private enterprise."[7] The one who draws the map asserts his or her control over the unknown, the mastery of geographic space unfamiliar to the map reader. In this way, the cartographer may be a kindred spirit with the dramatist, who also represents a hitherto unknown world on a flat surface.

Similar to the figures that populate Ortelius's cartouches, the characters in an English Renaissance drama are speaking pictures that represent both the audience's sense of its own cultural identity and the feared others of its imagination. As Linda McJannet shows in her analysis of *Pericles* and *The Comedy of Errors*, plays set in the Hellenistic culture of pre-Christian Greece could end on a note of reconciliation because the world they represented was bound by a single cultural tradition and, for the most part, by a shared language. By the time of Roman ascendancy, as Sara Hanna demonstrates in her survey of the Greek plays, that Hellenistic world was seen as the other in a binary opposition between Greece and Rome, between two different attitudes toward life, between different habits and customs.

The alien other came in many different shapes and colors to Elizabethan Englishmen. Any foreigner—were he or she German, Russian, French, or Spanish, not to mention Irish or Welsh—was to an ethnocentric culture inherently different and inferior. Of course, there were degrees of difference. The Catholic Spaniard, though corrupted by Catholicism and set apart by a different language, was more akin to the Protestant Englishman than the non-Christian, heathen Turk.[8] The tawny Moor, like the swarthy Spaniard, was perceived to be of darker hue than the white-skinned Englishman, but at least he or she was not black, the color of the devil.[9] Irish customs may have seemed as savage as those of New World natives, but at least the Irish were a known quantity.

The celebration of Englishness often entailed the disparagement of the stranger as a barbarian. As Richmond Barbour shows in his historical analysis of *The Masque of Blackness* and its reception, the exultation of British (and whiteness's) superiority could also betray nervousness that there might be more similarity with the alien other than could be admitted.

Love's Labor's Lost betrays similar concerns, as John Archer reveals. The court of Navarre begins with the desire to keep itself unpolluted by the female other; eventually, in pursuit of that other, it adopts the new and alien identity of "Muscovites," an appropriate choice because of the links between Russians and slavery, slavery and the discourse of romantic love. To map the woman's face can be seen as an act of colonization.

Anxiety about incorporating the other without becoming polluted—going native, so to speak—appears in early modern texts concerned with trade and commerce. The buying and selling of material artifacts can also be seen as an act of appropriation. The Englishman who buys a Persian rug and uses it in his own home transforms his space into something new, less "pure" than it was before. Similarly, the tourist's desire to take home a souvenir reflects the desire to possess, to own even a little piece of the country visited. As Barbara Sebek argues in her essay, commodity exchange was perceived in the Renaissance as threatening as well as desirable, as a process that could be disruptive and polluting, as well as lucrative.

The desire to conquer goes beyond notions of exchange to imply the transformation of another sort, whereby the conquered territory or people loses its original identity, becoming instead a mirror image of the conqueror. Tamburlaine's desire to expropriate the entire known world bespeaks, according to John Gillies, the uncanny, a dreamlike image "which is at once known and yet estranged." Tamburlaine's geography, one might add, is not a respector of difference. In his catalogue of the territories he has conquered, Tamburlaine makes few distinctions. Instead he flattens and conflates—all will become homogenized under his rule. He never mentions losses, yet that there were losses of culture and beauty (Damascus) we know, as Zenocrate tells us in her lament for the country of her birth.

Shakespeare's *Cymbeline* expresses a desire for union based on national identity rather than conquest. As Glenn Clark argues, the romance refracts James I's desire for a unified Great Britain—a harmonious confederation of England, Wales, and Scotland. Clark finds the only possibility of such harmony through Welsh ritual, which heals the breaches wrought in the corrupt English court. In the make-believe world of romance, the return to nature—to the uncultivated geographical space of Wales—can indeed spark a re-vision and healing. As James learned when his unification project failed, however, the political world is governed by harsher rules.

Anthony Miller expands on Renaissance political themes in

his analysis of Elizabethan and Jacobean appropriations of the Roman triumph. Elizabeth and James were frequently figured in public ceremonies as the "triumphator" who returns to Rome after the successful conquest of foreign territories and peoples. Though both monarchs preferred peacemaking to war, stressing conquest through benevolent largesse and Solomonic wisdom, the martial mode coexisted in pageants sponsored by militant Protestants who urged war against Europe's Catholic powers. London merchants also exploited the triumph motif in Lord Mayors' pageants that celebrated mastery over other countries through commercial ventures. Miller shows how these patterns are embedded in Shakespeare's Roman tragedies in ways that produce ambivalent responses to the Roman ideal of conquest.

As these essays demonstrate, the representation of geographic space and discourse varies from genre to genre. While the romances emphasize union by combining territories that had been radically separated under one beneficent ruler—Sicily and Bohemia at the conclusion of *The Winter's Tale,* Milan and Naples at the end of *The Tempest*—territory becomes a source of commodification and competition in *1 Henry IV* and *King Lear*. Moreover, just as the drama appears in a variety of genres, by the end of the sixteenth century, genres had also emerged in geographic thought. Within any dramatic text the two might be interconnected. Our subtitle, as must be apparent by now, resonates in this double sense: first, the genre of a play versus the type of mental map (commercial, political, patriarchal, etc.); second, the geography of the stage (the ways in which the action is mapped across it) and the geography of the greater world.

Our main title, *Playing the Globe,* is more obvious in import. The pun on Shakespeare's theater and the world itself has been with us ever since Prospero predicted that the great globe would dissolve, leaving not a rack behind.[10] If "all the world's a stage and all the men and women merely players," then to play the globe is to act out life itself on the broadest stage imaginable. The theater/theatrum connection suggests the English Renaissance's sense of endless possibilities and never-ending wonder in the world at large and in the smaller world of the playhouse.

By examining the ways early modern dramatists imagined the world and the peoples who inhabit it, *Playing the Globe* opens a window on cultural practices relating to the formation of individual and group identities. It surveys a variety of mental maps that continue to shape the ways the Anglo-American world imagines itself and its relationship to others and explores provocative new avenues into the world of English Renaissance drama.

Notes

I am grateful for assistance on this preface from Alden T. Vaughan, the staff of the Folger Shakespeare Library, and the staff of the Guy Burnham Map and Aerial Photography Library at Clark University.

1. See John Gillies, *Shakespeare and the Geography of Difference* (Cambridge: Cambridge University Press, 1994), 5.

2. For a discussion of England's reactions to the people of the New World, see Alden T. Vaughan, "People of Wonder: England Encounters the New World," in *New World of Wonders: European Images of the Americas, 1492–1700* (Seattle: University of Washington Press; distributed for the Folger Shakespeare Library, 1992), 11–23.

3. Robert W. Karrow, Jr., *Mapmakers of the Sixteenth Century and Their Maps* (Chicago: Speculum Orbis Press for the Newberry Library, 1993), 9. The discussion that follows is greatly indebted to this source and to John Goss, *The Mapmakers Art: An Illustrated History of Cartography* (New York: Rand McNally, 1993), 101–6. See also Gillies, *Geography of Difference*, 70–84.

4. R. A. Skelton discusses the origins of Ortelius's title in his introduction to the facsimile edition, *Theatrum Orbis Terrarum* (Cleveland, Ohio: World Publishing Co., 1964), vii.

5. See Gillies, *Geography of Difference*, 189.

6. Christopher Saxton, for example, was hired by the Privy Council from 1570–79 to map the counties of England and Wales. When he arrived in a town, he was to be "Conducted unto any towre, castle, high place or hill to view the country." See G. R. Crone, *Maps and Their Makers* (London: Hutchinson University Library, 1953), 108.

7. R. A. Skelton, *Maps: A Historical Survey of Their Study and Collecting* (Chicago: University of Chicago Press, 1972), 16–17.

8. For an interesting survey of English attitudes toward European foreigners, see A. J. Hoenselaars, *Image of Englishmen and Foreigners in the Drama of Shakespeare and His Contemporaries* (Rutherford: Fairleigh Dickinson University Press, 1992).

9. For a discussion of blackness in English Renaissance drama, see Anthony Gerard Barthelemy, *Black Face, Maligned Race: The Representation of Blacks in English Drama from Shakespeare to Southerne* (Baton Rouge, La.: University of Louisiana Press, 1987); Eldred D. Jones, *Othello's Countrymen: The African in English Renaissance Drama* (London: Oxford University Press, 1965); and Elliot H. Tokson, *The Popular Image of the Black Man in English Drama, 1550–1688* (Boston: G. K. Hall, 1982).

10. See Gillies, *Geography of Difference*, 84–92 for further discussion of the relationship between the Globe and geographical discourse.

Playing the Globe

Introduction: Elizabethan Drama and the Cartographizations of Space

JOHN GILLIES

In the England of 1500, maps were little understood or used. By 1600 they were familiar objects of everyday life. When Shakespeare wrote *Henry IV, Part 1* in 1597, he had Mortimer, Glendower, and Hotspur divide England and Wales between them by means of a map; these three historical characters in the early fifteenth century could not possibly have used a map in this way, but it is not surprising that Shakespeare—and his audiences—assumed they would.... But what made the cartographic revolution of the sixteenth century was not simply the discovery and acceptance of new techniques. Rather, it was the acceptance and spread of unfamiliar concepts. Far more than a revolution in the ways maps were made, it was a revolution in the ways of thought of those who used them.... What we see is successive extensions of an awareness of maps—of mapmindedness—until by the end of the 16c the map-maker could see any literate person as a potential customer.[1]

How many maps, in the descriptive or geographical sense, might be needed to deal exhaustively with a given space, to code and decode all its meanings and contents? It is doubtful whether a finite number can ever be given to this question.... It is not only the codes—the map's legend, the conventional signs of map-making and map-reading—that are liable to change, but also the objects represented, the lens through which they are viewed, and the scale used. The idea that a small number of maps or even a single (and singular) map might be sufficient can only apply in a specialized area of study whose own self-affirmation depends on isolation from its context.[2]

The essays gathered within this volume have two growing points. They arise simultaneously from a seminar of the 1995 conference of the Shakespeare Association of America and from a fertile confluence of the disciplines of geography, art history and literary/dramatic criticism—a moment of theorization in which the wider cultural investment of geographic practice (renaissance and modern) has become recognized and opened to a variety of hermeneutic approaches: semiotic, art historical, phenomenological, new-historicist, psychoanalytic, and post-structural.[3] These essays are the work of literary critics rather than of geographers and are accordingly about a special cultural mediation of geographic space (real, mapped, or imagined): that of Elizabethan "drama" (which term I shall hereafter adopt as shorthand for not just stage plays, but for the ritual practices of state, such as masque and pageantry, which are so richly present in the popular drama). Essentially, two kinds of questions are raised here. First, what is the relationship between the drama and the specifically cartographized construction of space that is recognized by cartographic historians (such as P. D. A. Harvey) as constituting one of the major cultural achievements of early modern Europe—and one of the most potent shaping forces in subsequent world history? Second, how are geographic and ethnographic discourses mediated by Elizabethan drama?

Both these kinds of question have been asked before. What makes these essays new is the way the questions are now being put. The first question was raised as early as the sixteenth century, when Sir Philip Sidney castigated the popular stage for its addiction to geographically expansive actions that it could not possibly hope to rationalize. For Sidney, the poverty of Elizabethan techniques of stage illusion—the sheer spatial givenness (and boundedness) of the stage—meant that the drama could have little legitimate business with geography. Chorography could not be directly translated into choreography. It could only hope to be represented at a verbal remove through the convention of "reported action."[4] Some decades later, a similar impatience with geographic ignorance would move Drummond of Hawthornden to complain that "Shakespeare in a play brought in a number of men saying they had suffered shipwreck in Bohemia, where there is no sea near by some 100 miles," (a fact he was unlikely to have known without a map).[5] Ben Jonson, of course, relates this remark with a smug consciousness of his own scrupulosity with regard to geographic detail—and (one may venture) an inferiority complex internalized from reading writers such as Sidney.

At about the turn of the twentieth century, a belated reaction to this traditionally low estimate of the geographical literacy of the Elizabethan drama emerged in the work of diverse critics. C. H. Coote, for example, argued that behind Shakespeare's mention of a "new map" in *Twelfth Night* was a particularly advanced world map (Edward Wright's *Hydrographiae Descriptio*), which itself argued that Shakespeare was both aware of the cartographic revolution and interested in the "augmentation of the Indies."[6] Other critics argued that the drama was informed by knowledge of voyage literature, that *The Tempest* was engaged with the discourse of the Virginia Colony, and even that Shakespeare (like John Donne) was a working associate of "the founders of liberty in America."[7] In similar spirit (if with greater cogency), Ethel Seaton vindicated the geography of the *Tamburlaine* plays, arguing that it owed more to a reliance on Ortelius's atlas, the *Theatrum Orbis Terrarum* (1570), than to random invention.[8] Regardless of what they make of it, all these critics, from Sidney to Seaton, are united by a concern for geographic literacy in the drama; *literacy* here being defined by reference to a largely unquestioned criterion of "mapmindedness," which is itself, as P. D. A. Harvey points out, a cultural invention of the sixteenth century.[9] In a different way, the same assumption can be sensed in a quite separate (and less agenda driven) body of critical literature on the drama's use of more literary or legendary or mythological or archetypal geographies. Such writing is generally uninterested in "real" geography.[10] The guiding assumption here is that literary geography means one thing and "real" geography another. Whether historicizing the cartography of what seem the least cartographized of Shakespeare's plays (the romances), or interrogating the ways in which mapping is mediated by the stage, the essays in this volume depart from traditional geographic criticism in attempting to rethink traditional approaches to the relationship between Elizabethan theater and mapmindedness.

What exactly is mapmindedness, and how can we pose it both in respect of the sixteenth-century culture it is thought of as entering and transforming? How, in a representative case, did the processes of cultural influence (intervention, propagation, and transformation) operate? Because it has already been well and recently discussed, the cultural effect of Saxton's atlas can serve as a model. Saxton was innovative not merely in producing the first national atlas in Europe but in itemizing and standardizing the national image at the level of each county.[11] Upon publication, this cartographic imagery was widely disseminated: "the county and national maps from that atlas were quickly copied, re-edited, and reduced in order to fulfil new roles as illustrations in books ... as diagrams in almanacks and traveler's guides, as curiosities in cabinets of wonder, as household tapestries, and even as images on sets of playing cards."[12] Produced and reproduced, then, Saxton's maps (it is asserted) played an important part in refashioning "existing mental geographies" of England.[13] How? Richard Helgerson provides us with one answer when arguing that Saxton's atlas initiated a process of splitting chorography (the image of the land) from history in the form of the English Chronicle-histories, which it had traditionally supplemented. A consequence of this, he argues, is that the newly cartographized image of the land began to divorce itself from the dynastic and monarchical associations and affects, which it had previously served to naturalize by virtue of its supplementation to chronicle history. So divorced, the cartographized image of England was free to become either politically neutralized (such as in the "Quartermaster's map" of 1644, which is thought to have been reworked from Saxton at the order and for the use of Cromwell) or affectively reinvested in ways that had nothing to do with monarchy (such as in Drayton's *Polyolbion*, where Saxton's remarkably uncluttered and unpeopled cartographic images are reinhabited by personified spirits of place rather than by rulers).[14] If Saxton's atlas may serve as a paradigm of cultural dissemination, then, mapmindedness appears as a paradoxical cultural phenomenon. Where, in one of its aspects the new cartography appears to oust "existing mental geographies" (or what John Noble Wilford calls "the topography of myth and dogma") with a more rationalized construction of space, in another of its aspects it appears as a site for the accumulation of traditional symbolisms and metaphors (as in the Ditchley portrait [see page 66], which depicts Elizabeth standing on a Saxtonian map of England).[15] More than a mere cultural loop is described here, however. Real change has occurred. While new maps may have become encrusted with old symbolisms, the relationship between the two has become more pliable, more supplementary; hence, while the symbolic investments fluctuate, the new cartography is relatively constant.[16]

If in one sense, mapmindedness inserted itself at the expense of the chronicle-based historicized picture of England described by Helgerson, then in another sense it might also have begun to insert itself at the expense of the theater. At one level at least, this must have seemed paradoxical. As I have argued elsewhere, there is a discursive link between theaters and atlases in the period.[17] The theater was linked to the discourse of "cosmography" via the topos of the *theatrum mundi*, whereas atlases—

from Ortelius's *Theatrum Orbis Terrarum* (1570)—were generically "theatres of the world." The meaning of this link is hard to assess. On one hand, the rhetorical and even structural parallels are extremely strong. Thus, Ortelius represents his atlas as a *theatron* in print: the printed equivalent of a renaissance map room, which the reader figuratively enters when turning the opening pages. Again the "Globe" theater courts construction as a geographic globe through both its title and emblem (Hercules bearing the world on his shoulders). Again, atlases adopting the convention of the *cartes à figures* surround maps of various cartographic entities (continents, countries, counties) with a kind of ethnographic cast (in the form of a sequence of vignettes of inhabitants dressed in regional garb), which in turn, encourages a reading of the map as a theatrical mise en scène. Finally, there is some evidence that real theaters took some pains to achieve a plausible level of ethnographic verisimilitude in costume and makeup, an effort that is surely not unrelated to the tradition of ethnographic handbooks, such as *The Fardle Of Facions* (London, 1555) of Johannes Boemus.

The question, however, is why—given the very strength of this tradition of affiliative rhetoric—the actual working relationship between cartography and theater is not stronger or more compelling than it strikes a modern reader, or as it must have struck contemporaries. Maps and theaters really are different after all. When a map is produced onstage, there is little sense of its being a kindred cultural product, and more sense of its being a kind of newfangled "oddity." Maps do not really belong in the same category as hell-mouths and other already theatricalized props of the type found in Henslowe's list.[18] There are several ways of answering this question. Helgerson's thesis suggests one kind of answer. If chorography split away from chronicle in the late sixteenth century—in the sense of being published in physically distinct forms, developing ever more divergent discursive practices, and producing an imagery of England detachable from the monarchical values sedimented in chronicle; then, the same motives were there for its splitting from theater. Notionally, atlases were "theatrical," and theaters "cosmographic" because geography was traditionally thought of as the "eye" of history. Supposedly, one went to the theater and looked at an atlas for the same reason—in order to "see" history brought to life in its proper mise en scène, or to "see" distant places as if through a magical window. Thus, in 1599 a Swiss traveler named Thomas Platter observed of the English that, "in the comedies they learn what is going on in other lands . . . since for the most part the English do not much use to travel, but are content ever to learn of foreign matters at home."[19]

Paradoxically, however, the very attempt to observe this injunction must have underscored its hollowness as the century wore on and the gap widened between the signifying practices appropriate to spatial representation or cartography on the one hand, and historical-theatrical modes of representation on the other. Thus, the characteristic cultural attitude of the Elizabethan drama to the map is one of deference. Maps are "cited" in the theater, such that when alluded to or when physically introduced to the stage, a whole portmanteau of signifying practices is similarly introduced into the dialogue and staging. This is the hallmark of cultural success. Maps reproduce their own cultural niche at every moment of their cultural dissemination, including within the theater. To appreciate this, one has only to compare the ways maps are used on the Elizabethan stage with the way they are used on the medieval stage. Surviving plats for *The Castle of Perseverance* and the Cornish *Ordinalia* effectively figure the stage in cartographic terms, with places (Paradise, Heaven, Hell) oriented much as on contemporary *mappa mundi* (themselves already absorbed into the drama of redemptive history).[20] Whereas, then, stage and map tend to collapse into each other in the medieval period, they become sharply distinct in the sixteenth century. The growing rift between cartographic and theatrical practice does not mean that there was no link between the two, but it does mean that the character of this link was essentially rhetorical. Rhetorical affirmations of the link between theater and cartography can be found as late as the Restoration when Sir Richard Baker, calling in 1662 for the reinstitution of the theater, urged his readers to "be content, as to see the wide world drawn as in a map, and a large history in an abridgement; so to see, and favour plays, which are nothing, but epitomes of the world's behaviour."[21] By this stage, one may surmise, the rhetoric had grown rather hollow. By 1662, cartography had grown vastly in prestige as a scientific discipline and as an instrument of government, navigation, war, discovery, and commerce. Theater, meanwhile, had virtually disappeared. Thus, whereas in Shakespeare's England, cartography could plausibly popularize itself by reference to theater in the Ortelian atlas, and theater could plausibly authorize itself by reference to cosmographic metaphor, the partnership was a good deal less equal by 1662. Cartography had done without theater for some twenty years and had no further need of it. Sir Richard Baker's appeal sounds more like begging than an equal cultural exchange.

If it is accepted that the sixteenth-century cartographization of space represents a major paradigm shift, how is it accounted for at the level of cultural mediations (such as drama) to which (unlike Drayton's chorographic epic) it has little intrinsic relationship? The danger here lies in totalizing, in assuming that all forms of cultural mediation are passive; that all other (earlier, alternative, nonscientific, marginal) forms of spatial thinking or enactment simply "melt into air" before the new cartographic discourse. To avoid falling into this trap, it is worth attempting to model the process of cultural intervention; effectively to map the new cartography onto the larger world of social practice that it is taken to be interrupting. Perhaps no one has thought more penetratingly (if abstractly) about the social dimension of spatial discourses than Henri Lefebvre. According to Lefebvre, the notion of "space itself" is the real problem here, one we have inherited from Descartes' positing of an unmediated physical space (res extensa) as the setting of the thinking subject (res cogitans). Rather than conceiving of space as real in the sense of existing independently of ourselves, Lefebvre proposes that we think of it as socially produced. In place of the Cartesian dualism, Lefebvre offers a conceptual triad. Space is to be grasped as the effect of three dialectical categories: "spatial practice," "representations of space," and "representational spaces." The spatial practice of any given society is whatever "secretes that society's space," whatever "propounds and proposes it ... masters and appropriates it."[22] This process of "secretion" will be largely, but not entirely, effected by the second category, "representations of space," which are defined in terms of

> conceptualized space, the space of scientists, planners, urbanists, technocratic subdividers and social engineers, as of a certain type of artist with a scientific bent—all of whom identify what is lived and what is perceived with what is conceived. This is the dominant space in any society (or mode of production).[23]

Finally, there is the category of "representational spaces" or "space as directly *lived* through its associated images and symbols, and hence, the space of 'inhabitants' and writers and philosophers, who *describe* and aspire to do no more than describe."[24] "Redolent with imaginary and symbolic elements," representational spaces "need obey no rules of consistency or cohesiveness . . . they have their source in history."[25] For all the depth of its historical roots, it is, however, "the dominated—and hence passively experienced—space which the imagination seeks to change and appropriate."[26] Two of these categories are familiar from existing discussions of Renaissance cartography. Thus, "representation of space" obviously corresponds to the cartographization of space, or to maps—especially "new" maps (some version of the word *new* is almost generic in the titles of Renaissance maps). "Representational space" just as clearly corresponds to literary or mythic or affective geographies (though it is a more comprehensive category, as it also grounds such affect–geographies in the bigger notion of a "living" of space). Also familiar is the way Lefebvre juxtaposes these two representational modes—with "representations of space" thought of as active and "representational space" thought of as passive. If (as I do) one might wish to quarrel with this idea that one type of spatialization is active and the other passive, an important qualification should be recognized. The polarization is true only of western "spatial practice," and only by virtue of the cartographization of space in the sixteenth century. The deeper point is that each modality of "spatial practice" has an in-principle claim to "secrete" the space of the society in which they arise.[27] Space does not exist independently of these "secretions;" hence, when either type of space is analyzed, it should be in full awareness of their dialectical character:

> Ethnologists, anthropologists and psychoanalysts are students of such representational spaces. . . . but they nearly always forget to set them alongside those representations of space which coexist, concord or interfere with them; they even more frequently ignore social practice. By contrast, these experts have no difficulty in discerning those aspects of representational spaces which interest them: childhood memories, dreams, or uterine images and symbols, holes, passages, labyrinths).[28]

Lefebvre, then, contributes to our project in two ways. He allows us to understand both the new cartography and the literary-mythological-ritual geographies of Renaissance drama as dialectically related (perhaps cooperating, perhaps competing) versions of spatial practice. He allows us to conceptualize the process of cultural mediation itself—and hence the role of the drama—in active and complex ways. Drama and ritual are not necessarily (as Sidney and Jonson supposed) the poor relations of the new cartography. Theoretically, by virtue of their mythological, legendary, and ritual basis alone—if by virtue of nothing else—they are equipped to challenge the Renaissance cartographization of space by engaging it with alternative norms of "spatial practice"—with, for example, a rich lore of "rites of passage," in which space is secreted primarily under the aspect of ritual traversal rather than detached vision. Examples would include itineraries, pilgrimages, the Roman Triumph, Renaissance pageantry (with its richly nonchorographic uses of geographic personifications), royal progresses, and the festive paradigm (of escape, sojourn, and reintegration).

Having fashioned, with Lefebvre's help, something of a conceptual model for the relationship between theater and cartography (a relationship that has never been thought of as in need of conceptual modeling), we can now turn to the ways in which cartography is mediated by the drama. As a first step, we might aim at characterizing the most common or elementary meanings which the word *map* and its cognates have in the drama. Here, however, we encounter the paradox that this apparently most straightforward of tasks has yet to be done. While proponents of the drama's affiliation with the "new geography" (and their opponents) were intent on highlighting the use of maps in the drama—the "new map" in *Twelfth Night*, for example; or "Marlowe's map" in *Tamburlaine*—they intended to overlook elementary usages in their haste to talk about a single class of map: world maps or maps of discovery.[29] Because the drama as a whole is somewhat unmanageable for present purposes, Shakespearean usage will have to serve as a rule of thumb. Shakespeare uses a variety of terms which either denote or imply maps or the activity of mapping or associated values: the word *map* itself and its variants (map, maps, mappry, mapp'd), also the words *card, plot, model*, and *form*. Probably the common denominator in all these words—when used with some cartographic implication—is that of the map as (in J. B. Harley's words) "a type of graphic tool to be used in . . . everyday business" for purposes of spatial modeling.[30] Thus, "I see (as in a map) the end of all" (*Richard III*, 2.4.54).[31] This example will also reveal how intrinsic the idea of cartography is to another conceptual activity. The speaker of this line seizes on the map as an analogy for predicting or modeling a future outcome. It is possible, however, that spatial practice informs not just the vehicle of the analogy (map) but also its tenor (the idea of modeling the future). This is because looking at a map could, in one sense, have been *literally* the same as looking at the plot of a fiction or a play. A plot was physically hung up backstage to provide the players of *Richard III* (equipped—not unlike the characters they played—only with their individual parts, not the complete script) with a bird's-eye view of the whole action—a grid of entrances, exits, and stage effects.[32] Interestingly, several of the surviving examples of such plots use the cognate form *plat*. According to the OED, both forms arose in the sixteenth century. Plat, the older and slightly more map-related variant, could mean any of four things: "a piece or area of ground ... of small extent," "a plan or diagram of anything, especially a ground plan of a building or any part of the earth's surface," "a plan of action or proceeding," finally, "the plan or scheme of a work of fiction, a drama, poem."[33] To these meanings, plot (used as a verb) added the meaning "to plan, contrive, or devise ... now always in evil sense."

What is common to all these senses of plotting and platting is a kind of teleology, a mode of projection. Whether one thinks of a plot as a model of space or as a model of an action yet to unfold in time, one is thinking of a schematic arrangement (whether of images or words) whereby some object or process is seized and outlined from the vantage of a particular *telos* or purpose or end. Significantly, it is just this teleological aspect of mapping that is uppermost in all *figurative* uses of *map* and its variants. Just over half (or nine) of all usages of this family of words (seventeen in all) are figurative.[34] This itself is remarkable if we pause to reflect that only two of the seventeen usages involve characters using maps to get from one place to another (probably the most intuitive associative context of maps today).[35] A few examples of figurative usage will suffice. *Sonnet 68* begins with the line "Thus is his cheek the map of days outworn." In *The Rape of Lucrece*, we find a similar image when Lucrece's face is imagined as "that map which deep impression bears" (1712). Again, we find Lucrece's hair "like golden threads play'd with her breath ... Showing life's triumph in the map of death" (400, 402).[36] Two revealing points might be made of these conceits. The first is that Shakespeare should have chosen to build them around maps rather than around paintings. The second is that the projective quality of maps—the quality whereby they epitomize what they depict along the axis of a given focus or instrumentality (so commonplace today that it is taken for granted) should routinely have given rise to poetic conceits. Both points tell us something about how the cultural impact of the map is registered in the sixteenth century. On the one hand, the map is clearly marked off from painting. It is less vivid, less immediate, less "present," but more schematic, more instrumental, more accessible. Maps, so to speak, offer themselves to be seen *through* rather than seen, such that the structure of the mapped object—or more precisely, only that aspect of structure which is pertinent—is rendered transparent to the gaze of the viewer. On the other hand, the opaqueness of the map—its artifactual identity—also qualifies routinely for poetic notice. A conjunction of both instrumental and artifactual qualities powerfully informs the most casual poetic usage. Taken casually, the conceit of a man's cheek as "the map of days outworn" yields a slight hint of the artifactual quality of engraving (the hint is that the face is deeply scored by wrinkles), a haunting suggestion of absence (the map shows not the presence of the days but their absence, their traces), and a powerful sense of projection, allowing us to grasp the whole pertinence of this face at a single glance. Taken in the full contexts of Sonnets 68 and 67, however, the image yields a surprisingly counterintuitive content—yet one that is dependent on the very same cartographic associations. "Thus" (the link word) exhorts the reader to view the beloved's cheek in graphic as distinct from painterly terms. So viewed, the cheek is no less young and beautiful, but it is nevertheless a sign of absence rather than a bearer of phenomenological presence. It is, so to speak, a living reliquary of the golden age; a "dead seeing" (Sonnet 67) or map of a vanished province of being.

Before moving on to consider more complex uses of maps in the drama, one more point needs to be stressed about these more elementary map images in Shakespeare. Of seventeen frequencies of the word *map* and its variants in Shakespeare, only seven are clearly geographic—in the sense that the geographic quality of the map operates as a vector of meaning. Of these seven, the best example is perhaps the image in *Twelfth Night*:

> ... He does smile his face
> into more lines than is in the new map, with the
> augmentation of the Indies; you have not seen such a
> thing as 'tis.
>
> (3.2.78–81)

What is clear in this image however, is that the cartographic quality operates independently of (if cooperatively with) the geographic quality. As in *Sonnet 68*, the primary idea is cartographic: Malvolio's smile wrinkles his face like the engraved lines on a map. The hint here is more specific of course. The image actually assumes familiarity with a particular map—a maritime map with an unusually dense cluster of rhumblines radiating from focal points. Only when this idea is grasped is the geography of the map brought into focus. It is important to know that this is a world map with a specific emphasis on maritime discovery, a map putatively showing an "augmentation of the Indies."[37] The new geography in the East and West—with its associations of desire, gender, wealth, sexualized discovery, and conquest—tells us precisely what animates this smile: a kind of domestic version of Jan Van der Straet's engraving of Vespucci "discovering" a naked America.[38] The point then is that while the geographic component of the image cooperates with the cartographic component, it remains independent. The image would still have worked without addition of the phrase "augmentation of the Indies." Mapmindedness then, is another—and arguably a more pervasive—cultural phenomenon than is geography (the writing or drawing of the earth). The deeper point is that geography—in various scales and types (national, regional, or global) and in all of its associated affects (patriotic and ethnocentric, or desire-driven and adventure-mad)—is but one of various ways cartographic images convey dramatic meaning.

Another way is represented by a class of allusions to military cartography. Before Bosworth (as we have already partly seen), Richmond makes the following request:

> Give me some ink and paper in my tent;
> I'll draw the form and model of our battle
>
> (5.3.23–24)

Richard, who also—and virtually simultaneously—asks for pen and paper, is distracted. The contrast here seems pointed, deliberate. Like a true Tudor—intellectually a man of the sixteenth century—Richmond draws a map. Once a Machiavellian "plotter," Richard suddenly seems medieval. The military application of cartography here identifies Richmond with two other Shakespearean soldier-technocrats: Ulysses and Michael Cassio. Unlike Richmond, however, both these soldiers incur the scorn of their cartographically untrained comrades. To Ulysses, the accusation of "mapp'ry" is equivalent to an attack on military science itself:

> They tax our policy, and call it cowardice,
> Count wisdom as no member of the war,

> Forestall prescience, and esteem no act
> But that of hand. The still and mental parts,
> That do contrive how many hands shall strike
> When fitness calls them on, and know by measure
> Of their observant toil the enemies' weight—
> Why, this hath not a finger's dignity.
> They call this bed-work, mapp'ry, closet-war,
> So that the ram that batters down the wall,
> For the great swing and rudeness of his poise,
> They place before his hand that made the engine . . .
> (1.3.197–208)

"Mapp'ry" here is associated with a whole set of technical practices involving "observant toil," "measure," and engineering, practices seemingly associated with the "closet" rather than the field itself. The same set of practices can be intuited from Iago's slighting mention of Cassio, who has—Iago supposes—been promoted over his head because his expertise in military science outweighs Iago's own practical experience on the battlefield:

> And what was he?
> Forsooth, a great arithmetician,
> One Michael Cassio, a Florentine . . .
> That never set a squadron in the field,
> Nor the division of a battle knows
> More than a spinster—unless the bookish theoric,
> Wherein the [toged] consuls can propose
> As masterly as he. Mere prattle without practice,
> Is all his soldiership.
> . . . . this counter-caster,
> He (in good time!) must his lieutenant be . . .
> (1.1.18–32)

Whether Cassio's work is specifically to do with drawing maps or not, it is plainly related to the same set of practices involving "measure" and calculation ("counter-casting"—use of a manual calculator). In the same way, as we shall see, maps are associated with a variety of other practices—governmental, commercial, and even magical—when cited in drama.[39]

So far we have been considering only the simpler ways in which mapmindedness is registered in Shakespeare (taking him as a rough guide for dramatic practice as such). What of the more complex varieties of citation in Elizabethan drama, those that tend to be constructed around the introduction of actual maps to the stage? Prime examples would be the moment in *King Lear*

(1.1) when the King calls for a map with the aid of which he proceeds to divide his kingdom, the moment in 1 *Henry IV* when Hotspur, Mortimer, and Glendower again use a map to divide the kingdom between them, and the moment in *Tamburlaine* at which the hero calls for a map upon which to trace his conquests and point to areas remaining to be conquered. To these, even though a map is not physically introduced, we might add the moment in *Macbeth* at which the witches map the movements of the pilot of the *Tiger* sailing to Aleppo, with the aid of an imaginary "seaman's card." It is precisely in moments such as these that we might best assess the ways in which the drama functions as a cultural mediation of cartographic values.

To reiterate, the question here is: does the drama serve as a conduit of such values, or does it play a more active and critical role, inflecting, qualifying, subverting, or challenging them? To my knowledge, few attempts have been made to address this question prior to the essays in this volume. In his preliminary survey of literary and dramatic usages of maps and globes in early modern England, the cartographic historian Victor Morgan works from the assumption that "literary references are likely both to have reflected and reinforced the values—practical and abstract—that were associated with maps."[40] Inadvertently (no doubt), this broad view seems borne out by the related argument of Phyllis Rackin, that the shift from chronicle to chorography (identified by Richard Helgerson) is registered in the discursive gap between *Richard II* and the second *Henriad*. The point here is that the image of England in the earlier play is an essentially chronicle-based and, therefore, medieval geographic image, whereas the image of England in the Henriad is chorographized and to that extent, more modern, secular, and friable.[41] This brings us to several of the essays that follow. Bruce Avery takes direct issue with the notion that the drama simply instantiates cartographic values and does so with special reference to the use of maps in *King Lear* and *1 Henry IV*. Drawing on Barbara Freedman's argument that the drama tended to destabilize the fixities of monocular perspective by virtue of the multiperspectivism of the Elizabethan stage, Avery insists that the drama can similarly be expected to destabilize the values of cartography (which is markedly dependent on the assumption of fixed viewpoint). Other essays, while not addressing themselves to the question of mediation as such, touch on it in revealing ways. Glenn Clark finds in *Cymbeline* a clash between a cartographic and a noncartographic construction of space (defined by reference to Lefebvre's distinction between "representations of space" and "representational spaces"). Underlying this rift, Clark suggests, is a clash of values: between a set of values dependant on cartographic practices of measure, calculation, itemization and commodification (the very practices and values which Iago affects to despise in Cassio) and a set of values that construe the geographic space of England (and Imogen, the human being who is identified with it) as, precisely, incommensurable, unmappable, singular, and unique (in the sense in which, in ancient and Renaissance geography alike, exotic lands—those beyond the bounds of the measured world—were marked by their possession of *thoma* or "wonders" or "singularity"). Working with a non-Shakespearean text—Heywood's *The Fair Maid of the West*—Barbara Sebek finds that it both transmits and yet destabilizes the mercantile cartography of Lewes Roberts's *The Merchant's Mappe of Commerce*. Here, the destabilization is less from critique than an almost embarrassing eagerness to fantasize motives concealed beneath the calculus of exchange in Roberts. All three essays concur in finding a far more complex and dynamic role for the drama than is found by Morgan.

That is certainly the view of this writer (a view to which he has been led by these and other essays of this volume). As the most complex instance of map usage in Shakespeare, Lear's map can be taken as an exemplary instance for testing the nature of dramatic mediation of cartographic values.[42] The opulent pastoralism of Lear's "reading" of his own map—with its "shadowy forests and with champains rich'd / With plenteous rivers and wide-skirted meads" (1.1.64–65)—strongly suggests a national map of the Saxtonian type. A distinctly cartographic value— the luxurious overlordship of the eye—is also implied in the rapturous invocation of "eyesight, space and liberty" (56) in Goneril's response. If it is accepted that this imagery is indeed map-informed, then it may be objected that this poetic map is working in a way quite counter to the typical instances noted earlier. The difference is that this map works like a picture, conveying a strong illusion of presence and fullness as distinct from the vacant instrumentalism noted in the map-conceit of *Sonnet 68*. It is just here, however, that the Saxtonian quality is felt most strongly. If one were to read the maps in Saxton in terms of the semiotic scheme developed by J. B. Harley, the link becomes clearer.[43] Adapting E. H. Gombrich's model of iconology, Harley proposes that Tudor maps be read at three levels. The first is iconic or pictorial, a level at which simplified visual codes, such as Saxton's "hills," "forests," "churches," "towns," and "fields," are registered "as tiny fragments of landscape" for the reason that "they are mimetic signs . . . bearing a visual resemblance to the features represented."[44] The second level is that of "conventional" signs without direct iconic significance, the level that (to revert to the example of Saxton) allows us to distinguish one of Saxton's county maps from another. "It is," writes Harley, "this practical dimension of renaissance cartography which is most frequently remarked on by historians of the period."[45] (Here one would be noticing nonrepeatable contour lines and the larger configurations they combine to form). The third level is that of "semantic interpretation, for which the term iconology is reserved."[46] A reading at this level:

> . . . seeks to establish the relationships between the philosophical, political and religious ideas in a society and the form and content of art. . . . In cartography, it is now suggested, these strata . . . have an exact counterpart. Put simply, the interpretation is now shifted from the reconstruction of real places . . . to a reconstruction of the ideological or symbolic undertones of images as they were now understood by cartographers, their patrons, or by individuals or groups in the society who came into contact with the image.[47]

If we now return to Lear's "reading" of his map, it can be seen that it operates—consciously at least—at the first or mimetic level (mostly) with some element of the third as well. The maps of Saxton's atlas convey an unusually powerful illusion of pastoralism for the reason that they are dominated by "tiny fragments of landscape" at the expense of utilitarian features, such as roads (which are completely absent). Town symbols and church symbols are shown in some profusion, but they are so tiny that they do not disturb the pastoral suggestion. That this was a compelling perception in the period (as well as for this writer) is testified to not merely by the popularity of Saxton's atlas and the broad cultural dissemination of the maps but by Drayton's *Polyolbion*, which can be read as an explicit elaboration of the pastoralism that is implicit in Saxton. Thus, on Drayton's frontispiece, Saxton's national map forms the pattern of the robe worn by a personified female Albion, while throughout the poem itself Saxton's county maps are reproduced with the addition of personified spirits of place (most often to be seen emerging from rivers and streams). If Drayton, then, bears testimony to the mimetic power of Saxton's maps, so (I suggest) does the onstage use of the map in *King Lear*.

However, just as pastoralism was not the only suggestion of Saxton's map of England (what Edward Lynam has called "this ethnocentric fugue of a map") so do further orders of meaning arise from the cartographic echoes in *Lear*.[48] These orders of meaning, while intimately connected to the pastoral, correspond to Harley's category of the symbolic and have to do with "the myth of national consciousness, unity and pride" articulated in Saxton.[49] The dramatic uses of this symbolism are subtle and layered. On one hand, the ethnocentric pathos of this Saxtonian landscape amplifies Lear's folly, for the reason that this geography—at once familiar and sacred—suggests the unthinkability of division. On the other hand, however, it suggests that division is inherent to the kingdom. Because maps exist precisely in order to draw lines of demarcation, they make geographic division eminently thinkable. Thus, Lear delineates Goneril's portion of the kingdom: "Of all these bounds, even from this line to this" (63). Two types of geographic line appear suggested here. "Of all these bounds" is more ample and less precise than "even from this line to this"; as if Lear were wishing to suggest full geographic extent in the first instance and precise cartographic limit in the second. The word *bound*, indeed, appears to include both geographic and cartographic values: the way this particular portion of the kingdom is defined as a whole by existing natural-geographic features (rivers, mountain ranges, the sea), as well as by abstract and imposed cartographic features ("even from this line to this"). Of these two types of geographical division—that based on geographic features and that based on purely cartographic values—the second seems what is most at stake at this moment of the play. Lear divides Goneril's portion from the rest of the kingdom not by means of existing natural features but by drawing a line.[50] As such, he uses his map in a particularly modern way, a way that could only have been made possible by an advanced cartographic culture. A contemporary audience must have found this as disturbing as it is exhilarating. The sheer arbitrariness of dividing a kingdom "even from this line to this" may have courted comparison with the notoriously arbitrary cartographic statecraft exemplified in the 1493 Bull of Pope Alexander VI which grandiosely donated to Spain:

> all the firme Lands and Ilands found or to be found, discouered or to be discouered, toward the West and South, drawing a Line from the Pole Artike to the Pole Antartike . . . a hundred Leagues toward

the West, and South, from any of the Ilands which are commonly called *De los Azores* and *Cape Verde*[51]

Equally, it might suggest the later amendment (under Portuguese pressure) whereby "That . . . Line of Partition, contained in the Bull of the Pope, should be extended 270. Leagues further to the West, all from thence Westward to remayne to the Castilian, and Eastward to the Portugall Nauigation and Conquest".[52] It is at this point that we begin to realise how much of the ethnocentric pathos of Saxton's map—at a symbolic level equivalent to that in John of Gaunt's invocation of "this sceptred isle" (*Richard II*, 2.1.40–66)—is here telescoped into the delusory pathos of Lear himself; cartographic ethnocentrism translating into personal egocentrism.

Even here, however, in his use of the map as a mirror of Lear's pride and folly, Shakespeare is still reflecting on another effect of the cartographic culture—what we might call the vanity factor in Renaissance maps. One has only to read a standard cartographic textbook or gaze at one of Vermeer's interiors featuring a wall map, to realize that an essential aspect of the appeal of the nation or continent scale map lay in a flattering imputation of spatial mastery and/or social aggrandizement. This could take several closely related forms. In William Cunningham's *The Cosmographicall Glasse* (London, 1559), mapmaking is praised for allowing one to traverse vast areas from the comfort of one's own home:

> Nowe I perceive by the makinge and describying of this onely Mappe . . . I may in like sorte at my pleasure, drawe a Carde for Spaine, Fraunce, Germany, Italye, Graece, or any perticuler regio: yea, in a warme & pleasant house, without any perill of the raging Seas: danger of enemies: losse of time: spending of substaunce: werines of body, or anguishe of minde.[53]

Mapmaking is made to seem comfortable precisely by being contrasted with the strenuousness of travel. Equally, a sense of proprietorship and pride is implied in the very ownership of a map. There is a subtle sense that the occupants of Vermeer's wall mapdominated interiors do in some way command—in the rhetorically "farsighted" way that "statues of eminent statesmen often overlook sweeping vistas"—the geographic vistas their maps open onto.[54] Framed against a national map, a simple gesture acquires a mysterious amplitude. In this, Vermeer intuits what Shakespeare does in *Lear*, that the opening of the domestic interior to the map of state brings the farsighted gaze of the state into the bourgeois home and hence into the psyche of a playgoing householder. Lear's use of his map as a flattering glass—a means of bolstering his own importance in his daughters' lives—represents a shrewd intuition about the rhetorical character of contemporary cartographic artifacts. Here it is worth reflecting that whereas in *Lear* this cartographized celebration of nationhood is elided with monarchical folly and egocentrism, in *Richard II*, the equation works in the opposite way. Thus, John of Gaunt's evocation of "this sceptred isle" is set *against* Richard's folly, not with it. Here there is no instrumental mediation between the "sceptred isle" and the whim of the sceptred ruler who leases it out as a "pelting farm" (2.1.60). In *Lear*, the map supplies this sense of instrumentation and the headiness that goes with it. There is, in short, very much a sense of the armchair general about Lear in this scene. The map, Lear seems to understand, contracts his far-flung power within the ambit of personal gesture precisely for the purposes of an ampler rhetorical expression of that power.

If we were to take our analysis of the drama's role in respect of mapmindedness no further than the directly cartographic imagery of *Lear*, 1.1, it should already seem that the role of the drama is far more complex than that of a cultural conduit. While it is true that the audience must have walked away from the play with an enhanced appreciation of maps and their cultural importance, it is also true that their appreciation should have been significantly nuanced, even disturbed. Disturbance of the cartographic paradigm seems just what is at stake as the action of the play descends into the chaos of the "heath" scenes, where (I would suggest) man's various contracts with social space, domestic space, and spatial practice are radically redefined.[55] A full-scale reading of these scenes as an extended commentary on mapmindedness lies outside the purview of an introduction. However, a few instances may be noted. First is the landscape Edgar evokes in the course of his metamorphosis into Poor Tom:

> The country gives me proof and president
> Of Bedlam beggars, who, with roaring voices,
> Strike in their numb'd and mortified arms
> Pins, wooden pricks, nails, sprigs of rosemary;
> And with this horrible object, from low farms,
> Poor pelting villages, sheep-cotes, and mills,
> Sometimes with lunatic bans, sometime with prayers,
> Enforce their charity.
>
> (2.3.13–20)

This vision of rural England is unSaxtonian precisely because so reminiscent of Saxton. It is no less uncannily reminiscent of the "sceptred isle" passage in *Richard II* (where the image of the "pelting farm" is also set in a counter-pastoral role). What is suggested here is not just another viewpoint (a close-up of what is concealed beneath Saxton's blandly pastoral codes), but an entirely different order of spatial practice altogether. This landscape is as it is because it is traversed on foot, not modeled from above. It is traversed with Cunningham's "werines of body" and "anguishe of minde." To interact with space in this way is to be Poor Tom:

> Poor Tom, that eats the swimming frog, the
> toad, the tadpole, the wall-newt, and the water;
> that in the fury of his heart, when the foul fiend rages,
> eats cow-dung for sallets; swallows the old rat and
> the ditch-dog; drinks the green mantle of the standing
> pool; who is whipt from tithing to tithing, and
> [stock]punish'd and imprison'd . . .
>
> (3.4.129–35)

This is not man defined visually against the landscape, nor is it man modeling and fetishizing the landscape as his proper *mise en scène*. Here man is dissolved into landscape and dissolves it in turn through the agency of his appetites and the senses of smell and touch. Tom's nonvisual experience of space also characterizes the blinded Gloucester who (stumbling when he saw) must now "smell / His way to Dover" (3.7.93–94). Again, the dissolution of self and landscape is evident in "the king himself" (4.6.84), who—as nature's piece against art—crowns himself with weeds as if in some crazy parody of Drayton's Albion.

If these experiences of space are countercartographic, because so physical, so uneconomised, so perspectiveless, they are also insistently ritualistic. For all the aimlessness of their several wanderings, Tom, Lear, and Gloucester have a directed experience of space. Inadvertent yet compulsive pilgrims, their tracks converge on Dover. In Tom, this sense is particularly strong. His way is measured in ritual leagues of pain ("whipt from tithing to tithing" 3.4.134); his presence is announced by prayers and "lunatic bans" (2.3.19). Gloucester too, travels a via dolorosa, a penitential journey (appropriately guided by Tom and the countryman who is Edgar's next persona). It is not merely then that these experiences of space are defined in terms of physical ordeal—beyond the comfort zone within which the map is made and experienced—nor only that they are so strikingly unvisual, but that they are directed and goal-oriented. Winding though these paths may be, in the end they all converge on Dover as on the sacred destination of a pilgrimage.[56] Here—as at a shrine—all three characters undergo cathartic spiritual transformations. Poor Tom is exorcised in the shape of the fiend who has haunted him through bogs and briars. Gloucester outlives his suicidal leap through the perspective of despair. Lear is awakened from anguish to bliss.

In these senses, then, the whole of *King Lear*—not just the scene of the map—can be read as an agonised fall from a privileged order of spatial practice (and its vision-based modality of percept and affect) to less privileged and more tangible forms of spatial practice. According to Yi-Fu Tuan:

> The structure and feeling-tone of space is tied to the perceptual equipment, experience, mood and purpose of the human individual. We get to know the world through the possibilities and limitations of our senses. The space that we can perceive spreads out before and around us, and is divisible into regions of differing quality. Farthest removed and covering the largest area is visual space . . . closer to us is visual-aural space . . . Next to our body is the affective zone, which is accessible to the senses of smell and touch . . . the relative importance of sight diminishes in affective space: to appreciate the objects that give it its high emotional tone our eyes may even be closed. We cannot attend to all three zones at the same time. In particular attendance to the purely visual region in the distance excludes awareness of the affective region.[57]

It is just this antagonism between sight and affectivity that is dramatized in *King Lear*. It is because "spatial dimensions are keyed to the human sense of adequacy, purpose, standing" (p. 400) that they are prominent in this tragic exploration of the breakdown of adequacy, purpose, and standing.

It is equally possible that the agonism between cartographic spatial practices based on sight and those based on earlier, more ritually-based paradigms is staged elsewhere in the drama. In the *Tamburlaine* plays, maps are either directly or indirectly used in fashioning several agonisms of this type. One such serves as prelude to the climax of the first play:

> I will confute those blind geographers
> That make a triple region in the world,

> Excluding regions that I mean to trace,
> And with this pen reduce them to a map[58]
> (1:4.4.81–84)

Far from being a simple paean to the new cartography and the empire building to which it is generically related, however, these lines take on a very dark resonance in their immediate dramatic context—Tamburlaine's refusal of Zenocrate's request that he spare Damascus, her father's city. It is as if the far-sighted gaze of the conqueror or the cartographer—each sharing an extensive vision of space and a remote "feeling tone" relative to that vision—is incapable of registering an intimate violation of his own "affective zone." In "Marlowe, the *Timur* Myth and the Motives of Geography" (following), it is suggested that the motif of cartographic expansionism is consistently juxtaposed with—and haunted by—a set of more ritually-based paradigms of spatial practice deriving from ancient geographic lore, whereby exotic conquest (and the crossing of certain key geographic thresholds) is marked as impious and transgressive. If, in certain instances, the danger of foreign conquest can be disarmed (such as in the ritual of the Triumph) this is only at the cost of exact ritual observation, an observation that Tamburlaine's triumphs are conspicuously without. Triumphal structures are also, of course, translated wholesale into Renaissance pageantry in which the theme of geographic imperialism is also prominent. Here too, there is a seemingly inherent conflict between the ritual mode of geographic imagination and the cartographic mode. Thus, Richard Helgerson defines the cartographic dimension of *Polyolbion* by its very opposition to the more ritually based geography of a passage in *The Faerie Queene* in which the world's rivers are imagined congregating to celebrate the marriage of Thames with Medway. This pageant-derived fantasy, as Helgerson remarks, "can never have been truly chorographical" because "it violates the very premise of chorography, fidelity to the natural disposition of the land" (p. 142).

The commerce between Elizabethan theater and Renaissance cartography is a paradoxical one. They were, as we have noted, rhetorically linked through the idea of the *theatrum mundi*. Yet those who drew attention to this link had looked backward rather than forward for their authorization—toward an ancient discourse that had no way of anticipating or accommodating the cartographic revolution that was driving a wedge between them. If, therefore, theater and cartography were related—as Ortelius and the proprietors of the Globe Theater liked to think—the relationship masked an intellectual, generic, and linguistic struggle in which the theater was at a decided disadvantage. Theater was at a disadvantage because cartography was setting the pace. Cartography was becoming so powerful as a means both of modeling and manipulating space that its need of the purely representational analogy of theater was no longer compelling. Theater, for its part, could hardly afford to ignore the new cartographic construction of space, not just because this was how space now "worked," but because of its own traditional monopolization of the mise en scène of human experience. With such pressures, theater could easily have drifted into a position of subordination in which—unable to take cartography over (as in the medieval drama)—it was doomed to serve as just another means of cultural dissemination.[59] As we have seen, however, the theater did not entirely succumb. In some cases (*Tamburlaine*, for example), it subverted the dominant paradigm while apparently advertising it. In other cases (*King Lear, Cymbeline*), it effectively mounted a conceptual challenge, confronting the cartographic construction of space with alternative—and more humanly responsive—"representational spaces." Potentially at least, the drama was always equipped to challenge cartography if only by virtue of the wealth of precartographic spatial practice sedimented in its generic structure. In fact, it did challenge cartography when (as in *Lear*) it represented cartographized space not as absolute but as contingent upon different human spatial practices and/or the human sensorium. In either case, space was shown to be not merely relative but heterogeneous. Different spatial practices begetting different spaces, and the sensorium begetting a progression of spaces—the far space of the eye, the near space of the ear and mouth, and the intimate space of touch and affect—which are, in humanly important ways, independent of each other. A drama that could demonstrate these facts could never be entirely subordinate to a cartographic revolution fetishizing and totalizing the space of the eye.

Notes

1. P. D. A. Harvey, *Maps in Tudor England* (Chicago: University of Chicago Press, 1993), 7, 15.
2. Henry Lefebvre, *The Production of Space*, trans. Donald Nicholson-Smith (Oxford: Blackwell, 1991), 85–86.
3. See Lefebvre, *The Production of Space*; Harvey, *Maps in Tudor England*;

Sarah Tyacke, ed., *English Map-Making, 1500–1650* (London: The British Library, 1983); Richard Helgerson, *Forms of Nationhood: The Elizabethan Writing of England* (Chicago & London: University of Chicago Press, 1992); S. Gale and G. Olsson, eds., *Philosophy In Geography* (Dordrecht: G. Reidel Publishing Co., 1979); J. B. Harley, "Meaning and Ambiguity in Tudor Cartography," in *English Map-Making*, ed. Tyacke 22–45; J. B. Harley, "Maps, Knowledge and Power," in *The Iconography of Landscape*, eds. Denis Cosgrove and Stephen Daniels (Cambridge: Cambridge University Press, 1988), 277–312; J. B. Harley, "Deconstructing the Map," in *Writing Worlds: Discourse, Text and Metaphor in the Representation of Landscape* eds. T. J. Barnes and J. S. Duncan (London and New York: Methuen, 1992); J. B. Harley and David Woodward, *The History of Cartography*, vol. 1 (Chicago and London: University of Chicago Press, 1987).

4. Sir Philip Sidney, *An Apology for Poetry*, in *Elizabethan Critical Essays*, 2 vols. ed. G. Gregory Smith (London: Oxford University Press, 1971), I, 148–207, 198.

5. William Drummond, "Conversations with William Drummond of Hawthornden," in *Ben Jonson*, ed. Ian Donaldson (Oxford and New York: Oxford University Press, 1985), 595–611, 599.

6. C. H. Coote, "Shakspere's 'New Map,'" pt. 1 of *New Shakspere Society's Transactions, 1877–79* (1878), 88–100.

7. R. R. Cawley, *Unpathed Waters: Studies in the Influence of the Voyagers on Elizabethan Literature* (London: Case, 1940); R. R. Cawley, "Shakespeare's Use of the Voyagers in The Tempest," *Proceedings of the Modern Language Association of America* 41 (1926): 688–726; Sir Sidney Lee, "The American Indian in Elizabethan England" in *Elizabethan and Other Essays by Sir Sidney Lee*, ed. Frederic S. Boas (Oxford: Clarendon Press, 1929), 263–301; C. M. Gayley, *Shakespeare and the Founders of Liberty in America* (New York: Macmillan, 1917). For useful overviews of the debate on the relationship between *The Tempest* and America, see Charles Frey, "The Tempest and the New World," *Shakespeare Quarterly* 30, no. 1 (1979): 29–41; Alden T. Vaughan, "'Shakespeare's Indian' The Americanization of Caliban," *Shakespeare Quarterly* 39 (1988): 137–53.

8. Ethel Seaton, "Marlowe's Map," *Essays and Studies* 10 (1924): 13–35.

9. There is considerable irony in the fact that prior to Ethel Seaton the geography of the *Tamburlaine* plays was assumed to be haphazard because it could not be squared with modern maps of the regions it covers. The fact that it might have been conscientiously geographic by the standards of its day—by the standards of Ortelius—was missed, possibly because Ortelius himself seemed conspicuously ungeographic to Seaton's readers. A similar irony is seen in J. D. Rogers's refusal of Coote's suggestion that Shakespeare was inspired by the new geography. In asserting that Shakespeare's interest was overwhelmingly confined to the Old World, Rogers likened Shakespeare's geographic understanding to that of pre-European China, ignoring the clear evidence in the concordances of Shakespeare's interest in the new cartography.

10. See C. L. Barber, *Shakespeare's Festive Comedy: A Study of Dramatic Form and Its Relation to Social Custom* (Cleveland, Ohio: World Publishing Co., 1963); Northrop Frye, *A Natural Perspective: The Development of Shakespearean Comedy and Romance* (New York: Columbia University Press, 1965); Frederic T. Flahiff, "Lear's Map," *Cahiers Elisabethians* (30 October, 1986, 17–33; Jeanne Addison Roberts, *The Shakespearean Wild: Geography, Genus, and Gender* (Lincoln, Nebr. & London: University of Nebraska Press, 1991).

11. See J. B. Harley, "Meaning and Ambiguity in Tudor Cartography," in *English Map-Making, 1500–1650*, ed. Tyacke 22–45, 24.

12. Ibid., 39.

13. Ibid., 24.

14. For Drayton's use of Saxton, see Helgerson, *Forms of Nationhood*, 107–47. For the "Quartermaster's map," see page 112.

15. See John Noble Wilford, *The Mapmakers* (London: Junction Books, 1981), 34.

16. See Helgerson, *Forms of Nationhood*, 107–47; John Gillies, "The Frame of the New Geography" in *Shakespeare and the Geography of Difference* (Cambridge: Cambridge University Press, 1994), 156–88; John Gillies, "Posed Spaces: Framing in the Age of the World Picture" in *The Rhetoric of the Frame*, ed. Paul Duro (Cambridge: Cambridge University Press, 1996), 24–43, especially page 33.

17. "Theatres of the World" in *Shakespeare and the Geography of Difference*, 70–98. The following paragraph summarizes the more detailed argument of "Theatres of the World."

18. Henslowe's list does mention "i globe" and "i crosers stafe" (though this may be a bishop's cross). See Andrew Gurr, *The Shakespearean Stage, 1574–1642* (Cambridge: Cambridge University Press, 1990), 171.

19. See E. K. Chambers, *The Elizabethan Stage*, 4 vols., vol. 2 (Oxford: Clarendon Press, 1923) 365–66.

20. See Richard Beadle, ed., *The Cambridge Companion To Medieval English Theatre* (Cambridge: Cambridge University Press, 1994), 60. There is a detailed comparison of map usage on the medieval stage with that on the Elizabethan stage in my "Posed Spaces: Framing in the Age of the World Picture," 26–31, 39–41.

21. Sir Richard Baker, *Theatrum Redivivum, or the Theatre Vindicated* (1662), cited in Victor Morgan, "The literary image of globes and maps in early modern England," in *English Map-Making, 1500–1650*, ed. Tyacke 54.

22. Lefebvre, *The Production of Space*, 38.

23. Ibid., 38–39.

24. Ibid., 39.

25. Ibid., 41.

26. Ibid., 39.

27. Lefebvre is careful to limit his antithesis between the active "representation of space" and the passive "representational space" to the West: "Whether the East, specifically China, has experienced a contrast between representations of space and representational spaces is doubtful in the extreme" (*The Production of Space*, 42).

28. Ibid., 41.

29. See notes 6, 7, and 8.

30. J. B. Harley, "Meaning and Ambiguity in Tudor Cartography," 27.

31. All Shakespeare quotations are taken from G. Blakemore Evans, ed., *The Riverside Shakespeare*, (Houghton Mifflin Company: Boston, 1974).

32. For facsimiles of surviving plots, see Sir W. W. Gregg, *Dramatic Documents From The Elizabethan Playhouses, Stage Plots: Actors' Parts: Prompt Books (Reproductions and Transcripts*, vol. 2, (Clarendon Press: Oxford, 1969).

33. The OED lacks any reference to the playhouse plots and plats, perhaps for the reason that Gregg's *Dramatic Documents* postdates it.

34. See, Martin Spevack, *The Harvard Concordance to Shakespeare* (Cambridge: The Belknap Press of Harvard University Press, 1973).

35. See under "mapp'd" and "maps" in Spevack, *The Harvard Concordance*. Antonio is described "Piring in maps for ports and piers and roads" in *The Merchant of Venice*, 1.1.19). Cloten speaks of being "near to th'place where they should meet, / if Pisanio have mapp'd it truly." (*Cymbeline*, 4.1.1–2).

36. This image is extensively analyzed in, Mercedes Maroto Camino, "'That Map Which Deep Impression Bears'": The Politics of Conquest in Shakespeare's *Lucrece*," in *Shakespeare: World Views*, eds. R. Eaden and T. Mares, (University of Delaware Press, 1996) 124–45. I am indebted to the editors for showing me this article.

37. C. H. Coote (note 6) made much of the fact that a particular world map, Edward Wright's *Hydrographiae Descriptio*, showed an "augmentation of the Indies" in arguing that this map was the source of the cartographic image in *Twelfth Night*. However, Rodney W. Shirley demurs: "The meaning of the phrase 'the augmentation of the Indies' is a little puzzling. The Wright-Molyneux map certainly delineates the East Indies and Japan fully, but in no greater detail than maps by others . . . in circulation during the previous decade" (*The Mapping of the World: Early Printed World Maps 1472–1700* (London: The Holland Press, 1987), 239.

38. The etching, for Jean Théodore de Bry's *Americae decima pars* (Oppenheim, 1619), is reproduced facing the title page in, Michel de Certau, *The Writing of History*, trans. Tom Conley (New York: Columbia University Press, 1988). Malvolio's daydream of coming from a daybed where he has left Olivia sleeping again suggests this fantasy.

39. Of the following essays, Glenn Clark's "The 'Strange' Geographies of *Cymbeline*" focuses on the theme of commensuration, while Barbara Sebek's "'Strange Outlandish Wealth': Transglobal Commerce in *The Merchant's Mappe of Commerce* and *The Fair Maid of the West, Parts I and II*," focuses on the commercial application of Renaissance cartography.

40. Victor Morgan, *The Literary Image of Globes and Maps in Early Modern England*, in *English Map-Making*, ed. Tyacke, 46–56, 46.

41. Phyllis Rackin, *Stages of History: Shakespeare's English Chronicles* (Ithaca and New York: Cornell University Press, 1990), 24–25.

42. Here I want to make it clear that my argument implies no disagreement with Bruce Avery's different argument on the dramatic role of Lear's map. I simply see myself as putting a more normative version of the case for the dynamism of the dramatic mediacy.

43. J. B. Harley, "Meaning and Ambiguity in Tudor Cartography," 22–45.

44. Ibid., 25

45. Ibid., 26–27.

46. Ibid., 28.

47. Ibid.,

48. Edward Lynam as cited in Harley, "Meaning and Ambiguity in Tudor Cartography," 37.

49. Edward Lynam, *British Maps and Map-Makers* (London: William Collins, 1947), 20; cited in Harley, "Meaning and Ambiguity in Tudor Cartography," 36.

50. As far as we can tell, the cartographic division of the kingdom between Hotspur, Glendower, and Mortimer in *1 Henry IV*, 3.1, seems to be drawn on

the basis of natural geographic features, such as "the smug and silver Trent" (3.1.101).

51. The translation is from *Purchas His Pilgrimes In Five Books* (London, 1625), 2, ch. 6, 17.

52. Ibid., b. 2, ch. 7, 26.

53. William Cunningham, *The Cosmographicall Glasse* (London: 1559); The English Experience, No. 44, (Amsterdam and New York: Da Capo Press, Theatrum Orbis Terrarum, 1968), fol. 120.

54. Yi-Fu Tuan, "Space And Place: Humanistic Perspective," in *Philosophy in Geography*, eds. Gale and Olsson (Dordrecht: G. Reidel Publishing Co., 1979) 387–427, 400.

55. In seeing the action of *Lear* as an *agon* between the cartographic construction of space (and its associated human values) and other modes of "spatial practice" (and their associated human values), I depart from F. T. Flahiff's view that the play enacts "the replacing of spatial by human relationships" ("Lear's Map," 19). The difference, in my view, is that space is engaged throughout the play.

56. There is a moving anonymous account of the last stage of a medieval pilgrimage to the shrine of St. James the Greater at Compostella in Victor Turner, "Pilgrimages as Social Processes," in *Dramas, Fields, and Metaphors: Symbolic Action in Human Society* (Ithaca & London: Cornell University Press, 1984), 166–230, 180–81. See also Turner's account of the link between pilgrimage and penitence; "pilgrimages were set down as adequate punishments inflicted for certain crimes" (p.175).

57. "Space And Place: Humanistic Perspective," 398–99.

58. Christopher Marlowe, *The Complete Plays*, ed. J. B. Steane (Harmondsworth: Penguin, 1975).

59. For cartography in medieval theater, see "Posed Spaces: Framing in the Age of the World Picture," 30–31.

Gelded Continents and Plenteous Rivers: Cartography as Rhetoric in Shakespeare

Bruce Avery

Student. And this, you see, is a map of the whole world. Look, here's Athens.
Strepsiades. Can't be; if it's Athens, where are the jurymen?
Student. No, I assure you, it is, and all this area is Attica.
Strepsiades. Well, what's happened to my own village, Cicynna?
Student. It's in there somewhere. Anyway, here's the island of Euboea, look, lying stretched out opposite us, all along here.
Strepsiades. Yes, I knew that already. It's been lying like that ever since me and Pericles and the rest of us knocked it out. Where's Sparta?
Student. Right here.
Strepsiades. Too near, too near! You'd better have another thought or two about that—get it to be a heck of a lot further away from us.
Student. We can't do that, silly.
Strepsiades. Can't you? Then take that! [*He strikes the student with his stick.*][1]

Aristophanes wrote this scene from *The Clouds* around 400 B.C., almost four centuries before Strabo composed his seventeen-volume *Geography*, and even longer—close to six centuries—before Ptolemy developed the sophisticated curved projection that lent authority to his own *Geography* well into the 1600s. It's a funny scene—although as a good modern pedagogue I cannot condone taking a stick to smart-aleck students—but I cite it here because it shows that playwrights have been interested in maps for about as long as maps have existed. It also shows that for just as long—and well before a modern writer made this phrase famous—plays have demonstrated that the "map is *not* the territory."[2]

I'd like to release some of the torque on a twist scholars have lately given that phrase. Richard Helgerson, Phyllis Rackin, and most recently John Gillies have suggested, in slightly various ways, that while the map isn't the territory, in important ways the play *is* the map.[3] Gillies points out that, given the number of early modern atlases that included the word *Theatre* in their titles, "an atlas was a theater for virtually all of Shakespeare's lifetime."[4] He then describes the ways maps and theater influence each other: maps, from Ortelius's 1570 *Atlas* onward, include depictions of historical voyages that edge toward narrative. More importantly theater, he argues, creates, as maps do, "a spatial understanding of things, concepts, conditions, processes or events in the human world."[5] Gillies is not alone in seeing parallel interests for theaters and maps.[6] Most of the others working in this growing cottage industry make similar claims, claims best summed up as follows: mapmakers creating images *of* the globe and the playwright creating images *for* the Globe had the same interests in depicting spatial relationships, so as each medium grew in popularity, it borrowed techniques, images, buzzwords, and, finally, authority from the other.

Now, although I'm not Marshall McLuhan, I do think that the medium is at least partly the message, and maps and plays are media with radically antagonistic formal properties. Barbara Freedman notes as much in her book *Staging the Gaze* when she argues that "the Elizabethan theater in the round offered an unusually provocative site for the performance of plays fascinated with subverting the truth of any private individual, or fixed vantage point."[7] Freedman adds that in Shakespeare

> right interpretation is presented as a virtual impossibility, requiring 360 degrees of viewing space and 120 minutes of absolute presence perfectly comprehended by one mind. Since individual viewpoint hampers rather than guarantees true sight, right interpretation is necessarily a communal activity.[8]

Freedman's argument traces the spatial qualities of Elizabethan theater that subvert the truth claims of media, such as maps, that construct monocular perspective. There really is, plays suggest, more than one way to look at things, and the contours of anything you look at are shaped in part by the position from which you gaze. I think this structural antagonism raises such interesting questions as Is it possible that Shakespeare's plays show an awareness of the brackets drama places around geographic knowledge? If they do, does that awareness result in a privileging of one form of knowing over another? Does Shakespeare's theater, in short, suggest that cartographic representations are no more, and in some cases less, valid ways of understanding the world than theatrical representations? The short answer to these questions is yes. The long answer follows.

In recent years, Richard Helgerson and historians of cartography such as Sarah Tyacke have reexamined the work of John Norden. Norden was a surveyor, historian, and cartographer who, following the example of the famous Christopher Saxton, sought Elizabeth's patronage for his own compendium of English county maps. Helgerson's account details the troubles Norden had with the Queen and her advisors. For reasons that remain clouded, patronage was not forthcoming and Norden fell into financial trouble.[9] My interest is in a different sort of trouble, the sort Norden experienced at the other end of the social scale when he went out among the public to execute his surveys. He wrote about it in his book *The Surveyor's Dialog*, which pits a farmer against a surveyor in a dispute over the cartographic project.[10] The farmer's prevailing tone echoes in a phrase he utters early in the first section of the book. Accusing the surveyor, he complains that "customs are altered, broken, and sometimes perverted or taken away by your means."[11] In voicing this objection, Norden's dialogue admits that maps and the surveyors creating them offered a convenient focus for anger rising out of transformations occurring in English culture. In response and to facilitate their acceptance by a suspicious public, Norden, John Speed, and others worked hard to frame their maps within social and religious traditions, which implied maps were not really changing anything, they were simply depicting what was out there in a more accurate, but still traditional, way. They had ample motivation; there was money to be made, position to be attained. Saxton had shown that maps were an effective tool—a tool for which certain people, Lord Burleigh and the Queen among them, would pay handsomely.[12] Mapmakers, in turn, provided landowners with the means to quantify and control their holdings and the state with the means to manage territory. Norden's farmer, then, was right after all. Cartographers were not simply mirroring the world, they were transforming understanding of just what the world is. Yet mapmakers and those employing them made a concerted effort to create maps that represented themselves as something other than they really were, a radical change in the orientation of subjects toward their world.

Because of this reorientation, maps also provoked reactions other than fear, namely, excitement and awe. They stimulated an almost giddy interest, to the extent that members of the nobility included them in their "cabinets of wonders," collections of cultural desiderata and curiosity.[13] I think that such an intense interest in maps suggests that bringing one onstage in a play, such as *King Lear*, could produce a spectacular effect on the Globe audience. Early maps dazzled readers; they would probably dazzle theater audiences, too. Dazzle is just what Shakespeare's King Lear is trying to do when he gestures toward his map in the first scene, because for many onstage, his deed is more than a little frightening, and by keeping them focused on his map, he can help them ignore their fears. Lear, just like Norden's surveyor, alters borders and attitudes toward territory in a way that is potentially dangerous to those lower down the royal food chain, for whom a kingly tantrum can mean death or banishment. He relies heavily on the map to carry out his darker purpose, to make his complicated motivations appear to be larger than life, greater than the transient desires of his family. He intends to alienate his own version of reality from the present circumstances of the other characters so that it appears natural and transcendent—something that goes, as they say, with the territory.

It seems curious that for such a vital purpose the map's role is so brief, limited to just one scene in the first act, where Lear's daughters must speak well to get their several dowers.[14] The old man represents those dowers cartographically, ordering a functionary to "Give me the map there" (1.1.37).[15] Lear uses the map to provide a focal point centered on the discourse of patrimony, a magical place where obedience and gratitude result in "gifts" of land during that familiar ritual, the passing of the torch. A useful way to read such rituals was developed by anthropologist Maurice Bloch in the 1960s and 1970s. Bloch argues that hierarchy is inscribed in ritual performance and that ritual rhetoric compels acquiescence in that hierarchy from its performers. Formalized language, formalized body gestures, and so on tend to move by a momentum that predates a specific historical moment, and participants sense that in performing their roles they enact something that transcends themselves, something not subject to their own desires, nor even to their questions. Bloch explains ritual structures such as this one in specifically linguistic terms, revealing the content of their form. "If you have allowed somebody to speak in an oratorical manner," writes Bloch, "you have practically accepted his proposal."[16] The traditions ritual oratory invokes, that is, carry a strong persuasive charge regardless of the content of the oration itself. In Lear's opening speech, the verb *say* of line 51, "Which of you shall we say doth love us most," highlights the rhetorical push of his words. The King wants to force his daughters to claim to love him so he might convince everyone, including, perhaps, himself, that he really is so kind a father.

In act 1, scene 1 of *King Lear*, then, the participation of cartography in a political ritual touches off a complex play of political and psychological discourses that highlight the map's rhetorical purpose. Certain characters fall under the sway of the ritual system and the map's rhetorical force; others do not. Goneril does; she plays her role, obediently offering up a list of nouns that do not measure up to her love:

> Sir, I love you more than words can wield the matter,
> Dearer than eyesight, space, and liberty,
> No less than life, with grace, health, beauty, honor;
> As much as child e'er lov'd, or father found;
> A love that makes breath poor, and speech unable:
> Beyond all manner of so much I love you.
>
> (1.1.54–61)

Strikingly, the thirteen nouns of her response hang on the single verb *love*. This static construction reflects passivity, and the attenuated syntax displays the speech's ritual function. It is practically a rote reply to a prompt—not really a speech at all in any independent sense, and so the line "a love that makes . . . speech unable" is Goneril's particularly apt, albeit unconscious, description of her lack of verbal agency. She is under the constraint, then, of the conception of love inscribed in the ritual's oratory by her father. The strain shows in the tangled metrics of the speech: feminine endings in lines 54, 56, and 58; three extra syllables in line 54.

Cordelia, too, is under that verb's control, though she breaks it from Lear's rhetorical orbit and claims to actualize it when she whispers

> What shall Cordelia speak? Love, and be silent.
>
> (1.1.62)

In other words, by making *love* an imperative verb directed at herself, she will perform the action it describes, and so not only prove to herself she's better than Goneril, but also, perhaps, prove it to her father as well.

Regan, on the other hand, *describes* herself as performing the love that Goneril was only able to name:

> I am made of that self metal as my sister,
> And prize me at her worth. In my true heart
> I find she names my very deed of love;
>
> (1.1.69–71)

Like Cordelia, Regan claims to be actualizing Goneril's mere words, but she does so in a public way. By this deft move, she outdoes both her sisters yet avoids disrupting the ritual's structure and thereby challenging her father. Cordelia, of course, disrupts everything, and we know what happens to her.

The two daughters who play by the rules, however, get a piece of the map, so Goneril and Regan literally see themselves, as does the rest of the court, taking possession of their lands. They get more than just the map: the opulence of Lear's verbal landscape rewards Goneril for her rhetoric. It offers fewer nouns than she did but gives her a bounty of adjectives, e.g., "shadowy," "wide-skirted," "plenteous," in payment for her obedience, as well as the space, liberty, and wealth she says mean less to her than Lear himself. In this scene, then, we have moved into a world of symbolic exchange where the currency isn't just territory, it's also the representation of it in ritual language and images, such as the map. The map itself, that is, because of its ability to display possession (and therefore generosity) and represent power (and therefore Lear's self-image), becomes as important as the territory that forms the actual possession.

Lear highlights the map's importance in the scene's ritual structure when Goneril responds as he wants her to. Turning to the map (1.1.62–66), he makes of it a sacrament that confirms her obedience, fussing over its details and displaying for everyone her share of the new kingdom. More importantly, the gesture projects in impressive scope Lear's generosity—literally makes it spectacular—because he is able to show everyone he is giving his daughter an immense gift: from rivers to meadows, fields to lakes. One could never see it all without the aid of cartography. What this also shows is that he, Lear, is *giving* it to her, that he is generous to Goneril beyond mere human measure, beyond, even, anyone's capacity to see with the naked eye. Regan, too, is getting as much as Goneril is, a kingdom "no less in space, validity, and pleasure than that conferred" on her sister (1.1.80–81).

But she is getting absolutely no more. We learn that from the play's first lines, when Gloucester tells Kent that "now in the division of the kingdom it appears not which of the dukes he values most, for equalities are so weighed that curiosity in neither can make choice of either's moiety" (1.1.3–7). We learn early on, then, that the king has cleverly balanced his bequests to his eldest daughters, so their curious husbands, try as they might, can find nothing to envy in the other's share. That fact is crucial, because the map must then perforce display Lear's darker purpose for him, since once he has marked off the borders of the kingdom Cornwall gets through Regan, everyone can see that a third portion of the kingdom, more opulent and larger, remains, and that share belongs to Cordelia. The map then stands as a landscape, projected in grand scale, of the humiliation of Lear's eldest daughters, a powerful symbol reminding everyone that while the King may be rendering control of the land to his daughter's husbands, he intends to retain psychological control over the women themselves.[17]

By retaining such control, Lear displaces the desire for economic and physical control, a desire patriarchal tradition requires him to relinquish to the men they marry. He displaces it to an altogether murkier realm where borders are not clear and defenses are weak. The scene renders in stark outline a world where women are made to jump and beg, to swoon and cajole, for "gifts" of land that pass directly through them from their fathers to their husbands. Note, for example, that when Lear disinherits Cordelia, he says

> ... Cornwall and Albany
> With my two daughter's dowers digest this third.
> (1.1.127–28)

He sees the property going not to his daughters but to his "beloved sons"; hence, the scene represents the process through which patriarchy inscribes its organization of space on a medium—the map—that obscures its origins in patriarchal social practice and represents it instead as something that is literally part of the landscape.[18]

Lear plans, of course, to sweep this ritual to a close with a final, sumptuous description of each detail on Cordelia's portion of the map. He has concluded the other daughters' obedient responses with a turn to his chart and a formal demarcation of their reward; clearly, he will sacramentalize Cordelia's obedience in the same fashion. The problem is that she does not obey; the ritual has failed to coerce her. This shows in her language, which features questions, analysis, and logic:

> Why have my sisters husbands, if they say
> They love you all? Hap'ly, when I shall wed,
> That lord whose hand must take my plight shall carry
> Half my love with him, half my care and duty . . .
> (1.1.98–101)

In contrast to her sister's static speech, Cordelia's sentences defy the grammar of ritual. They interrogate and speculate, and as Bloch writes, ritual favors speech without logic and causality.[19] The effect on Lear and his map is immediate. Just at the moment when he should turn to the projection in grand fashion and make it speak for his overwhelming generosity, he instead releases a tirade. Abruptly, the map falls from the center of the stage action—no one refers to it again in the play. Once Cordelia breaks into motivated dialogue, focus must turn toward her and her father, to the dramatic contours of their relationship and away from the static spectacle of the map onstage. The first scene of the play, then, presents the upstaging of cartography's visual spectacle in a theater where the audience can see Lear attempt to herd his court into the narrow confines of his map's perspective so that *King Lear*, finally, shows the map to be just another form of rhetoric.

While *King Lear* displays a failed attempt at coercive cartography, the other Shakespearean map I am interested in here shows how maps can fail at fostering community. Shakespeare's source for *1 Henry IV*, Holinshed's *Chronicles*, does not mention cartography.[20] This suggests to me that he chose to put the map in this play, as he did in *King Lear*, because he was interested in its dramatic resonances with his characters and because he was skeptical of its use in political alliances. As act 3 scene 1 unfolds, Mortimer and Glendower reveal that they intend the map to function as what J. B. Harley has called a "cartographic *lingua franca*"; a device that gives the conspirators a common language so they might turn away from divisive squabbles and give more productive attention to a common goal.[21] As a result, the map in *1 Henry IV* finds its meanings created not by rigorous fidelity to territorial reality, but by the communal, political transactions of

Hotspur and his coconspirators. In those transactions, their uses and interpretations of the map bend to the sway of discourses of gender and honor circulating through the structures of dynastic patriarchy.

Mortimer enters act 3 scene 1 hoping for a quick ratification of the Archdeacon's brokered deal. They will take the crown from King Henry IV and split the island three ways. Hotspur follows him in parody of courtly graciousness, pointedly giving the others their honorifics: "*Lord* Mortimer," "*Cousin* Glendower," and "*Uncle* Worcester" (my emphasis). This graciousness he deflates by following Worcester's name with "a plague upon it! / I have forgot the map." (3.1.5–6) Tonally, the curse jars with the elaborate formality of Hotspur's previous lines and with the general Foreign Office solemnity of a meeting whose function is essentially diplomatic. More than his language, Hotspur's forgetfulness threatens the stability of the scene—without the map to enforce a perspective, each confederate threatens to retreat to positions opposed to and focused on each other, rather than on their common goal. This would then replicate the uncivil England Henry complains of in act 1, where

> Those opposed eyes,
> Which, like the meteors of a troubled heaven,
> . . . .
> Did lately meet in the intestine shock
> And furious close of civil butchery . . .
>
> (1.1.9–13)

Yet for the first of three times, Glendower settles things down. His "No, here it is" completes the pentameter line that Hotspur's "I have forgot the map" began, restoring to the ritual its proper poetic form. If, however, Glendower must rescue the scene from Percy three times, either Hotspur wants badly to end it, or he wants to make everyone believe he does as a rhetorical ploy, because such a belief would make them more likely to cater to his wants.

I think the latter explanation more convincing, and because Glendower in particular seems to go out of his way to be conciliatory, it proves to be an effective ploy. Its ultimate success results in the anticlimax of the scene, when Glendower says, "Come, you shall have Trent turn'd" (3.1.134). That capitulation allows Hotspur to reveal a disenchanted view of exchange in the economy of power, as he responds

> I do not care. I'll give thrice so much land
> To any well-deserving friend;
> But in the way of bargain, mark ye me,
> I'll cavil on the ninth part of a hair.
>
> (3.1.135–58)

Hotspur shows everyone that the bargain itself matters more to him than the territory over which they contend. He not only knows his stature rests upon the practice of exchange itself, instead of on the land he expects to gain, but it's also clearly important to him to let everyone else know he knows it. This sort of self-consciousness can turn every utterance to an insult or retort in a zero-sum economy of power relations. In Hotspur's case, every conversation is a discussion of, and a battle for, his status, his masculinity, his honor. What he shows at the end of act 3 scene 1 is that it's more honorable to take from Glendower than it is to receive from him, because as Harry Berger puts it, "if to receive honor as a gift from others is to be diminished, emasculated, reduced to a minion, then the gift must be refused so that honor may be taken by force."[22]

This curious pattern of refusal and seizure follows two speeches, which Mortimer and Glendower clearly intend should close the proceedings. I will deal with those speeches later, but after they have been uttered, Hotspur prevents closure, extending the scene by pointing to the map and saying

> Methinks my moi'ty, north from Burton here,
> In quantity equals not one of yours.
> See how this river comes me cranking in,
> And cuts me from the best of all my land
> A huge half-moon, a monstrous cantle out.
> I'll have the current in this place damned up,
> And here the smug and silver Trent shall run
> In a new channel fair and evenly.
> It shall not wind with such a deep indent,
> To rob me of so rich a bottom here.
>
> (95–104)

The river, when it comes "cranking in," takes some of the land Hotspur thinks should be his. The word *crank* carries with it not only the meaning of "winding" but also an association with military defeat and weakness. Its Old English root verb, according to the OED, meant "to fall in battle," and "to shrink, give way, become weak or ill." Eventually, it evolved to mean shifty and devious, as well as developing the sense of twisting and turning for which the OED cites this passage as exemplary. Given what we know of Hotspur and his conspirators, it's not pushing too hard on this word to see all of these meanings suspended in it at once, so his use of it hints at his fear that the map and its river might represent the ebbing of his power.[23] The association of the monarch's body with territory was increasingly common in Renaissance England. Queen Elizabeth often employed the royal-person-equals-country metaphor herself, and various maps made efforts to elide the two images.[24] A glance back at act 2 scene 1 shows us Gadshill mocking this equation when he talks to his friends who "pray continually to their saint the commonwealth, or rather not pray to her, but prey on her . . ." (79–80). The same association forces Hotspur to interpret a cut in his lands with an assault on his manhood. Taken together, these confusions subordinate the map to Hotspur's anxious encounters with the discourses of gender and honor; thus, they dislodge it from its locus as a stable representation of the conspirators' desire. Mortimer feels their pressure too when he speaks of the river "gelding" the opposed continent (106), using a word that specifically invokes the cutting off of testicles. He too appears to be anxious about gender and power.

To see how this anxiety urges on Hotspur's language, consider now the honor speech of act 1 scene 3:

> By heaven, methinks it were an easy leap,
> To pluck bright honor from the pale-faced moon,
> Or dive into the bottom of the deep,
> Where fadom-line could never touch the ground,
> And pluck up drowned honor by the locks,
> So he that doth redeem her thence might wear
> Without corrival all her dignities;[25]

(201–7)

Observe that his image displays honor as a conquered woman, dragged drowned from the water, redeemed by the male whose redemption consists in plundering her of her clothes and putting them on himself. The metaphor betrays Hotspur's anxiety about the relationship between masculinity and honor, which stems from the sense that the other nobles are trying to diminish his power. Beneath the bravado of the oration is the knowledge, as his language shows, that he cannot acquire honor by his own brave exploits: the *were* of line 201 makes the mood subjunctive. What he is saying, then, is that were it possible, it would be much easier to acquire honor by leaping to the moon than by the manner in which one actually acquires it. Unfortunately, as the subjunctive tells us, he knows such a leap would be fruitless: honor, as philosophers from Aristotle to Hobbes have pointed out, is in the mouth of the other; you must either compel it from there by force, or it must be given to you. Shakespeare's plays persistently expose the anxieties and dangers with which such gifts are fraught.[26]

The discourses of gender and power that run through this passage also emerge when he taunts Glendower in act 3 scene 1. By provoking him, Hotspur controls the scene. By making others react to his words, he interrupts the call and response of their litany of rebellion. His insults also encourage the Welshman's contrarian boasting, egging him on to refute Hotspur by proving his birth was indeed uncommon and mystical. By this strategy, Hotspur urges Glendower to play the role of the Welshman, to occupy the space of the foreign other in this group of English lords. Glendower, at first obliges, explaining how the earth moved at his birth. Then he says,

> Where is he living, clipt in with the sea
> That chides the banks of England, Scotland, Wales,
> Which calls me pupil or hath read to me?
>
> (3.1.43–45)

Glendower suggests here that while Hotspur may want to marginalize him as the foreign other, he is not merely a mystical, war-beaten rustic, but also a well educated, accomplished courtier—just like the rest of the men in the room. Hotspur responds, "I think there's no man speaks better Welsh. / I'll to dinner" (3.1.49–50). The word *Welsh* has a history of associations with foreignness—in Old English it means literally "foreign"—as well as with notions of racial inferiority. It also appears to mean something like "It's all Greek to me." Just when Glendower asserts his community with the other Lords, Hotspur retorts that he has never been more foreign and less comprehensible. Next, he threatens to end the scene with the compact unratified. Mortimer interjects a plea for peace, but it fails, and then he asks them to end "this unprofitable chat."

Hotspur answers by raising the tension with a curse, and chaos threatens to break the scene apart. This is the moment when Glendower draws out the map in an attempt to refocus everyone's attention on their original purpose, to "divide our right / According to our threefold order ta'en" (69–70). It should also reestablish a common language, a *lingua franca*, invoking the sacred icons of political power: borders and rivers, the terms of geography. Mortimer intones that

> The Archdeacon hath divided it
> Into three limits very equally:
> England, from Trent and Severn hitherto,
> By south and east is my part assign'd;
> All westward, Wales beyond the Severn shore,
> And all the fertile land within that bound,
> To Owen Glendower; and, dear coz, to you
> The remnant northward lying off from Trent.
>
> (3.1.71–8)

There are two things to remember here: first, that these borders have already been agreed to by the deputies of the interested parties; second, that Mortimer is using the map as a demonstration of that agreement. It symbolizes the common ground they have already achieved. He employs relatively chaste language in describing its contours. He sticks to value-neutral place names and directional indicators, intending to shore up the tone of inevitability with which the ritual began. Bloch characterizes this sort of inevitability in an epigram when he writes that "You cannot argue with a song."[27] That is, once the rhythms and refrains of ritual begin, they carry a meaning far more important and compelling than their actual words: that the speakers are in control and the auditors are not. Mortimer employs his oratory with just that notion in mind, but since Hotspur has shown himself keen to argue nonetheless, Mortimer must try something else, hoping that even Hotspur cannot argue with a map.

It seems to work—at least initially. Mortimer manages ten lines that suggest conclusion and agreement without an interruption from Hotspur—a difficult feat in this play. Then Glendower makes a comment he intends as a farewell, but that unfortunately suggests that Hotspur and Mortimer are too much in love with their wives:

> For there will be a world of water shed
> Upon the parting of your wives and you.
>
> (93–94)

The implication that he might be subject to the feminizing influence of excessive love for a female, even though the play shows clearly that he indeed loves Kate, and she him, is too much for Hotspur. He looks at the map and threatens once more to disrupt the meeting. At the same time, his language reveals an attitude that sees cartography not as a stable representation of what already exists but as a prop to serve his political needs. He wants to solve the dispute by changing the course of the river. For him neither the landscape nor the map are fixed entities—they can be arranged to suit him.

Glendower's attitude towards it, in contrast, colors his riposte to Hotspur's suggestion when he says "Not wind? It shall, it must, you see it doth" (105). The rhetorical ladder of "shall . . . must . . . doth" reveals the relationship of desire for political power to the representation of that power through cartography. When Glendower says "It shall," he argues that the river will wind because he wants it to; it gives him a great increase in fertile landholdings. When he moves on to say "it must," he means that the river has to stay as it is because an alteration would reflect a loss for him and so impugn his honor. When the "must" evolves into "doth," he portrays the map as fixed, drawn on paper, and therefore unchanging, stable. If the map cannot be changed, then neither can the world it represents. For Glendower, the irreducible fact is that the river on the map winds, and Hotspur cannot erase it. He takes the map, in short, as Mortimer intended. It is not something to be argued with. Given that he profits from his acceptance of the map as it is, Glendower's naiveté is, at least, convenient and perhaps strategic.

Hotspur, though, has imposed on that paper his own concerns with honor, political power, and gender and will, therefore, fight over it just as he has done over everything else bound up with his anxieties. For a change, Glendower refuses to compromise, telling Hotspur directly that he will not allow the map to be altered. Hotspur responds, "Let me not understand you then, / Speak it in Welsh," (118) again using the discourse of ethnicity to lure Glendower away from their real argument. Glendower rises to the bait and protests he can speak English as well as anyone and can even write poetry. Hotspur then hooks him by associating poetry with effeminacy, and Glendower gives in—showing that he, too, knows about the rhetorical use of gender categories. Therefore, when Glendower answers "Come, you shall have Trent turned," the effect of Hotspur's disruption becomes clear. The map is now unstable, arbitrary, and malleable not just for Hotspur but for everyone else in the room, and finally for the Globe audience, as well.

At the same time, the decision to "have Trent turned" reflects a rather violent, and even comic, understanding of the word "geography"—earth writing. It is as if they take as a serious option Strepsiades's advice to the student to move Sparta further away from Athens for safety's sake in the excerpt from *The Clouds* with which I began this essay. It seems from here no great leap to argue Hotspur and his cronies see the territory as a representation of the map. Rather than simply rewriting the map—say, drawing a new boundary across the disputed territory—the conspirators want to rewrite the *territory*, so the subsequently drawn map will reflect the "natural" boundary between Glendower and Hotspur. Never mind that the new channel will be artificial, and forget that a map evoked the desire for the change in the first place. The conspirators want to preserve the image of the map as a mimetic, not proscriptive, representation, because such an image is necessary to maintain its rhetorical force. That need requires them to make the "natural" world tell the map what they want the map to show, so it will appear once more as if the map is, after all, the territory. Unfortunately for them, it's not. As the play has made clear, and as J. B. Harley has argued, maps are nothing more than "perspectives on the world at the time of their making."[28]

But neither is theater a map. Theater does organize space; it does not represent space graphically as a fixed, homogenous entity viewed from a single, authoritative perspective, and at least in Shakespeare's theater, attempts to represent space that way appear to be of dubious value. What Shakespeare's theater does do is stage characters in the act of constructing space and establishing perspectives on it. In the process, it shows both the limits of the single point of view and the rhetorical motives that determine its focus. Maps, in contrast, show space not as something actively constructed but as an object passively perceived.

That, I think, is what John Speed had in mind when he titled his atlas *The Theater of the Empire of Great Britaine*. He wanted his readers to think of the map as a theater of spectacle, not of plot. In Shakespeare's plays, however, the plots question the very certainties that found cartography's truth claims. Perspective, borders, territory all appear to be subject to and often expressions of the petty motives of nobles with limited vision. The maps they formed may indeed have begun as the Theater of the Empire, where the authorized version of history could, in dazzling fashion, strut and fret its hour upon the stage, but as they entered the playhouse, they began to look like just another way to tell the same tales idiots always tell, the tales about the globe that the onlookers within the Globe learned to view with jaded eyes.

Notes

1. Aristophanes, *The Clouds*, trans. A. H. Sommerstein (Chicago: Bolchazy-Carducci,). 1985)
2. Jonathan Z. Smith, *Map Is Not Territory* (Leiden: E. J. Brill, 1978).
3. Richard Helgerson, *Forms of Nationhood* (Chicago: Chicago University Press, 1992), 139ff. Phyllis Rackin, *Stages of History* (Ithaca: Cornell University Press, 1990) argues that "the movement from *Richard II* to *Henry V* resembles the movement in Renaissance historiography from chronicle to chorography, from the history of the royal dynasty to the maps and geographical descriptions that assembled a picture of national identity from the component parts of the land." 137.
4. John Gillies, *Shakespeare and the Geography of Difference* (Cambridge: Cambridge University Press, 1994), 71.
5. Ibid., 91.
6. The essays for this volume are drawn from a seminar at the Shakespeare Association of America conference on Shakespeare and geography. Most of them see the relation between theater and geography as one of similarity.
7. Barbara Freedman, *Staging the Gaze* (Ithaca: Cornell University Press, 1991), 25.
8. Ibid., 24.
9. Helgerson, *Forms of Nationhood*, 125.
10. Bruce Avery, "Mapping the Irish Other: Spenser's 'A View of the Present State of Ireland'" *ELH* 57/2 (1990): 263–79.
11. John Norden, *The Surveyour's Dialogue* (London, 1607), 7.
12. The bibliography in this area is extensive. See, for example, G. R. Crone, *Maps and Their Makers* (London: Hutchinson, 1953); J. B. Harley, "Meaning and Ambiguity in Tudor Cartography," in *English Map-Making, 1500–1650*, ed. S. Tyacke (London: The British Library, 1983), 22–45; Chandra Mukerji, *From Graven Images* (New York: Columbia University Press, 1983); Peter Stallybrass, "Patriarchal Territories: The Body Enclosed," in *Rewriting the Renaissance*, ed. M. W. Ferguson (Chicago: University of Chicago Press, 1986), 123–142; and finally Sarah T. Tyacke and John Huddy, *Christopher Saxton and Tudor Map-Making* (London: The British Library, 1980).
13. Victor Morgan, "The Cartographic Image of the Country in Early Modern England," *Transactions of the Royal Historical Society* 5/29 (1979): 136–137.
14. David Young, *The Action to the Word* (New Haven: Yale University Press, 1990), sees the map as "the leading image of the play's expansive tendencies," 87. As a heuristic image this is perhaps so, but the map as a dramaturgical object has a very limited half-life on stage.
15. All citations of Shakespeare's works are from G. Blakemore Evans, ed., *The Riverside Shakespeare* (Boston: Houghton Mifflin, 1974).
16. Introduction to *Political Language and Oratory in Traditional Society*, ed. Maurice Bloch (London: Academic Press, 1975), 9.
17. Underlying my interpretation here is the reading of *King Lear* advanced by Harry Berger, Jr., most recently in "What Did the King Know and When Did

He Know It?: Shakespearean Discourses and Psychoanalysis." *South Atlantic Quarterly* 88 (winter 1989): 811–62.

18. Thus, it describes the "history of space" Henri Lefebvre discusses in *The Production of Space*, trans. Donald Nicholson-Smith (Oxford, Basil Blackwell, 1991), 127.

19. Maurice Bloch, "Symbols, Song, Dance, and Features of Articulation: Is religion an Exteme Form of Traditional Authority?" *European Journal of Sociology* 15 (1974). Bloch writes that linguistic "units in ritual do not follow each other logically, but sequentially, since there is no power in the articulation which links them . . ." 76.

20. Geoffrey Bullough, *Narrative and Dramatic Sources of Shakespeare*, (New York: Columbia University Press, 1957). Holinshed describes the arrangement in terms that Shakespeare adopted but mentions no map: "Heerewith, they by their deputies in the house of the archdeacon of Bangor, divided the realme amongst them, causing a tripartite indenture to be made and sealed with their seales, by the covenants whereof, all England from Severne and Trent, south and eastward, was assigned to the earle of March: all Wales, & the lands beyond Severne westward, were appointed to Owen Glendower: and all the remnant from Trent northward, to the lord Persie," 185. The map does not appear either in another possible source for the play, Samuel Daniel's *The First Fowre Bookes of the Civile Wars Between the Two Houses of Lancaster and Yorke*. See Bullough, 208–11.

21. Harley, "Meaning and Ambiguity in Tudor Cartography," 35.

22. Harry Berger, Jr., "Food for Words: Hotspur and the Discourse of Honor" (Forthcoming).

23. OED

24. Christopher Hibbert, *The Virgin Queen* (Reading, Mass.: Addison-Wesley, 1991), 167.

25. This passage is a textual crux. The first five quarto printings attribute the lines to Northumberland. The 1613 nd 1622 quartos give them to Hotspur, as does the first folio. I accept the folio lineation because, at least in my reading, it makes more sense that the words come from Hotspur.

26. Obviously, I take issue with Phyllis Rackin's assertion that "Hotspur's honor is never questioned in the play." *Stages of History*, 77. If his honor is never in question, one has to wonder why he himself is so concerned with it, polices it, and finally feeds his anxieties about it into the map in act 3 scene 1.

27. Bloch, "Symbols, Song, Dance," 71.

28. J. B. Harley, "Silences and Secrecy: The Hidden Agenda of Cartography in Early Modern Europe," *Imago Mundi* 40 (1988): 71.

A Room Not One's Own: Feminine Geography in *Cymbeline*

RHONDA LEMKE SANFORD

I

IN the literature of travel and exploration, the language of desire is frequently used to advertise new discoveries enticingly. Columbus described the New World alluringly as "a land to be desired, and, seen, it is never to be left."[1] Similarly, Sir Walter Raleigh described Guiana invitingly as "a Countrey that hath yet her Maidenhead, neuer sackt, turned, nor wrought."[2] These short excerpts reflect the abundance of sexual references in the literature of exploration, where the land is frequently figured as a woman to be ravished and the pun on the word *country* to refer to women's genitals (as in Hamlet's "country matters" (3.2.116)) was commonplace. In America, colonies named for queens are dubbed "Maryland" and "Virginia"—the latter coinage cleverly eliding the name of the monarch, emphasizing instead the virgin state of both queen and land (both of which presumably have yet their maidenheads), thus inviting seduction(s) far away that seem infeasible, and by now quite unlikely, at home). Tellingly, even colonies named after kings are feminized: Carolina for Charles and Georgia for George. The land thus feminized, discovery, exploration, invasion, and conquest are frequently figured as seduction, penetration, and rape. Iconographically, Jan Van der Straet's etching of Americo Vespucci standing erectly over a recumbent, nude, and female "America" illustrates vividly the initiation of what Michel de Certeau calls the "colonization of the body by the discourse of power."[3] Annette Kolodny, too, aptly captures the sexual innuendo involved in this colonization in the title of her book on the American pastoral, *The Lay of the Land*.[4]

Topographic images of women go beyond travel and exploration narratives and iconography of the New World, showing up in both the cartography and the literature of Renaissance England. In this essay, I will examine the pervasiveness of the image of the land gendered as feminine and the explorer-cartographer as masculine along with the attendant prevalence of the imagery of sexual congress and rape to characterize the act of surveying and of mapping. I will demonstrate a link between the portrayal of Imogen in *Cymbeline* with iconography of Elizabeth I and show how the scene in which Jachimo invades Imogen's chamber enacts the process of mapping and represents the action of rape. I will also show how Jachimo deviates from his intended mapping project and finally abandons this project altogether to concoct a traveler's tale that ironically turns out to be more convincing than the intended map. Finally, I will show the consequences of the "soil of rape"[5] on Imogen and on "Britain" using feminist and postcolonial theory.

In the English Renaissance, some of the most prominent images of woman-as-land-to-be-conquered are cartographic images of Queen Elizabeth I. A Dutch engraving of 1598 features Elizabeth as Europa; her head is Spain, her breast (singular, since she is portrayed as an Amazon) is in France; her right arm is Italy; and her left sword-wielding arm is England (armed against the papal invasion off her coast). Juxtaposed on several countries, Elizabeth's body thus becomes vulnerable to attack at many places—every cartographic inlet provides an orifice for invasion, or rape, as the name Europa reminds us. Similarly, the famous portrait of Elizabeth I by Marcus Gheeraerts the Younger (commonly referred to as the Ditchley portrait) shows Elizabeth standing on the map of England; in this iconography, Elizabeth the monarch becomes England the country, or island. Here, woman figured as island is as vulnerable to attack as woman figured as continent as we can see the tiny ships sailing under Elizabeth's skirt; this incursion, either commercial or, more menacingly, military, may remind us of Lucrece, the "late-sack'd island" of Shakespeare's poem, with blood flowing around her (*The Rape of Lucrece* 1740). In *Cymbeline*, Imogen's reference to herself as "Britain" (1.6.113) and Jachimo's comment that she is "fasten'd to an empery" (1.6.120) recall the Ditchley portrait.[6]

But the iconography of Queen Elizabeth's person associated with mapping does not stop with islands and countries. On the cosmographic scale, in a woodcut from John Case's "Sphæra Civitatas," Elizabeth's portrait looms above and embraces an outdated Ptolemaic universe in which the outermost sphere is Elizabeth's name and the concentric circles (representing the officers of the Court of Star Chamber) make invasion a matter of

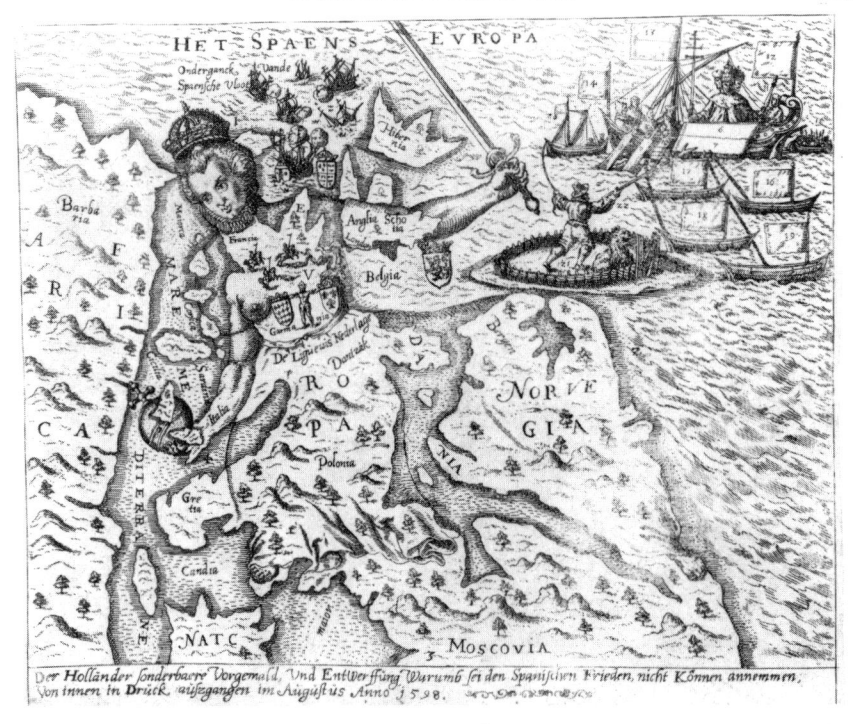

Elizabeth as Europa, an anonymous Dutch engraving. By permission of the Ashmolean Museum, Oxford University.

degrees, implying greater and greater intimacy within this "map" of the royal body. On a smaller scale, the emblem of the ideal woman in the Renaissance is the *hortus conclusus*, the enclosed garden—also the emblem of the Queen's virginity and of England the island.[7]

Also inscribing the royal body, I would argue that poems such as John Davies' *Hymnes of Astræa* represent a move to a different sort of mapping of the monarch. Describing the Queen in the formulaic manner of the acrostic—a form in which latitude and longitude seem implicit—certain features are highlighted, which taken cumulatively, might represent a map of Elizabeth's terrain. For example, in "Hymne III: To the Spring," the first *E* in the recurring acrostic ELISA BETHA REGINA tells us that "Earth now is greene"; the B - E - T of *Betha* gives us "Blasts are mild, and seas are calm, / Every meadow flowes with balme, / The earth wears all her riches"—much like the jewel-encrusted Elizabeth of many of her portraits. Thus, we have at least a partial delineation of a map inscribed in the monarch's name, the letters of

Elizabeth I by Marcus Gheeraerts the Younger (1592?), known as the "Ditchley" portrait. By courtesy of the National Portrait Gallery, London.

Woodcut from John Case's *Sphoera Civitatis*. By permission of the Houghton Library, Harvard University.

which may be seen as the cross-reference points of that map. In "Hymne XII: To her Picture" the poet chastises the painter for his "rude counterfeit"; a better rendering would have "each lyne, and each proportion right" as would an accurate map; Davies' insinuation here is of course that a poem is a better means of mapping (or portraiture) since the poet must feel by writing these lines that he indeed did get "each lyne, and each proportion right" in his metrics, his diction, and in this particular sequence of poems, in his inscription of each line within the body politic represented by the name of the monarch. Words, in fact, supplant pictorial representation in this mapping of the monarch and are powerful enough to bring this poet to something of a sexual climax in "Hymne XXIII" in his "delightful paine"; and to images of ejaculation in the middle of "Hymne XXVI."[8]

Just as Davies's acrostics divide the monarch's name in order to describe her, Donne's "Elegy 13: Love's Progress" divides a less regal woman's body while describing it. The poet, figured as a sailor, makes a voyage on his mistress' body, describing her from the top down in geographic terms. Her brow, when smooth, is a "paradise" for the lover but when furrowed can "shipwreck" him. The lover's face is mapped out in terms of meridians and compass points: "The nose like to the first meridian runs / Not 'twixt east and west, but 'twixt two suns" (47–48). Later, the cheek is a "rosy hemisphere" and the "swelling lips" are the "Islands Fortunate" where the lover "anchors" for "they seem all" (49–55). The poet continues with his voyage on the woman's body past the "Sestos and Abydos of her breasts" (61) and sails "towards her India, in that way / Shall her fair Atlantic navel stay" (65–66); here, the genitals are equated with exotic locales and are, of course, the real goal of this navigatory inventory.[9] In fact, after leading us through an inventory from the head down, where the lips seem all (and hint at the genital labia), the poet suggests that we "consider what this chase / Misspent, by thy beginning at the face" (71–72). The better route for "love's progress" would be from the bottom up: "rather set out below" (73)—since there would be fewer distractions along the way before arriving at this "first part that comes to bed" (80).

Composing a poem with certain cross references to a woman's name or "incorporating" an itemized list of geographical features into a poem may seem like an innocuous pastime, but Nancy Vickers discusses how the French poetic *Blasons anatomiques du corps femenin* (1543), which divides the woman's body while describing it, can be dangerous.[10] In such poems as *The Rape* of *Lucrece,* where breasts are at first "a pair of maiden worlds unconquered" (408), description leads to competitive desire, rape, and eventual death. Vickers discusses how descriptions of women can be dangerous:

> The canonical legacy of description in praise of beauty is, after all, a legacy shaped predominantly by the male imagination for the male imagination; it is, in large part, the product of men talking to men about women. In Lucrece, occasion, rhetoric, and result are all informed by, and thus inscribe, a battle between men that is first figuratively and then literally fought on the fields of woman's "celebrated" body. (96)

Likewise, in the hands of a character such as Jachimo in *Cymbeline,* the activity of description in a boasting game between men destroys the reputation of a princess just as surely as the enticing tales of the New World prompted its conquest. Having provided a bit of background on the common association of women's bodies with geography in the Renaissance, I would like to explore the dangers of describing women in terms of cartography and travelers' tales using the specific case of Shakespeare's *Cymbeline.* Like Columbus, Raleigh, and Donne, Shakespeare figures the woman Imogen as a country to be conquered, and Jachimo's penetration and mapping of her chamber represents his attempt at conquest.[11] Because Jachimo's actual failure of physical penetration of Imogen's body would effect his loss of the boasting game in which he is involved, he must fabricate false evidence of conquest based on his penetration of Imogen's bed chamber in order to win the game. Since the evidence Jachimo initially presents to Posthumus is a mental map, I would like to frame the first part of my discussion of Jachimo's description in terms Renaissance cartography.[12]

II

Because the mapping of England was a huge political project in Elizabethan England, the commissioning of a map was a manifestation of power. Because of their uses in defense, land ownership, travel, and colonization, the accuracy of maps was taking on greater import; thus, new maps included claims to greater accuracy than their predecessors had provided. In the boasting game central to *Cymbeline,* Posthumus's "map" of his wife, Imogen, as chaste is being questioned for its accuracy. If Posthumus is wrong about his wife, Jachimo's proposed map will correct or replace Posthumus's own inaccurate or outdated map of Imogen. In fact, Jachimo and Posthumus are engaged in a contest similar to that of Elizabethan cartographers over the accuracy of their maps. Consider, for example, the case of William Camden's *Britannia* (1594) and of Ralph Brooke's "A Discoverie of certaine errours published in the much-commended *Britannia*" (1594), followed by another edition "to which is added Mr. Camden's answers to this Book."[13] Like these Renaissance mapmakers, Jachimo, in his initial encounter with Imogen, extols his own skills and proclaims his corrections of previous inaccuracies as he rhapsodizes on Imogen's qualities:

> What, are men mad? Hath nature given them eyes
> To see this vaulted arch and the rich crop
> Of sea and land, which can distinguish 'twixt
> The fiery orbs above, and the twinn'd stones
> Upon the number'd beach, and can we not
> Partition make with spectacles so precious
> 'Twixt fair and foul?
>
> (1.6.32–38)

Here, Jachimo chastises the absent Posthumus for not seeing clearly what a prize Imogen is. Posthumus and other men may have eyes with which to appreciate the "vaulted arch" of heaven, the ability to comprehend the geographic features of "sea and land," the "fiery orbs" of the stars, as well as other features of the landscape, but they (and especially Posthumus) seem unable to truly appreciate that bit of geography with which Jachimo is now faced. Jachimo, as mapmaker, intends to "make partition"— he will use his own cartographic vision, his "spectacles" to chart "twixt fair, and foul," to draw boundaries and to capture the essence of Imogen within those boundaries.

Jachimo's vocation of mapmaker at Posthumus's behest requires that he gather certain information, certain knowledge about his "new found land," to steal blatantly from Donne's "Elegy 2."[14] Thus, when Jachimo enters Imogen's chamber via a trunk, he postures himself as both explorer and rapist: he compares himself to "Tarquin ... ere he waken'd / The chastity he wounded" (2.2.12–14) as he arrives in something like a bark and begins to explore both the sleeping Imogen and her chamber.[15] As he describes Imogen in typical Petrarchan terms—her eyes are "enclosed lights, now canopied / Under these windows, white and azure lac'd / With blue of heaven's own tinct" (21–23)—he nearly forgets himself in his desire for a kiss and he must remind himself of his mission:

> But my design!
> To note the chamber, I will write all down:
> [*Takes out his tables.*]
> Such, and such pictures; there the window; such
> Th' adornment of her bed; the arras, figures,
> Why, such and such; and the contents o' th' story.
> (2.2.23–27)

Jachimo's use of the words *design, note,* and *write* as well his locating certain features as reference points ("there the window") all figure in the mapmaking process, but with all of his sketchy "such and suches" we may begin to wonder how accurate a mapmaker Jachimo really is. Actually, Jachimo seems merely to be sketching notes for a map he intends to draw in greater detail later; the poetry, too, suffers here, marking the move from poetic description to notetaking.

While Jachimo begins by jotting notes about Imogen's chamber and her more accessible features, a change takes place when he realizes that more compelling evidence would be "some natural notes about her body" which would enrich his "inventory" (28–30). The actual transformation of Jachimo's mission takes place, however, when the word *voucher* (39), usually taken to mean written proof, is used to describe Imogen's cinque-spotted mole. In an ironic sense, Jachimo himself becomes a *voucher* who realizes he need no longer sketch out his proof and that the usual tools of mapmaking are superfluous to this assignment. The text inscribed on Imogen's body is converted to an oral transmission of a traveler's tale rather than the written proof of the map he intended to draw when he first took out his "tables." In fact, once he realizes the potency of this voucher, he abandons his "design" of writing, declaring, "No more: to what end? / Why should I write this down that's riveted, / Screw'd to my memory?" (42–44). Jachimo is certain that he can "vouch" for Imogen's supposed inconstancy with this evidence. Not coincidentally, this moment of recognition coincides with textual allusions to rape and sexual fulfillment as Jachimo notices that Imogen's book is marked "where Philomele gave up" (46), reinforcing his earlier rape allusion to "our Tarquin"; and he realizes he has had "enough" (46), underscoring the sexually satisfying nature of his invasion.[16] As he sees the "dragons of the night" (48), he reenters his trunk. He leaves Imogen's chamber with the rudiments of his intended map but also with the sexual fodder for a traveler's tale he will relate with embellishments later. Jachimo's ocular survey or voyeuristic rape might again remind us of the sexual anticipation in Donne's "Elegy 2: To His Mistress Going to Bed":

> Licence my roving hands, and let them go
> Behind, before, above, between, below.
> O my America, my new found land,
> My kingdom, safeliest when with one man manned,
> My mine of precious stones, my empery,
> How blessed am I in this discovering thee.
> To enter in these bonds is to be free,
> Then where my hand is set my seal shall be.
>
> (25–32)

In an ironic way, Jachimo's reentry into the trunk sets him free from the temptation he might have felt, along with Donne's poetic persona, to let his hands rove "behind, before, above, between, [and] below." Oddly, though, Jachimo has what he came for—he too has a "new found land." His eyes have "discovered" her "behind," "above," and so on, and his mouth can report her attributes with embellishments. Being back in the trunk renders Jachimo free from being discovered himself—allows him or "licenses" him to tell of the "voyage upon [Imogen]" (1.4.158) that he has figuratively made as satisfaction of his wager with Posthumus. Jachimo's ambiguous statement that he lodges in fear, "though this a heavenly angel, hell is here" (2.2.49–50), might refer to his fear before he reenters the trunk that either Imogen's beauty or the "hell" of her vagina might tempt him—an interesting twist on Donne's more blatantly sexual "to enter in these bonds is to be free."[17]

The nature of Jachimo's penetration as a figurative rape is reinforced ridiculously in the next scene when another kind of penetration is planned by Cloten to win the love of Imogen (2.3). Here, Cloten plans to "give her music a' mornings," because "they say it will penetrate" (11–13). As if to reinforce the idea of penetration, the stage direction, "Enter musicians," follows with further rather suggestive directions from Cloten: "Come on, tune. If you can penetrate her with your fingering, so; we'll try with tongue too. If none will do, let her remain; but I'll never give o'er" (14–16). If the music does not penetrate, he accuses music itself of being a vice, the "voice of unpav'd eunuch . . . can never amend" (27–31). Several uses of the words *come* and *arise* and references to being "up" both late and early make clear the sexual nature of this attempted penetration; the double figuring of castration in "unpav'd eunuch" makes it clear that this penetration does not "come off," a point restated by Cloten to Cymbeline: "I have assail'd her with musics, but she vouchsafes no notice" (39–40). In an odd way, too, this "penetration" reflects the move from the written to the oral ("fingering" to "tongue") that Jachimo enacted in Imogen's chamber.

Meanwhile, upon Jachimo's return to Rome, he reports of the night he had "in Britain" (2.4.45), and as he amplifies his "knowledge" of Imogen (51), he replicates the move from the written inventory for the intended map to the oral transmission of the traveler's tale first inspired within Imogen's chamber. Some of the details of Jachimo's "map"—for example, the tapestry of "proud Cleopatra, when she met her Roman" (70)—are dismissed by Posthumus as possible hearsay Jachimo may have gathered, even in Rome. This dismissal also seems to be an ironic allusion to other mapmakers having explored "Britain," and Mediterranean mapmakers were famous for their portolan maps of England;[18] thus, Jachimo must provide greater detail. He realizes that "more particulars / Must justify [his] knowledge," as he goads Posthumus with sexual innuendo in an obvious pun on "knowledge" (78–79). As Jachimo describes the "chimney," the "chimney piece," and "chaste Dian" (80–82) with likely implications of vagina, mons veneris, and hymen), he has set forth some compass points for his map. By establishing the chimney as the south, we might position the Cleopatra tapestry on the north (since it is of a directly opposing theme to that of "chaste Dian"). Delineations of north and south, however, do not satisfy Posthumus who says that "This is a thing / Which you might from relation likewise reap, / Being, as it is, much spoke of" (2.4.85–87). These lines might prompt us to ask just who would be speaking "much" about the details of Imogen's private chamber—how many others might have "reaped" there. This reference that figures Imogen as land to be cultivated and harvested seems to echo the discussion of Cleopatra by Enobarbus and the Romans: consider Agrippa's comment that "She made great Caesar lay his sword to bed; / He ploughed her, and she cropp'd" (*Antony and Cleopatra* 2.2.227–28). Besides the more usual sense of harvesting, the OED lists one "obscure" verb meaning for *reap* "to take away by force"—Posthumus's suggestion in this anagram of "rape" seems not implausible here since Philario and then Posthumus will soon also accuse Jachimo of stealing Imogen's bracelet. Likewise, Jachimo's further details [the roof of the chamber (87–88), and the andirons or the guards to the chimney (88–91, despite their metaphoric allusions)], are hardly enough to convince Posthumus that Jachimo has compromised Imogen's "honor" (91) or that he has been "on her" to invoke the common pun. Although Posthumus praises Jachimo's remembrance, merely having accurately mapped (or sketched, or described) the chamber is not enough for Posthumus. Even the physical evidence of the bracelet does not suffice because it might have been stolen.

It is, of course, finally with the description of the "cinque-spotted mole," the "corporal sign," that Posthumus is convinced of his wife's adultery. Jachimo continues:

> If you seek
> For further satisfying, under her breast
> (Worthy her pressing) lies a mole, right proud
> Of that most delicate lodging. By my life,
> I kiss'd it, and it gave me present hunger
> To feed again, though full. You do remember
> This stain upon her?
>
> (2.4.133–139)

Here, the description of the mole and Jachimo's affidavit of truth ("by my life"), his embellishment of its virtues ("worthy her pressing"), its paradoxical ability to provoke desire even while satisfying it, together become a traveler's tale of the fantastic reminiscent of Columbus's earlier reference to the New World or Enobarbus' description of Cleopatra's paradoxical ability to make hungry even while satisfying (likewise reported back in Rome, in *Antony and Cleopatra* 2.2.190–239).[19] Jachimo the fabulist now inspires complicity in Posthumus who is, after all, a fellow traveler and, since they are both involved in the competition of the boasting game, can do nothing but concur when Jachimo poses his question, "You do remember / This stain upon her?" To answer "no," would be to admit his own lack of "knowledge" of Imogen.[20] This question is definitely "worthy [Jachimo's] pressing" since it wins him the game. Posthumus's response, too, becomes embellished: the "stain," in fact, becomes "as big as hell can hold" (2.4.140) as he implores Jachimo to "spare your arithmetic, never count the turns. / Once, and a million!" (142–43). Here, once again allying Imogen with Cleopatra, Posthumus greatly multiplies Antony's epithet for the Egyptian "triple-turn'd whore" of Imogen's tapestry (*Antony and Cleopatra*

4.12.13) so that Imogen may as well have "turned" a million times in bed with Jachimo and other men. Posthumus's condemnation of women, too, is greatly multiplied as he implicates all women and finally all things feminine in his "woman's part" speech in the next scene (2.5.1–35). The mole, a "voucher" at the site of description, only becomes a "stain" at a distance—can only be exaggerated and embellished once Jachimo is out of the chamber, and in fact, like Enobarbus, back in Rome.[21]

As a cartographer within Imogen's chamber, Jachimo is limited to accurate recording of topographical features because he can only correct Posthumus's previous map in a verifiable way, but the traveler's tale offers a better medium for Jachimo's purposes because of its tolerance of improvisation. Annette Kolodny enumerates the range of the journeys on which travelers' tales are based: "some planned, some already executed, some wholly imaginary, and some a confusing combination of the three" (11). Thus, the very circumstances under which the traveler's tale is written (or invented)—away from the subject locale and often based on a thumbnail sketch such as Jachimo's—allow for improvisation, expansion, exaggeration, and complete fabrication. Jachimo may have undertaken to draw an accurate map, but he cannot be objective about a subject that threatens to carry him off in the rapture which prompts Imogen's "What, dear sir, / Thus raps you? Are you well?" (1.6.50–51). He is never sufficiently detached and, ironically, the traveler's tale he improvises turns out to be more convincing.

François Hartog outlines a rhetoric of otherness at work in travel literature, such as Herodotus' *History*, that is useful to my discussion of Jachimo's voyage to Imogen's chamber. Herodotus (ca. 480–425 B.C.), referred to as both the "father of history" and the "father of liars," wrote what is accepted as the first ethnography about those living outside Greece in his day. According to Hartog, the problem facing a writer of ethnography becomes one of translation; in other words, "how can the world being recounted be introduced in a convincing fashion into the world where it is recounted?" (212). The degree to which ethnographers (and travelers) are able to convince their audience is evaluated based on who is speaking and on the claims of experience made by the traveler. Firsthand experience, seeing with one's own eyes, or "autopsy," is the best evidence; next is hearsay evidence or experience that is reported by others; least convincing is that which is created by the traveler. Key phrases employed by Herodotus are used by Hartog to answer the question, "Who is speaking and to whom?" These key phrases correspond with the evidentiary hierarchy so that "I have seen" ranks higher and indicates more direct experience and the greatest likelihood of truth. "I have heard" ranks next, and the phrases "I say" and "I write" most likely indicate fabrication. Since vision is connected with persuasion, Jachimo succeeds because he is able to elevate pure fabrication into evidence of "autopsy" status.[22] Posthumus's objections to Jachimo's initial evidence also seem to depend on this evidentiary hierarchy. Thus, Jachimo's initial description of Imogen's chamber (his map) is rejected because it is evidence that is low on the hierarchy: Jachimo could have *heard* about some of the details from others, because they are "much spoke of." Jachimo eventually succeeds because he uses evidence that both he and Posthumus have *seen with their own eyes*. To secure his claim, however, Jachimo adds another element that Hartog also considers essential to the traveler's tale—marvels and curiosities (the Greek *thoma*), like the statues that are so lifelike they are "likely to report themselves" (2.4.83) and the cinque-spotted mole with its mystical properties. By presenting *thoma*, Jachimo wins the wager because he claims to have seen something of great wonder *with his own eyes*.

In fact, Jachimo was never able to render an accurate map because the boasting game requires that Posthumus remain involved, and only a traveler's tale allows and accommodates such participation, such complicity. In fact, the rules of this game of description were established when Posthumus, as Jachimo later tells Cymbeline, began

> His mistress' picture, which by his tongue being made,
> And then a mind put in't, either our brags
> Were crak'd of kitchen trulls, or his description
> Prov'd us unspeaking sots.
>
> (5.5.175–78)

Thus, in their initial meeting, Posthumus, too, began with a thumbnail sketch of Imogen, and it is Posthumus's own traveler's tale, this "picture" made by his tongue, requiring embellishment and complicity by his listeners ("and then a mind put in't"), and his own boasting and "publishing," which are to blame for prompting Jachimo's action. Jachimo's tale, as he finally unravels it, shows that while he may have been capable of drafting a true map of Imogen's terrain (Posthumus does commend the accuracy of his remembrance, after all in 2.4.92–93), the competition requires an embellished traveler's tale instead. It requires (in effect) that a "mind [be] put in't."

Nancy Vickers discusses this kind of description where "on the one hand, the describer controls, possesses, and uses that matter to his own ends; and, on the other, his reader/listener is extended the privilege or pleasure of 'seeing.'"[23] Considering the voyeuristic nature of Jachimo's sexual drive, his pleasure is indeed great and his lavish descriptions demonstrate how much he values that pleasure. The "pleasure" extended to Posthumus, however, brings only pain. Because of the nature of the boasting contest in *Cymbeline*, Posthumus is in the peculiar position of being both rival mapmaker and, in a sense, patron to the mapmaker Jachimo. However, by the time Jachimo returns with his "map," the paradigm seems to have changed from patronage to purchase (as it did in Renaissance cartography)—and Posthumus is simply not "buying" Jachimo's map. Jachimo and Posthumus are now united in the eyewitness of the traveler's tale and are jointly enthralled by their descriptions and expansions. Back in Rome, they look from a distance upon Imogen and Britain as other, just as Enobarbus and his Roman peers relished a communal (and imaginary) gaze upon Cleopatra thanks to Enobarbus' evocative description. Jachimo's descriptions, taken together, were deemed by Posthumus to show that Imogen's "bond of chastity [is] quite crack'd" (5.5.207) and to associate her stained honor with that other "triple turned whore." Just as Vickers discussed the "buying" and "selling" of description (97), explorers cracked the chastity of the New World with the selling and buying of fantastic tales. By becoming the subject of description, by being mapped, by becoming the "new found land"—and like that land being turned a million times—Imogen has lost the innocence implied by her more likely name "Innogen."[24] For her "transgression," Posthumus orders her murder. Of course, Pisanio is unable to carry out his master's orders, but Imogen is nevertheless punished for having been the subject of description. She is exiled to the edge of the map in Wales, where she becomes a wandering womb (unmappable and unreadable because of her male garb) and lives in a cave in the highly feminized but savage geography of Milford Haven for two acts before she returns to her father's court for her final humiliation.

It is significant, too, that much of the imagery in both Jachimo's initial meeting with Imogen and his penetration of her chamber alludes to navigational matters, foreshadowing his later move to the tale of wonder. Jachimo's mission, according to Posthumus was, after all, to "make your voyage upon [Imogen]" (1.4.158). As we have seen, Jachimo initially becomes so transported, seasick, or "mad" by his own lust over this new terrain that Imogen has to bring him back to reality with the query, "What, dear sir, / Thus raps you? Are you well?" (1.6.50–51). At Jachimo's initial meeting with Imogen, he is able to observe only her surface qualities—her shoreline or border, if you will—and can only speculate about what he might find with a survey of the interior of this continent:

> All of her that is out of door most rich!
> If she be furnish'd with a mind so rare,
> She is alone th' Arabian bird.
>
> (1.6.14–17)

In fact, here Jachimo may appear to be describing a portolan map; as a Roman, he is viewing Imogen, and Britain, as the other to be mapped with his reference to the exotic, the wonderful "Arabian bird"—the phoenix.[25] He will continue with his further penetration of Imogen's terrain via a trunk, a smaller vessel than the one in which he would have initially arrived. Like a good navigator, when he emerges from his trunk, he notes the time of day: "The crickets sing, and man's o'er labor'd sense / Repairs itself by rest" (2.2.11–12). He also notes the weather conditions: "'Tis her breathing that / Perfumes the chamber thus. The flame o' th' taper / Bows toward her" (2.2.18–20). His description here is reminiscent of explorers in the New World described by Annette Kolodny in *The Lay of the Land*:

> On the second of July, 1584, two English captains, Philip Amadas and Arthur Barlowe, entered the coastal waters off what is now North Carolina and enjoyed "so sweet and so strong a smell as if we had been in the midst of some delicate garden abounding with all kinds of odoriferous flowers."
>
> (10)

Exotic smells are a common report of travelers to the New World, and Jachimo's description of this experience places him squarely in the genre of travel and exploration literature.

In another Shakespearean romance, Antonio proclaims that "Travellers n'er did lie, / Though fools at home condemn 'em" (*The Tempest* 3.3.26–27), but his proclamation is made after Prospero's magic has produced "*strange SHAPES, bringing in a banket.*" These same "shapes" then "*dance about it with gentle actions of salutations"* (3.3. SD following 19). Resembling reports of hospitality by New World natives, this same bit of theatrical artifice prompts Sebastian's avowal:

> Now I will believe
> That there are unicorns; that in Arabia
> There is one tree, the phoenix' throne, one phoenix
> At this hour reigning there.
>
> (21–24)

Shakespeare seems to be poking fun at these castaways who suddenly believe in wonders after viewing a bit of theater, but Jachimo's own bit of improvisation has a similar, but more explosive, effect on Posthumus.

III

Turning for a moment to modern literature, I would like to suggest a parallel between Imogen's status at the end of *Cymbeline* and that of a character in a story by Indian writer Mahasweta Devi. In Devi's "Douloti the Bountiful,"[26] Douloti, the daughter of a tribal bonded worker in India, becomes a bond slave prostitute who, after achieving the highest status in a house of prostitution, descends to the lowest rung in that same hierarchy. Finally, having contracted venereal disease and too sick to continue in her profession, she makes a journey to a hospital for treatment, only to be directed to a more remote hospital. She decides instead to walk back to her family's village. She doesn't make it home but collapses in the night on the comforting clay of a schoolyard and dies. A rural schoolmaster, Mohan, had drawn a map of India in the clay of the schoolyard in order to teach his students nationalism in preparation for an Independence Day celebration during which he was to place the Indian flag in the middle of the map. In the morning, Mohan and his students discover Douloti on the map. Gayatri Spivak explains the ambiguous ending: "The story ends with two short sentences: a rhetorical question, and a statement that is not an answer: 'What will Mohan do now? Douloti is all over India.'" Spivak continues:

> The word *doulot* means wealth. Thus *douloti* can be made to mean "traffic in wealth." Under the last sentence—"Douloti is all over India" [*Bhrat jora hoye Douloti*]—one can hear that other sentence:

Jagat [the globe] *jora hoye Douloti.* What will Mohan do now?—the traffic in wealth [douloti] is all over the globe.

I end, somewhat abruptly, with a text for discussion: Such a globalization of douloti, dissolving even the proper name, is not an overcoming of the gendered body. The persistent agendas of nationalisms and sexuality are encrypted there in the indifference of superexploitation.[27]

Similarly, by having maps and tales "encrypted" on her geography, Imogen has experienced a metaphoric death during the play even though she has escaped the actual death that Posthumus ordered for her. In the end, Imogen is "fasten'd to an empery" in the manner of the dead Douloti, all over India, rather than like the erect and stately Elizabeth of the Ditchley portrait, with the "traffic in wealth" that her jewels and the tiny ships suggest. Like Douloti, Imogen's proper name (as the next Queen) has been dissolved. After all, she was sole heir to her father's kingdom at the beginning of the play and it seems not coincidental that her brothers, who were kidnaped twenty years earlier and believed dead, have discovered their own identities even while hers has been tainted. Interestingly, Jachimo's lewd penetration of Imogen's chamber is not enough to resurrect them—only after the *telling* of the traveler's tale do they appear; in other words, they don't appear until after she is "stained."

As readers, we too have been diverted with a traveler's tale, since the boasting game is based on such a tale. Ironically, one translation of the story from Boccaccio's *Decameron* that is a likely source for Shakespeare begins by warning of the dangers of description:

> Wherein is declared that by over-liberal commending the chastity of women it falleth out (oftentimes) to be very dangerous, especially by the means of treacherers, who yet (in the end) are justly punished for their treachery.[28]

In this translation of Boccaccio, those "dangers" and their consequences are incumbent upon the describer, or "treacherer"—who, in Boccaccio's story, ends up being impaled naked on a stake, anointed with honey and devoured by wasps and mosquitoes. In another possible source, *Frederyke of Jennen*, the treacherer, John of Florence, too, suffers a "shamefull death" of beheading.[29] In *Cymbeline*, by contrast, the treacherer Jachimo is forgiven—is told to "Live, / And deal with others better" (5.5.419–20)—in effect, to "go and sin no more." Imogen, not so fortunate, is the real loser here, moving from her role as heir apparent to a role of near insignificance as part of the land and the masses to be ruled; this, despite having her reputation cleared. Ironically, Britain, for which Imogen has been the sometimes metonymic equivalent, again pays the tribute to Rome despite having won the battle at Milford Haven. Oddly enough, in this play, winners are losers, and losers, such as Jachimo, are forgiven.

A pun on tail/tale in Petruchio's retort to Kate when she asks him to leave, "What, with my tongue in your tail?" (*The Taming of the Shrew* 2.1.218), works well in the story of Imogen. By having her "tail" become the subject of "tales" of travelers, especially those who would like to "make their voyage on her," Imogen has indeed ceased being "Virginia," the virgin land. Her chastity, as well as her chamber, by being explored, mapped, described, and published has been "cracked." Jachimo has figuratively had his tongue in her "tail" by his lewd and voyeuristic sexual fantasies, and he has had his tongue in her "tale" by describing and publishing his knowledge of her chamber and her person to others. The continued momentum of this descriptive competition is evident even in the final scene when Posthumus reverses his opinion of Imogen and creates yet another, or a sort of "counter-traveler's tale" to Jachimo's, based on the same formula of the boasting game which initiated this dangerous competition of description: Posthumus describes further wonders, too, as he now realizes that Imogen is indeed a "temple / Of Virtue" (5.5.220–21). Concluding that Jachimo's map was a forgery and that his traveler's tale was false, Posthumus's former map of Imogen is reinstated, if not a little embellished with newfound "wonders."

Even the "happy ending" has this competing traveler landing on Imogen's shore as Cymbeline tells us, "See, / Posthumus anchors upon Imogen" (5.5.392–93). Thus, Imogen continues as the "new found land" once again being colonized by the discourse of power that makes her subject to having all of her aspects published broadly. She is left with neither a room nor a womb of her own.

Notes

1. Christopher Columbus, *Select Documents Illustrating the Four Voyages of Columbus*, trans. and ed. Cecil Jane (London: Hakluyt Society, 1930) 1:12.

2. Walter Raleigh, *The Discoverie of the Large, Rich, and Bewtiful Empyre of Guiana* in (London: Imprinted by Robert Robinson, 1596), 96.

3. Michel de Certcau, *The Writing of History*, trans. Tom Conley (New York: Columbia University Press, 1988), xxv–xxvii. Louis Montrose also offers an excellent discussion of this etching in "The Work of Gender in the Discourse of Discovery," *Representations* 33 (Winter 1991):1–41.

4. Annette Kolodny, *The Lay of the Land: Metaphor as Experience and History in American Life and Letters* (Chapel Hill: University of North Carolina Press, 1984).

5. Catherine Stimpson uses this evocative title for her discussion of rape in *Titus Andronicus*, *The Rape of Lucrece*, the "darkly comic study of imagined rape" of Imogen by Cloten in *Cymbeline*, and Jachimo's theft of Imogen's good reputation, which "like his penetration of her bedchamber, is a psychic equivalent" (61). Stimpson links rape in Shakespeare's works with the tainting of patriarchal property rights in "Shakespeare and the Soil of Rape," in *The Woman's Part: Feminist Criticism of Shakespeare*, ed. Carolyn Ruth Swift Lenz, Gayle Greene, and Carol Thomas Neely (Urbana and Chicago: University of Illinois Press, 1983), 56–64.

6. Indeed, in *Cymbeline*, England is even "clothed"—in a "salt-water girdle" (3.1.80).

7. Using the popular iconography of the Queen along with other emblems of chastity, Peter Stallybrass discusses women's chastity as a "patriarchal territory" that must be safeguarded. Using as his model Bakhtin's distinction between the classical ("finished, completed") body and the grotesque body (which is "unfinished, outgrows itself, transgresses its own limits"), Stallybrass shows how women, as possessions of men, were subject to constant surveillance of three specific areas: the mouth, chastity, and the threshold of the house. The three areas are often collapsed into each other so that linguistic fullness and/or frequenting public space might be associated with wantonness. "Patriarchal Territories: The Body Enclosed," in *Rewriting the Renaissance: The Discourses of Sexual Difference in Early Modern Europe*, ed. Margaret W. Ferguson, Maureen Quilligan and Nancy J. Vickers (Chicago: University of Chicago Press, 1986), 123–42.

8. John Davies, "Hymne XXVI":

> **B**ehold how my proud quill doth shed
> Eternal nectar on her head;
> The pompe of coronation
> Hath not such power her fame to spread,
> As this my admiration.

Here the pen is the mighty instrument of description that successfully competes with pictorial representation but is also figured sexually; for certainly a writer of Davies' skill in manipulating letters is also playing on the anagram for "Hymne"—hymen. *Hymnes of Astræa*, ed. Alexander Grosan (1869), *The Complete Poems of Sir John Davies* (Ann Arbor: University Microfilms, 1969).

9. This type of imagery is very much with us today; I am reminded, for example, of Michael Franks' recent recording of "Popsicle Toes": "You've got the nicest North America this sailor ever saw, / I'd like to feel your warm Brazil and touch your Panama," from Michael Franks, *The Art of Tea*, Warner Bros. Records, 1975.

Similar images appear in Maya Angelou's "Africa," from *Oh Pray My Wings*

Are Gonna Fit Me Well (New York: Random House, 1975) and in Sharon Olds' "Topography," in The Gold Cell (New York: Knopf, 1987).

10. Nancy Vickers, "'The Blazon of Sweet Beauty's Best': Shakespeare's Lucrece," in Shakespeare and the Question of Theory (New York: Methuen, 1985), 95–115. Patricia Parker also ties together blazon, inventory, and exploration in "Rhetorics of Property: Exploration, Inventory, Blazon," chap. 7 in Literary Fat Ladies: Rhetoric, Gender, Property (New York: Methuen, 1987), Linda Woodbridge, too, discusses the land-as-woman trope and aligns seige and rape in Titus Andronicus, Lucrece, and Cymbeline in "Palisading the Elizabethan Body Politic," Texas Studies in Literature and Language, 33, no. 3 (Fall 1991): 327–54. She also proposes a change in the body-political image of England with the death of the Virgin Queen and the accession of James I.

11. Shakespeare also uses this connection between geography and woman in The Merry Wives of Windsor where Falstaff describes Mistress Page as "a region in Guiana, all gold and bounty" (1.3.69) and where he articulates his plans to seduce both Mistress Page and Mistress Ford: "They shall be my East and West Indies, and I will trade to them both" (71–72), for example. In The Comedy of Errors, Dromio of Syracuse orates a lengthy and very bawdy description of Luce as "spherical, like a globe" wherein, he swears, he could "find out countries" (3.2.112–43).

12. Richard Helgerson presents an excellent outline of Elizabethan projects of mapping England in Forms of Nationhood: The Elizabethan Writing of England (Chicago and London: University of Chicago Press, 1992). Peter Barber offers two excellent chapters in Monarchs, Ministers, and Maps that deal specifically with the mapping of England: "England I: Pageantry, Defense, and Government: Maps at Court to 1550," and "England II: Monarchs, Ministers, and Maps, 1550–1625," in Monarchs, Ministers, and Maps: The Emergence of Cartography as a Tool of Government in Early Modern Europe, ed. David Buisseret (Chicago and London: University of Chicago Press, 1992), 26–98. John Gillies connects these mapping projects with theater in Shakespeare and the Geography of Difference (Cambridge: Cambridge University Press, 1994).

13. Less polemic claims of accuracy and correction are often touted in the titles of new maps, such as Thomas Porter's "The Newest and Exactest MAPP of the most Famous Citties LONDON and WESTMINSTER . . ." (1655).

14. "To his Mistress Going to Bed." Also frequently anthologized as Elegy 19, John Carey's edition of Donne's poems has it as Elegy 2. John Donne (Oxford and New York: Oxford University Press, 1990).

15. The image is again reminiscent of Van der Straet's etching of Vespucci surveying the recumbent "America." Compare, too, Troilus's description of Cressida:

> Her bed is India, there she lies, a pearl;
> Between our Ilium and where she [resides],
> Let it be call'd the wild and wand'ring flood,
> Ourself the merchant, and this sailing Pandar
> Our doubtful hope, our convoy, and our bark.
> (Troilus and Cressida 1.1.100–105)

16. Georgianna Ziegler asserts that "the woman's room signifies her 'self,' and the man's forced or stealthy entry of this room constitutes a rape of her private space." "My Lady's Chamber: Female Space, Female Chastity in Shakespeare," Textual Practice 4, no. 1 (Spring 1990): 71–90. Patricia Parker, too,

remarks that "the association of a female body with a 'chamber' is finally inseparable from the violation of the chamber to which her sexuality is reduced" (*Literary Fat Ladies,* 136). See also Note 5.

17. Of course, he could be posing an opposition between this heavenly angel and the "hell" under the stage, to which he will now return via the trunk.

18. See Barber, "England II: Monarchs, Ministers, and Maps, 1550–1625," 65–66.

19. Compare also Jachimo's initial impression of Imogen filled with oxymorons, Shakespeare's frequent refuge for characters under pressure:

Jachimo.	Sluttery, to such neat excellence oppos'd Should make desire vomit emptiness, Not so allu'd to feed.
Imogen.	What is the matter, trow?
Jachimo.	The cloyed will— That satiate yet unsatisfied desire, that tub Both fill'd and running—ravening first the lamb, Longs after for the garbage.
Imogen.	What, dear sir, Thus raps you? Are you well?

(1.6.44–51)

20. Of course, in his "woman's part" speech in the next scene, Posthumus admits to a rather disappointing connubial union in which Imogen "restrain'd" him of his "lawful pleasures" and "pray'd me oft forbearance" (2.5.9–10).

21. Although they are indeed very different women, a compelling resemblance is constructed in many of the scenes involving Imogen between her and Cleopatra: in particular, both are portrayed as "other," exotic, female, and transgressive by Roman men for the titillation of other men in Rome and away from the site of the wonders themselves.

22. See Francois Hartog, "The Eye and the Ear," chap. 7 in *The Mirror of Herodotus: The Representation of the Other in the Writing of History,* trans. by Janet Lloyd (Berkeley: University of California Press, 1988), 260–309, for a discussion of this hierarchy of evidence. See also Stephen Greenblatt, *Marvellous Possessions: The Wonder of the New World* (Chicago: University of Chicago Press, 1991), for a thorough discussion of marvels and wonders of the New World.

23. Vickers, *Shakespeare and the Question of Theory,* 96. Patricia Parker's discussion of *enargeia* in "Shakespeare and rhetoric: 'dilation' and 'delation' in *Othello,*" is germane to this point, as well, *Shakespeare and the Question of Theory,* ed. Patricia Parker and Geoffrey Hartman (New York: Routledge, 1990), 54–74. Iago, too, is able to describe Desdemona's supposed infidelity so vividly that Othello accepts a mere description as "ocular proof" and responds with, "I see" (*Othello,* 3.3.360ff).

24. J. M. Nosworthy suggests that "Imogen," while used throughout the 1623 folio, may be a misprint for "Innogen" (or Jnnogen), the name Simon Forman used in his diary when describing the 1611 staging of the play. Nosworthy also points out the occurrence of a mute Innogen, wife of Leonato, in the 1600 Quarto of of *Much Ado About Nothing,* demonstrating a long association of the of the names of this hero and heroine (Posthumus's family name is Leonatus.) *Cymbeline,* The Arden Shakespeare (New York: Routledge, 199), 7.

Also important, I think, is Innogen's status as a mute or "ghost" character in *Much Ado*, similar to Imogen's status by the end of *Cymbeline*.

25. Although it has been noted that Elizabeth seems to be standing on a composite of Christopher Saxton's county maps (1579) in the Ditchley portrait, I think Jachimo's initial glimpse at Imogen's more public features invites an alternative reading of this foundational map as a portolan map. We get the coastline and not much more—she hides the *terra incognita* beneath her skirts.

26. The story is found in Devi's *Imaginary Maps*, trans. Gayatri Chakravorty Spivak (New York: Routledge, 1995), 19–92.

27. Gayatri Chakravorty Spivak, "Woman in Difference: Mahasweta Devi's 'Douloti the Bountiful," *Cultural Critique* (Winter 1992):105–128.

28. *The Decameron*, The Second Day, The Ninth Novel. Trans. unknown. (London, 1620).

29. "Than toke the officers John of Florence and brought hym besyde of the galowes, where the Justice should be done. And whan that he had made his prayers and all doone, than made the hangman him knele downe and smote Johann of Florence head of, and after that laied his body vpon a whele, and the head he stycked on a stake and set it by, ouer the head a galowes: all after the maner as the kyng had iudged him; and than retourned home againe. And in this maner was John of Florence serued for his great falshed and thefte that he hadde done to that trewe wyfe and mayde" (*Frederyke of Jennen*, reprinted in J. M. Nosworthy, *Cymbeline*, 203).

Genre and Geography: The Eastern Mediterranean in *Pericles* and *The Comedy of Errors*

LINDA MCJANNET

WITH exception of *The Tempest*, the romances have not been seen as prime texts in which to examine Shakespeare's handling of geography, history, or other markers of cultural otherness. Like their improbable plots (whose symbolic or mythological meaning seems their chief claim on our attention), the space and time of the romances have been seen as that of myth or fairy tale: a never-never land and a mythical "no-time," or a hodge-podge of "real places," used, without regard to geographic or historical fidelity, for their decorative, exotic, or other generic value. Editorial bemusement at the presence of the "seacoast" in the Bohemia of *The Winter's Tale* stands as an exemplum of this view. Bohemia is seen as a literary, pastoral landscape, not a "real country" that can be (or needs to be) meaningfully located in history or placed in the *theatrum mundi* of Ortelius. To the extent that history and geography often seem to be erased in these plays, the romances may seem irrelevant to our attempt to recover the symbolic geography and history of the period. I say "geography *and* history" since the two cannot be easily separated. In referring to a geographical location, one also implies to some degree a historical period. Cities (to focus on the geographical unit most relevant in these plays) thrive and decline, change their names, or have them changed by invaders; they suffer destruction, and new cities rise from the ashes.

The two plays I propose to discuss, *Pericles* and *The Comedy of Errors*, are set in pre-Christian, and apparently pre-Roman, times in the eastern Mediterranean.[1] Their *oikumene* or "home world," to borrow John Gillies' phrase, is the Greek or Hellenized cities of the Levant, although at any given moment a particular locale may be constructed as *eschatia*, exotic, strange, and other.[2] In adapting this setting from their respective sources, both plays contain examples of anachronism and geographical confusion. In *Errors*, Shakespeare switches the setting from Epidamnum (as in Plautus) to Ephesus, but he makes no explicit reference to this city's famous Temple of Diana. Instead, he places a "Priory" and an "Abbey" in the town. In *Pericles*, Thaliard promises to kill Pericles if he comes "within my pistol's length" (1.1.166), and in Pentapolis, Pericles competes in a tournament with other "knights," whose shields bear mottos in Latin and "Spanish" (Italian). In this episode, the sources are more faithful to the Greek customs of the original story than the play.[3]

Nonetheless, the handling of geography, and therefore of historical and cultural otherness, in these two plays merits attention for several reasons. First, setting is operative in both plays as both a literal and a symbolic marker; place-names echo in *Pericles* almost as frequently as in *Antony and Cleopatra*, where setting is crucial. According to Marvin Spevack's concordance, in *Antony and Cleopatra* the key place-names (Rome, Alexandria, Egypt) are mentioned a total of seventy-eight times. *Pericles* mentions the six locales of the action (Tyre/Tyrus, Tharsus, Mytilene, Ephesus, Pentapolis, and Antioch) seventy-five times.[4] Second, comparing the early play, *Errors*, to the later, *Pericles*, suggests at the very least an increased effort to maintain historical and geographic coherence.[5] Third, what I shall argue is a relatively benign view of the East in these plays (and, in the case of *Pericles*, in their sources) suggests a paradoxical relation between humanist veneration for ancient Greek culture and Christian hostility to the Muslim Turks. In brief, the humanist habit of naturalizing or assimilating the Hellenized East to one's own moral universe in the long run may have contributed to demonizing the infidels who, in the eyes of early modern Christians, had usurped and enslaved the venerable locales of the ancient world.[6]

Since both plays ultimately derive from Greek sources, it is not surprising that they are set in the Greek cities of the eastern Mediterranean. *Errors* is, of course, based on *The Menaechmi* of Plautus, whose plays were "freely adapted into the Latin vernacular from the New Comedy of the Greeks."[7] Although Plautus is synonymous with "Roman comedy" for us, he sets this play in a Greek city on the Adriatic coast of Macedonia, and he uses its Greek name, Epidamnum, not its Roman one, Dyrrhachium. As is equally well known, *Pericles* is a retelling of *Apollonius of Tyre*, a tale that provides the clearest evidence of a "direct connection" between later medieval romance and its roots in Greek prose narratives of the first century B.C. to the third century

A.D.[8] The geography of the two plays is that of the Greek diaspora and, in the case of *Pericles,* the cultural moment and locales of the late Hellenistic kingdoms that governed and fought over Alexander's empire after his death. The Seleucid monarchs, centered in Antioch, and the Ptolemies in Alexandria developed the imperial blend of Macedonian kingship and Egyptian/Persian absolute monarchy initiated by Alexander. The cities of these twin empires nurtured a homogenous culture (at least for those who wished to join the elite) based on a common language ("Koine Greek"), facilities for travel and commerce, Greek institutions (such as the gymnasium and the worship of the Olympian gods), and Greek styles of dress and living. Although eventually dominated and influenced by Rome, the culture of the East retained much of its Hellenistic character, and the Romans were "Orientalized" even as the East was "Romanized."

The two plays take place in (or significantly allude to) eight cities prominent in the Greek world and, therefore, well known through literary works of classical antiquity and the Renaissance. The same cities are also prominent in several of the historical maps in the supplement or "Parergon" included in the later editions of Ortelius's *Theatrum Orbis Terrarum.* It has, in fact, been suggested that one of these, a map of the eastern Mediterranean locations visited by St. Paul ("Peregrinatio D. Pauli"), was a source for both of these plays.[9] Seven of the eight ancient cities mentioned or represented in these plays are clearly visible on the original of this map.[10]

The following annotations provide a brief sketch of the Hellenistic background of seven of the eight cities.[11]

> Antioch, ancient city of Syria, now the southeast coast of modern Turkey. Founded by the Greeks about 300 B.C. Center of the Seleucid Kingdom.
>
> Tyre, an ancient Phoenician seaport and center of trade, now in modern Lebanon. Parent city of Carthage. Famous for its seven-month resistance to Alexander. Part of the Ptolemaic Kingdom initially, but in 200 B.C., it came under Seleucid rule.
>
> Tharsus (Tarsus), ancient city near southeast coast of modern Turkey on the Cydnus River (site of the first meeting of Antony and Cleopatra). Excellent harbor of Rhegma. Known for its fertile soil and its school of Greek philosophy.
>
> Ephesus, ancient city in Ionia on the Aegean coast, now modern Turkey. Famous for the Temple of Diana/Artemis, one of the seven wonders of the ancient world.

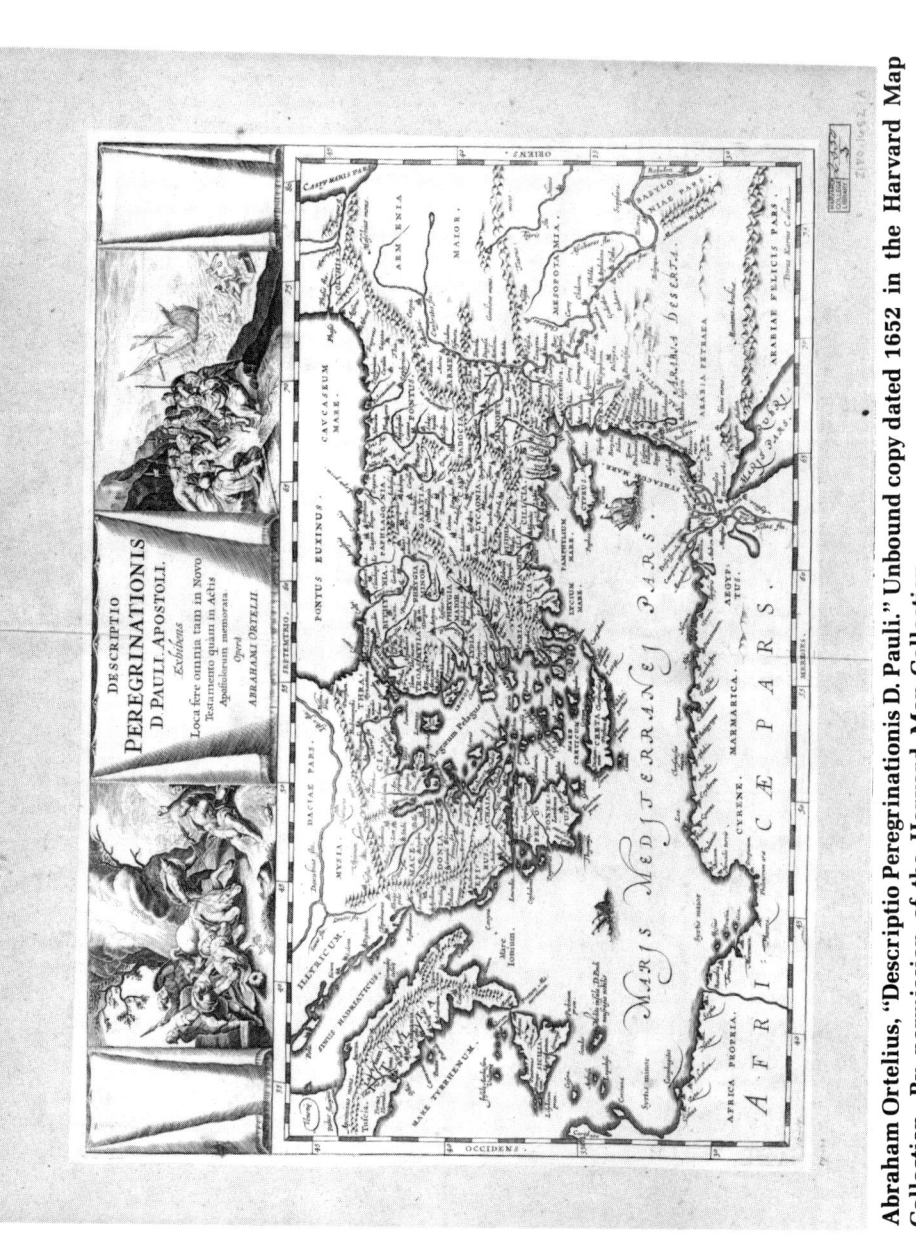

Abraham Ortelius, "Descriptio Peregrinationis D. Pauli." Unbound copy dated 1652 in the Harvard Map Collection. By permission of the Harvard Map Collection.

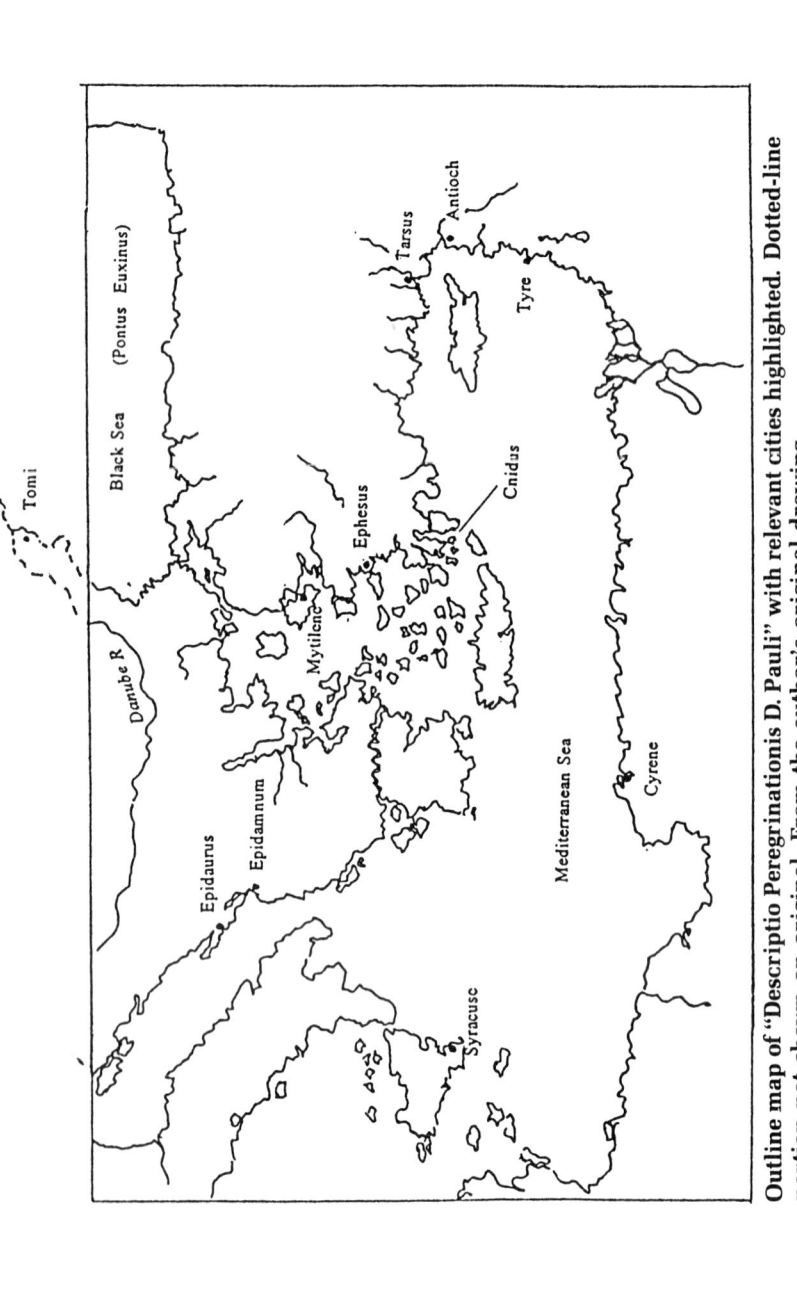

Outline map of "Descriptio Peregrinationis D. Pauli" with relevant cities highlighted. Dotted-line portion not shown on original. From the author's original drawing.

Epidamnum, a Greek city founded in the seventh century B.C. on the Adriatic coast of what is now Albania. Called Dyrrhachium by the Romans; now known as Durres.

Mytilene, port city on the island of Lesbos, off the west coast of Asia Minor. Greek theater discovered there in 1958. Known for its poets and Greek culture in the Archaic period (seventh to sixth century B.C.).

Syracuse, on the southeast coast of Sicily. Founded by Greeks from Corinth in the eighth century B.C. Famous for repelling a Carthaginian invasion in 480 B.C. and later the Athenians. Independent until Roman conquest in 211 B.C.

Locating the eighth city, Pentapolis, is more problematic. Some scholars identify it with Cyrene, chief of five cities settled by Greeks as early as 630 B.C. on the coast of what is now Libya. Cyrene is to be found on the map of St. Paul's journeys, but under this name, not as Pentapolis. If Cyrene is the city meant, it constitutes the major geographical anomaly in *Pericles*. First, it is not "in our country of Greece," as the fishermen claim (2.1.64); second, a wind *from* the north ("When I was born, the wind was north," 4.1.51) could not drive Pericles' ship north*ward* from Cyrene on the African coast to the waters off Ephesus in Asia Minor, where Thaisa gives birth and apparently dies. However, there were seven Pentapolises known in the ancient world, and two that are geographically consistent with these details have been proposed: Tomi, a coastal city in Thrace, and Cnidus, an island near Rhodes.[12] Although neither candidate is entirely satisfactory, the case for Tomi, on the Black Sea south of the Danube mouth, seems the stronger of the two. Tomi is located in Thrace, territory often classified as part of Greece. It was visited by Jason and colonized by Greeks at an early date. It lies north of Ephesus, and traveling from Tomi to Tyre, Ephesus is about halfway, the point at which the storm is said to commence ("Half the flood / Hath their keel cut," says the Chorus, 3.Cho.45–46.) Cnidus, which lies slightly south of Ephesus, is consistent with the general path of Pericles' travels but not with the distances.[13] If Tomi is the original of Shakespeare's Pentapolis, it was well known as the place of Ovid's exile; Ortelius explicitly labels it as such.[14]

After perusing the Ortelian map of St. Paul's journeys, I suggest one other possibility. The map shows five cities on or near the northern coast of the Aegean whose names end in "-polis": Philippopolis, Hadrianopolis, Neapolis, Traianopolis, and Amphipopolis. If Shakespeare knew this map, as it has been argued that he did, he might have coined his own Pentapolis from the suggestive five-fold repetition of this classical suffix. If so, this invented place-name would have its origins in a logical geography; thus, though one cannot know for sure which Pentapolis Shakespeare was thinking of, one need not assume that it represents a geographic anomaly.

Now, it is obvious that the plays do not require us to know all this, nor are all of these details relevant to plot and theme. To a great extent, however, the setting and action of both plays is consistent with and illuminated by a Hellenistic construction of these locations.

The action of *Errors*, for example, transpires exclusively in Ephesus. The unrelievedly middle-class, urban locale peopled with servants, courtesans, goldsmiths, and merchants is rare in Shakespeare's comedies and romances, most of which feature aristocratic principals in a "court and country" setting. Those that are set in cities offer at least a token pastoral respite: Venice is contrasted with idyllic Belmont, and venal Vienna is set off by Marina at her moated grange. (The closest we come to a green world in either *Errors* or *Pericles* is an allusion to the locus of Marina's school as "The leavy shelter that abuts against / The island's side" [5.1.51–52]; the action never takes us to this setting.) The urban emphasis makes sense in an Greek setting, however, where the *polis* was the heart of cultural and commercial life. This was especially true of the Greek cities of the Levant; the city was the locus of Hellenic culture, while the indigenous culture remained dominant in the surrounding countryside.

Despite the restriction of the action to a single city, references in *Errors* to other locales suggest the larger Hellenistic world, at once far-flung and homogeneous. The heroic scope of the Syracusan Egeon's search for his lost son is vividly suggested:

> Five summers have I spent in farthest Greece,
> Roaming clean through the bounds of Asia,
> And coasting[15] homeward, came to Ephesus;
> Hopeless to find, yet loath to leave unsought
> Or that, or any place that harbors men
>
> (1.1.132–36).

In the comparable passage in Shakespeare's source, a 1595 translation of Plautus, the traveling twin's servant recalls a slightly different itinerary: "Six years now have we roamed about thus: Istria, Hispania, Massilia, Illyria, and all the upper sea, all high

Greece, all haven towns in Italy."[16] By comparison, Shakespeare's list is consistently more Eastern and Hellenistic, and less Roman—no references to Hispania or Italy. Further, Egeon and the other travelers experience no language barrier in the play. The cities mentioned in the action (Syracuse, Epidamnum, Corinth) appear to share a common language, as they would have in Hellenistic times.

In addition, Egeon remains a merchant as in Plautus, and he refers to his commercial activities, which are typical of those that bound the cities of the Hellenized East:

> With her I liv'd in joy, our wealth increas'd
> By prosperous voyages I often made
> To Epidamnum, till my factor's death,
> And [the] great care of goods at randon [sic] left,
> Drew me from the kind embracements of my spouse. . . .
> (1.1.39–43)

Shakespeare adds to the plot the hostile relations between Ephesus and Syracuse, which threaten Egeon's life; but the anti-Syracusan laws arise from an unhappy episode in formerly brisk commercial dealings between the two cities (1.1.5–10), not from xenophobia or pure cultural prejudice. On the contrary, the Duke refers to them as "intestine [that is, internal] jars" (1.1.11) and expresses his regret that he cannot be an "advocate" for Egeon in his distress (1.1.145).

At the same time, as one might expect in so dispersed a cultural community, the various cities do not always treat or view each other's citizens kindly, and each may on occasion be arbitrarily seen as other. Thus, the Syracusan twin, both in Shakespeare and his source, views the city of his sojourn (whether Ephesus or Epidamnum) in a negative light. Shakespeare's Ephesus is known to the travelers as a place of witchcraft and sorcery (a prejudice they feel to be borne out by the strange treatment they receive there):

> They say this town is full of cozenage:
> As nimble jugglers that deceive the eye
> Dark-working sorcerers that change the mind. . . .
> (1.2.97–99)[17]

Similarly, Emilia describes how she and two of the boys were saved from the sea by "men of Epidamnum," but "by and by rude fishermen of Corinth / By force took Dromio and my son"

(5.1.350–52). So far, the geography, language, and commercial, urban culture of the play are in keeping with a Hellenistic image of Ephesus.

The play is cheerfully inconsistent, however, in its representation of the political and religious setting. Solinus is "Duke" of Ephesus, an anachronistic title, and frequent Christian allusions suggest no attempt was made to preserve the pagan religious background of the source. Examples of Christian allusions include Syracusan Dromio's exclamation, "O for my beads! I cross me for a sinner" (2.2.188), references to Pentecost (4.1.1) and Satan (4.3.48–49), and the attempt to exorcise the Ephesian Antipholus with the aid of Doctor Pinch. Satan and God are mentioned not only by lower class characters (whom Shakespeare often Anglicizes while aristocrats in the same play are depicted as Greek or Roman) but also by the middle-class characters. S. Antipholus expostulates with E. Dromio: "Now, as I am a Christian, answer me, / In what safe place you have bestowed my money?" (1.2.77–78). The famous Ephesian Temple of Diana is not mentioned; it is translated into the abbey, or perhaps Shakespeare did not bother to elaborate on the landmarks (if he was then aware of them) of his substitute setting.

Further, while some of the characters' names are Greek or Roman (Solinus, Egeon, Antipholus) and one is at least originally Asian (Balthasar), others are more at home in Renaissance Italy (Angelo, Luciana, Adrianna). Since the play has no framing device, no presenting character or chorus distances us from the action in time; its Greek setting is the chief and most consistent marker of its otherness from Elizabethan London, but this otherness is not very marked.

By contrast, the geographical and historical setting of *Pericles* is far more consistently developed. The chorus[18] initially represents the play merely as an old "song," and its antiquity is not specifically classical:

> To sing a song that old was sung,
> From ashes ancient Gower is come,
> ... It hath been sung at festivals,
> On ember-eves and holy [-ales] ...
>
> (1.Cho. 1–6)

In line 6, the chorus refers to the Christian calendar ("ember-eves" or "ember days" being those that precede a fast-day). As part of the narrative frame, the line legitimately alludes to the historical popularity of the Apollonius tale throughout the Christian Middle Ages. It does not import Christian customs *into* the play proper. A few lines later, the chorus clearly and self-consciously locates the story in space and time:

> This Antioch, then; Antiochus the great
> Built up this city for his chiefest seat,
> The fairest in all Syria—
> I tell you what mine authors say.
>
> (17–20)

The setting is similarly described in the two main sources of the play, Gower's *Confessio Amantis* and Twine's *Pattern of Painfull Adventures*, so this specificity is not new. Gower's presence as chorus "cites" the play's authoritative source, much as Gower's narrator in *The Confessio* cites his (the *cronike* of *Panteone* [or Pantheon]). The presence of Gower, however, is as literary as it is historical. The rhetorical strategy of invoking one's authors is as much a convention of "old tales" as it is of history.

More clearly historical is the allusion to Antiochus the Great and the reference to Syria. Syria is an accurate name for the territory surrounding ancient Antioch. The epithet "the Great" is associated with Antiochus III, who ruled the Seleucid Kingdom from 190–187 B.C. Since the chorus (like both Gower and Twine) also describes him as the one who "Built up" and/or named the city after himself, Antiochus I Soter ("Savior," ruled 292–261 B.C.) may be meant, or the two monarchs may be conflated.[19] In either case, these references establish a Hellenistic setting for the play, and this setting is, more consistently than in *Errors*, developed. In particular, the urban locales; the geography of Pericles' voyages; the political nomenclature; and the treatment of religion, language, and education are largely consistent with the East in Seleucid times.

The urban locations of the play are, as noted previously, all cities prominent in the Hellenistic East. The urban emphasis lends coherence to the otherwise miscellaneous feeling of its scene being (as the Signet editor puts it) "dispersedly in various Mediterranean countries."[20] Given the primacy of the city in Hellenistic culture and in the play, *countries* seems the wrong word. If an eastern European Pentapolis is accepted instead of the North African Cyrene, all of Pericles' voyages can (as we shall see) be coherently charted among the Greek cities of the Levant. One additional geographic error has been alleged in the play.

When Pericles relieves Tharsus, the citizens cry, "The gods of Greece protect you / And we'll pray for you" (1.4.97–98). This has been interpreted as evidence that Tharsus is also imagined to be in Greece. However, since the Greek gods were worshiped throughout the East (witness the Temple of Diana in Ephesus), this seems to me an unwarranted conclusion. On the contrary, the line seems to preserve the sense of a dual heritage in these Greek cities in Asia Minor, in which the gods of Greece were reverenced along with local gods. With the possible exception of Pentapolis, the geography of the play works logically in accordance with a Hellenistic map of the ancient world.

Tharsus, known for its fertile soil and wheat production (1.4.22), is experiencing an uncharacteristic dearth. Pericles is able to relieve the city with his shipload of wheat, emphasizing the thriving exchange of commodities in the area.[21] The subsequent path of his travels is geographically consistent with the navigational practices of ancient times, which usually entailed sailing along the coast, keeping land in sight.[22] Indeed, even in the sixteenth century, Mediterranean navigation was primarily coastal, both for safety and for trade among the port cities.[23] For example, in act 2, Pericles travels west from Tharsus along the coast of Asia Minor and is shipwrecked somewhere north of Ephesus (Pentapolis). After his marriage, he is alerted to trouble at "home" (3.Cho.31). Leaving the north for Tyre, as a brief glance at the map indicates, it is plausible that he should be driven south by a storm to a point off Ephesus (to which city Thaisa's body washes ashore), continue east to Tharsus, where he leaves the infant Marina for her safety, and then sail south to Tyre to reassert his kingship. Years later, he returns to Tharsus to search for Marina. Departing from Tharsus, he is again tempest-tossed, eventually arriving in Mytilene. Recovering Marina there, his vision of Diana directs him back to Ephesus, where he is reunited with Thaisa.

Like the geography of the voyages, the political relationships in the play are far from purely fanciful. The play's political nomenclature is more consistent with the reign of the Seleucid monarchs than that of either source. The Seleucids held sway over lesser kings and princes or ruled through governors. In the play, Cleon and Lysimachus are accurately called "Governors" of Tharsus and Mytilene, respectively. In Gower, Cleon is a "Burgeis riche of old and fee" (l.551), and Lysimachus's counterpart is called the "lorde ... of that citee" (l.1621); Twine calls him "Prince" (455). More important, if a Hellenistic setting is assumed, Pericles's flight from Tyre need not be ascribed to immaturity or an errant desire for travel. His fear of Antiochus's revenge is understandable in light of the latter's far greater power and status. Antiochus's empire included Tyre and all of the other locales of the play, except (perhaps) Pentapolis.[24]

Culturally, as would have been the case in Hellenistic times, Pericles experiences little otherness as he journeys from city to city. Though he is called a "stranger" in Pentapolis (2.2.43 and 53), he can speak with the natives, and he is familiar with the arts of the tourney and having proven his merit is a suitable son-in-law for "the good king Simonides." Near the end of the play, the chorus alludes to the supposed linguistic liberties taken in the play:

> By you being pardoned, we commit no crime
> To use one language in each several clime
> Where our scene seems to live
>
> (4.4.5–7)

Here, in an effort to emphasize historical awareness, the chorus errs in supposing that the cities mentioned did not share a language. Evidently, the playwright and his audience were not aware that *Koine* Greek served as a lingua franca of travelers and citizens alike, which is why the Pericles of the source does not need a translator. (The apology is rather belated; this is third time that the action has shifted to Tharsus, and on the previous occasions, no comment was made. I have not spotted a similar comment in Gower.)

The emphasis on Marina's musical and intellectual accomplishments also resonates with the Hellenistic setting, recalling the gymnasium and the Greek emphasis on education. The lost daughter in this romance is not found at an idyllic sheep-shearing festival; rather, she uses her wit and learning to escape from a brothel and then earns her living as a scholar. Having "gained / Of education all the grace" (4.Cho.8–9), she persuades the bawd's man to advertise her lawful talents:

> Proclaim that I can sing, weave, sew, and dance,
> With other virtues which I'll keep from boast;
> And I will undertake all these to teach.
> I doubt not but this populous city will
> Yield many scholars.
>
> (4.6.183–87)

Later, the chorus verifies that "Deep clerks she dumbs" (5.Cho.5).

Finally, the desire to maintain a consistently pagan (or at least pre-Christian) world with respect to religion is far more evident in *Pericles* than in its sources or in *Errors*. In Gower and Twine, pagan and Christian references appear side by side. Amid many references to pagan gods and practices, Twine includes specifically Christian religious terms. Thaisa is placed at the "Temple of Diana" to protect her chastity, but her community is referred to not only as "religious women" but as "holy Nunnes" (450). Marina in her trials prays to "God" and the narrator ascribes her apparent rescue by pirates to "the providence of God" (454). Further, when she is instructed to worship Priapus, she replies, "God forbid, master, that I should worship such an idoll" (456). (Later in this same conversation, she is knowledgeable about different pagan cults, inquiring if the bawd is a "Lapsentenian . . . because the Lapsentenians doe worship Priapus" [456]). Again, when Pericles flees from Tyre, his people, among other signs of mourning, abandoned worship: "no man repaired unto the Churches" (430).

Not surprisingly, given the early date of the *Confessio* (1393, printed 1483), Gower is similarly inconsistent, alternating between references to pagan and Christian deities. Although Pericles' vision directs him to the temple of Diana to "do there his sacrifice" (l.1803), the origin of the vision is "The hie god, which wolde him kepe" (l.1798). When the wind changes to blow him to Ephesus, Pericles knows well that "god it wolde [willed]" (l.1818). Further, upon entering the temple, he performs a most Christian act: "Within his herte he made his schrifte" (l.1847). Preparing for the great recognition scene, the narrator explains that Pericles' wife was "by goddes grace . . . Abesse there" (ll.1855–57).

By contrast, the religious details in *Pericles* preserve a consistently pagan setting, especially in comparison to *Errors*. Spevack's concordance shows that the gods (plural) are invoked forty-five times in *Pericles* compared to only once in *Errors*; God in an apparently Christian sense is alluded to only twice in *Pericles* compared to ten times in *Errors*. Both plays employ such quasireligious terms as *heaven(s)* (twenty-one and five times, respectively) and *Fortune* upper and lower case (eleven and three times, respectively, but *Pericles* alone refers to specific gods (Diana, eleven times; Zeus, four times; Neptune, four times; Juno, twice) and to the temple as place of worship (five times) although the word *church* is also used twice, once in an emphatically

Christian context ("parish, church steeple, bells and all" 2.1.34). By contrast, *Errors* alone refers to angels twice, an abbey eight times and an abbess five times. In *Pericles*, the chorus calls Thaisa a votaress (4.Cho.4). Pericles appears to refer to her once as nun, but this word is Collier's emendation for Q1's "mum" at 5.3.14; Q4 has "woman."[25] Overall, the frequency of pagan religious terms in *Pericles* is in keeping with plays, such as *Julius Caesar* and *Timon*, usually seen as faithful to their classical sources. The contrast with *Errors* is more striking since in that play Shakespeare introduced Christian references while adapting a classical source, whereas in *Pericles*, he removed many of the anachronisms of his Christianized sources.

To stress the historical consistency of the geography of *Pericles* is not to diminish its symbolic function. The chorus frequently stresses the extent and intensity of Pericles's wanderings as a trope for his sufferings and Fortune's cruel reign. For example, when Pericles flees Tharsus, the chorus emphasizes his being tossed "by waves from coast to coast" (2.Cho.34), and elsewhere the litany of place-names increases the scope of the play's "fast-growing scene":

> Imagine Pericles arriv'd at Tyre,
> Welcom'd and settled to his own desire.
> His woeful queen we leave at Ephesus,
> Unto Diana there 's a votaress.
> Now to Marina bend your mind,
> Whom our fast-growing scene must find
> At Tharsus. . . .
>
> (4.1.Cho.1–7)

In the two recognition scenes, geographical terms play a major role as tokens of identity. Pericles asks Marina about her identity: "What countrywoman? / Here of these shores?" and she responds "No, nor of any shores" (5.1.102–3). "Where were you bred?" he demands, and the answer, "Tharsus," helps to confirm her identity (5.1.115, 170). Similarly, when in Diana's temple Pericles rehearses aloud the path of his wanderings, he sparks Thaisa's outburst, and their joyful rediscovery of each other is partly confirmed by establishing where her body was abandoned and recovered:

Cer. Upon this coast, I warrant you.
Per.   'Tis most certain.

Cer. Early one blustering morn this lady
    Was thrown upon this shore.

(5.3.20–23)

It seems important to note, however, that the geography of the play functions logically and historically as well as poetically.

As constructed in these romances, the themes of voyaging and encounters with distant peoples clearly serve a different mythos than that of the tragedies.[26] They reflect, I have been suggesting, not the terrible laying down of the boundaries of the home world in sacrificial blood, but the easier interchange among Greeks and others sharing a common Hellenistic culture (albeit an imported or imposed one). Pericles' travels are reluctant and politically enforced, not extravagant, and their outcome is the joyful reconstitution of the family and the state. Similarly, Egeon's and S. Antipholus's voyages are motivated by the desire to restore the family to unity. Patience and fortune, rather than errant travel or pollution, are the dominant themes. To put it another way, these plays seem to have absorbed from their sources the Greek notion of a decentralized, cosmopolitan empire of the world, rather than the Italocentric image of empire cherished by the Romans.[27]

No doubt, the benign view of the eastern Mediterranean in these plays is possible because they are set in ancient times. Unlike the Turks, Arabs, and others who inhabited the cities represented in these plays at the time that they were written, their Hellenistic inhabitants, while pagan, were not guilty of being infidels or of rejecting or opposing Christianity. Having lived before Christ, they could be accorded the status of the virtuous pagan, like the classical worthies in Dante's First Circle. Paradoxically, a historical approach to the pre-Christian antiquity of these locales and peoples naturalizes them and assimilates them into the reader's moral universe.

This humanist construction is not new with the plays; it can be found in their sources. In Gower's *Confessio*, for example, Pericles is blown off course and arrives:

    Upon this towne of Mitelene
    Which was a noble cite tho.*   *then
    And happeneth thilke tyme so
    The lordes bothe and the commune
    The high festes of Neptune
    Upon the stronde at the rivage

>   As it was custumme and usage
>   Solempneliche thei be sigh.*   *attended to
>   (ll.1618–25)

The presence of a narrator interpreting ancient customs points to the gap in time and culture between the characters and the reader. At the same time, since the customs described are ancient and classical, they are not threatening. These pre-Christian souls are simply following their "custumme and usage" prior to the Good News. Although, it seems to be implied, Mytilene may be alien and degraded now, it "was a noble cite [then]."

Further, in addition to being safely remote in time, the settings of these plays are naturalized for the reader or viewer by being "Greek." Though the cities in question might now be in the grip (a popular metaphor) of the "mis-beleeuing Turke,"[28] they were once part of the glory that was Greece. In stating their admiration for and assimilation of Greek learning, Renaissance writers often contrasted past and present. For example, Ortelius's atlas contains this commentary on Greece:

> Formerly the mother and father of all beneficial studies, who by reason of her rich land and excellent virtues was lord of the greater part of the world, Greece in this age has been so reduced (since fortune and time overturn all things) that no remnant of her greatness remains that is not subject to the yoke of Turkey or the servitude of Venice, or made into a tributary state.[29]

In John Speed's *A Prospect of the Most Famous Parts of the World*, the earliest atlas to bear the name of an English compiler, Speed contrasts Greece's ancient glory with its contemporary decay in very similar terms:

> However now she lyeth deiected, and groaned under a miserable servitude: yet once shee had as well the preheminence of Rome in glory, as the precedence in time. For to say truth, shee was the wisest of any people, that were not inlightened with the knowledge of that great mysterie: she set a patterne for gouvernment to all succeeding ages; and (in brief) she was the mistressse almost of all Sciences. . . . [30]

> It was once the seate of the worlds Empyre, and flourished farre beyond all others in every kind of humane learning, which to this day is received by all ciuill Nations as their rule. . . . but the inhabitants are now curbed and kept low . . . by the tyrannie of the Turke.[31]

Similar encomiums of ancient Greece might be cited from the culture wars of our own day.

English travelers, such as William Lithgow, John Cartwright, George Sandys, and Lucius Carey, Viscount Falkland, also emphasized the contrast between past and present in Greece, and poets and other men of letters who commented on their accounts reiterated the theme. Lithgow, in his *Rare Adventures*, writes:

> In all that countrey of Greece I could finde nothing to answer the famous relations ... of the excellency of that land, but the name onely; the barbarousnesse of the Turkes and Time having defaced all the Monuments of Antiquity.[32]

Michael Drayton, responding to similar remarks in Sandy's *Relation of a Journey*, laments that:

> Th' unlettered Turk, and rude Barbarian trades
> Where Homer sang his lofty Iliads.[33]

This dual vision, contrasting the ancient and the contemporary merits of a classical people or locale, was also applied to Asia (and especially Asia Minor). In Speed's atlas, Asia has pride of place; as he explains:

> ... our generall description of the World gives Asia the prerogative, as well for worth as time. Europe shall not want her due, in her due place. ... But in Asia did God himselfe speak his miraculous worke of the Creation. There was the Church first collected; there was the Savior of the world borne. ... And if we should compare her [Asia] to the rest, in that earthly glory of Kingdoms, Empires, and nations, which sounds fairest to men's sense, shee would still keep her ranke. ... However, now [she] is left (for her Infidelity) to the punishment of a Propheticall curse ... and is delivered vp into the hands of Turkes and Nations that blaspheme their Creator, and therefore doth not flourish in that height as heretofore.[34]

At one point in the atlas, Speed distinguishes the peoples of those (western) provinces of Asia that "were onely accounted Greekes," and he lists (among others) Ionia and Ephesus. He goes on to say, however, that though they were called "Barbarians," the "other Provinces of *Asia Minor* have their stories worth the memorie."[35] He proceeds to link Tarsus with St. Paul and mention other New Testament and classical worthies associated with the more eastern provinces. In his antiquarian and generous mood, even the term *barbarian* is treated skeptically. He traces its etymology from the Arabs' derogatory term for the rough speech of the Berbers:

> And thence the Grecians call them *Barbarians* that spake a harsher language than themselves. After, the Latines, and now we, esteeme the people of our owne Nation barbarous if they ever so little differ from the rudeness either of our tongue or manners.[36]

This enlightened view seems to me to suggest that although the Elizabeth antiquarian could not bring himself to view the contemporary East as anything but other, the humanist fascination with the Greek and Levantine past at least exerted benign effects, whether expressed in works of geography or in works of romance.[37] At the same time, it must be admitted, glorifying and appropriating the Hellenic past may, in the end, have further demonized contemporary non-Christian others with whom the nascent British empire was eventually to struggle for dominance in the East.

Notes

1. I include *Errors*, a play not normally classed with the romances, because of its romance plot and because of its setting in Ephesus. Citations from the plays are from G. Blakemore Evans, et al., eds., *The Riverside Shakespeare* (Boston: Houghton Mifflin, 1974).

2. John Gillies, *Shakespeare and the Geography of Difference* (Cambridge: Cambridge University Press, 1994), 8.

3. John Gower's *Confessio Amantis* refers to "games" with the contestants "naked" (ll.674, 691), and his Latin marginal glosses refer to *ludus gimnasii*, giving the games a specifically Greek flavor. Laurence Twine in *The Pattern of Painfull Adventures* has his hero play at "tennis" with the king and his men, but he preserves the Greek custom of their repairing afterwards to the baths: the hero ingratiates himself by "wash[ing] the king very reverently in the Baine" (435). The play is the most anachronistic of the three versions in its presentation of this episode, but the knights of the play do hail from appropriately Hellenic and Eastern locales: Sparta, Macedon, and Antioch. Citations from *Confessio Areantis* are by line number from G. C. Macauley, ed., *The Complete Works of John Gower*, vol. 3 (Oxford: The Clarendon Press, 1901). Citations from Twine are by page number from Geoffrey Bullough, ed., *The Narrative and Dramatic Sources of Shakespeare*, vol. 6 (London: Routledge, 1966).

4. Marvin Spevack, *A Complete and Systematic Concordance to the Works of Shakespeare*, 6 vols. (Hildesheim: G. Olms, 1968–70).

5. For the purposes of this paper, I am ignoring the authorship issue in *Pericles*. If the play is a collaboration, that would not diminish its interest as a reflector and shaper of geographical awareness and cultural attitudes.

6. No doubt, the critical impulse (in this case, mine) to locate the settings

of the plays on our mental maps also says something about our own ways of asserting control and authority over our world and the plays.

7. Harry Levin, ed, *The Comedy of Errors* (New York: New American Library, 1965), 116. This edition contains the text of W. W.'s translation of Plautus's *Menaechmi* (1595) from which all the following citations are taken.

8. [Eugene Vinaver and Frederick Whitehead,] *Encyclopaedia Britannica*, 15th ed., s.v. "Romance (Literature)."

9. See George B. Parks, "Shakespeare's Map for *The Comedy of Errors*," *JEGP* 34 (1940): 92–97; and Joan Hutton Landis, "From Epidamnum to Ephesus: *The Comedy of Errors*, *Pericles*, and Romance Geography" (paper presented at the meeting of the Shakespeare Association of America, 1995). I am indebted to Landis for pointing out the relevance of these maps to the plays.

10. The map is given slightly different titles in different editions of Ortelius's atlas. The version of the map reproduced here is an unbound (and therefore, more easily photographed) version dating from 1652. The full title of this version is "Descriptio Peregrinationis D. Pauli Apostoli Exhibens Loca fere omnia tam in Novo Testamento quàm in Actus Apostolomm memorata: Operà Abrahami Ortelii." The identical map with a different marginal illustration appears in the Parergon of the editions of 1584 and 1592 in the Harvard Map Collection, and Joan Landis, in the essay previously cited, reproduces it from the 1595 edition.

11. The information on each city is taken from their respective entries in *Encyclopaedia Britannica*, *Micropaedia*, 15th ed.; Epidamnum is described under the entry for its modem name, "Durres." I have also relied on the *Macropaedia*, s.v. "Ancient Greek Civilization." The New Testament significance of many of these same locations has been profitably explored by Joan Hutton Landis, in the unpublished essay previously mentioned.

12. Tomi is proposed by Clifford J. Renan, "The Onemastics of Shakespeare's Works with Classical Settings," *Literary Onemastics Studies* 3 (1981): 47–69; Cnidus is defended by Georges Lambin, "De Longues notes sur deux brefs passages Shakespearians," *Études Anglaises*, 20 (1967): 58–68. Cnidus is shown on the Ortelian map; Tomi lies on the west coast of the Black Sea, just north of the top edge of the map and south of the mouth of the Danube, the river visible near the top on the left-hand side.

13. See the Ortelian map and Lambin's own map, "De Longues notes," 65.

14. Ortelius's map of the Black Sea (or Pontus Euxinus) in the Parergon annotates the place-name of Tomo/Tomi with the phrase "Ovidae poetae exilio nobilis." The volume I consulted was the 1592 edition in the Harvard Map Collection; the map follows p. 15 of the Parergon.

15. For the navigational and geographical significance of "coasting homeward," see the discussion of the path of Pericles' travels.

16. Levin, *Comedy of Errors*, 124.

17. Plautus's travelers are likewise wary of their host city: "a place of outrageous expenses, exceeding all in riot and lasciviousness . . . ," Ibid.

18. The poet John Gower serves as chorus, but to avoid confusion with references to the historical Gower and his version of the tale (one of the play's sources), I shall refer to the play's Gower as "chorus." For simplicity, when comparing the play with its sources, I shall also refer to all characters by the names given them in the play.

19. Several of the Seleucid monarchs who took the name Antiochus, including the two just mentioned, implemented conscious policies of Hellenization.

They encouraged immigration from Greece, the founding of new cities, and the growth of Greek culture and institutions. *Encyclopaedia Britannica Micropaedia*, 15th ed., s.v. "Antiochus."

20. Ernest Schanzer, ed., *Pericles, Prince of Tyre* (New York: New American Library, 1965), 44.

21. In Twine, Pericles takes the Tarsinns' money and then restores it to maintain his "dignitie of a prince," but after the loss of his family, he determines to "exercise the trade of merchandize" (Bullough, *Narrative and Dramatic Sources*, 443, 441). In the play, he is more princely from the beginning, but why the prince should flee on a ship laden with wheat is not explained.

22. It was not until the late Middle Ages that innovations in sail and rudder design and in navigational aids (such as astronomical charts and the magnetic compass) made open ocean sailing a common practice.

23. See Fernand Braudel, *The Mediterranean and the Mediterranean World in the Age of Philip II*, trans. Siân Reynolds, vol. 1 (New York: Harper and Row, 1972), 103. The practice is mentioned by Marlowe when Barabas speculates regarding one of his vessels: "Belike they coasted round by Candy [Crete's] shore / About their oils, or other business." (*The Jew of Malta*, ed. N. W. Bawcutt [Manchester: Manchester University Press, 1990], 1.1.91–92).

24. Cyrene, the Pentapolis" in North Africa, was under the Ptolemies; the other candidates for Pentapolis would have been under Seleucid rule.

25. See Evans's textual notes.

26. See Gillies's discussion of Ovid and the tragic paradigm, *Geography*, 103–8.

27. See Gillies, *Geography*, 12, and his reference to Lidia Storoni Massolani, *The Idea of the City in Roman Thought: From Walled City to Spiritual Commonwealth*, trans. S. O'Donnell (London: Hollis and Carter, 1970). See also my discussion of Antony and the Greek image of empire, "Antony and Alexander: Imperial Politics in Plutarch, Shakespeare, and Some Modern Historical Texts," *College Literature* 20 (October 1993):1–18, and Sara Hanna's discussion in this collection of dispersion and decentralization as hallmarks of the Greek world view.

28. John Speed, *A Prospect of the Most Famous Parts of the World . . . together with . . . The Theatre of Great Britaines Empire* (London, 1631), 11. Harvard Map Collection.

29. Abraham Ortelius, *Theatrum Orbis Terrarum* (Antwerp, 1592), 86. Harvard Map Collection, my translation.

30. John Speed, *A Prospect of the Most Famous Parts of the World* (London, 1627), ed. R. A. Skelton (Amsterdam: Theatrum Orbis Terrarum, Ltd., 1966), 8.

31. Speed, *A Prospect . . . together with . . . The Theatre of Great Britaines Empire* (1631), 11.

32. Quoted in Samuel C. Chew, *The Crescent and the Rose: Islam and England during the Renaissance* (New York: Octagon Books, 1965), 133.

33. Quoted in Chew, *The Crescent and the Rose*, 134. Chew also quotes passages with similar themes from the works of Carey, Henry King, the Earl of Stirling, and Phineas Fletcher; see 134–35.

34. Speed, *Prospect* (1627), 3. In commenting on the present essay, John Gillies pointed out that this view of Asia is in keeping with the moralized and "biblicized" world map in works such as Hugh Broughton's *A Concent of Scripture* (c. 1590). In this "resilient" tradition, the continents were given by

Noah to his three sons, Asia going "the blessed S[h]em." See Gillies, *Geography,* 174–77.

35. Speed, *Prospect* (1627), 3.
36. Ibid., 5.
37. For a different view, see Constance C. Relihan, "Liminal Geography: *Pericles* and the Politics of Place," *Philological Quarterly* 71 (Summer 1992):281–99. She argues that hostility toward the Islamic East was such that contemporary Christians could not separate Greece's past from its present, and therefore, one must "qualify automatic associations between *Pericles's* cultures and those of the ancient Greek or New Testament worlds" (284).

Shakespeare's Greek World: The Temptations of the Sea

SARA HANNA

WHILE Shakespeare's Roman works (*Lucrece, Titus,* and the Plutarchan plays) reveal a certain family resemblance in their focus on history and their gravity, the Greek works (*Venus and Adonis, Comedy of Errors, Midsummer Night's Dream, Twelfth Night, Troilus and Cressida, Timon of Athens, Pericles, Winter's Tale,* and *Two Noble Kinsmen*) form a motley group seemingly more remarkable for their diversity than for any kinship or coherent representation of Greek culture. Unlike the Roman works, which are all tragedies set at least in part in or near Rome, the Greek works range through a variety of genres and settings. The possibility that Shakespeare knew enough about Greece to represent it in these works was not entertained before the twentieth century. In the first study of Shakespeare's classical works to include Greek plays, *Shakespeare et l'antiquité* (1879), Paul Stapfer defended the historical verisimilitude of Shakespeare's Roman world against those who scoffed at the anachronisms in the Roman plays, but he felt that the plays with Greek settings lacked "all trace of a Greek spirit or of the local coloring of Greece."[1] Major studies of the classical heritage in Western literature from the middle of the twentieth century still subscribed to this view.[2] In fact, the Greek works are not uniformly Greek in character. Strictly speaking, only *Timon, Troilus,* and *Pericles* offer some type of sustained representation of Greek culture, while the other six works present amalgamations of various elements: Greek, Roman, Italian, French, and British. The Greek features in these six works, however, support and amplify the fascinating conception of Greek culture developed in the core Greek works.

Critical efforts to account for Shakespeare's conception of Greek culture have focused largely on Roman and medieval derogation of the Greeks, picked up by numerous Renaissance authors, including Shakespeare.[3] Elisabeth Wolffhardt surveyed

Roman, medieval, and Renaissance attitudes toward the Greeks, demonstrating the pervasiveness of the Greek notoriety for drunkenness, dissipation, luxurious living, mendacity, and levity.[4] T. J. B. Spencer advanced the case for the influence of Roman views on Shakespeare's portrayal of Greece, insisting that "there was little to resist the influence of the prevailing Roman attitude to the Greeks, namely that they were licentious, luxurious, frivolous, bibulous, venereal, insinuating, perfidious, and unscrupulous."[5] As Wolffhardt and Spencer have shown, the Elizabethan epithets "mad Greek" and "merry Greek" cover a variety of revelers, rogues, harlots, liars, cheats, deceivers, panders, drunkards, and parasites. Shakespeare, certainly familiar with this tradition, offers his own variations on the theme. Hearing about Helen's flirtation with Troilus, Cressida quips, "then she's a merry Greek indeed" (Troilus, 1.2.109). Mistaking Feste's solicitations for pandering, Sebastian remarks, "I prithee, foolish Greek, depart from me" (Twelfth Night, 4.1.18). After a drinking bout in the cellar of the Boar's Head, Prince Hal staggers out to proclaim himself "a Corinthian, a lad of mettle" (1 Henry IV, 2.1.12); and a page describes Falstaff's drinking companions as "Ephesians ... of the old church" (2 Henry IV, 2.2.150).

For several reasons, however, the reduction of Shakespeare's Hellas to a reflection of Roman derogation must be challenged. In the first place, Shakespeare knew several Greek authors, at least Plutarch, Homer, and Lucian; and various works of other Greek authors were translated into English in the sixteenth century: Aesop, Herodotus, Thucydides, Xenophon, Isocrates, Demosthenes, Euripides, Aristotle, Theocritus, Longus, Heliodorus, and Achilles Tatius.[6] Moreover, Shakespeare undoubtedly gleaned Greek thought from a variety of secondary sources: dictionaries, mythographies, collections of wisdom, and works of contemporaries. While the popular literature of the Renaissance capitalized on the vices of the Merrygreeks, humanist educators in England had been promoting the study of Greek throughout the sixteenth century, and humanist literature is often extravagant in praise of the ancient Greeks.[7] Although Shakespeare's knowledge of the Greek language was slight, probably limited to New Testament Greek,[8] it is difficult to imagine his teacher of Greek imparting to students none of the humanist enthusiasm for Greek thought. Finally, the Romans were by no means unanimous or unequivocal in their attitudes toward the Greeks. Roman opinions of the Greeks range from admiration for Greek accomplishments in arts, literature, and sciences to contempt for the vices associated with the Greek national character.

One must also consider the reasons for Roman disparagement of the Greeks, a subject too complex for this essay since Roman attitudes vary over the long course of Roman domination of the Mediterranean world. In broad outline though, the argument remains roughly the same: Greek philosophy, arts, and vices will corrupt Rome by destroying the traditional customs, values, and skills that brought the city to greatness. Such is the position of Cato the Censor in the Early Republic, whose principal efforts throughout his career were directed toward preserving Rome as an agrarian and military society through a program of stern moral conservatism. Reacting against the influx of Hellenistic scholars and visitors and against the Hellenism of the Scipios, Cato considered the luxurious ways and liberal ideas of the Greeks a threat to Roman identity and hegemony.[9] Two main types of Greeks pose problems: fortune hunters and philosophers. With regard to the former, Cato's worst fears seem to have been realized some two centuries later in Juvenal's contemptuous satirical portrait of the successful invasion of Greek parasites, who have insinuated their way into every household through flattery and deceit, spreading vice and corruption throughout Roman society.[10] The philosophers, however, posed the more serious threat to Roman hegemony. Against the conservative exclusionist policies designed to ensure the supremacy of Roman citizens, Hellenistic philosophers were promoting the concept of universal brotherhood, of social, racial, and legal equality of all peoples under one divinely inspired monarch. These cosmopolitan assimilitionist ideas they associated with Alexander in part because he adopted the manners and dress of conquered nations, married a foreigner, and claimed divine descent.[11] Shakespeare would most likely have read of such matters in Plutarch, who speaks of Alexander's wise policy of promoting accord with foreign nations by "mixture and enterchaunge of manners" rather than by "force" (*Lives*, 3:371); and who credits Alexander with realizing Zeno's concept of a universal "common-wealth well governed by Philosophicall lawes," which treats "all men" as "felow citizens, & of the same country."[12]

While Roman attitudes toward Greek influences on Roman society are vital to understanding Shakespeare's Greeks, they provide only a limited perspective. We can perhaps approach Shakespeare's conception of the Greek world more clearly by focusing on the geography of Greece and the contrasting ways Greek and Roman authors perceive that most prominent feature of Greek geography, the sea. The earliest "geography" of Greece is, in fact, Homer's catalog of ships from Book 2 of the *Iliad* with its bewildering array of territories, cities, and islands. Enough of these place names in Chapman's translation are identifiable on Renaissance maps (in particular, Ortelius) to demonstrate that while mainland Greece provided the bulk of the naval forces, lesser contributions came from many islands of the Aegean, from Euboea east to Samos off the coast of Asia Minor and south to Rhodes and Crete, thus forming roughly a circle around the southern Aegean and the interesting concept of a nation whose center is the sea.

Herodotus's *History* presents the earliest extended geography of the Western world. From a core of Greek peoples centered on the Aegean, who share a temperate climate, as well as common language, religion, and customs, Herodotus's vision extends outward in all directions to non-Greek, "barbarian" lands of more extreme temperatures containing incredible riches and wonders, even monsters and savages in most distant lands.[13] Although only the first two books of the *History* were translated into English (by B. R. in 1584), they represent Herodotus's conception of foreign lands well through such descriptions as the wealth of Persia, the splendors of Babylon, and the pyramids and exotic animals of Egypt. Herodotus, however, never loses sight of the importance of the sea to Greek civilization. In Book 1, he tells of the great seafaring Phocions, who, rather than submit to the Persians who were besieging their city, embarked the whole population on ships and sailed to Corsica to found a new city. For Herodotus, the single skill that preserved Greece from barbarian dominion was navigation, namely, the Athenian defeat of the Persians in the naval battle at Salamis. This event, beyond the translated portion of Herodotus, Shakespeare could have read about in Plutarch's lives of Themistocles and Cimon. For all the exotic wonders of the non-Greek lands that Herodotus reports, he would undoubtedly have agreed with his contemporary Sophocles on the greatest wonder of the world and the first skill that merits attention:

> Wonders are many on earth, and the greatest of these
> Is man, who rides the ocean and takes his way
> Through the deeps, through wind-swept valleys of perilous seas
>   That surge and sway.[14]

How important seafaring was to the development of civilization from the Greek point of view Shakespeare might have learned from the opening of Thucydides' *Peloponnesian War*, translated by Thomas Nicolls in 1550. For Thucydides the earliest era on the Greek mainland prior to seafaring was one of shifting tribes, constantly threatened by foreign invaders and ever ready to abandon their territory to save their lives. No large cities were built, and agriculture was not developed beyond immediate needs because settlements lacked fortifications to protect surplus from invaders: "they had not amonge them any trade of marchaundyse nor any entrecourse by sea nor by lande, but all in feare."[15] Seafaring changed this life of migration and insecurity, making possible the development of stable societies. After an early period of piracy, Minos developed the first navy and drove the pirates out of coastal settlements, "who lyuing in more suertie, gave them self more to exersise merchaundyse" (fol. 16r). With their new resources the stronger cities built walls, protected the weaker, then began voyaging further abroad. The intimidation of a stronger navy made it possible for Agamemnon to raise the expedition to Troy, the first united effort of Greece. After the Greeks returned from Troy, strife in the cities led to colonization of Ionia, Italy, and Sicily. The next period of Greek history saw an increase in shipbuilding and the development of the powerful navies of the Corinthians, Ionians, Samians, and Phocians. Thucydides's brief survey of early Greek civilization culminates, as did Herodotus's whole *History*, in the naval battle of Salamis.

For a striking contrast to Thucydides's vision of how navigation enabled the development of civilization, we might turn to the most famous passage on seafaring in Roman literature, the second chorus of Seneca's *Medea*, in which navigation causes the corruption of civilization. Seneca (in John Studley's 1566 translation) identifies the mythical voyage of the *Argo* as the event that ruined "the golden worlde," where "all were content to live at home in rest" without seeking trade or warefare abroad: "The Thessail shyp together now hath set, / The Worlde that well with Seas dissevered lay."[16] The voyage appears as "a wicked journey," appropriately rewarded by "Medea accurst" (p. 71). But the consequences have been much more far-reaching:

> Eche whirry boate now scuddes aboute the deepe,
> All styntes and warres are taken cleane away,
> The Cities frame new walles themselves to keepe,
> The open worlde lettes nought rest where it lay:
> (p. 71)

As John Gillies notes, Seneca's chorus goes beyond Euripides's focus on the miscegenation between Greek and barbarian to condemn "the fundamental transgressiveness of voyaging," which brings about massive confusion throughout the known world.[17] Thus, two centuries after Cato, we still hear the echo of Roman conservatism in the nostalgic vision of one who has experienced a more "open world," including a high degree of assimilation of foreign peoples and ideas brought about by more extensive Roman conquests. Seneca goes on to predict a time "When Ocean wave shall open every Realme," which in Studley's translation culminates in a final conception of the whole world losing its stability: "The wandering World at will shall open lye" (p. 71).

Cicero, well versed in Greek language and thought, uses the Greek passion for seafaring to develop a psychology of the Greek national character. Thoroughly familiar with Roman conservatism as well, Cicero builds on Cato's anti-Greek arguments to formulate a contrast between Greece and Rome, but he adds a whole new dimension to Cato's thinking by basing his assessment of the proclivities of the two cultures purely on geography. Cicero attributes the "corruption and degeneration of morals" in Greece to the fact that the country is largely composed of maritime cities. These cities

> receive a mixture of strange languages and customs, and import foreign ways as well as foreign merchandise, so that none of their ancestral institutions can possibly remain unchanged. Even their inhabitants do not cling to their dwelling places, but are constantly being tempted far from home by soaring hopes and dreams; and even when their bodies stay at home, their thoughts nevertheless fare abroad and go wandering. In fact, no other influence did more to bring about the final overthrow of Carthage and Corinth, though they had long been tottering, than this scattering and dispersion of citizens, due to the fact that the lust for trafficking and sailing seas caused them to abandon agriculture and the pursuit of arms. Many things too that cause ruin to states as being incitements to luxury are supplied by the sea, entering either by capture or import; and even the mere delightfulness of such a site brings in its train many an allurement to pleasure through either extravagance or indolence. And what I said of Corinth may perhaps be said with truth of the whole of Greece. . . .[18]

By contrast says Cicero, the site of Rome inland on the Tiber promotes agriculture, stability, and a sense of national identity.

There is much to suggest that Shakespeare discerned contrasting tendencies in Greek and Roman civilizations in some ways similar to Cicero's. Rome has often been called the protagonist of the Roman plays. As strong center, principal setting, and source of power and ideology, the city gives the Roman plays a unique coherence. For Shakespeare, as for Cicero, lack of a single strong center characterizes the Greek world. The Greek plays range throughout the Mediterranean world with three set in Athens, two in Ephesus, and other settings extending from the mainland west to Sicily; northwest to Illyria;[19] east to Tyre, Antioch, and Tharsus; northeast to Mytilene and Troy; either south, east, or north to Pentapolis, depending on whether one locates it in Africa, Asia Minor, or Thrace,[20] and even beyond geography to the fantasy island of Delphos.[21]

Even more important than the sheer diversity of settings in Shakespeare's Greek world is what Cicero identified as the temptation of the sea, drawing people away from home. The dominant tendency in Shakespeare's Roman world is movement toward the center: all roads do indeed lead to Rome. Even from Egypt, Antony and Cleopatra feel threatened at the prospect of being led in triumph into Rome. By contrast, the dominant tendency in the Greek plays is away from the center, an eccentric, even centrifugal tendency. In six of the Greek plays, the sea plays a significant role as setting, symbol, or means of trade, adventure, warfare, escape, and even suicide. To use Cicero's terminology, "lust for trafficking and sailing the seas" scatters the family of Egeon (appropriately named for a sea) to distant shores in *The Comedy of Errors*; "soaring hopes and dreams" of conquest or beautiful women precipitate the sea ventures of *Troilus and Cressida* and *Pericles*; and shipwrecks or escapes by sea launch major actions in *Twelfth Night*, *The Winter's Tale*, and *Pericles*. The eccentric tendency can also lead characters out into nature in general, not just the sea. Venus and Adonis have gone out to sport in the woods; and the lovers of *A Midsummer Night's Dream* flee from Athens to the woods, incidentally, a flooded woods under the influence of the "wat'ry moon" (2.1.162). Perhaps *Timon* offers the clearest demonstration of the eccentric tendency, as the hero abandons Athens for the neighboring woods, steadily moving closer to the sea until his strange suicide on the seashore.

Genre certainly enters into the eccentric tendency in Shakespeare's Greek works. Although the *Odyssey* and the *Argonautica* with their voyages into realms of wonders, monsters, and barbarian races were not available in English translation, Shakespeare knew enough of these stories to allude to incidents from them deftly. In addition to scattered allusions to Circe, the Cyclops, the Sirens, and Scylla and Charybdis in his plays, Shakespeare develops Autolycus into a true descendant of his thieving Homeric namesake and draws upon the Homeric tradition of the intelligent, enduring Greek seafarer for the characterization of Pericles.[22] The quest for the golden fleece appropriately enters into the mercantile, maritime world of the great Italian Renaissance sea power in *Merchant of Venice*.[23] Moreover, the most popular of the Greek literary genres available in translation, the Hellenistic sea romances of Heliodorus and Achilles Tatius and the Hellenistic pastorals of Theocritus and Longus, send characters either out into the Mediterranean for a myriad of improbable adventures or out into fanciful, idyllic natural settings.

While history (and historical sources) to a large extent dictate action in the Roman works, such that all of them at least give the impression of historical verisimilitude, the Greek works offer the dramatist the opportunity to explore worlds of fable, myth, and fantasy; to escape the more severe constraints of verisimilitude; and to experiment with genre. As Clifford Leech put it, Greek works gave Shakespeare "the freedom to speculate."[24] Indeed, they are unusually experimental. *Venus and Adonis* was his first narrative poem; *Comedy of Errors*, probably his first comedy; *Midsummer Night's Dream*, his only representation of a fairy world, *Troilus and Cressida*, an anomalous play of uncertain genre; *Timon*, his oddest, most atypical tragedy; and *Pericles*, probably his first late romance. Among the Greek works, we also find some of Shakespeare's boldest departures from the unities of time, place, and action, as well as some of the most interesting combinations of genres. The Roman works all take the form of serious historical tragedies that contain very little comedy (with the exception of some Egyptian scenes in *Antony and Cleopatra*); the Greek works defy typical generic conventions even more blatantly than do other plays in the Shakespearean canon, especially the distinction between comedy and tragedy. *Venus and Adonis*, a comical, tragical, pastoral, mythological poem that would delight Polonius, Shakespeare contrasts to the "grauer labour" (Dedication, *Venus*) of *Lucrece* that he plans to undertake next, thus evoking the traditional distinction between Greek levity and Roman gravity. The Greek romance schemes of *Comedy of Errors*, *Twelfth Night*, *Winter's Tale*, and *Pericles*, as well as the death of Arcite in *Two Noble Kinsmen*, introduce a larger amount of grief than is customary in other Shakespearean comedies; and the two plays with significant tragic action, *Timon* and *Troilus*, contain so much satire that it threatens to undermine their status as tragedies.

Genres of the three plays I have identified as core Greek works deserve perhaps slightly fuller consideration. What, if anything, Shakespeare knew of Greek tragedy remains speculation. One Greek tragedy, Euripides's *Phoenician Women*, was available in English translation; and Emrys Jones argues that Shakespeare may have known two others, Euripides's *Hecuba* and *Iphigenia in Aulis*, in Latin translation.[25] None of these Greek tragedies seems to have much bearing on Shakespeare's Greek "tragedies" with their decidedly un-Greek preponderance of satire. *Troilus and Cressida* has been called comedy, tragedy, history, and satire, as well as "comicall satyre" and "tragic satire."[26] I think we could appreciate the satirical dimension of this play more fully as Shakespeare's version of Greek satire in contrast to the Roman satirical tradition coopted by his associate Ben Jonson. Although two forms of Greek comic satire, Old Comedy and satyr plays, were not available in translation, their reputation was fairly widespread.[27] A third type of Greek satire, Lucian's dialogues, had gained some popularity among the educated through the Latin translations of Erasmus and More, and four of the dialogues were available in English. In defining his "Roman" form of satire, Jonson takes care to dissociate his methods from the notorious excesses of the Greek satirical tradition, in particular extreme ferocity, scurrility, personal abuse, and attacks on people in high places[28]—precisely the practices Shakespeare employs in *Troilus and Cressida*. In Greek satire anything goes, nothing is sacred, and no one is safe. That same freedom from restraint informs *Timon of Athens*, perhaps more thematically than generically, although Lucian's satirical dialogue *Timon* (in Latin or French translation) is generally accepted as one of the sources for the play; and another principal source, Plutarch's *Life of Antony*, features a Roman breaking away from Roman traditions to indulge in the luxurious "orientalism" that Rome associated with the whole eastern Mediterranean—Greece, Egypt, and Asia. That "freest" of all Greek genres, the odyssey and its successors, the Hellenistic romances, in which anything can happen, anywhere, any time, attracted Shakespeare from the beginning of his career to the end, finding its purest expression in *Pericles*.

Freedom is, of course, also the key concept in the political machinations of ancient Greece. From Homer through the fifth century the Greeks sought freedom from external restraint, from any central authority beyond the petty kingdom or the *polis*.

While the Romans adopted the concept of the *polis*, the self-ruling city-state, from the Greeks, they turned it into something that would have been anathema to the ancient Greeks—an ever expanding central power, as the city absorbed each new territory into the empire, extending Roman law and administration. Prior to and immediately after Alexander, Greece had no single political leader, center, or form of government. Even the most cursory reading of Plutarch's *Lives* reveals the uniqueness of each city-state, with governments ranging from monarchies through oligarchies to democracies and each state jealously guarding its individuality and independence. Plutarch's history of ancient Greece is one of continuous rivalries, wars, and shifting alliances among the various city-states in their efforts to maintain their identity and sovereignty and to defeat any one city's efforts to attain supremacy. Herodotus merely confirms the picture of incessant warfare among rival cities, abated only when threat from Persia required a united effort to preserve the liberty of Greece; and Thucydides presents the culmination of internecine warfare in the Peloponnesian War.

Antagonism between city-states, whether derived from sources or invented, enters into several of Shakespeare's Greek plays—Syracuse and Ephesus in *Comedy of Errors*, the sea captain Antonio's unnamed city and Illyria in *Twelfth Night*, Sicilia and Bohemia in *Winter's Tale*, Athens and Thebes in *Two Noble Kinsmen*—although none of these hostilities arise from the kind of threats to independence that wrought such havoc throughout early Greek history. For rivalries more typical of the ancient Greeks, including unwillingness to submit to a central authority, Shakespeare draws to some extent from Homer in *Troilus and Cressida* for his interpretation of the loose confederation of Greek forces in the Trojan War, in which the power struggles among Greek heroes (each a king or prince in his own domain) threaten to defeat the Greek enterprise. Shakespeare emphasizes one feature much more strongly than does Homer: the weak center, the inability of the supreme commander to control the Greek forces. Homer's Agamemnon is an egotistical, hot-tempered leader, an imposing figure whose presence dominates the first nine books of the *Iliad*. Shakespeare's retiring Agamemnon with his mixed stoic fatalistic philosophy[29] and his ready acquiescence to whatever Ulysses proposes, lacks power, drive, and initiative. Indeed, Ulysses's diagnosis of the disease of "emulation" (1.3.134) in the Greek camp subtly implies that Agamemnon has failed as a leader, and Hector confirms that impression:

"I was advertis'd their great general slept, / Whilst emulation in the army crept" (2.2.211–12).

For Cicero, the internal politics of Athens reveal much the same problem as do relations among city-states: lack of responsible central control. Cicero charges the Athenians with political ineptitude with regard to their constant dissensions and their libertine form of democracy:

> Greece of ancient times, once so flourishing in its wealth, dominion, and glory, fell through this single evil, the excessive liberty and license of its meetings. When untried men, totally inexperienced and ignorant, had taken their seats in the theatre, then they would decide on harmful wars, put troublemakers in charge of public affairs and expel from the city the citizens who had served it best.[30]

The last item, the notorious ostracism, Plutarch also presents as the most characteristic problem of ancient Athens, explaining how this curious practice was connected with the ancient Athenians' idealization of liberty and equality. Of their banishment of Themistocles, he says, "For this manner of banishment for a time, called *Ostracismon*, was no punishment for any faulte committed, but a mitigation and taking away of the envie of the people, which delited to plucke downe their stomaks that to much seemed to exceede in greatnes." Other nations considered the practice ridiculous. When the banished Themistocles arrived at the Persian court, the king "besought his great god Arimanius, that he would allwayes send his enemies such mindes, as to banishe the greatest, and wisest men amongest them" (*Lives*, 1:223, 228–29). The opposing tendencies of Athens and Rome are perhaps most clearly reflected in the ways the two cities characteristically dealt with their finest military leaders: the ostracism and the triumph.[31]

In "Timon in Shakespeare's Athens," Robert Miola has demonstrated how thoroughly classical and Renaissance political theoreticians condemned the democracy of ancient Athens as a form of government in which excessive liberty among the people inevitably led to disorder, even chaos. Although in *Timon* Shakespeare does not interpret the ostracism as a method of ousting a largely virtuous leader (as Plutarch had), he does, nonetheless, use the political climate associated with ancient Athenian democracy in presenting the central events of the banishment of Alcibiades and the self-ostracism of Timon. The result in Athens is absence of a strong center, or, as Miola puts it, summarizing the opinions of theoreticians from Plato and Aristotle through the Renaissance: "In a democracy there is no center of authority, no clear voice of reason to settle controversies, to make judgments—just the confusing din of claims and counterclaims...."[32] *Timon of Athens* thus presents both a prominent version of the power vacuum at the center and in the hero of the play the most exaggerated version of the eccentric tendency.

Although Plutarch condemns the excesses of democracy, he sees the problems of this form of government in contrast to an equally disturbing tendency in Roman politics. These contrasting tendencies he traces in his earliest Athenian and Roman rulers:

> But both Theseus and Romulus being naturally geven to rule and raigne, neither the one nor the other kept the true forme of a King, but bothe of them dyd degenerate alike: the one chaunging him self into a popular man, the other to a very tyranne.... But he that is more severe or remisse then he should be, remaineth now no more a King or a prince, but becommeth a people pleaser, or a cruell tyrante: and so causeth his subjects to despise or hate him. (*Lives*, 1:68)

To some extent, this contrast holds true throughout Plutarch's *Lives*. Athens risks degenerating into a mindless popular government, ultimately anarchy, while Rome is ever threatened by tyranny. Although Shakespeare's Greek tragedies present different forms of freedom carried to excess, the geographical image at the end of both is telling: in *Troilus* anarchy on the seashore; in *Timon* the hero's grave on the seashore.

Patterns of expulsion or escape from the center are not confined to any particular form of government in the Greek plays, nor are all the rulers weak or incompetent. However, among Greek characters problem solving often takes the form of flight, evasion, or eviction. In *The Two Noble Kinsmen*, Theseus banishes Arcite; and in *The Winter's Tale*, Leontes sends the baby Perdita out to sea, undoubtedly a variation of the exposure of a baby in a climate of riddling prophecies in the Oedipus story. Granted, these two examples arise from Shakespeare's sources, yet among lovers in the Greek plays, escape from the jurisdiction of the central power seems to be the natural impulse, as Lysander and Hermia flee from Athens toward a neighboring city and Perdita and Florizel readily agree to Camillo's plan to seek refuge in Sicily. A part of this inclination toward flight undoubtedly arises from the fact that the geographical dominion of any one

Greek city is very limited, in contrast to the vast extent of Roman power. For Antony and Cleopatra, Egypt offers no refuge. None of the powers of Greek cities extends quite so far. When Polixenes escapes from Sicilia, Leontes lacks the power to attack Bohemia. Although Antiochus threatens Tyre and even Tharsus, Pericles is able to find safe haven farther abroad in Pentapolis. In fact, a number of Greek characters (Pericles, Marina, Thaisa, Perdita, Camillo, Viola, Antipholus and Dromio of Ephesus, Aemilia) are able to make lives for themselves in places remote from their origins, whereas for Roman characters there is really no arena for activity outside of Roman dominion, no "world elsewhere" (3.3.135), as Coriolanus would like to think, no chance for Antony to realize the alternative he seeks after defeat, to live as "a private man in Athens" (3.12.15).

Shakespeare uses a striking reversal of an ancient Greek geographical image—the island of earth surrounded or bounded by the sea—to express the psychology of one of his earliest Greek characters: "The sea hath bounds, but deep desire hath none" (line 389), declares Venus (the goddess born from the sea) in her effort to seduce Adonis by explaining natural, instinctual passion. The narrator of the poem frequently likens the heroine's passions to elemental forces pent up and threatening to burst out (fire, flood, and earthquake). It is just this boundless, uncontrollable power of passions that characterizes a number of Shakespeare's Greeks. To be sure, passions rage out of control throughout Shakespeare's plays, but in the Greek works emotional excess seems almost a principle of character. One thinks of the sudden desire of Palamon and Arcite for Emilia, which immediately destroys their friendship, or of the sudden irrational jealousy of Leontes, which one critic has likened to the fits of madness that Greek gods inflicted on mortals.[33] In the heroines of his two early poems, Shakespeare seems to have developed a contrast between passionate excess and rational excess that will come to typify his Greek and Roman characters, Venus seeking purely emotional and sensual gratification, Lucrece driven by superego (Roman ideology) to commit suicide. Timon is obviously the prime example of emotional excess in his swing from extravagant philanthropy to raging misanthropy; in part, he seems more like a boundless elemental power than a realistic character—a flood of love and hatred (and water imagery is pervasive throughout the play), a torrential river returning to the sea. That type of character stands in sharp contrast to the rigid self-control exercised by typical Roman characters, such as Titus and Brutus, when they refuse to let emotional attachments interfere with what they consider duty to the state.

Venus, however, functions as a prototype of Greek character psychology in other ways as well, particularly in her Ovidian metamorphic pattern. While Lucrece through her suicide affirms Roman ideology, literally identifies with the Roman ideal of chastity (thus in a lesser way imitating the upward metamorphosis into gods that Ovid associates principally with Rome), Venus follows the dominant pattern of Ovid's Greek world—of downward metamorphosis, of emotional excess leading to transformation into natural phenomena: birds, beasts, streams, trees, etc. This, of course, is only hinted in the metaphorical progression of the poem as Venus descends from predatory birds through milch doe to snail in pain. In more serious contexts, such as the tournament of *Two Noble Kinsmen* or the final battle of *Troilus and Cressida*, downward metamorphosis takes the form of regression into savagery and bestiality. The "universal wolf" (1.2.121) that Ulysses warned of in the early Greek council scene becomes reality in the final battle scenes, as the Greeks "proclaim barbarism" (5.4.16), enraged rivals in love try to destroy each other, and the forces of Achilles resort to the tactics of a wolf pack. Other intense moments of emotional excess, regression into bestiality, and loss of human identity are associated with the sea. It is clearly intentional iconography that the scene of Leontes's rage in the Sicilian court, where his leonine tendencies take control, is followed by the scene on the Bohemian seacoast: Perdita abandoned on the seashore is Leontes' lost identity. Immense grief over the loss of Marina reduces Pericles to a mute bestial man (with unwashed face and uncut hair), a shattered creature drifting aimlessly on the wayward sea, and of course, "transformed Timon" (5.4.19), who digs for roots and rages about the woods like a beast, ultimately (in fine Ovidian form) simply vanishes into nature, submerging his identity in the sea.

As with Venus, the "soaring hopes and dreams" of the Greeks (the lack of central, rational control) often take the form of delusion, particularly in the pursuit of beauty. Invariably this pursuit involves some kind of blindness on the part of the pursuer to the object of his or her attentions: Adonis wants to hunt, not dally; Shakespeare's Helen (unlike Homer's) shows no remorse for her infidelity and no desire to return home; Emilia does not want to be the prize of a brutal contest. Even Pericles, Shakespeare's most nearly ideal Greek hero, reveals his Greek origins simply in setting out on a quest for beauty and further, when he first sees the lady, immediately succumbing to the delusion that beauty necessarily entails virtue: "See where she comes, apparelled like the spring, / Graces her subjects, and her thoughts the king / Of every virtue gives renown to men" (1.1.12–14).[34] Timon's delusions are the most grandiose but of a kind with those of his fellow Greeks—at one extreme the beautiful dream of an ideal society of brotherly love, reflected in the perfect Greek symposium, along with the sheer inability to perceive the reality of corruption around him; at the opposite extreme, fantastic visions of cosmic chaos and finally obsession with lavish images of the sea washing over his grave.

The temptation of the sea toward fantasy, this form of the eccentric tendency, does not always produce delusion and disaster. The willingness to venture forth on the seas even at great risk to oneself (as well as the inquisitiveness of the first great Greek mariner Odysseus) Shakespeare has made the heroic impulse of his first comedy with a Greek setting, expressed in the Sicilian Antipholus's gentle lament:

> I to the world am like a drop of water,
> That in the ocean seeks another drop,
> Who, falling there to find his fellow forth
> (Unseen, inquisitive), confounds himself.
> So I, to find a mother and a brother,
> In quest of them (unhappy), ah, lose myself.
>
> (1.2.35–40)

Equally heroic, if perhaps less fanciful, Egeon has sailed to "farthest Greece, / Roaming clean through the bounds of Asia" (1.1.131–32) in search of his son. Moreover, in the Greek comedies, unrestrained fantasy gives rise to delightful confusions of identity and amusing suggestions of downward metamorphoses in atmospheres of geographical wonders. In *The Comedy of Errors* with its exotic place names (Centaur, Phoenix, Propentine), fantasies about sorcery, witchcraft, and demonic possession threaten to veer out of control, as Antipholus of Ephesus is locked up as a madman, and Antipholus of Syracuse, convinced that "we wander in illusions" (4.3.43) is about to take flight on the next ship. At the climax of confusion, Duke Solinus (probably named for the classical geographer) declares that the whole city has "drunk of Circe's cup" (5.1.271). *Twelfth Night*, too, combines a touch of exotic geography through inn and ship names (*Elephant, Tiger, Phoenix*) with confusion of identities to bring Sebastian to the point of wondering whether he is mad or dreaming. Through the Greek romance framework of these plays, as well as in the later Greek romances, *Pericles* and *The Winter's Tale*, Shakespeare expresses the Greek inclination toward fantasy with resolutions beyond the wildest or most "soaring hopes and dreams" of his characters.

In the Greek comedies and romances, sailing the "open world" and marrying foreign women do not raise the problems that Seneca foresaw or that Shakespeare exploited in the Roman plays through Tamora and Cleopatra. On the contrary, Pericles encounters the most serious trouble with a marriage prospect nearest to Tyre in Antioch. Whether we locate Shakespeare's Pentapolis in Africa, Thrace, or Asia Minor, Pericles finds an ideal wife and an ideal kingdom much further broad, interestingly though, not in a seaport but a "half day's journey" inland (2.1.107). Though Polixenes tries to thwart the alliance between Perdita and Florizel, his arguments are based on class not race; and ultimately, all the characters are thrilled by this rather extreme instance of miscegenation between a Greek and a Bohemian. In Shakespeare's two versions of Theseus's Athens, the Amazonian women, far from posing any threat, contribute valuable qualities to the society. Hippolyta of *Midsummer Night's Dream* shows warmth and humor, as well as an inclination to believe in fantasy that supports the young lovers' stories of their woodland adventures. In *Two Noble Kinsmen*, the Amazons are more compassionate than Theseus, who refuses to halt his marriage ceremony until Hippolyta and Emilia kneel and join the petition of the Theban queens. While Theseus ordains that one of Emilia's suitors must die, Emilia would rather die than cause the death of either. Assimilation and intermixture clearly strengthen the societies of Shakespeare's Greek comic worlds.

Although England may have had a wet season in 1594, this obviously cannot account for the flooded woods of *Midsummer Night's Dream*, especially since directly after the business about the floods Shakespeare takes pains to evoke extended seascapes of Titania sitting with the Indian boy's mother on "Neptune's yellow sands / Marking th' embarked traders on the flood" (2.1.126–27) and of Oberon perched "upon a promontory" by the sea where he heard "a mermaid on a dolphin's back" singing (2.1.149–50) and watched Cupid shoot his wayward arrow. The flooded nightime, fairy woods with its irrational loves, illusions, and marvellous downward metamorphosis, as much as Shakespeare's other Greek worlds, reveals the temptations of the sea. Moreover, as the lovers awake from their woodland adventures confused about reality and dream, it is certainly no accident that imagination becomes the central theme of the final act of this Athenian comedy. As a wise Athenian leader (who anachronistically knows his Platonism), Theseus recognizes the tendency toward imaginative flights among his subjects and tries to curb them with derision and scepticism or (more like an Aristotelian) to channel them into appreciation of the arts.

Cicero concluded his analysis of the geography of Greece with the notions that the sea supplies "incitements to luxury" which ruin maritime cities and that "the mere delightfulness of such a site" brings "many an allurement to pleasure through either extravagance or indolence." Although not concerned with geography, other classical authors support this conception of ancient Greece. Horace traces the degeneration of Greece from early military greatness into a whimsical, childish indulgence in arts and pleasures:

> From the day she dropped her wars, Greece took to trifling, and amid fairer fortunes drifted into folly: she was all aglow with passion, now for athletes, now for horses; she raved over workers in marble or ivory or bronze; with eyes and soul she hung enraptured on the painted panel; her joy was now in flautists, and now in actors of tragedy. Like a baby-girl playing at its nurse's feet, what she wanted in impatience, she soon, when satisfied, cast off.[35]

The portrait sounds very much like the follies of Shakespeare's Timon, as he contemplates the offerings of poet, painter, and jeweler; regales his friends with horses and greyhounds; and arranges his masque of Amazons, music, and dancing as the culmination of his extravagant banquet. Once again Shakespeare presents Amazons at the heart of Athens. It has been suggested that the Amazons in Timon's Athens signal a menace, given what Shakespeare's audience would have known of their warlike qualities;[36] but the greater threat seems to be the overdomestication of these once fierce women. While the Amazonian women in the comedies contribute an appropriate touch of refinement, fantasy, or compassion, the gorgeous dancing Amazons of Timon's masque suggest an overly luxurious soft center.

Plutarch, too, condemns the extravagances of Athenian preoccupation with the arts, citing a wise Spartan's view of the excessive expense and magnificence of dramatic productions in Athens:

o how farre amisse and out of the way are the Athenians, to dispend so much money, and imploy such serious study in games and fooleries: surely they defray in the furniture and setting out of a theatre as much as would serve to set aflote a royall armado at sea, and mainteine a puisant army upon the land. (*Morals*, 985–86)

Plutarch also presents a derogatory description of a dramatic procession in Athens as a parody of a military triumph, wherein musicians, artists, actors, and all manner of theatrical trappings march in a vast train, "attending upon a tragoedie, to tricke and trim her, or to beare up her traine, and carry her litter, as if she were some stately or sumptuous dame" (*Morals*, 985). With these personifications of Greece as a baby girl and Athens as Dame Tragedy, it sounds like we have come full circle back to traditional disparagement of the Greeks, but not quite.

Although Horace condemns the excessive tendency of Greeks toward novelty and frivolity, neither does he favor the Roman slavish attachment to the past or excessive preoccupation with economic and practical concerns (*Ars Poetica*, 477–79). Nor can we forget his advice to Roman poets: "For yourselves, handle Greek models by night, handle them by day" (*Ars Poetica*, 473). Cicero, too, gives the Greeks great credit in arts and sciences, especially in impractical areas like music and poetry.[37] The context of Plutarch's comments on Athenian extravagance mitigates the severity of the censure. This essay on Athenian fame also gives Plutarch the opportunity to praise Athens as "the fruitfull mother and kinde nourse of many and sundry arts" (*Morals*, 982). And in other places Plutarch presents the early Romans as a barbaric warlike nation, completely lacking in humanitarian and artistic qualities until they learned those from the Greeks.[38] Moreover, the English title of Plutarch's principal work, *The Lives of the Noble Grecians and Romans*, should give us pause before we lump Shakespeare too readily together with other popular Renaissance authors who show nothing but contempt for Merrygreek vices.

Shakespeare presents the dominant tendencies of Greece and Rome antithetically: the Roman centralizing tendency and the Greek eccentric tendency that pervade many aspects of each culture. In this regard, the two classical types of virtue, Roman and Greek, might be characterized as virtues of continence (based on the ideal of authority) and virtues of expansiveness (based on the ideal of freedom). The central Roman virtue of piety (duty to family, state, and religion) requires a consciousness of tradition and an emphasis on restraint and self-control, in general, the philosophical attitude of stoicism. Greek outgoing virtues involve curiosity, sympathy, spontaneity, and openness, as well as delight in the present rather than concern with tradition. The distinction is, of course, also historical: Greece is the youth of Western civilization; Rome is a more mature culture. As Horace observed, either tendency can become destructive. If Greece was susceptible to ruinous indulgence and childish preoccupation with novelty, Rome was threatened by a no less ruinous practicality and an obsession with the past. Plutarch presented a variation on the idea in his observation about the tendency of his first Roman leader to be too strict and his first Greek leader, too remiss.

Among Shakespeare's plays, the clearest exemplification of these antithetical tendencies occurs in the characters of Titus and Timon. Titus's tragedy arises from a too extreme piety that admits of no sympathy. Bound to tradition, he errs in being too self-controlled and in adhering too closely to law and custom. We want him to break out of this rigidity in the opening scene— to feel pity for Tamora's son, to choose Bassianus over Saturninus despite primogeniture, to have sympathy with Bassianus's claim to Lavinia, and to stand with his sons in their support of Bassianus. Instead, he murders one of his sons in a fit of misguided piety, and murder at the center of the monumental city obviously captured Shakespeare's imagination again later in his career. By contrast, the words *free* and *freely* ring through the first acts of *Timon* to describe the hero, who it appears, "outgoes / The very heart of kindness" (1.1.274–75) with his expansive brotherly love, generosity, and hospitality. However, we quickly learn that his generosity is extravagant and indiscriminate, captured appropriately through metaphors of excess—"raging waste" (2.1.4), "flow of riot" (2.2.3), and "prodigal course" (3.4.12). At the peak of his sentimentality during the banquet, Timon breaks down in tears of happiness at the thought of friends commanding one another's fortunes. Later, however, we hear that Timon's steward has often wept at his master's prodigality, and still later we see Timon's servants weeping just before they go their separate ways. All these images of flowing waters and tears culminate in the final speech of the play as Alcibiades envisages "vast Neptune" weeping over Timon's "low grave" (5.4.78–79). And disasters on seashores seem to pervade Shakespeare's imagination in the Greek plays.

Neither type of virtue, Roman or Greek, is ignoble, and neither tendency in moderation is destructive. Indeed, the eccentric tendency of the Greeks produced great adventurers and explorers of the mind and the physical world, and the Merrygreek pursuit of beauty, arts, and pleasures has attractive qualities. If the fragile political organizations of the Greeks failed, their culture, nonetheless, survived. The same anarchic impulse that led to their political decline also contributed to their cultural greatness—a marvellous emotional and imaginative freedom that gave rise to fascinating mythology, enduring philosophies, and brilliant works of art—some of which inspired Shakespeare's various Greek worlds.

Notes

1. Paul Stapfer, *Shakespeare and Classical Antiquity: Greek and Latin Antiquity as Presented in Shakespeare's Plays*, trans. Emily J. Carey (1880; reprint, New York: Burt Franklin, 1970), 259.

2. Gilbert Highet, convinced that Shakespeare lacked familiarity with Greece, noted that "the Greek plays are not like Greece." *The Classical Tradition: Greek and Roman Influences on Western Literature* (Oxford: Oxford University Press, 1949), 197; R. R. Bolgar observed that "while Shakespeare's Romans are indeed Roman and carry their stoicism with an authentic solemnity, his Greeks are hardly Greek." *The Classical Heritage and its Beneficiaries* (Cambridge: Cambridge University Press, 1954), 327.

3. There have, however, been tentative efforts to look beyond traditional disparagement in assessing Shakespeare's conception of Greece. Emphasizing the complexity of characters in *Troilus* and *Timon*, Clifford Leech concluded that the two plays demonstrate "no simple exposure of decadent Greeks." "Shakespeare's Greeks," *Stratford Papers on Shakespeare*, ed. B. W. Jackson (Toronto: W. J. Gage, 1964), 18. John Velz granted that Renaissance bias contributed to the portrait of "a corrupt Hellas" in *Timon* and *Troilus*, but he also noted that this view does not account for the other Greek works. "The Ancient World in Shakespeare: Authenticity or Anachronism? A Retrospect," *Shakespeare Survey* 31 (1978): 6.

4. Elisabeth Wolffhardt, *Shakespeare und das Griechentum* (Weimer: G. Uschmann, 1920), 1–53.

5. T. J. B. Spencer, "'Greeks' and 'Merrygreeks': A Background to *Timon of Athens* and *Troilus and Cressida*," *Essays on Shakespeare and Elizabethan Drama in Honor of Hardin Craig*, ed. Richard Hosley (Columbia: University of Missouri Press, 1962), 231.

6. For fuller lists of Greek works available in English translation, see Henry Burrowes Lathrop, *Translations from the Classics into English from Caxton to Chapman 1477–1620* (New York: Octagon Books, 1967), 311–18; and R. R. Bolgar, *Classical Heritage*, 508–24.

7. See John Edwin Sandys, *A History of Classical Scholarship*, vol. 2 (New York: Hafner Publishing, 1958), 219–50.

8. T. W. Baldwin, "Upper Grammar School: Shakspere's Lesse Greeke," in

William Shakspere's Small Latine & Lesse Greeke, vol. 2. (Urbana: University of Illinois Press, 1944), 617–61.

9. See Plutarch, *Life of Marcus Cato,* in *The Lives of the Noble Grecians and Romances,* 5 vols., trans. Thomas North (1579 and 1603; reprint, London: Nonesuch Press, 1929–30), 3: 182–212. Subsequent citations of Plutarch's *Lives* are to this edition.

10. Juvenal, Satire 3 in *The Sixteen Satires,* trans. Peter Green (New York: Penguin Books, 1967), pp. 87–98.

11. Lidia Storoni Mazzolani, "The Precedent of Alexander," in *The Idea of the City in Roman Thought: From Walled City to Spiritual Commonwealth,* trans. S. O'Donnell (Bloomington: Indiana University Press, 1970), 82–98.

12. Plutarch, "Of the Fortune or Vertue of K. Alexander," in *The Philosophie, commonlie called the Morals,* trans. Philemon Holland (London: Arnold Hatfield, 1603), 1267. Subsequent citations of Plutarch's *Moralia* are to this edition.

13. See James S. Romm, *The Edges of the Earth in Ancient Thought: Geography, Exploration, and Fiction* (Princeton: Princeton University Press, 1992), 32–41; and his "Herodotus and Mythic Geography: The Case of the Hyperboreans," *Transactions of the American Philological Association* 119 (1989): 97–103.

14. Sophocles, Chorus 2 of *Antigone,* in *The Theban Plays,* trans. E. F. Watling (New York: Penguin Books, 1947), 135.

15. Thucydides, *The hystory writtone by Thucydides,* trans. Thomas Nicolls (London, 1550), fol. 14r. Subsequent citations are to this edition.

16. Seneca, *Seneca: His Tenne Tragedies,* vol. 2., ed. Thomas Newton (1581; reprint, New York: AMS Press, 1967), 70. Subsequent citations are to this edition.

17. John Gillies, *Shakespeare and the Geography of Difference* (Cambridge: Cambridge University Press, 1994), 23–25.

18. Cicero, *The Republic,* trans. Clinton Walker Keyes, Loeb Classical Library (Cambridge: Harvard University Press, 1961), 117. Subsequent citations are to this edition.

19. Greek colonization of the Illyrian coast began in the seventh century B.C.E. Among Greek colonies in Illyria, Shakespeare shows some familiarity with Epidamnus (Epidamium in *Comedy of Errors*). Thucydides identifies the dispute between Corcyra and Corinth over Epidamnus as the earliest contributing factor to the Peloponnesian War.

20. For location of Pentapolis in Thrace, see Clifford J. Ronan, "The Onomastics of Shakespeare's Works with Classical Settings," *Literary Onomastics Studies* 8 (1981): 47–69; for its location in Asia Minor, see Georges Lambin, "De longues notes sur de brefs passages Shakespearians," *Études Anglaises* 20 (1967); 62–66.

21. This notorious geographical error (quite possibly an intentional fallacy designed to evoke an atmosphere of fantasy) interestingly combines the birthplace of Apollo on the island of Delos (roughly the geographical center of the southern Aegean and Homeric Greece) and the oracle of Apollo at Delphi (the spiritual center of Greece).

22. See Thelma N. Greenfield, "A Re-Examination of the 'Patient' Pericles," *Shakespeare Studies* 3 (1967): 51–61.

23. See Gillies, *Shakespeare and the Geography of Difference,* 135–37.

24. Leech, "Shakespeare's Greeks," 19.

25. Emrys Jones, *The Origins of Shakespeare* (Oxford: Clarendon Press, 1977), 85–118.

26. See Oscar James Campbell, *Comicall Satyre and Shakespeare's "Troilus and Cressida"* (San Marino: Huntington Library, 1938); and G. K. Hunter, "Troilus and Cressida: A tragic satire," *Shakespeare Studies* 13 (Tokyo 1974–75): 1–23.

27. See George Puttenham, *The Arte of English Poesie*, ed. Gladys Willcock and Alice Walker (1936; reprint, Cambridge: Cambridge University Press, 1970), 31–32. Several of Plutarch's Athenian lives refer to the comic poets' mockeries of political leaders.

28. Jonson defines his own practices, sometimes over against ancient Greek methods in several places; for his fullest criticism of Old Comedy, see *Timber*, in *Ben Jonson*, vol. 8, eds. C. H. Herford and Percy and Evelyn Simpson (Oxford: Clarendon Press, 1947), 643–44.

29. See Robert K. Presson, *Shakespeare's "Troilus and Cressida" and the Legends of Troy* (Madison: University of Wisconsin Press, 1963), 407.

30. Cicero, *Pro Flacco*, trans. C. Macdonald, Loeb Classical Library (Cambridge: Harvard University Press, 1976), 459.

31. One immediately thinks of the banishment of Coriolanus as an exception to this contrast. Certainly, early republics, Greek or Roman, can function similarly. Cicero insists, however, that the Greek practices should have no place in Rome: "Indeed there is no lack of instances of the fickleness [*levitas*] and cruelty of Athens toward her most eminent citizens; and this vice, originating and spreading there, has, they say, overflowed even into our own powerful republic." *Republic*, 19–21.

32. Robert S. Miola, "Timon in Shakespeare's Athens," *Shakespeare Quarterly* 32 (1980): 28. See also his discussion of the ostracism, 26–27.

33. E. M. W. Tillyard, *Shakespeare's Last Plays* (1938; reprint, London: Chatto and Windus, 1958), 11.

34. Perhaps Antony should be mentioned in this context for his impractical decision to fight at sea rather than on land and for the moment he loses his last chance at Roman power by pursuing his Hellene-Egyptian across the sea.

35. Horace, Epistle 2.1 in *Satires, Epistles, and Ars Poetica*, trans. H. Rushton Fairclough, Loeb Classical Library (1916; reprint, Cambridge, Mass.: Harvard University Press, 1970), 405. Subsequent citations of Horace are to this edition.

36. See Robert C. Fulton, "Timon, Cupid, and the Amazons," *Shakespeare Studies* 9 (1976): 283–99.

37. Cicero, *Tusculan Disputations*, trans. J. E. King, Loeb Classical Library (1927; reprint, Cambridge: Harvard University Press, 1966), 3–5.

38. Plutarch, *Life of Numa*, 1:117–18; *Comparison of Pericles with Fabius*, 1:346; *Life of Marcus Cato*, 2:208; *Life of Marcellus*, 2:131–33; *Life of Caius Marius*, 2:312–13.

Britain and the Great Beyond: *The Masque of Blackness* at Whitehall

RICHMOND BARBOUR

WHEN Abraham Ortelius named his great volume *Theatrum Orbis Terrarum* (1570), he made the same metaphor Shakespeare's company made in 1599 when it renamed the Theatre, reassembled bankside, the Globe. Given the master trope of the world as a stage, a book of maps can be a theater, and a playhouse can be a three-dimensional map of the world.[1] The question is where and how one views the world, who gets to look, and what such vision does to viewers. The Globe warranted its name in part because its geography was utterly flexible. Its staging centered on the human body and voice. Stage devices were indicative—bed, throne, arbor—not comprehensively illusionistic. As the term *audience* suggests, the playhouse was an auditorium and did not display a separate or necessarily located world.[2] Speech and gesture, and properties defined as much by use as by appearance, generated a sense of place there. Such place is rhetorical: it resides in the audience's complicit mind.

Masques at the Jacobean court, on the other hand, situated themselves more concretely, addressing the cartographic challenge with peculiar thoroughness and visible force. As the crown's guests, viewers at Whitehall witnessed unique performances featuring sumptuous illusionistic scenes and machines. A proscenium arch framed much of the spectacle; perspective sets deployed themselves before the King's focal eye. On certain gilded nights, the Great Hall transformed itself into a machine for representing the world, into a model of the universe,[3] which took its center at Whitehall. While plays in the public theater roamed the world with the freedom of thought (for instance, *Tamburlaine*, *Antony and Cleopatra*), masques, operating in a triumphal mode, explicitly—and riskfully—returned the world to England.

Jacobean masques, then, provided signal occasions for a nascently imperial British court to consider its relations to the encompassing world. Performed not long after the term *Great Britain* was proposed, Ben Jonson's premiere assignment in this genre, *The Masque of Blackness* (1605), offers an arresting formulation of early Stuart England's geography: the masque celebrates Britain's difference from distant, "darker" worlds. The exoticism welcome to masques, and a tradition of black impersonation at the English court and in civic festivals, may have prompted Queen Anne's wish that she and her ladies appear as Africans: "it was her majesty's will to have them blackamores at first," Jonson writes. In an English court unaccustomed to seeing the Queen as a masquer, any role she took might prove disturbing to some, but there was nothing necessarily subversive about the design for blackness.[4] Eldred Jones details popular and aristocratic traditions of such mimicry in England: festive villagers danced the "Morisco" or Morris, often with blackened faces; in mummings the king of Egypt had a black face; devils in cycle plays were often black; in 1510, Henry VII and the Earl of Essex, dressed as Turks, were escorted by torchbearers "lyke Moreskoes, their faces blacke" into a show featuring ladies whose "faces, neckes, armes and handes, [were] covered with fyne plesaunce blacke ... so that the same ladies seemed to be ... blacke Mores."[5] Jones rehearses similar evidence from the reigns of Edward VI and Elizabeth and points out that the tradition continued after Jonson's *Blackness* (e.g., in Campion's *Squires Masque* [1613] and Townshend's *Tempe Restored* [1631]). Further, Lord Mayor's shows not infrequently featured a king of Moors, sometimes, like the more usual "green men," tossing squibs into the crowd to clear the way. Records of the 1585 show note "him that rid on a luzern [lynx] before the Pageant, apparelled like a Moor." Escorted by six tributary ingot-bearing kings in 1616, a king of Moors riding a golden leopard scatters gold and silver.[6] By presenting the Moor as a scary or magnificent presence already harnessed to domestic pomp, such pageants thrilled, without deeply threatening, London's spectators. In *The Triumph of Truth* (1613), for instance, Thomas Middleton's king of Moors reports, presumably straight-faced, that the "Religious Conversation / Of English merchants" abroad has converted him, "my Queene and people all" to Christianity.[7]

If the classic Roman triumph, by offering foreign captives up to the city's view, displayed imperial power, Jacobean London's adaptation of the genre, with English actors, displayed instead imperial fiction. Blurring the differences it pretended to clarify,

King of Moors from Anthony Munday's *Chrysanaleia* (1616), reproduced courtesy of the Guildhall Library, London.

such ritual containment of the showy other remained problematic; and Jonson's masque, I argue, founders on the matter. Given the Queen's will and a workable tradition of black shows at court, around this material the poet produced a fiction of unprecedented elaboration and consistency. One of his chosen imperatives was geographic: the dark nymphs must arrive from a region that has a place on the map and a rhetoric of its own. That Jonson was attentive to geography and its staging we know from his famous quip to Drummond on *The Winter's Tale:* "Shakespeare . . . brought in a number of men saying they had suffered shipwreck in Bohemia, where there is no sea near by some 100 miles."[8] Jonson finds the inaccuracy risible. He knows the mileage to the coast. His London-based plays are crammed with pertinent place-names: specific urban topography helps make meaning. For instance, *Every Man Out of His Humour* (1600) begins outside London, passes through various city stations—a merchant's house, Paul's walk, a tailor's shop, outside a notary's office—proceeds by oars to Whitehall, and concludes with an exploded feast at the Mitre and a fop's imprisonment at the Counter. By no accident, this trajectory not only sketches the course of Jonsonian ambition, frustration, and vengeance; it also traces the unstable venues of London's playing companies, who rehearse in marginally situated playhouses to make the occasional royal performance and then return to their ways.[9]

His alertness to place at once streetwise and bookish, Jonson carefully specifies an origin for the nymphs: they come from the Niger:

> Pliny, Solinus, Ptolemy, and of late Leo the African, remember unto us a river in Ethiopia famous by the name of Niger, of which the people were called *Nigritae*, now Negroes, and are the blackest nation of the world. This river taketh spring out of a certain lake, eastward, and after a long race falleth into the western ocean (ll.13–17).[10]

If Jonson has chosen the region because its people are "the blackest nation of the world," he still wants to locate the river. However, his account leaves us perplexed. Does the Niger flow "eastward" and then issue into the west, or does he simply mean that the lake lies to the east? His note compounds the problem:

> Some take it to be the same with Nilus, which is by Lucan called *Melas*, signifying *niger*. Howsoever, Pliny . . . hath this: "The river Niger has the same nature as the Nile; it produces reeds, papyrus and the same animals."[11]

If Jonson prefers Pliny's "same nature as" to Lucan's "the same with," he lacks information to decide between them. Thus, the "Introduction into Cosmographie" of *The Most Noble and Famous Travels of Marcus Paulus* (1579) proposes, unhelpfully, that "among all Rivers, onelie Nilus entereth into two Seas, . . . one braunche into the East Sea, and another braunche into the West Sea." Consulting Leo Africanus, whose *Geographical Historie of Africa* (1600) was translated into English by a man in attendance at the *Masque of Blackness*, John Pory, we see perhaps why Jonson has left the Niger's identity and course unclear:[12]

> This lande of Negros hath a mightie river, which taking his name of the region, is called Niger: this river taketh his originall from the east out of a certaine desert called by the foresaide Negros Sen. Others will have this river to spring out of a certaine lake, and so to run westward till it exonerateth it selfe into the Ocean sea. Our Cosmographers affirme that the said river of Niger is derived out of

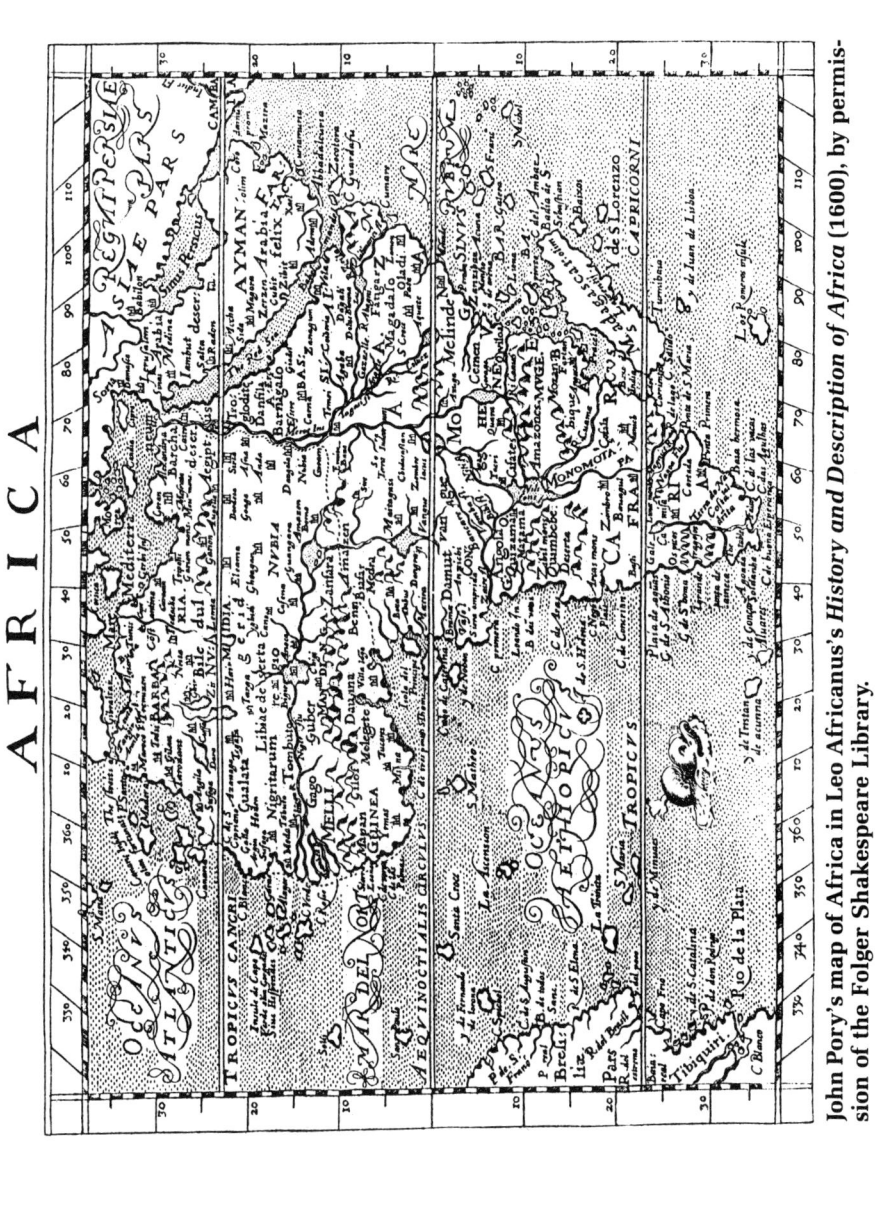

John Pory's map of Africa in Leo Africanus's *History and Description of Africa* (1600), by permission of the Folger Shakespeare Library.

Nilus, which they imagine for some certaine space to be swallowed up of the earth, and yet at last to burst forth into such a lake as is before mentioned. Some other are of opinion, that this river beginneth westward to spring out of a certaine mountaine, and so running east, to make at length a huge lake: which verily is not like to be true.[13]

Niger's source is an eastern desert, or a lake, perhaps subterranean currents of the Nile; or, more dubiously, it flows eastward from a mountain into a vast swamp. The masque requires westward issue, for the Daughters of Niger meet Oceanus near Britain's shore. The "some other" whom Leo-Pory-Jonson thus correct prominently include Ptolemy, whose *Nigris* ("ostia est regnum Senega") "Facit autem . . . Nigrite paludem," makes the Nigritae marshes. Both Ptolemy's early "Tabula Africa IV" and Münster's 1540 "Nova Tabula" in the same volume depict the Niger running, without issue, between two lakes in "Libya interior" (though the latter curiously names the river Dara). Like Jonson's, Leo's text puts the river in Aethiopia, a name extending more widely in Münster than in Ptolemy. Nevertheless, Jonson stays with Ptolemy's observation, "Meridionalis ripae homines sunt omnino nigri."[14]

Jonson's haziness about the Niger is functional then, a product not of inattention but of uncertainty. The authorities differ; he takes from them what the masque requires. In the service of Jacobean mythology, which would locate imperial Roman culture in London now, he combines ancient and modern geography.[15] In Homer, Oceanus is the great river encircling the world, bordered by the Pillars of Hercules on one side, the Elysian Fields and Hades on another. In asking his son Niger why "thou, the Ethiop's river, so far east, / Art seen to fall into th'extremest west / Of me" (11.90–92)—that is, into the regions of Elysium—Jonson's Oceanus addresses a river the poet has located in the latest African "geographical history" in print. To renew the classical world makes for contradiction, yet what matters for the masque is that the Niger is an exotically distant river whose name indicates blackness and whose daughters may reach the westward sea and Albion, which name Jonson glosses as "white land." The spirit of this geography is poetic and post-Columbian: that the Niger is imperfectly known, variously rumored, is vital to its fascination.[16]

The African equivalent to English uncertainty about Africa, of

Ptolemy's map of Africa in Münster's *Geographia* (1540), reproduced courtesy of the James Ford Bell Collection, University of Minnesota.

Sebastian Münster's map of Africa (1540), reproduced courtesy of the James Ford Bell Collection, University of Minnesota.

course, is Niger's quaint (to English eyes) ignorance of Britain. This river-father cannot decipher the white cliffs of Dover:

> Niger. What land is this that now appears to us?
> Oceanus. This land that lifts into the temperate air
> His snowy cliff is Albion the fair,
> So called of Neptune's son, who ruleth here.
> (ll.178–81)

As from Asia, Marlowe's verse invokes distant "Europe, where the sun dares scarce appear / For freezing meteors and congealēd cold," so this passage invites the English audience to conceive its own terrain exoticized in others' eyes.[17] This is the land Niger has been seeking: where black skin may be made white. Niger tells how his daughters have fallen into despair at their blackness, which he finds beautiful, proof of the sun's overzealous love. Expansive European ideology has confused them:[18]

> Yet since the fabulous voices of some few
> Poor brainsick men, styled poets here with you,
> Have with such envy of their graces sung
> The painted beauties other empires sprung,
> Letting their loose and winged fictions fly
> To infect all climates, yea, our purity;
> As of one Phaeton, that fired the world,
> And that before his heedless flames were hurled
> About the globe, the Ethiops were as fair
> As other dames, now black with black despair;
> . . . .
> Which when my daughters heard, . . .
> . . . . fear and care
> Possessed them whole
> (ll.130–39, 142–44).

Niger is made to look foolish because he does not know where he is; and that he finds his daughters' black skin beautiful in part because "Death herself (herself being pale and blue) / Can never alter their most faithful hue" (ll.124–45) is bizarre (praising lovely daughters by imagining them dead?). His viewpoint is garbled and forcefully contained, then; yet he does voice an Afrocentric esthetic. Their "purity" has been "infected" by Western contact. Intending to correct Niger's vision of things, the masque must first present it. The likeness between his (comic) ignorance of England, and England's of Africa, silently undercuts Jacobean complacency.

His daughters have learned in a vision that the answer to their trouble abides in a land "Whose termination, of the Greek, / Sounds -*tania*" (ll.164–65); and, industrious but not quick, they have tried "Black Mauretania" (Morocco), "Swarth Lusitania" (Western Spain, Portugal) and "Rich Aquitania" (Southwest France) so far (ll.173–75). The moon, recognized by Niger as the goddess Aethiopia, appears with happy news: this is the place. "Britannia, which the triple world admires, / This isle hath now recovered for her name" (ll.211–12). The name's recovery contributes to the Jacobean classical project: as Jonson's great teacher Camden had expounded in *Britannia* (1586), "the most ancient Greeks (... were they that first gave the Island that name) ... *Brith*, and *Brithon;*" and they passed the term to the Romans: "Lucretius and Caesar, the first Latines that made mention therof, [called it] more truely *Britannia*."[19] However ambivalently—for much of Britain was conquered by Rome, whose writers described the natives as barbarians—the name grounds James's polity in the Roman world.

It is also a "new name" (l.221). James desired his accession to the English throne to effect the union of England, Scotland, and Wales. He strove fruitlessly to make the name for this empire, Great Britain, official.[20] Honoring old-new Britannia, Jonson proclaims James' peaceful rule over a united island:

> With that great name Britannia, this blessed isle
> Hath won her ancient dignity and style,
> *A world divided from the world*, and tried
> The abstract of it in his general pride.
> For were the world with all his wealth a ring,
> Britannia, whose new name makes all tongues sing,
> Might be a diamond worthy to enchase it.
>
> (ll.216–22)

Thus, the masque adapts the familiar conceit of England as a separate, more exalted world.[21] This complacent geography, however, as Jeffrey Knapp has persuasively argued, holds unsettling implications. To think of England as a "little world"[22] insinuates that, for all its refinements, the island kingdom may be irrelevant to the larger world—a commonwealth of triflers. The British were, and knew themselves to be, belated about their Renaissance and their empire building. While he encouraged trade and plantation, the pacifistic James was no monarch to renew continental—or to initiate Eastern, African, or New World—conquest. He was intent on his project for Scotland in Parliament, insular, narcissistic.[23] He met Africa in his own shows, where for instance black nymphs—rather, Englishwomen costumed as black nymphs—arrive to adore his transformative power. Analogously of the people, Swiss visitor Thomas Platter observed in 1599, "for the most part the English do not much use to travel, but are content ever to learn of foreign matters at home, and ever to take their pastime."[24] Uneasy about such habits, Shakespeare's Prologue in *Henry V* (1599) begs pardon for presuming to cram "The vasty fields of France . . . / Within this wooden O": for the circular, self-regarding playhouse is a type of islanded Britain itself, where audiences thrill to domestic renderings of distant worlds.[25] Thus, Niger's ignorance of Albion raises a major question: who is really provincial here? Niger arrives from an immense continent whose interior the English have never seen. They have given him no occasion to notice their existence.

Of course, the masque proceeds confidently, assuming that the world, insofar as it manages to discover Britain, finds itself sublimed. The realm is

> Ruled by a sun that to this height doth grace it,
> Whose beams shine day and night, and are of force
> To blanch an Ethiop, and revive a corse.
> His light sciential is, and, past mere nature,
> Can salve the rude defects of every creature.
>
> (ll.223–27)

One cannot but declare: Even given the hyperbolic occasion, these lines risk self-parody. Of course, James, bearer of "light sciential," was an intellectual; and his glance might redeem a dead career. As his favorites discovered, his attentions were indeed transformative. Sound Neoplatonic doctrine supports Jonson's conceit: illuminating their object, the King's purifying eye-beams are to the sun's tanning rays as Plato's Ideal Beauty is to Sensible Beauty.[26] The masque's problem, however, was that the monarch failed to effect this miracle on the spot: the court ladies arrived in blackface, and so, after the dancing, they departed. It would be three years until their rarefied return in *The Masque of Beauty*. This awkward gap between poetry and spectacle— indeed, the strategy of taking on blackness to begin with—made for trouble.

Thus Dudley Carleton describes the Queen and her ladies:

> Their Apparell was rich, but too light and Curtizan-like for such great ones. Instead of Vizzards, their Faces, and Arms up to the El-

bows, were painted black, which was Disguise sufficient, for they were hard to be known; but it became them nothing so well as their red and white, and you cannot imagine a more ugly Sight, then a Troop of lean-cheek'd Moors.[27]

As Orgel argues, Carleton is disturbed by a breach of decorum: masquers' roles should represent the dignity of the persons performing them, and these nymphs, however costly, look available. That some of them did in fact live rather freely probably added to Carleton's discomfort: promiscuity is not a happy topos for a Jacobean masque.[28]

But what most strikes readers today is the racist edge to Carleton's mislike. For he finds the costumes "Curtizan-like," it would seem, not because they are too revealing, but because they reveal black skin. In *The Masque of Beauty* (1608), which celebrates the ladies' ravishing return to whiteness, one of the masquers appeared "In a robe of flame color, naked-breasted, her bright hair loose-flowing" (1.159); yet the record holds no complaint about "too light" attire here. Viewers admired rather "the wealth of pearls and jewels that adorned the Queen and her ladies."[29] Carleton's 1605 antipathies spring, as several critics have argued, from an equation of blackness with unbridled sexuality. That women should embody this linkage only heightens his unease: racial fears combine with patriarchal anxieties about female lust and generativity. Because black women may be fantasized to erase white paternity in their children, Boose suggests, to represent black women in Jacobean England is a queasy matter. Particularly as objects of desire: "Theyr black faces, and hands wch were painted and bare up to the elbowes, was a very lothsome sight," Carleton writes again, "and I am sorry that strangers should see owr court so strangely disguised."[30]

The terms of Carleton's critique, however, indicate a specifically theatrical provocation as well: The women are "strangely disguised." As we noted in Henry VIII's courtly disguising, long black gloves, stockings, and velvet masks had done the trick before; similarly in 1547, "hugh Eston the kynges hosyer" received payment for fourteen "peyres of nether stockes of lether black for mores;" in 1579 one Willyam Lyzard was paid probably for designing skin-covers: "for patorns for the mores maske that should have served on Shrovetuesday." Arguing that it "became them nothing so well as their red and white," Carleton mocks the new cosmetics.[31] "Instead of Vizzards, their faces" were shown, looking perhaps more "lean-cheek'd" than with a mask. Moreover, the masque gave him sound occasion to protest. For if their blackness had been effected with the usual gloves and masks (they wore full-length dresses), the nymphs' transformation into daughters of Albion should have been achievable within a few seconds. The look of verisimilar skin, probably an item of Inigo Jones's illusionistic agenda, called for painting that obscured the fiction's central conceit.

Thus, the novel means of representation exacerbates racial and sexual anxiety: what troubles Carleton is that, in effect, the masquers' skin is indelibly black. Vizards would signal a safer distance between the women and their roles, and they represent a notoriously lustful nation. Leo Africanus, a Christianized Spanish Moor less familiar with the "lande of Negros" than with Africa's more northern regions ("Barbaria, Numidia, Libya") (1:123), reports that when discovered by Muslims,

> Negros . . . lived a brutish and savage life, without any king, governour, common wealth, or knowledge of husbandrie. Clad they were in skins of beasts, neither had they any peculiar wives: in the day time they kept their cattell; and when night came they resorted ten or twelve both men and women into one cottage together, using hairy skins instead of beds, and each man choosing his leman which he had most fancy unto.[32]

Promulgating stereotypes pertinent to the Jacobean occasion, Leo associates blackness with ungoverned lust: "there is no nation under heaven more prone to venerie."[33] Carleton was surely not the only spectator to think the same; the idea was reinforced by the myth that black Africans were the children of Chus, who was punished with blackness for his father Ham's sexual disobedience.[34]

In a "great concave shell" flanked by "six huge sea-monsters" (ll.46, 51), the masquers arrive to the singing of two sea-maids and a triton:

> Sound, sound aloud
> The welcome of the orient flood
> Into the west.
>
> (ll.76–78)

In eroticized cross-cultural transit, Niger and his daughters, in whom Africa and the Orient already commingle, penetrate the aptly named Whitehall. However welcome, their passage is aswarm with submarine anxieties about gender, race, and cul-

1 Masquer: A Daughter of Niger

A Daughter of Niger from *The Masque of Blackness* (1605), painted by Inigo Jones. Courtesy of Philip Wilson Publications, London.

ture, as well as spectacular sea monsters. That the women move with the masculine force of Niger's current aggravates whatever unease viewers may take from their blackness: this is flagrant display of vigorous, polymorphic sexuality. That the Queen, her hieroglyph "A golden tree laden with fruit" (ll.244–45), was almost seven months pregnant surely added to the impact.[35] Having recently posited its isolate unity as Great Britain, now the land opens itself to "the orient flood." Such traffic may not be manageable.[36] The masque confidently proclaims that Britain's sun "refines / All things on which his radiance shines" (ll.234–35); but as we have seen, no such demonstration was made that evening. To the contrary, invited to dance, writes Carleton, the Spanish Ambassador "took out the Queen, and forgot not to kiss her Hand, though there was Danger it would have left a mark on his Lips."[37] As they were "infected" by white ideology, so Niger's daughters, willingly or not, may impart their hue in Albion.

A small and separate realm, Britain is at once susceptible and resistant to foreign excitations. Thus, Camden, in Holland's translation, praises its ambiguous geography:

> [T]he most famous Island, without comparison of the whole world; severed from the continent of Europe by the interflowing of the Ocean, lieth against Germanie and France triangle-wise; by reason of three Promontories shooting out into divers parts ... Disjoyned from those neighbor-countries all about by a convenient distance every way, fitted with commodious and open havens, for traffique with the universall world, and to the generall good, as it were, of mankind, thrusting it selfe forward with great desire from all parts into the sea.[38]

Into a sea that is both barrier and thoroughfare, Britain reaches out, longing to embrace the world. Though an Elizabethan, Camden does not call up the insular mythos of impenetrability embodied in the Virgin Queen. His island is androgynous and ready for action: its members "thrusting ... forward with great desire," its harbors "commodious and open." Unlike, say, Carleton, he is remarkably calm about Britain's availability, not fearing that "generall good" will eclipse domestic identity. Promiscuity is strength: for Camden, commerce vivifies both Britain and the world. He is proud that Romans made the island into "the very barne, garner, and storehouse of victuals of the West Empire" (3). He trusts the native resiliency of Britons:

> [A]lthough the Romans, Saxons and Normans have subdued them and triumphed over them; yet hitherto have they preserved their old name and originall language safe and sound: notwithstanding the Normans sought to abolish the same (22–23).

Such tenacious ethnicity—which Camden grounds, decisively, in language—will not be greatly threatened by commerce.

Of course, by Camden's account, Britain's identity, produced through successive histories of invasion and resistance, requires discursive maintenance. His *Britannia*, defining the nation, performs part of the task. Recalling "the vices of . . . the Britans, or the inhumane outrages of the barbarous enemies, or the insatiable crueltie of our Fore-fathers the Saxons," Camden continues:

> But since that for so many ages successively ensuing, we are all now by a certaine engraffing or commixtion become one nation, mollified and civilized with Religion, and good Arts, let us meditate and consider, both what they were, and also what wee ought to be: lest that for our sinnes likewise, the supreame Ruler of the world, either translate other nations hither, when wee are first rooted out, or incorporate them into us, after we are by them subdued (110).

Writing two years before the Armada, Camden suggests that God sent invasions into England to punish its cruel and irreligious peoples, and now that the resulting "commixtion" is "civilized," complete, regression might invite reprisals. Spiritual and cultural achievement must maintain the island's integrity. Thus, Britain's isolation—"Disjoyned . . . by a convenient distance every way"—remains a great comfort, allaying fears about "traffique with the universall world" (1) and freeing the nation to cultivate moral, before military, readiness.

Welcoming the orient flood, Jonson's masque promotes Camden's equanimity about peaceful "engraffing or commixtion" that matures into "one nation." Yet the spectacle cannot contain the threat it ritually assumes. The dark nymphs must be expelled. Their happy reception—"yourselves, with feasts, / Must here remain the Ocean's guests" (ll.304–5)—remains liminal. The show concludes with a prescription for thirteen full-moon lavings in venerean sea-foam somewhere else: "'Back seas, back nymphs, but with a forward grace / Keep, still, your reverence to the place" (ll.333–34) They will be welcome to return when white.

To late-twentieth-century eyes, this ending is deeply obnoxious, a prophesy of racism. The masquers, however, still painted, had in any case to depart after the dancing. It would be a mistake to confound Jonson's vision with Carleton's, as in effect Boose does by arguing that the black-white oppositions of *Blackness* and *Beauty* constitute racist discourse.[39] Jonson had recourse to the Niger because its people were supposedly "the blackest nation in the world" (ll.15–16). What concerns him is exoticism, not a linkage between skin tone and differential human essence. Black and white are opposites: for purposes of color-coded spectacle, the land of Niger is the furthest one can get from Albion's shore. "Black Mauretania," "Swarth Lusitania," and "Rich Aquitania" separate central Africa from England. Residing at the other end of a spectrum of difference, blackness is its most compelling instance, not the trait of a unique race. Thus, the masque is surprisingly nonchalant about the ethnicity it stages. Despite the cartographic concerns of Jonson's preface, the river Niger is hailed not as the "African" or the "Southern" but as the "*orient* flood." His daughters, as if to confirm the adjective, wear Persian mitres.[40] Like Munday's king of Moors in 1616, scattering silver and gold from a leopard's back, they display England's confusion of Africa with the opulent East.[41]

Jonson's masque plays out vital contradictions in early Stuart Britain's sense of its relation to the wider world—an island at once confident of its own culture and deeply threatened by the foreignness it desires to embrace. *Blackness* wants to take in Africa and the East—on condition that they anglicize themselves and turn white. Reverse metamorphosis, the darkening of Albion, must be denied. While something like racism is nearing formulation here, the masque also argues, to the contrary, that differences between peoples are conventional, not essential. Jonson's fiction assumes that "racial" difference is a matter of skin tone, an exterior sign, not of essence: nothing but pigment—appliable, removable, an effect of the tropic sun—detains the Daughters of Niger from becoming Albion's daughters. This is, to be sure, an ethnocentric, even xenophobic, but not a racist, view. Pory and Jonson conceive the people of Niger as a "nation," not a subspecies. In marked contrast to George Best's genealogical account, which finds "the curse [of Ham] & natural infection of bloud" in blackness, Jonson's masque supposes that definitions of human beauty are products of environment and education, culturally relative.[42] Masques aggrandize their audiences, and *Blackness*, of course, assumes Britain's definitions superior. Yet its hyperbolic praise of Albion works only if spectators find Niger's daughters, as their father does, *already* beautiful—an effect that Jones's costumes, whatever their impact on Carleton, were designed to secure. We could say, then, that the Jacobean court trifles with blackness by putting it on and taking it off at pleasure. On the other hand, they are asserting that "race" is a product of geography and culture and that the human race is mobile.

Given the masque's attention to pigment, does painting the body falsify one's person? The antitheatricalist in Jonson would say so. He satirizes women's use of beauty products repeatedly; in this vein, Niger aims sarcasm at the "painted beauties" whose praise has dismayed his (ironically black-painted) daughters.[43] A governing assumption, however, in masques as opposed to plays—whose performers are social ciphers, make-believe aristocrats—is that courtly ostentation reveals the truth; thus, power displays itself. This is why Carleton is upset (do the ladies mean to declare themselves as lustful as blackamores?). If appearance, not inwardness, is of the essence, then differences are negotiable. There is no absolute organic mystery to race.

Studying Roman Britain, Camden makes a fascinating argument:

> Caesar, Mela, Plinie, and the rest doe shew, that the Britaines coloured themselves with woade, called in Latine *Glastum* (and *Glass* at this day with them signifieth *Blew.*) What if I should conjecture, that they were called Britains of their depainted bodies? For, ... that word *Brith* among the Britans, implieth that which the Britans were indeed, to wit, *painted, depainted, died,* and *coloured.*[44]

As Camden explains it, the name by which Jacobean culture affirms its authenticity, proclaiming a heritage at once indigenous and Roman, bespeaks artifice and barbarism. Ancient Britons were remarkable not for innate whiteness but for the stains they made on their skin. Camden, moreover, associates white skin not with native virtue but with teutonic invaders—"those faire white folke, the martiall Germans"—and he insists, "I would have no man ... raise a slander upon the Britans, or thinke them to bee issuede from the savage cruell Hunnes" (*op. cit.*, 12, 114). Body-painting distinguished Britons from "those most fierce Saxons, a people foully infamous, odious both to God and man, ... let into this Island" (p. 109). Picts correspondingly marked their bodies ("And whence should they bee called *Picts*, if it were not because they depainted themselves?"): "*their Nobilitie and Gentry thus spotted, ... carry these skarres about them,* in their painted pounced limbes, as badges to be knowne by. Shall we thinke now, that those *Picts* were Germans, who never used this manner of painting?" (116, 115).

An expert in heraldry, Camden implicitly reverses the dark-light valuations typical of "Western" thought:[45] for ancient Britons, he proposes, stains, spots, and scars confer distinction. Whiteness is the savage ground against which they assert ethnicity and class, inscribe their culture. Thus, "in the names, of well neere all the most ancient Britaines, there appeareth some signification of a colour" (26). Noting a rite strikingly close to that performed in Jonson's masque, Camden cites Pliny: "*the women of Britaine, as well married wives, as their young daughters annoint and die their bodies all over; resembling by that tincture the color of Aethiopians, in which manner they use at some solemne feasts and sacrifices to goe naked.*"[46] For them, presumably, the dark hue was honorific.

To recognize Jonson's indebtedness to Camden—the "reverend head," as the poet names him in *Epigram* 14, "to whom my country owes / The great renown and name wherewith she goes" (1, 3–4)—is to understand the ideological labor in Jonson's celebration of "Britannia" in *The Masque of Blackness*. To identify Britain with Albion, that "white land," and to naturalize an equation of whiteness with beauty and civility, the poet must suppress powerful contestatory discourses, alternate histories, that Camden derives from the name. Pretending to reclaim Britain's "ancient dignity and style" (l.217), Jonson elides originary resemblances between Britons and Ethiopians, just as he sets Britain's "new name" in "th'extremest west" (ll.221,91) of Oceanus's stream, as far from Africa as the old geography allowed. History and geography, nevertheless, converge on Whitehall in the masque, carrying more than the Jacobean royal mythos would admit.

Other cultures recognized Britons as a people, Camden proposed, only insofar as they made their bodies "British," painted themselves. This is what they "were indeed." For the word that Imperial Rome took for them was their own word. Although the term is indigenous, such naming makes British identity a necessarily hybrid thing. It is forged in the encounters of Celts, Greeks, and Romans. To understand that ethnicity is carried in language and inscribed on bodies, to recognize that "racial" identities are cross-cultural semiotic constructs—enacted, imputed, changeable—contests racist thinking. Here, if not in its valuation of whiteness, the masque is in accord with Camden; yet to see ethnicity as such a provisional construct may prove as disturbing as liberating. It challenges insularity; it may become an argument for empire. Distinctions between self and other, domestic and strange, turn slippery: ever-present but factitious, perhaps exploitable.

As I have argued, *The Masque of Blackness* commits itself to confidence. At the stable center of the chosen world, Whitehall transforms, sublimes, its visitors. This fiction, of course, is the easier to sustain because the exotic performers are all English. Even domestic facts, however, may prove unmanageable. Objects of ethnocentric celebration, the ladies of *The Masque of Beauty* return to their floating island at the close:

> Now use your seat—that seat which was before
> Thought straying, uncertain, floating to each shore,
> And to whose having, every clime laid claim;
> Each land and nation urged as the aim
> Of their ambition beauty's perfect throne,
> Now made peculiar to this place alone . . .
> . . . .
> Th'Elysian fields are here.
>
> (ll.319–24, 345)

There is deep poignancy in such communal prayer. For surrounding the charmed circle of performance was, necessarily, a contentious, hungry world. Thus, Carleton on *Blackness*:

> The confusion in getting in was so great, that some Ladies lie by it and compliance of the fury of the white staffs [doormen]. In the passages through the galleries they were shutt up in several heapes betwixt dores, and there stayed till all was ended. And in the coming out, a banquet wch was prepared for the king in the great chamber was overturned table and all before it was skarce touched.[47]

Albion's Elisian display was indeed endangered by a human flood, and the source was local, not "oriental."

Notes

1. See John Gillies, *Shakespeare and the Geography of Difference* (Cambridge: Cambridge University Press, 1994), 70–98.

2. In a typical phrase, Beaumont's Prologue describes playgoing as an aural experience: "If there be any amongst you, that came to *heare* lascivious *Scenes*, let them depart" (*The Woman Hater*, qtd in Andrew Gurr, *Playgoing in Shake-*

speare's London [Cambridge: Cambridge University Press, 1987], 221; my emphasis).

3. Stephen Orgel, *The Illusion of Power: Political Theater in the English Renaissance* (Berkeley and Los Angeles: University of California Press, 1975), 58.

4. Stephen Orgel, ed., *Ben Jonson: The Complete Masques* (New Haven: Yale University Press, 1969), 48. "The problem of incorporating the monarch into the masque was considerably simplified if he was himself one of the masquers, if he took part literally as well as figuratively. This Queen Elizabeth did only rarely, and her successor, never" (Stephen Orgel, *The Jonsonian Masque* [Cambridge, Mass.: Harvard University Press, 1965], 19). Of Queen Anne's plan Jonson's Oxford editors note, "The idea was anything but novel, disguising as negresses having been a favourite fashion with the ladies of Elizabeth" (C. H. Herford and Percy and Evelyn Simpson, eds., *Ben Jonson*, 11 vols. [Oxford: Clarendon, 1925–52] 2:265). Kim Hall argues, on the other hand, that in Jacobean times, "growth of actual contact with Africans, Native Americans, and other ethnically different foreigners" made such shows increasingly disruptive (*Things of Darkness. Economies of Race and Gender in Early Modern England* [Ithaca, N.Y.: Cornell University Press, 1995], 129); Lynda Boose suggests that the Queen's proposal perhaps harbored subversive intent ("'The Getting of a Lawful Race,'" eds. Margo Hendricks and Patricia Parker, *Women, "Race," and Writing in the Early Modern Period* [London: Routledge, 1994], 51). In a forthcoming essay, Stephen Orgel maintains to the contrary that black mimicry was not specifically controversial and that critics have misread *Blackness* by taking Dudley Carleton's frequently cited trouble with the show for a typical response.

5. Eldred Jones, *Othello's Countrymen. The African in English Renaissance Drama* (London: Oxford University Press, 1965), 58.

6. Quoted in John Gough Nichols, ed., *Chrysanaleia, or The Golden Fishing*, 2d ed. (London: Fishmongers' Co., 1859), 14. See also Jones, *Othello's Countrymen*, 29–36; John Nichols, ed., *The Progresses, Processions, and Magnificent Festivities of King James the First*, 5 vols. (London: 1828; New York: Franklin #118), 3:204; Nichols, *Chrysanaleia*, 6.

7. Peter Fryer, *Staying Power. The History of Black People in Britain* (London: Pluto, 1984), 25; Nichols, *James I*, 2:689.

8. Ian Donaldson, ed., *Ben Jonson* (Oxford: Oxford University Press, 1985), 599.

9. The argument that public playing was in fact rehearsal for royal performance was a serious defense of public theater. Thus, Sir Francis Walsingham to the Lord Mayor in 1583: "without frequent exercise of suche plaies as are to be presented before hir majestie, her servantes cannot conveniently satisfie hir recreation and their owne duties" (E. K. Chambers, *The Elizabethan Stage*, 4 vols. [Oxford: Clarendon, 1951], 4:296). See Stephen Mullaney, *The Place of the Stage* (Chicago: University of Chicago Press, 1988) on the liminal placement of playhouses.

10. Orgel, ed., *Ben Jonson*, 48.

11. Orgel, ed., *Ben Jonson*, 509.

12. John Frampton, trans., *The Most Noble and Famous Travels of Marco Polo*, ed. N. M. Penzer (London: Argonaut, 1929; New York: Da Capo, 1971), 5. In a letter to Jonson's friend Sir Robert Cotton, Pory notes that *Hymenaei*'s masquers (1606) "sate somewhat like the ladies in the Scallop-shell the last year" (Herford and Simpson, *Ben Jonson*, 10:466). (Jonson describes the device

as "a great concave shell like mother of pearl" [Orgel, ed., *Ben Jonson*, 49].) It is likely that Pory and Cotton saw *Blackness*. Whether or not Pory made personal contribution to the masque's conceit (had the Queen been reading or conversing with him?), his translation of Leo's *Geographical Historie* may be more important to the conception of *Blackness* than Jonson's single reference indicates.

13. Leo Africanus, *The History and Description of Africa*, trans. John Pory, 1600, ed. Robert Brown, 3 vols. (New York: Franklin; original pub. Hakluyt Soc., 1st Ser. No. 92, 1896), 1:124–25.

14. Claudius Ptolemaeus, *Geographia*, ed., Sebastian Munster (Basle, 1540), Intro. R. A. Skelton (Amsterdam: Theatrum Orbis Terrarum, 1966), 75 (Book 4, Ch. 6).

15. On Jacobean Romanism, see Jonathan Goldberg, *James I and the Politics of Literature* (Baltimore, Hopkins University Press, 1983), esp. "The Style of Gods," 28–54 and David Riggs, *Ben Jonson. A Life* (Cambridge: Harvard University Press, 1989), 14.

16. Orgel, ed., *Ben Jonson*, 51; "the reference," Orgel notes, "is taken from Camden's *Britannia* (London, 1586)" (*Ben Jonson* 511): in the Holland translation (1637), "of *Albus*, that is, White" (p. 26). On post-Columbian cartography, see Gillies, *Shakespeare*: "For perhaps the first time in the history of world cartography, world maps post-1492 began to privilege the unknown and unpossessed over the known and possessed. This is the *semiosis* of desire" (62).

17. *Tamburlaine* I.1.10–11.

18. Cf. Hall, *Darkness* 133.

19. "The Name of Britain," in *Britain, or A Chorographicall Description of the Most Flourishing Kingdomes, England, Scotland, and Ireland*, trans. Philemon Holland (London, 1637), 27; the translation was first published in 1610. In a passage Jonson has found useful, Camden continues, "besides our Britaine, a man shall not find, over the face of the whole earth above three countries of any account and largeness, which end in the determination TANIA: and those verily lying in this west part of the world, namely, MAURETANIA, LUSITANIA, and AQUITANIA" (27). On Camden's decisive importance to Jonson, see Riggs, *Ben Jonson*, 14, 114; Anne Barton, *Ben Jonson, Dramatist* (Cambridge: Cambridge University Press, 1984), 45, 170–72; and *Epigram* 14:

> Camden, most reverend head, to whom I owe
>   All that I am in arts, all that I know,
> (How nothing's that?) to whom my country owes
>   The great renown and name wherewith she goes;
> Than thee the age sees not that thing more grave,
>   More high, more holy, that she more would crave.
>
>   (ed. Donalson, ll.1–6)

20. See Bruce Galloway, *The Union of England and Scotland 1603–1608* (Edinburgh: John Donald, 1986).

21. Camden writes in the *Remains Concerning Britain* (1605):

Britaine ... is ... well knowne to be the most flourishing and excellent, most renowned and famous isle of the whole world: ... if the most Omnipotent had fashioned the world round like a ring, as hee did like a globe, it might have beene most worthily the onely gemme therein (ed. R. D. Dunn [Toronto: University of Toronto Press, 1984], 5).

The conceit is common; see Josephine Waters Bennett, "Britain Among the Fortunate Isles," *SP* 53 (1956): 114–40; and the fascinating study by Jeffrey Knapp, *An Empire Nowhere. England, America, and Literature from Utopia to The Tempest* (Berkeley: University of California Press, 1992).

22. William Shakespeare, *Richard II*, II.i.45.

23. Thus, I am uncomfortable with Hall's conviction that *Blackness* is all about "the growing pains of imperialism" (*Darkness* 140); those would come later. Cf. R. Malcolm Smuts: "The imperial theme was now [under James] associated almost exclusively with the internal peace and prosperity of the British Isles and the dynastic union of England and Scotland, rather than with dreams of overseas dominions" (*Court Culture and the Origins of a Royalist Tradition in Early Stuart England* [Philadelphia: University of Pennsylvania Press, 1987], 25). Distinguishing England's Virgin Queen from her treaty-minded Scot succesor, Hall sharply opposes "Elizabethan insularity" (126) to Jacobean expansionism: "the country earnestly stretched its imperial grasp . . . when James became king" (127). I would argue that England was neither so "inward" (126) with Elizabeth, nor so forcefully imperial with James, as Hall proposes.

24. Quoted in Chambers, *Elizabethan Stage*, 2:366. As Lawrence Stone observes, by the turn of the century, the "Grand Tour" was an increasingly popular, but still novel, practice (*The Crisis of the Aristocracy, 1558–1641*, Abr. ed. [London: Oxford University Press, 1967], 317.) While English maritime ventures increased during the late-Elizabethan and Jacobean periods, expeditions were conceived in tardy emulation of the Iberians and the Dutch. See John Parker, *Books to Build an Empire: A Bibliographic History of English Overseas Interests to 1620* (Amsterdam: N. Israel, 1965); Knapp, *Empire*; and Mary C. Fuller, *Voyages in Print. English travel to America, 1576–1624* (Cambridge: Cambridge University Press, 1995).

25. *Henry V*, Prologue, 11. 12–13.

26. See Orgel, ed., *The Renaissance Imagination. Essays and Lectures by D. J. Gordon* (Berkeley and Los Angeles: University of California Press, 1980) on the masques' systematic Neoplatonism, esp. 143–44.

27. Herford and Simpson, *Ben Jonson*, 10:448.

28. Orgel, *Jonsonian Masque*, 68–69, 118. Hall notes that the masque "featured . . . women who resisted patriarchal standards of female decorum.... From the first entrance of James into England, the court ladies are associated with lawless, transgressive behavior" (*Darkness*, 137). As if to confirm that *Blackness* promoted "light and Curtizan-like" ways, Carleton notes that "one woeman amongst the rest lost her honesty, for wch she was caried to the porters lodge being surprised at her business on the top of the Taras" (Herford and Simpson, *Ben Jonson*, 10:449).

29. Orgel, ed., *Ben Jonson*, 67; Herford and Simpson, *Ben Jonson*, 10:457.

30. Herford and Simpson, *Ben Jonson*, 10:449. Hall notes that Carleton's "connection of face painting with their 'Curtizan-like' apparel points to a time-honored association of blackness with lechery" (*Darkness*, 130). Boose proposes, "What challenges the ideology [of early modern England] enough to require erasure is . . . the black female-white male [union], for it is in the person of the black woman that the culture's pre-existing fears both about the female sex and about gender dominance are realized. Through her, all free-floating anxieties about 'the mother's dark place' contaminating the father's designs for perfect self-replication become vividly literal" (Boose, "'The Getting of a Lawful Race," 46).

31. Jones, *Othello's Countrymen*, 30–31. Hall observes that Carleton describes a new technique for representing black skin, but like other commentators, she does not distinguish his trouble with the novel disguise from his trouble with blackness *per se* (*Darkness*, 130–31). Cf. Jones: "the masquers used paint (and not the usual velvet masks) to disguise their complexions" (*Countrymen*, 33). Anthony Gerard Barthelemy also notes that *Blackness* marks "the first recorded use of blackening to actually darken the skin of the royal maskers" (*Black Face, Maligned Race* [Baton Rouge: Louisiana State University Press, 1987], 20.

32. Leo Africanus, *The History and Description of Africa*, 1:123, 3:819.

33. Ibid., 1:180. Leo also explains that, like the English, "Negroes . . . ne yet are desirous to travell out of their owne countrie"—Niger has never seen Dover—and "Some of them performe great adoration unto the sunne rising" [3:819–20]—an action easily imagined of Niger, proud that the "glorious sun" shows his daughters "fervent'st love" (Orgel, ed., *Ben Jonson*, 52). Barthelemy reviews the traditional European linkage of blackness with concupiscence (*Black Face*, 2–6).

34. Thus, George Best on the results of Ham's trespass against God's demand for sexual continence on the ark (1578):

> a sonne shuld be borne, whose name was Chus, who not only it selfe, but all his posteritie after him, should be so blacke & lothsome, that it might remaine a spectacle of disobedience to all the Worlde. And of this blacke & cursed Chus came al these blacke Moores which are in Africa . . .
> Thus you see, yt the cause of ye Ethiopians blacknesse, is the curse & natural infection of bloud (quoted in Fryer, *Staying Power*, 143; see also Paul Edwards, *The Early African Presence in the British Isles* [Edinburgh: Centre of African Studies, 1990], 6).

Taking blackness for a physically inherited sign of moral depravity, this deeply racist account is tempered in some versions by the climatological hypothesis, whereby the equatorial sun generates difference: Chus' white wife bore sometimes white, sometimes black, children; he assigned the latter to tropic climes more comfortable to them (Fryer, *Staying Power*, 143).

35. Boose, "Getting," 307.

36. Cf. Gillies: "Technically, foreign merchants were simply forbidden to conduct business [in London] . . . London was to be protected from the Babel-like 'openness' of Venice and Antwerp" (*Shakespeare*, 130).

37. Herford and Simpson, *Ben Jonson*, 10:448.

38. Camden, *Britain*, 1.

39. "Jonson . . . pushes the discourse of color difference outside any framework conducive to tolerance, let alone affirmation. In the production of the incipiently racist binary that makes 'Beauty' the antithesis of 'Blackness,' what gets dismantled is the 'black and comely' feminine ideal of the Song of Songs; what gets produced is a model of racial opposition constituted specifically along the axis of gender" (Boose, "Getting," 50). Yet Niger praises a comeliness in his daughters that was supported by their opulent dress and dazzling arrival in Jones' design; indeed, the masques' praise of James' Britannia rings both hyperbolic and true only if the dark nymphs strike spectators as already beautiful. We cannot assume that Carleton's mislike, which applies not just to the painted dancers but to the entire production, was normative. Jonson and Jones received more commissions. As Carleton notes, the Spanish ambassador, for one, took the blackface Queen for a beautiful woman.

40. Line 76, my emphasis. Orgel and Roy Strong, *Inigo Jones: The Theatre of the Stuart Court*, 2 vols. (London: Sotheby Parke Bernet; Berkeley: University of California Press, 1973), 1:96, 98, determine that the headdress is based on that of a Thessalonian bride in Vecellio.

41. As with Columbus, the confusion extends, of course, to the New World: the tributary kings in Munday's pageant wear feathered headbands like American Indians and carry ingots associated rather with New World mines than with Eastern, bullion-consuming, markets. I thank John Gillies for bringing Wickham's reproduction of Munday's king of Moors to my attention (*Early English Stages 1300 to 1660* [London: Routledge, 1963], vol. 2, plate 26). Barthelemy explores far-flung applications of the term "Moor" (*Black Face*, 6–17).

42. Quoted in Fryer, *Staying Power*, 143; see note 34.

43. See, e.g., *Sejanus* II.i.53f; *Epicoene* IV.vii.78f. On Jonson and antitheatricalism, see Jonas Barish, *The Antitheatrical Prejudice* (Berkeley and Los Angeles: University of California Press, 1981), 132–54. See Hall on the ironies of "painting" (*Darkness*, 130–32).

44. *Britain*, 26.

45. On the cultural history of black vs. white, see Barthelemy, *Black Face*, 1–17; and Hall, *Darkness*, 1–24.

46. Camden, *Britain*, 31. The blue pigment of "woad" links Britons to Africans. According to Edwards, "As in Irish and Icelandic, and in the descriptions of Black figures in medieval English drama, the word used to describe racial colour appears commonly to have been 'blue,' as well as 'black', as in an entry in a mid-15th century accounts book, referring to a payment made in 1468 to 'Richard Fyrthing, a blewmane'" (*Early African Presence*, 7). Pertinently, Ceasar's account of native Britons, quoted by Camden, indicates their striking resemblances to Leo's "Negros" (see above, 131): "The Inlanders for the most part sow no corne, but live of milke and flesh; and clad themselves in skins. . . . Ten or twelve of them together use their wives in common, and especially brethren partake with brethren, and parents with their children" (29).

47. Herford and Simpson, *Ben Jonson*, 10:449.

Slave-Born Muscovites: Racial Difference and the Geography of Servitude in *Astrophil and Stella* and *Love's Labor's Lost*

JOHN MICHAEL ARCHER

WHEN the lovers entered the stage disguised as Russians in early performances of *Love's Labor's Lost*, they were evidently preceded by "Blackmoors with music."[1] These figures come from nowhere; there is no indication that they are also in disguise, and they do not participate in the ensuing action, apart perhaps from providing the music for some portion of it. Twentieth-century scholarship notices them only in connection with the question of Russian disguise and its sources. The claim was made long ago that Shakespeare's blackmoors are related to the "Negro-Tartars" of the Gray's Inn Revels of Christmas 1594–95. The Prince of Purpoole received an Ambassador from the Emperor of Russia and two of his colleagues, suitably costumed. They thanked the Prince for the services of his six Knights of the Helmet against the "Bigarian" and the curiously spelled "Negro-Tartars" on behalf of the Emperor. The knights themselves had entered just before, leading in three prisoners.[2] The differences between the Gray's Inn episode and *Love's Labor's Lost*, however, are at least as striking as the similarities. The blackmoors are musicians, servants of a sort but hardly captives. The Gray's Inn prisoners were dressed as "Monsters and Miscreants" with no mention of racial disguise. They were, in fact, allegorical personifications picked up on the return from Russia, named Envy, Malcontent, and Folly.[3] The name *Negro-Tartar* appears a little later in the text of the entertainment; I would suggest that it is a corruption, perhaps unknowing but probably willful and humorous, of Nogai or Nagay Tartar, terms given by Elizabethan travelers in Russia to the inhabitants of the area around the lower Volga River, a warlike people who had recently made peace with the czar. Bigarian may similarly be a play upon Boghar or Bokhara (modern Bukhara), a city beyond the Caspian Sea associated with the Persian trade in slaves from Russia and eastern Europe.[4]

It is true, however, that an association between Russia, its environs, and blackness is evident in English texts well before the middle of the sixteenth century. Edward Hall chronicled a device of 1510 in which two lords appeared at Henry VIII's court in Muscovite costume along with two other lords and six ladies dressed as "Nigers, or blacke Mores;" the ladies' faces and armes were covered in thin black cloth. Hall's account was reprinted in the second edition of Holinshed in 1587.[5] In Richard Eden's compilation *Decades of the New World* (1555), we find "many blacke men, lackynge th[e] use of common spech" who come from Lake Kitai in Siberia to trade precious stones.[6] Giles Fletcher wrote in his influential travel account *Of The Russe Commonwealth* (1591) that Russia was divided under its ancient name of Sarmatia into "White" and "Black": "*Blacke Sarmatia* was all that countrey that lieth southward, towards the *Euxin*, or *Black Sea*."[7] Of Tartars in general he remarks, "For person and complexion they haue broad and flatte visages, of a tanned colour into yellowe and blacke" (p. 72 recto). These references are all very different, but together they suggest that a discourse linking Russian travel and an increasingly racialized blackness was emerging around the time of *Love's Labor's Lost*.[8] This complex, I suggest, lies behind both the Russian-blackmoor pairing in Shakespeare's play and the rather different case of the Negro-Tartars of Gray's Inn, whatever the lines of local influence may or may not be. The reason for the association of Russia and blackness is bound up with the geography of slavery between the fifteenth and seventeenth century. Slavery hardly seems the point in the Russian disguise scene with its blackmoor musicians, and we should not be too quick to assume that it is being represented on stage. Slavery lies behind the love-play of the text, however, concealed in the court of Navarre's fascination with blackness, beauty, and the gentler servitude of erotic courtship. The action of the play unites male and female aristocrats in the middle of western Europe by setting them against various social and cultural groupings on their borders, real and fantastic.

Well before the formal enserfment of the Russian peasantry began in the early 1590s, Russia was chiefly associated with servitude of one sort or another by western Europeans. Richard Hellie has shown that slavery existed in Russia from medieval times, and that it was a diverse institution governed by its own laws and, after 1571, a separate Chancellery. Early modern Russia was unique among large slaveholding societies in that Russians regularly enslaved each other; slavery did not depend upon ethnic difference. Perhaps 10 percent of the population was enslaved, and about half of these slaves were hereditary. The other half was largely given over to various forms of voluntary slavery.[9] In addition to the enslavement of Russians by each other, there was also the very different matter of the Tartars' enslavement of Russians and other eastern Slavs, a trade that passed into the hands of the Ottoman Turks during the last quarter of the fifteenth century. By the first half of the seventeenth century, Russia may have lost on average some 4,000 people a year to this trade, although a figure such as this is hard to verify.[10]

Beyond Russia's borders, slavery was at least as likely to bring Russians to mind as Africans during the sixteenth century, despite the burgeoning trans-Atlantic slave trade. According to Abraham Ortelius, "It is a wilie and deceitfull people, and is rather delighted to liue in seruitude and slauery, than at large and in liberty."[11] The corruption of the inhabitants is regularly linked with their enslavement to the absolute power of the czar, or emperor as he is usually styled, in contemporary English travel writings on Russia. There are a number of such accounts—the Elizabethans were more concerned with Russia than America or Africa during the later sixteenth century. "This trade," as two merchants wrote in 1568, "will maynetene thirtie or fortie greate shippes, ... vent the most part of our coullarid clothes, & in shorte tyme if neade requier all the Karsayes maid within the realme, whereby her maiesties subiectes may be sette a wourke."[12] English travel in Russia was driven by the need to trade in staple goods like rugged kersey cloth, as well as the twin dreams of northeast and southern passages to the riches of Asia.

The Muscovy Company of merchant adventurers was chartered by the Crown in 1555, two years after its founders sponsored the first English voyage to Russia.[13] An account of the 1553 expedition based largely upon the observations of Richard Chancellor, its surviving leader, appeared in Hakluyt's *Principall Navigations Voiages and Discoveries of the English Nation* (1589). Chancellor was raised in the Sidney household, and the narrative contains a long speech attributed to Company member Henry Sidney, friend to Edward VI and father of Philip Sidney, praising Chancellor upon his election. The captain will "commit his safety to barbarous and cruel people," Sidney is supposed to have declared, a prediction partly born out by the subsequent description of "the barbarous Russes" and their idolatrous ways.[14] Chancellor's first contact with the inhabitants comes when he boards a fishing boat in the White Sea. The fishermen prostrate themselves in terror, but the English captain gained their trust, "comforting them by signs and gestures, refusing those duties and reverences of theirs, and taking them up in all loving sort from the ground." This incident, we are told, lent the English a reputation for gentleness and courtesy among the common people, who brought them food and were willing to trade—"except they had been bound by a certain religious use and custom not to buy any foreign commodities without the knowledge and consent of the king" (p. 18). The shadow of the emperor falls across this scene of contact, threatening commerce and underlining the unexpected servility of the people.

Like many later accounts of English travel into Russia, the Chancellor narrative is ostensibly about an exchange of letters between sovereigns. The travelers tell their hosts that they were sent by Edward VI to deliver "certain things" to their king, and eventually they are brought to Moscow and attain an interview with the emperor himself, Ivan IV ("The Terrible"). The description of this meeting and the feast that follows illustrates the majesty and power of the emperor among his nobles in the Kremlin. He ceremonially bestows a piece of bread to each of his courtiers and names them all when he leaves, but the Russians inform their visitors that this "was to the end that the emperor might keep the knowledge of his own household, and withal, that such as are under his displeasure might by this means be known" (p. 27). Later, Chancellor marvels at the willing subjection of wealthy men who give up their riches to the emperor for failing to fight in his wars. As for the poor, he notes, "there are some among them that use willingly to make themselves, their wives, and children bondslaves unto rich men to have a little money at the first into their hands, . . . so little account do they make of liberty" (29–30, 34).

The preeminence of the Russian emperor in this hierarchical society contrasts with the absence of a firm center of English power during the period covered by the narrative. When the English ships left Greenwich, the current location of the court, they discharged their cannon:

> it was a very triumph (after a sort) in all respects to the beholders. But, alas, the good King Edward, in respect of whom principally all

this was prepared, he only by reason of his sickness was absent from this show; and not long after the departure of these ships, the lamentable and most sorrowful accident of his death followed.

(14)

The letter from the emperor that Chancellor carries back from Russia is addressed to a dead king. In his place reigns Mary I, who is saluted at the end of the narrative with a promise that her renown will spread through the newly opened lands. At the same time, it may be significant that the preceding account of Russian customs stresses, somewhat inaccurately, that women cannot inherit property unless the emperor allows them a portion; without a male heir all lands fall back into his hands (29). An implicit comparison of Russian ways with English runs throughout the text, squarely it would seem to the disadvantage of the former. The barbarity and obedience of the Russians is not uniformly denounced. They make excellent soldiers who eat little and sleep happily upon the hard ground: "How justly may this barbarous and rude Russe condemn the daintiness and niceness of our captains, who, living in a soil and air much more temperate, yet commonly use furred boots and cloaks" (28). The Chancellor account reveals an undercurrent of anxiety about the power of the emperor and the resources at his command in contrast to the English Crown and its merchant adventurers.

The absolute power of the czar and the barbarity of his people became a constant refrain in English writing about Russia. Even the diplomatic Anthony Jenkinson, who visited Russia four times in the 1550s and 1560s on behalf of the Muscovy Company, notes in his first voyage of 1557 that

> This emperor is of great power, for he hath conquered much as well of the Livonians, Poles, Latvians, and Swedes, as also of the Tartars, and gentiles called Samoyeds, having thereby much enlarged his dominions. He keepeth his people in great subjection; all matters pass his judgment be they never so small.[15]

Jenkinson's juxtaposition of imperial expansion with domestic oppression was not accidental. The two are mutually dependent in the Elizabethan discourse of Russia. The great map of Russia and Tartary that Jenkinson produced in 1562, dedicated to Henry Sidney and included in Ortelius's atlas eight years later, similarly sets the commanding figure of the "Imperator" Ivan IV beneath his baldachin of state in the northwest corner against the exotic and legendary scenes that ring the eastern and southern borders

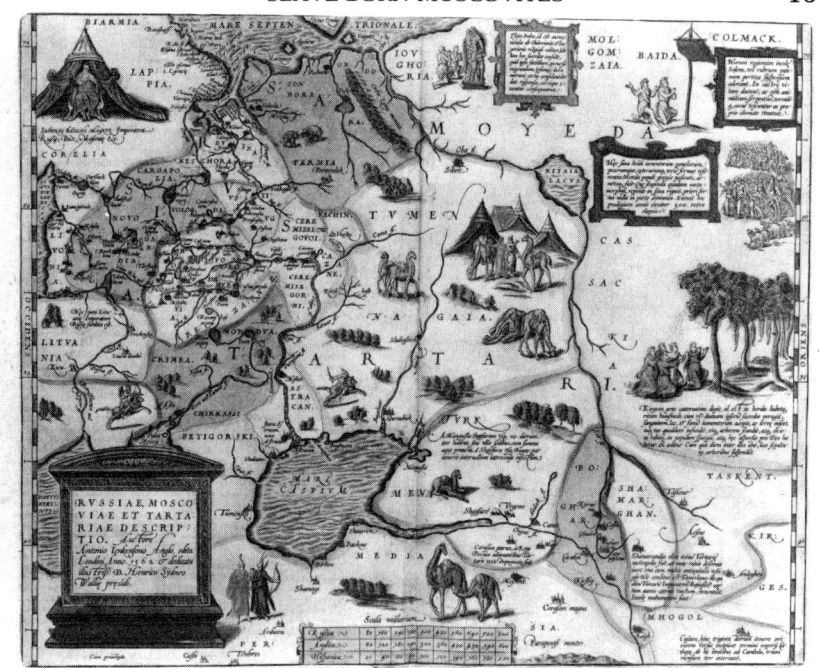

Jenkinson's map of Russia and Tartary (1562), from Abraham Ortelius's *Theatrum Orbis Terrarum* (1606). By permission of the Folger Shakespeare Library.

of his domains, a dense cluster of villages and place-names in the midst.[16]

We will return to Jenkinson's adventures below. The least diplomatic report of Russian barbarity is to be found in three poems by George Turberville, verse letters in poulter's measure evidently written while their author accompanied Thomas Randolph on his difficult embassy to Russia in 1568. Randolph himself patiently recounted in bland prose the strict treatment and months-long delays his party had been subjected to by the emperor's servants.[17] In the epistle "To Dancie" his secretary Turberville was less circumspect in commenting on their hosts, "A people passing rude, to vices vile inclin'd, / Folk fit to be of Bacchus' train so quaffing is their kind."[18] He goes on to specify the vices of the Russian peasant:

> Perhaps the muzhik hath a gay and gallant wife
> To serve his beastly lust, yet he will lead a bugger's life.
> The monster more desires a boy within his bed
> Than any wench, such filthy sin ensues a drunken head.

> No wonder though they use such vile and beastly trade,
> Sith with the hatchet and the hand their chiefest gods be made.
>
> (76)

The charge of sodomy places Russia outside Christendom and civilization but not without implicating the wandering Englishman who observes all this as well.[19] Turberville's letter "To Spencer" concludes by invoking the informal censorship that his economic mission with Randolph entails:

> Who so shall read this verse, conjecture of the rest,
> And think by reason of our trade that I do think the best.
> But if no traffic were, then could I boldly pen
> The hardness of the soil and eke the manners of the men.
>
> (80)

The "vile and beastly trade" of the Russians is partly cloaked here by "our trade" with Russia itself. Expansion and commerce bring risks to identities as well as investments. Travel casts the sturdy domestic bond among men conventionally invoked at the beginning of each verse letter in an unfamiliar light. Turberville greets his "Dancie dear" and professes his love to Spencer; he describes his sleeping arrangements with Stafford, "that was my mate in bed," while decrying the muzhik's desire to share his bed with a boy (75, 77, 80). It is clear that Turberville can recognize absolutely no similarity between himself and the monstrous people among whom he is forced to dwell. In the very process of casting the Russians as totally other to himself, however, the English observer betrays the danger that travel and trade will bring out the other within the self as well.[20]

The danger of sexual transgression extends to women—the peasant's spurned wife seeks other men, resorting to cosmetics, "Wherewith she decks herself and dyes her tawny skin. / She pranks and paints her smoky face, both brow, lip, cheek, and chin" (77). Here we find another explanation for the dark skin associated with the Russians, "brown by reason of the stove and closeness of the air" (81). Complaints about makeup are common in the Juvenalian mode of satire that Turberville adopts, but the excessive use of cosmetics by Russian women is also found in other travel accounts.[21] Painting and sodomy both represent the lawless excess that Turberville and his fellow travelers paradoxically discover beneath the surface of the emperor's absolute control. The final epistle, "To Parker," dwells on the combination of disorder and power that its author found:

> In such a savage soil where laws do bear no sway,
> And all is at the king his will to save or else to slay.
> . . . .
> Conceive the rest yourself, and deem what lives they lead
> Where lust is law, and subjects live continually in dread.
> (83)

The emperor's lust ultimately absorbs the petty transgressions of his subjects. As an incarnation of the traditional tyrant, he embodies an abusive power that has taken the place of law, natural, human, and divine: "So Tarquin ruled Rome" (83).

Giles Fletcher dwells on the excessive power of the emperor and the contradictions it conceals in *Of the Russe Commonwealth*. Dispatched by Queen Elizabeth as ambassador to the czar in 1588, he stayed for barely a year, arguing the Muscovy Company's case against competition by Dutch and rival English traders and forestalling a Russian alliance with the Hapsburgs. Fletcher provided the most comprehensive account of Russia during the period despite his short visit, supplementing his observations with reading in history and antiquities. Despite the relative success of his mission, the Muscovy Company petitioned against the publication of his book in 1591 and succeeded in having it withdrawn. The Company, fearing harm to their agents and property in Russia from an angry Kremlin, listed Fletcher's unflattering references to the emperor's power and person in their complaint to Lord Burghley, ironically confirming the book's picture of an oppressive kingdom. Turberville's earlier apprehension about censorship for the sake of trade was born out.[22]

Of the Russe Commonwealth begins with the antiquity of its subject, originally called Sarmatia. Fletcher discounts Strabo's derivation of Russia from the nation of the Roxellani. The country was renamed because

> it was parted into diuerse small, and yet absolute gouernments, not depending, nor being subiect the one to the other. For *Russe* in that tongue doth signifie as much as to parte, or diuide. (1 recto)

Four brothers in the north and four others in the south divided the kingdom among themselves in the ninth century. The lack of fit between "diverse small" and "absolute" goes unremarked, but it sets the tone for rest of the treatise, in which absolute power is subtended by division, weakness, and even the lawlessness that Turberville likewise glimpsed.[23]

Fletcher denies that Sarmatia came from Asarmathes, the nephew of Heber, cutting Russia off from the lineage of Shem (2 recto). Later, however, he conjectures that Moscow, the "Metropolite citie," was named after another, quasi-biblical figure. Citing an influential fifteenth-century forgery of a supposedly ancient historical source, he writes:

> *Berosus* the *Chaldean* in his 5. book telleth that *Nimrod* (whom other profane stories cal *Saturn*) sent *Assyrius, Medus, Moscus,* & *Magog* into *Asia* to plant Colonies there, and that *Moscus* planted both in *Asia* and *Europe*. Which may make some probability, that the city, or rather the river whereon it is built, tooke the denomination from this *Moscus:* the rather because of the climate or situation, which is in the very farthest part and list of *Europe*, bordering vpon *Asia*. (12 recto-verso).

Russia is both European and Asian at once, its metropolis virtually defining the border between the continents. Fletcher traces Moscow, and Muscovy, back to a primal scene of global colonization, evoking absolute power and its inevitable division once again.

With the evocation of antiquity comes the evidence of degeneration and decline. Moscow, roughly the size of London, was sacked by the Tartars in 1571 and now lies partly in waste (13 recto). "The other townes," Fletcher informs us, "haue nothing that is greatly memorable, saue many ruines within their walles. Which sheweth the decrease of the *Russe* people, vnder this gouernment" (14 recto). Fletcher pities "the poore people that are now oppressed with intollerable servitude" (17 recto). The rule of the emperor is responsible for his kingdom's decay. "The State and forme of their gouernment," he asserts, "is plaine tyrannicall, as applying all to the behoofe of the Prince, and that after a most open and barbarous manner" (20 recto). It is hard to say which is greater, the cruelty of the inhabitants or the "intemperancie" they practice, "so foule and not to bee named." Sodomy is almost certainly meant here; the whole country overflows with it, "And no marueile, as hauing no lawe to restraine whoredomes, adulteries, and like vncleannesse of life" (116 verso) As in Turberville, the seeming contradiction between lawlessness and imperial rule is allowed to stand. Not only the common people, but burghers and even nobles are accounted "as seruants or bond slaues that are to obey, not to make lawes" (22 verso, 46 recto). Fletcher is particularly distressed by the lack of social mobility in Russia: "This order that bindest euery man to keepe his rancke, and seuerall degree, wherein his forefathers liued before him, is more meet to keep the subiects in a seruile subiection and so apt for this and like Common-wealths, then to aduance any vertue" (49 recto). In this, he may well have reflected the secret misgivings of the very English merchants who protested his book most loudly.

For English commerce was in some sense at odds with the sovereign power under which it sheltered, at home as well as in Russia. Fletcher nervously describes the imperial expansion of the czar's absolutism in his chapter "Of their Colonies, and mainteyning of their conquests, or purchases by force" (61 verso), noting the rapid beginnings of what Fernand Braudel has called "the invention of Siberia." Russia's need for an apparently boundless tract of exploitable territory paralleled Europe's incorporation of the Americas in its world economy.[24] His obsession with Russian absolutism leaves Fletcher less impressed with the imperial army than Chancellor. The Russian soldier "is farre meaner of courage and execution in any warlike seruice" than the English, he claims, "Which commeth partly of his seruile condition, that will not suffer any great courage or valure to growe in him" (59 recto-verso). More clearly than Chancellor and the other English authors I have treated, Fletcher expresses an anxiety about the relationship between metropolitan oppression and imperial expansion in Russia that is related to England's own expansive enterprise in a complex way. It is the sheer size of Russia and its empire that has made the thorough despotism that Fletcher describes necessary:

> This manner of gouernment of their Prouinces and townes . . . might seeme in that kinde to bee no bad nor vnpollitique way, for the conteyning of so large a Commonwealth, of that breadth and length as is the kindgome of *Russia*. But the oppression and slauerie is so open and so great, that a man would maruell how the Nobilitie and people shoulde suffer themselues to bee brought vnder it. (33 recto-verso)

What if the English sovereign were to attain a territorial empire or even an economic sphere of influence as large as Russia's domain? What would the consequences be for the merchants who supported it and the commoners and aristocrats at home?

Space itself, the sudden possibility of covering such vast distances inland as well as across the oceans, offered a dizzying prospect to English observers at the end of the sixteenth century. Such worries seem laughably premature, but they would be less so a century, or even a few decades, later. *Of the Russe Commonwealth* was republished in 1643 and again in 1657, when it was read as an indictment of monarchy in the eras of civil war, interregnum, and the consolidation of the American colonies.

Fletcher's dedicatory letter to Elizabeth, omitted from the seventeenth-century editions, insists on the graciousness and dignity that supposedly characterizes her reign in England. In his work, the Queen may see "A true and strange face of a *Tyrannical state,* (most vnlike to your own) without true knowledge of GOD, without written Lawe, without common iustice." Elizabeth's people may well be thankful that "you are a Prince of subiectes, not of slaues, that are kept within dutie by loue, not by feare" (A3 verso, A4 recto). Despite Fletcher's parenthetical assurance, the book is a mirror for magistrates, Elizabeth in particular. The subsequent censorship of his volume was a reminder that the English Crown itself could exercise oppression on behalf of expansionism. *Of the Russe Commonwealth*, of course, is very far from a tract against monarchy, despite its later appeal to Parliament-men. It does, however, uncover a latent unease about the subject's status within a suddenly expanding world that might require extreme methods of control and domination.[25]

Russia came to stand for this unease in Elizabeth's England. Her subjects regarded all Russians as virtual bondslaves in a far-flung, if somewhat vulnerable, empire. Philip Sidney's poet-lover in *Astrophil and Stella* 2 at first submitted reluctantly to love's decrees, but now

> even that footstep of lost liberty
> Is gone, and now like slave-born Muscovite
> I call it praise to suffer tyranny.[26]

The words *slave* and *slav* are in fact etymologically linked through the medieval Latin word *sclavus*.[27] Fletcher offers a slightly different explanation:

For the people called *Sclaui*, are knowen to haue had their beginning out of *Sarmatia*, and to haue termed themselues of their conquest *sclauos*, (that is) famous or glorious, of the word *Sclaua*, which in the *Russe* & *Slavonian* tongue, signifieth as much as *Glory*, or *Fame*. Though afterwards being subdued and trod vpon by diuers nations, the *Italians* their neighbors haue turned the worde to a contrary signification, and terme euery seruant or peasant by the name *sclaue*, as did the *Romanes* by the *Getes* & *Syrians*, for the same reason. (48 verso-49 recto)

The word *slave*, then, supposedly contains within itself the kind of reversal of fortune the Elizabethans perversely delighted in. Astrophil, suffering "full conquest" by love, calls it praise to suffer tyranny, just as the Slavs name themselves glorious conquerors with a word that other peoples have long since made a term of abuse.

In a confusion typical of sixteenth-century western Europe, Sidney blends the subject's servitude to the czar, chattel slavery of Russians by other Russians, and the enslavement of Russians within the Ottoman empire in his sonnet sequence's complex geographical allusions. In *Astrophil and Stella* 30, busy wits press the reluctant poet-lover for geopolitical intelligence:

> Whether the Turkish new moon minded be
>   To fill his horns this year on Christian coast;
>   How Pole's right king means, without leave of host,
> To warm with ill-made fire cold Muscovy.
>
> (lines 1–4)

Poland was at war with Russia from 1580 to 1581. The poet's father, Henry Sidney, whose Deputy Governorship of Ireland is mentioned in line 9, had been connected with Russian travel as well. An early member of the Muscovy Company, he patronized Chancellor and his name is prominently displayed on Jenkinson's map. Philip is subtly invoking his family's long-standing involvement in administration and foreign policy in this sonnet, in eastern and northern matters as well as Irish affairs. The lines on Turkey are usually taken as a reference to an impending attack on Spain, but Turks, with the help of the Tartars, had traditionally enslaved Russians and others from eastern Europe captured in battle. The possibility that the juxtaposition of Turkey and beleaguered Muscovy may refer indirectly to the "Russian slavery" complex is strengthened by the concluding lines of the previous sonnet with its stress on coasts and military conquest: "And I, but for because my prospect lies / Upon that coast, am giv'n up for a slave"—a slave to Stella's love, of course, but on the Muscovite model once more (29.13–14). Fellow Europeans were fully complicit in the trade in slaves during the middle ages, employing slaves from all regions. According to Immanuel

Wallerstein, "Slavery followed the sugar" from the Mediterranean islands where sugar was first cultivated to America between the fifteenth and sixteenth centuries, and "As it moved, the ethnic composition of the slave class was transformed."[28] As late as Jenkinson's time in the late 1550s, Russian slaves were still being traded in the market at Bukhara. He matter-of-factly notes that the Persians trade cloth and silk there for "redde hides with other *Russe* wares, and slaues which are of diuers Countries."[29]

Jenkinson also records his return across the Caspian Sea toward Russia "with 25. Russes, which had been slaues a long time in *Tartaria,* nor euer had before my comming, libertie, or meanes to gette home, and these slaues serued to rowe when neede was." The Hakluyt Society editors proclaim this "the first successful attempt on record of the rescue of Russian slaves in Central Asia."[30] It might give us pause to note the necessary use to which the "rescued" slaves were put on the voyage home. Given the constant criticism of the Russians for their servile attitude in the travel writings, it comes as a surprise to learn (one of those unsurprising surprises) that the English themselves employed slaves in the cloth factories of the Muscovy Company. A letter from the Muscovy Company in London, dated 18 April 1567 (old style), instructs the factors in Russia: "We wold vnderstand how many slaues be sett to that worke, whether they be apt to that arte; if nead be we will sende more men from hence, but if slaues there be docible it weare better to traine them vp (for diuars considerations) then haue many of our nation from hence except it be master of the work."[31] Management comes from the home office, while labor is kept as inexpensive as possible, a pattern repeated on a world scale in today's international division of labor.

Astrophil and Stella can further help us to understand the connections among Russia, blackness, and servitude in *Love's Labor's Lost.*[32] The ill-made fire that may warm cold Muscovy in sonnet 30, though Polish in origin, is tied to other metaphors of burning and branding in the sequence. In sonnet 47, the poet cries:

> What, have I thus betrayed my liberty?
>   Can those black beams such burning marks engrave
>   In my free side? or am I born a slave,
> Whose neck becomes such yoke of tyranny?
>
> (lines 1–4)

Again, love–service—here submission to Stella's dark eyes—has absorbed and troped the violence of slavery. If slavery is associated with blackness in *Astrophil and Stella*, it is principally the blackness of the brand burned onto the flesh and not the color of the flesh itself. Slavery is an artificial condition, it seems, enforced by a mark that signifies conquest in battle and the loss of honor, the "liberty" of the aristocratic warrior. This is an old, in some sense "pre-racial" notion of slavery. The example of the "slave-born" Muscovite, however, suggests that one can also be born a slave whose neck "becomes" the yoke of tyranny as well as suits it. *Astrophil and Stella* marks a transitional phase in the English conception of slavery, a gradual process of racialization in which branding is turned into a different, putatively essential kind of blackness. The Muscovite embodies this transition. A member of a nation that unsteadily straddles the boundary between Europe and Asia, the Muscovite is also assimilated to the racial typology of color increasingly associated with the massive system of African slavery in the Americas. The triangular trade, after all, was one of those methods of extreme domination that the new world of the sixteenth and seventeenth centuries ostensibly required, one practiced by, rather than upon, European subjects.[33] Conflated with the Tartars and Turks on their borders who participated with Europeans in the earlier slave system, Russians are "othered" as subservient and "black" in a number of sixteenth-century English texts. The Muscovite, nevertheless, continues to represent the possibility of "white" slavery that comes to haunt the anxious proprietors of the new geography, a possibility they must exclude from its operations.

It is strange that the process of exclusion should be played out through aristocratic love discourse in texts like *Astrophil and Stella* and *Love's Labor's Lost*. I will suggest one set of reasons for this connection in turning at this point to Shakespeare's play. The most striking thing about erotic relations between men and women at the court of Navarre is how they are rendered in spatial, almost in cartographic, terms, long before the fanciful Muscovites appear in Act V. The King decrees "that no woman shall come within a mile of my court" (1.1.119–20). Don Armado accordingly informs on Costard, having witnessed him dallying with Jaquenetta: "But to the place Where? It standeth north-north-east and by east from the west corner of thy curious-knotted garden" (1.1.244–46). The comic superimposition of large-scale cartographic space on the tiny locale of the court intensifies with the arrival of the Princess of France and her ladies. She is an ambassador from her father, sent to reclaim part of Aquitane from Navarre. That this situation may refer to a 1579 mission by the historical Marguerite de Valois to her husband Henri of Navarre over a dowry that included Aquitane only confirms the link between territory and courtship that the play's fictional action fulfills.[34] No map appears in the stage directions to his negotiation with the Princess in Act I, but the episode, nevertheless, looks forward to the more sober map scenes in *King Lear* and *1 Henry IV*.[35] The King says he would prefer a sum of money to Aquitane, "so gelded as it is" (2.1.148); *geld* is a technical term signifying the reduction in value of land, but it clearly implies a sort of castration as well. Gelded Aquitane serves as an obstacle between the King and the Princess; a more pressing obstacle is the King's own decree against admitting women to his little academy, which in its turn is rendered spatially when the ladies are forced to encamp outside the court.

The microcartography of the court is cumbrously overlaid with the macrocartography of international politics. Diplomacy, as the travel writings consistently demonstrate, provided the framework for the English conception of Russia. The Kremlin's painstaking ceremonies oddly compliment the awkward barbarism attributed to the czar's people. Russian missions to England confirmed the impressions of English travelers. Ivan IV's ambassador came to England to woo Lady Mary Hastings, Elizabeth's cousin, on behalf of his alliance-seeking master in 1582. According to the contemporary manuscript account of Jerome Horsey, who served some eighteen years in Russia himself, the emissary's unsuccessful proposal was comically abject.[36] It has long been thought that this episode lies behind the elaborate courtship of the French noblewomen by Navarre and his "Muscovites" in *Love's Labor's Lost*. The play's Russian masquerade might well have been intended to overcome the self-distancing of dynastic courtship by symbolically, and parodically, negotiating and diminishing its difficult terrain by contrast. The space between the Princess's camp and the King's court, or even between France and Navarre, is seemingly eclipsed by the difference between Europe and barbarous, servile Muscovy.

Given the contemporary association between Russia and male-male sodomy, however, Muscovite disguise may not have been the best choice for a group of courtiers determined to escape a self-imposed vow to avoid women's company.[37] The ladies take the stratagem as "mockery merriment," and determine to answer it "mock for mock" by masking themselves and jumbling their identities (5.2.139–44). The scene is marked by a quibbling failure in communication:

> King. Say to her we have measur'd many miles,
> To tread a measure with her on this grass.
> . . . .
> Ros. It is not so. Ask them how many inches
> Is in one mile: if they have measured many,
> The measure then of one is eas'ly told.
> (5.2.184–85, 188–90)

Courtly dancing measures are confused with measurement itself as the women refuse to play along. There is something maplike in the pedantic concern with units of measurement. In Anthony Jenkinson's map of Russia, for instance, a chart converting Russian versts into English miles and Spanish leagues occupies the bottom center of the layout. The narrative of Jenkinson's first trip to Russia displays a matching scrupulosity where distances are concerned: "the way to Moscow is as followeth: from Vologda to Commelski, twenty-seven versts; so to Olmor, twenty-five versts, so to Teloytske, twenty versts," and so on (52). Jenkinson's precision looks back to the itinerary format of medieval travelers, but it became associated with the charting of a vast territory that was almost totally new to the English. The conceit of Russia in *Love's Labor's Lost* fails to overcome the apprehension about limitless space and lawless excess, and may actually have aggravated it.

The language of economic calculation runs throughout the Muscovite scene. Like scales of measurement, the cash nexus almost counteracts the anxiety about limitlessness by offering a means of parceling out space and managing it. As Henri LeFebvre argues, however, the early modern sense of space canonized in Descartes's notion of "extension" is perfectly compatible with commodification and the money-form, since each system reduces reality to a homogenous code or measure.[38]

Terms of praise become conditions by which people are made equivalent to property. Acting as herald, Moth hails the Princess and her company as "the richest beauties on the earth," and "A holy parcel of the fairest dames"; Boyet remarks that they are no "richer" than the taffeta they wear (5.2.158–60). The Russians ask them to "Price you yourselves: what buys your company?", but the women will not be bought (5.2.224–26). It is the Russians who eventually offer their "service" to each lady (5.2.276, 284).

The Elizabethan association of Russia with commercial ventures and an ambiguous relation to servitude also lies behind these exchanges.

It is here that the presence of the blackmoors on stage becomes important as well. Berowne asks the ladies: "Vouchsafe to show the sunshine of your face, / That we (like savages) may worship it" (5.2.201–2). These lines, like the reference to "sun-beamed eyes" at line 169, recall the burning marks of *Astrophil and Stella*. They also look back to an earlier passage, tying the Russian scene to a larger complex of racial difference in the play. "Who sees the heavenly Rosaline," Berowne asks,

> That (like a rude and savage man of Inde),
> At the first op'ning of the gorgeous east,
> Bows not his vassal head, and strooken blind,
> Kisses the base ground with obedient breast?
> (4.3.217–21)

The figure of the savage or "Indian" worshipping the sun and perhaps being darkened by it assimilates love-service to an emerging scene of racial difference. It is connected to the discourse of Russia through the idea of servility and the "gorgeous east." Berowne's praise of Rosaline in these terms is complicated by her own appearance, which is in some way "dark" as Katherine's badinage early in act 5 attests (5.2.20–42). "By heaven, thy love is black as ebony," the King states in act 4, to which Berowne replies by praising the exotic wood, a valuable commodity (4.3.244–45).

His defense of Rosaline's black beauty is offset by the King's well-known words on black as the badge of hell, the school of night, and, significantly, the hue of dungeons, linked through conquest and captivity with slavery (4.3.250–51). Dumaine's earlier praise of Katherine as so white she would make Jove swear Juno was an "Ethiop" confirms the King's opinion (4.3.115–16).

Berowne, however, declares that his companions' mistresses use cosmetics. Women should paint themselves black like Rosaline if they want to imitate her natural beauty—"Your mistresses dare never come in rain, / For fear their colors should be wash'd away" (4.3.259–61, 266–67). A glancing reminiscence of the Russian women in the travel accounts, perhaps, in a play that also stages the popular view of Muscovite men.

Chimney sweepers, colliers, and Ethiops boast a similar complexion to Rosaline, Berowne's friends retort (4.3.262–63). *Love's*

Labor's Lost initially suggests a southern Europe where people are darker in complexion than the English audience (as in "tawny Spain," 1.1.173). The historical Navarre, a border area like Russia, was situated amid France, Spain, and the Mediterranean world, and Moriscos were still to be found in its vicinity during the later sixteenth century.[39] Perhaps we are to conceive of the blackmoor musicians as undisguised natives of Navarre, despite their pairing with the mock Russians.

Ultimately, however, the play subjects this hybrid world to the metaphorical difference of white and black. Even Berowne, despite his suggestive name and rhetorical efforts on behalf of black beauty, imagines Rosaline's hand as "white" (5.2.230, 411). The relation of blackness to beauty remains unstable in the play, but in general it consolidates the ideal of whiteness by offering a contrast to it.[40] The blackmoor musicians almost serve the same purpose in the Russian scene, but the ladies reject their Muscovite suitors, who remain bound up with the blackness and crudity associated with Russia in the travel material. It is left to the pedants and the clowns, with their pageant of the Nine Worthies (another geohistorical farrago), to offer the contrasting image that brings aristocratic men and women together, until dynastic politics intervenes once more with the French King's death ("'tis some policy," as Berowne remarks, "To have one show worse than the King's and his company": 5.2.512–13).

The consolidation of "white" aristocrats, including Berowne and Rosaline, is made possible by class and economic difference, as well as a developing sense of racial difference. The constant association of all Russians, including aristocrats, with bond-slaves in the travel material assimilates "race" to class; in fact, this may be the distinguishing feature of Russia in early modern European discourse, a feature that made the figure of the Muscovite an engaging one for upwardly—and downwardly—mobile subjects in a widening world. Economic movements, then, may provide a provisional explanation for why the process of othering is figured through sexuality and gender as well, as in the love discourse of Sidney and Shakespeare. Berowne's Rosaline is not so much black as a mixture of shades:

> Of all complexions the cull'd sovereignty
> Do meet as at a fair in her fair cheek.
>
> (4.3.230–31)

The pun is daring—Rosaline, like world commerce, is "fair" in that like a fair she unites contrasting principles for common profit. The slave market of Bukhara also comes to mind, but chattel slavery is subsumed in the language of courtship, in the desire to possess women on the one hand and the offer to serve them on the other. To some extent, love is one of several types of elite discourse behind which the shift in global labor and its racial character can be worked out. It is, however, more than an ideological screen. Women, aristocratic and bourgeois alike, were assigned the role of consumer in the expanding commercial consciousness of Europe, both glorified and scapegoated as the source of the demand for luxury goods that drove an expanding world system.[41] Love discourse, with its preexisting ambivalence toward the exalted but capricious lady, dictated that elite men serve their women, providing them with exotica, including, as in *Love's Labor's Lost*, outlandish knowledges and images as well as commodities. Of course, Shakespeare's play parodies the failure of the exotic. As Berowne vows to Rosaline:

> And I will wish thee never more to dance,
> Nor never more in Russian habit wait.
> . . . .
> Henceforth my wooing mind shall be express'd
> In russet yeas and honest kersey noes.
>
> (5.2.400–1, 412–13)

Both kersey cloth, largely associated with the Russia trade, and the commodities of the gorgeous East were produced within a developing system of global labor and exchange that made the desires of European women its pretext. The terms of heterosexual courtship became intimately bound to the lost labors of slavery and other forms of economic servitude.

Notes

1. William Shakespeare, *Love's Labor's Lost*, 5.2.157 SD, in *The Riverside Shakespeare*, eds. G. Blakemore Evans et al. (Boston: Houghton Mifflin, 1974). Further references to the play are from this edition and will be cited in the text.

2. *Gesta Grayorum, 1688*, ed. W. W. Greg (Oxford: Malone Society, 1914), 44–46. The Prince of Purpoole went on a trip to Russia himself, returning later in the Revels ill from his fictional journey at sea and so unable to greet Queen Elizabeth (54–55)—this is often compared with Rosaline's comment that the undisguised Berowne is "sea-sick, I think, coming from Muscovy" (5.2.393). Earlier in the week, a performance of a "Comedy of Errors," probably Shakespeare's, was mounted after a chaotic embassy from the Temple to Gray's Inn (22). For a summary of past scholarship linking *Love's Labor's Lost* to Gray's

Inn, see the introduction to the Arden edition of the play, ed. Richard David (London: Methuen, 1956), xxx–xxxi.

3. *Gesta Grayorum*, 43–44.

4. "The voyage of M. Anthony Ienkinson . . . in the yere 1558," in E. Delmar Morgan and C. H. Coote, eds., *Early Voyages and Travels in Russia and Persia* (London: Hakluyt Society, 1886), 51–52, 89.

5. Raphael Holinshed, *Chronicles of England, Scotland, and Ireland* (London, 1587), 3. 805; Fred Sorensen, "The Masque of the Muscovites in *Love's Labor's Lost*," *Modern Language Notes* 50 (1935): 499–501.

6. Eden, in *The First Three English Books on America*, ed. Edward Arber (Edinburgh: Turnbull & Spears, 1885), 323. The source is Sigismund von Herberstein, *Rerum Moscoviticarum Commentarii* (1549). English translation: *Notes upon Russia*, 2 vols., trans. R. H. Major (London: Hakluyt Society, 1851–52), 2: 40.

7. Fletcher, *Of the Russe Common Wealth. Or Maner [sic] of Gouernement by the Russe Emperour, (commonly called the Emperour of Moskouia) with the manners, and fashions of the people of that Countrey* (London: T. D. for Thomas Charde, 1591), 2 verso. Subsequent citations will be included in the text.

8. Larry Wolff has recently noted the link between Russians and Africans in the developing racial typology of eighteenth century Europe. See *Inventing Eastern Europe: The Map of Civilization on the Mind of the Enlightenment* (Stanford: Stanford University Press, 1994), 46, 105, 345–46.

9. Richard Hellie, *Slavery in Russia, 1450–1725* (Chicago: University of Chicago Press, 1982), 15–16, 30–33; 46–47, 716.

10. Hellie, *Slavery in Russia*, 23.

11. Ortelius, *The Theatre of the Whole World* (London: John Norton, 1606; reprint, Amsterdam: Theatrum Orbis Terrarum Ltd., 1968), 104 recto. I quote from the English version of 1606; the Latin original appeared in 1570.

12. Morgan and Coote, *Early Voyages*, 259. The trade in kerseys was thought to be particularly important (see lxiv, 221, and passim), although it may not have been as vital as contemporaries often claimed (Willan, *Early History of Muscovy Company*, 186).

13. The standard work for the sixteenth century is T. S. Willan, *The Early History of the Muscovy Company, 1553–1603* (Manchester: Manchester University Press, 1956). See also Robert Brenner, *Merchants and Revolution: Commercial change, Political Conflict, and London's Overseas Traders, 1550–1653* (Princeton: Princeton University Press, 1993), 13, 20–21. For a recent discussion of the Muscovy Company and Marlowe's *Tamburlaine* plays, see Richard Wilson, "Visible Bullets: Tamburlaine the Great and Ivan the Terrible," *ELH* 62 (1995): 47–68.

14. Chancellor, "The First Voyage to Russia," in *Rude and Barbarous Kingdom: Russia in the Accounts of Sixteenth-Century English Voyagers*, eds. Lloyd E. Berry and Robert O. Crummey (Madison: University of Wisconsin Press, 1968), 13, 18, 38. Further references in parentheses.

15. Jenkinson, "A Voyage to Russia in 1557," in Berry and Crummey, *Rude and Barbarous Kingdom*, 56. Further references to the first voyage are from this edition.

16. Ortelius, *Theatre of the Whole World*, between 104 and 105.

17. Randolph's account is included in Berry and Crummey, *Rude and Barba-*

rous Kingdom, 65–70. On the circumstances of his ultimately successful embassy, see Willan, Early History of Muscovy Company, 94–111.

18. Turberville, "Verse Letters from Russia," in Berry and Crummey, Rude and Barbarous Kingdom, 75. The poems were published in Tragicall Tales (1587), and again in Hakluyt's Principall Navigations (1589). Further references in the text.

19. On "sodomy" as the demonic opposite of Christianity see Alan Bray, Homosexuality in Renaissance England (London: Gay Men's Press, 1982), 19–31. He discusses Turberville's depiction of the Russians on pages 25 and 75.

20. For different examples of "enjoyment of the other" and its scapegoating between "West" and "East," and within the "East," in the current east European context, see Slavoj Žižek, "Eastern Europe's Republics of Gilead," in Dimensions of Radical Democracy: Pluralism, Citizenship, Community, ed. Chantal Mouffe (London: Verso, 1992).

21. See, for instance, Fletcher, Russe Common Wealth, 113 recto-verso.

22. For the petition and its result, see Lloyd E. Berry, The English Works of Giles Fletcher, the Elder (Madison: University of Wisconsin Press, 1964), 150–53. Berry describes Fletcher's embassy (367–75) and the composition of his book (135–44).

23. For a related explanation of the name Russia, see Herberstein, 1: 3.

24. See Braudel, Civilization and Capitalism, 15th–18th Century, vol. 2: The Perspective of the World, trans. Siân Reynolds (New York: Harper & Row, 1984), 455.

25. On the "new geography" in early modern Europe and the sense of instability it brought with it, see José Rabasa, Inventing America: Spanish Historiography and the Formation of Eurocentrism (Norman: University of Oklahoma Press, 1993), 180–209, and John Gillies, Shakespeare and the Geography of Difference (Cambridge: Cambridge University Press, 1994).

26. Astrophil and Stella 2, lines 9–11, in Katherine Duncan-Jones, ed., Sir Philip Sidney: Selected Poems (Oxford: Clarendon, 1973). Further references in the text.

27. Charles Verlinden, "Encore sur les origines de sclavus = esclave," in Verlinden, L'esclavage dans l'Europe médiévale (Gent: Rijksuniversiteit te Gent, 1977), 2: 999–1010.

28. Wallerstein, The Modern World-System, vol. I (New York: Academic Press—Harcourt Brace Jovanovich, 1974), 88–89.

29. Morgan and Coote, Early Voyages, 89.

30. Ibid., 95 and note.

31. Ibid., 211. Until 1627/28, foreigners were in effect permitted to own Russian slaves in Russia. Even after this date, the exclusion was based not on nationality but religion, since only Orthodox masters henceforth were allowed to hold Orthodox slaves. The change in the law was specifically intended to limit Westerners in Russia, however (Hellie, Slavery in Russia, 73–74).

32. The connection between slavery and love servitude in the play and Astrophil and Stella has been noticed by R. S. White, without reference to blackness: "Muscovites in Love's Labour's Lost," Notes and Queries 33 (1986): 350.

33. Following C. L. R. James and Toni Morrison, Paul Gilroy has suggested that the African slave system was one of the first institutions of modernity. See The Black Atlantic: Modernity and Double Consciousness (London: Verso, 1993), 221.

34. See Shakespeare, *Love's Labor's Lost*, Arden ed., xxxiii.

35. Gillies, *Geography of Difference*, 45.

36. Horsey, "Travels," in Berry and Crummey, *Rude and Barbarous Kingdom*, 301. Ivan's insistence on Mary Hastings or some other English bride was cut off by his death in 1584 during the embassy of Jerome Bowes. The marriage business may have added to uneasiness about a commercially expansive England's potential similarity to imperial Russia. Ivan, like Elizabeth's father Henry VIII, had already been married seven times during this quest for an eighth wife; his seventh was still living. His death was announced to Elizabeth's ambassador with the curious phrase "the English Emperor was dead," meaning it would seem the emperor who had favored England. For the negotiations, see Willan, *Early History of Muscovy Company*, 161–66.

37. On sodomy and other forms of the "preposterous" throughout the play, see Patricia Parker, "Preposterous Reversals: *Love's Labor's Lost*," *Modern Language Quarterly* 54 (1993), 435–82. Parker discusses the implied reversals of 5.2 without relating the "Muscovites" to sodomy, although the travel material supports her reading of the text here (466–67).

38. LeFebvre, *The Production of Space*, trans. Donald Nicholson-Smith (Oxford: Blackwell, 1991), 71–79. John Gillies brought this passage to my attention.

39. Fernand Braudel, *The Mediterranean and the Mediterranean World in the Age of Philip II*, trans. Siân Reynolds (New York: Harper & Row, 1973), 785.

40. My ideas on this point, and on racial difference throughout this paper, are deeply indebted to the work of Kim F. Hall. See "Sexual Politics and Cultural Identity in *The Masque of Blackness*," in *The Performance of Power: Theatrical Discourse and Politics*, ed. Sue-Ellen Case and Jenelle Reinelt (Iowa City, Iowa: University of Iowa Press, 1991), 3–18. See also Hall, *Things of Darkness: Economies of Race and Gender in Early Modern England* (Ithaca, N.Y.: Cornell University Press, 1995).

41. See Maria Mies, *Patriarchy and Accumulation on a World Scale: Women in the International Division of Labour* (London: Zed Books, 1986), 100–3, and Laura Brown, *Ends of Empire: Women and Ideology in Early Eighteenth-Century English Literature* (Ithaca, N.Y.: Cornell University Press, 1993), 44–45.

"Strange Outlandish Wealth": Transglobal Commerce in *The Merchant's Mappe of Commerce* and *The Fair Maid of the West, Parts I and II*

BARBARA SEBEK

SIXTEENTH-CENTURY England witnessed the emergence of commodity exchange on an increasingly larger scale, a form of exchange that was seen to disrupt the grounds on which traditional social relationships were established and maintained. Throughout the period, a national economy gradually solidified, and it came to depend on market forces that operated beyond the local or even the national level. Given the expanding scope of international trade as the seventeenth century progressed, commerce—broadly conceived—became a prominent constitutive category in the early modern geographical imagination. I want to begin laying out this broad conception of commerce with a brief look at the tangled transactions in *The Comedy of Errors*.

Egeon, whose "factor" has died and forced him to tend to his own business at sea, opens the play at the mercy of a hostile foreign host's trade restrictions. He explains how his participation in maritime traffic initially precipitated his family's dispersal: "my factor's death / And the great care of goods at random left / Drew me from kind embracements of my spouse" (1.1.41–43).[1] Herself drawn over stormy seas by her husband's departure, Emilia's movement results in the displaced birth of the identical twins, their separation from each other, and the farce of mistaken identity and chaotic exchange played out in Ephesus. Overseas trade, in short, confounds identity, and that confusion takes the form of mistaken exchanges, as Antipholus of Syracuse remarks:

> There's not a man I meet but doth salute me
> As if I were their well-acquainted friend,
> And every one doth call me by my name.

> Some tender money to me; some invite me;
> Some other give me thanks for kindnesses;
> Some offer me commodities to buy.
> Even now a tailor call'd me in his shop
> And show'd me silks that he had bought for me
> And therewithal took measure of my body.
> Sure, these are but imaginary wiles
> And Lapland sorcerers inhabit here.
>
> (4.3.1–11)

The passage equates being acknowledged as oneself—being called by one's name, or hailed in a social gesture, the salute[2]—with participating in exchanges of various sorts: buying and selling, giving and receiving money, proffering and accepting invitations or expressions of gratitude for "kindnesses" previously rendered. Even the validation of physical existence—the "measure of my body"—is part of an ongoing transaction.[3] More intriguing, perhaps, is how Antipholus of Syracuse's discomfitted catalogue of baffling exchanges culminates by attributing his confusion to that which is geographically remote, unfamiliar, and exotic. Only sorcery intruding from the outer (or upper) reaches—well beyond even the dispersed world of Hellenized Greece, where the play is set—can account for the perplexing social exchanges our twin experiences. Antipholus of Syracuse and the dramatic structure of *The Comedy of Errors* demand that we understand commerce as a means of both constructing and expressing—enacting and symbolizing—identity. Understanding exchange in this way and considering the ever-widening geographical scope of trade in our period, we see why representing English ventures *beyond* the shores of "the maiden isle" becomes an especially weighted arena of cultural work.[4]

I will look at two texts that engage in this work—Lewis Roberts's commercial atlas, *The Merchant's Mappe of Commerce* (1638), and Thomas Heywood's two-play series, *The Fair Maid of the West, Part I* (c. 1597) and *Part II* (c. 1630). I will focus on the vision of commerce enacted in a particular locale, the region of northern Africa most commonly referred to as "Barbary" by contemporaries. The well-documented Elizabethan trade with Barbary in the second half of the sixteenth century has been called a "promiscuous, straggling, and dispersed trade."[5] This "promiscuity" and dispersal notwithstanding, Lewis Roberts admiringly characterizes the capital city's public marketplace as a strong-walled "court or exchange" that provided "security of goods and persons" for the "merchants of diverse nations" before the recent civil wars (sig. H2ᵛ). Despite his admiration for this circummured commercial space, Roberts's *Mappe* enacts a larger geographical vision in which all singularity collapses, raising the conceptual threat of the figurative promiscuity that accompanies the solvent power of the money form. The potential for literal sexual promiscuity comes to the fore in Heywood's plays, which figure Fez as a place of dangerous eroto-commercial, cross-cultural commerce. *The Fair Maid* embarks on the unevenly successful project of asserting cultural difference in exchange, demonizing cultural others who are positioned beyond the economic nation. By positing Moors as denigrated transactors, *The Fair Maid* attempts to purify English efforts to bring wealth home from the outlands. The drama reveals that women play a crucial role in this ideological enterprise.

* * *

Antipholus of Syracuse's sense of wonder at exchange in Ephesus is not absent from the commendatory poems that preface the *Merchant's Mappe*. Rather than the sorcery of Laplanders, however, it is the bewitching abilities of the merchant-voyager and his commercial instruments that dazzle Roberts's readers. Poem after poem revels in the commercial advantage that Roberts shares and in the mastery of vision that his book grants. According to J.H., the reader gains a panoramic and masterful view of the entire world and its commerce: "For here that Massy Ball and all its traffique / At once is seen, as through a perfect optique" (sig. A4ᵛ).[6]

If the text offers its readers a global vista, it also carries something back into the home country, doing so without travail or travel on the part of its consumers. In the verse of one Robert Roberts:

> I've perusd thy Booke, and there have seene
> A Worke of wonder; and though have not beene
> Farr from my Native home; yet now I find
> The Worlds worth closed within thy knowing Minde;
> See the Riches of each Countries soyle
> By this thy Art brought home, without our toyle.
> I find the Rarities of each Place and Towne
> Brought to our view with ease, and thou hast drawne
> All forreigne Coines to Ours, and ours to theirs;
> Their Weights and Measures too, to us appeares
> All but One thing; thy most industrious hand

> By this thy skill, ha's crowned thus this Land
> With strange Outlandish wealth ...
>
> (sig. A2)

This verse sets up a contrast between the geographically remote and the "native Home." The admiring poet marvels at the merchant's ability to procure "strange Outlandish wealth" while emphasizing how, in order to do so, the merchant-mapper uses his commercial instruments to convert all oddities and singularities to "one thing," to reduce difference to equivalence. We will have more to say later about the "one thing" into which Roberts converts the "Rarities of each Place and Towne." For now, I want to stress how this poem delights in the reader's "ease" as opposed to the merchant-mapper's industry. This delight approximates that of an apprentice cosmographer from the 1580s who gleefully makes his map "in a warm & pleasant house, without any perill of the raging Seas: danger of enemies: losse of time: spending of substance, weriness of body, or anguishe of minde" (quoted in Gilles 9). This "armchair Tamburlaine," as John Gillies calls him, offers a panegyric to the safety of the sedentary, a view that Thomas Heywood shares with his readers in the epistle to the printed version of *The Fair Maid of the West, Part II*. He says that his readers have

> heard the beginning of [the English heroes'] troubles, but are not yet come to the end of their travels, in which you may accompany them on land without the prejudice of deep ways or robbers, and by sea free from the danger of rocks or pirates, as neither using horse or ship more than this book in thine hand and thy chair in thy chamber. (95)

Perusing the play is like tracing a map, keeping the home fires burning all the while. Although they might at first seem like radically different cultural forms, then, both plays and commercial atlasses are seen to bring the world home to sedentary textual consumers. Both maps and plays engage their onlookers in literal transactions in the space of the theater or the printer's shop, while providing them with a spectrum of imaginative possibilities for envisioning themselves as social transactors.[7]

In *The Merchant's Mappe of Commerce*, Lewis Roberts offers a work of cartography, a commercial atlas, and a wide-ranging and systematic explication of "exchanges mysteries" (sig. a4^v).[8] In an Epistle to English Merchants and general readers, Roberts says that he spent twelve years collecting information for his map "during my abode and imployment in many parts of the

World" (sig. A5). The desire for profit ensures membership in the community of merchants constructed in the *Merchant's Mappe;* it is those compelled by "the motive Profit" (sig. B1) to travel and trade in foreign lands whom Roberts enjoins to read and thereby "profit" from his work. In a universalizing claim like John Wheeler's notion that "all the world choppeth and changeth, runneth and raveth after Marts, markets and Merchandising, so that all things come into Commerce, and pass into traffic (in a manner) in all times, and in all places" (sig. B2), Roberts says that trade is driven by "the natural inclination of Mankind to enrich themselves" (sig. B6). He persists, however, in constructing a community of traders: "conceiving that as my intentions (joyned to my labour and pains herein) tended only to the good of others, and principally of Merchants and their Factors, that reside or negotiate in foreign parts, so they will in requital be induced to have a good opinion thereof, as a reward to me, for the benefit that shall redound to them by the same" (sig. A4^v). As Roberts's repetition of "redound" underscores, the brotherhood of merchants who "reside or negotiate in foreign parts" is held together by a bond of allegiance and good will, a will expressed in the terms of an ongoing exchange of labor, profit, and gratitude, of travel and travail.

After several pages of prefatory epistles and commendatory verses, *The Merchant's Mappe* consists of three main sections. The first is a fifty-page introduction. The second is an extended descriptive section of each of the "four principal parts" of the world—America (11 pages), Africa (47 pages), Asia (110 pages), and Europe (262 pages), with a separate map at the beginning of the section on each region. Each continent's section is divided into chapters on the various countries, kingdoms, provinces, and cities of trade to be found there. The third main "Exchanges" section consists of almost two-hundred pages of currency conversion tables. These tables iron out all of the singularities Roberts has catalogued, flattening them into a single continuum of value, a "kind of geographic stock exchange."[9] The text offers a geographic vision that moves from an extended catalogue of "rarities" to the establishment of universally commensurable equivalencies.

Obviously, such a work would have immense practical value for a merchant or traveler. It is, nonetheless, difficult to characterize briefly because of the number of generic categories in which it falls, or that it invents. The *Merchant's Mappe* can be read as a work of proto-economic anthropology or as a kind of history of national and international trade, as its descriptions of the commodities and cities of various regions include many passages detailing particular discoveries or episodes in national and international trade relations. As Roberts's claim to have been compelled to merchandizing by "adverse fortune" might suggest, he is somewhat defensive about his profession. The *Merchant's Mappe*—particularly the prefatory materials and the ten chapter introductory section—is likewise an apologia for the "art of Merchandizing."[10] The first commendatory verse scornfully asserts that it is only "our ruder Country-men" who "despise / The mysteries of trade and merchandise" (sig. A1). Roberts himself defines merchandizing in celebratory terms:

> truly considered in itself, and rightly practised . . . [merchandizing is] an art or science invented by ingenious mankind for the publike good, commodity and welfare of all commonwealths; for thereby some places and kingdomes are supplied and furnished with those necessary things, whereof Nature herself hath proved deficient in, and which in some other places or kingdoms hath abounded, tending either to the need, ornament, or commodity of human life, and is performed by exporting the superfluities that are found in the one to furnish the defects and wants that are found in the other. (sig. B6^v)

Roberts's merchant is a benign distributive agent who compensates for the deficiencies of nature. By asserting that the merchant furnishes those "necessary things where of Nature herself hath proved deficient in," Roberts posits a merchant rather like Philip Sidney's poet in the *Defense of Poesy* who, "disdaining to be tied to any such subjection [to nature] . . . doth grow in effect another nature, in making things either better than nature bringeth forth, or, quite anew, forms such as never were in nature."[11] Roberts's international merchant does not bring forth "new" forms, however, but instead redistributes "necessary things" from one place to another, acting as an agent of geographical relocation. If Sidney's poet creates "forms such as never were in nature," Roberts's merchant, by means of his extensive conversion tables, reduces all manner of forms into "one thing."

Although he levels all differences between that which he maps and catalogues, Roberts offers a heroic notion of the merchant himself—a merchant who remains aloof from the very equivalencies he establishes. In fact, starting in America and working back to Europe (and, ultimately, London) through Africa and Asia, his text is a kind of commercial epic, with its merchant-Odysseus, the text's narrator, wending his way homeward.[12]

Rather than epic catalogues of ships, armaments, or angels, Roberts offers catalogues of commodities. In his epistle to general readers, Roberts describes the "continual toyle and search" (sig. A4) that went into his project and the obstacles that he, "the wind-scanted seaman" (sig. A4^v), had to overcome. Not satisfied with the collections of his precursors,[13] and aware of the advantage that the completion of his work could bring to England, Roberts persists in his efforts despite his difficulties:

> I have at last by due sounding of the Channel, safely sailed over the Ocean . . . and brought my Bark to an Anchor in her desired Harbour; and I hope so well observed the depths, shoulds, rocks and sands thereof, that he that navigates after me, and by this my Map, shall be secured from all dangers, and thereby bring his accounts to that wished Port, that my prove both to his owne profit and Commoditie. (sig. A5)

Endangering himself in order to ensure the physical and financial security of his followers, Roberts and his map become the heroic figures on whom the fate of the economic nation rests. Once the merchant-voyager makes his way back home, he brings the world home with him in the form of the book, which itself, of course, is a commodity.

For Roberts, then, to map the world is to catalogue and measure commodities. He offers a cosmography in which the map of the world is a map of commerce. To paraphrase J.H.'s commendatory poem, this "massy ball is its traffique." Within Roberts's cosmography, spaces, places, cities, and kingdoms, are sets of potential commodities, commodities whose values are reducible one into another. As the title page says, in this work, the "weights and measures of all eminent cities and townes of traffique [are] collected and reduced one into another." Equivalence rendered by the money form underlies the diversity of places and things that Roberts reports.

Roberts goes on to praise the divine creator for filling the earth with the "singular" metal gold, which has the power to reduce "the rarities of each place and town" into "One thing." Roberts celebrates the power of money to map geographical singularities onto a single continuum of value:

> amongst all the diversity of Metals which God the Creator hath shut up in the closet and concavitie of the earth, none is accounted more singular and excellent than silver and gold, of which the communication and Commerce of mankind, have framed and invented the use

of money and coin, which money and coin may be properly termed to be the universall measure of all things in the world.... And thereby it is evident and manifested that all things are obedient and in subjection to monyes. (28)

A passage which begins as praise of God transforms into a song of obeisance to the universally desingularizing power of money, the "universall measure of all things in the world." According to the Hebrew wisdom writer in Proverbs 20:10, "Diverse weights, and diverse measures, both of them are alike abomination to the Lord." Roberts's cosmography consists of the abominable system of valuation by which all things and places are "collected and reduced one into another."

Theorizing the commodity process, Igor Kopytoff would describe what we have been noting in Roberts as the creation of "value equivalence ... the mysterious process by which things that are patently unlike are somehow made to be alike with respect to value." Creating value equivalence "involves taking the patently singular and inserting it into a uniform category of value with other patently singular things."[14] Kopytoff balances this "drive to commoditization" against the cultural confusion that the process can cause. He suggests, following Durkheim, that "societies need to set apart a certain portion of their environment, marking it as 'sacred'" (73). This social and cultural countertendency toward "sacralization"—the creation of singularity—is one that Roberts's cosmography, as we have seen, unremittingly undermines. Describing the college in the city of Fez, for example, Roberts surveys its elaborate artistry, carvings, mosaics, and inlay work, and then sends them to the mint, so to speak, tallying the building's value in gold sultans, English pounds, and measuring it against the pound value of Westminster Chapel (sigs. H2^v-H3).[15]

The Moroccan people, on the other hand, are seen to be quite adept at sacralization in the following account of the architectural wonders in Marrakesh:

The Castle is also very large and strong, of the bignesse of a reasonable Towne, in the midst whereof is a Temple, which hath a Towre, whereon is fixed a spindle of Iron passing through three great round Globes made of pure gold, and weighing 130 thousand Barbary duckets, which is 58500 li, sterling, which divers Kings have gone about to take downe and convert into money; but have all desisted, by reason of some strange misfortunes that have been inflicted on them, so that the common people imagine they are kept by a guard of spirits. (sig. H4)

Men might have exhumed the "singular" metal gold from the deep "closet and concavitie" of the earth, but these three great round globes of gold remain perched atop the iron spindle, try as monarchs might to dislodge them. Resisting this lesson in the cultural relativity of value formation, Roberts only grudgingly acknowledges a social process of sacralization that is utterly alien to the European commodity cosmographer. The sort of magical property that Mauss associates with the "spirit of the gift" inheres in these massy balls, but in stark opposition to such gifts, these globes are objects whose circulation is magically proscribed. In these golden orbs, Roberts butts up against *irreducible* singularity, difference that cannot be converted. The pure gold globes might be weighed and valued, but they will not be sent to the literal mint to be converted into duckets or pounds sterling. For our merchant-voyager, this is an alien notion indeed. In the face of these "imaginary" yet all too successful wiles, Roberts is forced to quietly change the subject, returning to his commodity catalogue and establishment of equivalencies.

* * *

Trade beyond the shores of the "maiden isle" (*FMWI* 5.1.90)— the shared experience of ranging across the globe, impelled by the "motive Profit"—unites the members of the brotherhood of London merchants constructed in the prefatory materials of Roberts's *Merchant's Mappe*. Thanks to the public theaters, not only those directly involved in foreign trade are invited to reflect on the implications of commerce with distant cultures. I now turn to two plays that explore how to deal with the social and sexual threats that transglobal commerce is perceived to entail.[16] Thomas Heywood's *The Fair Maid of the West, Part I* and *Part II* explore how to exchange with cultural others, and how to do so without establishing exchange-generated bonds that corrupt, or more interestingly, compete with and win out over the exchange relations among Englishmen and those between Englishmen and Englishwomen. While Roberts's merchant-mapper, the establisher of equivalencies, remains heroically aloof from the difference-eradicating processes that transglobal commerce potentially entails, Heywood's characters—particularly his tavern maiden Bess Bridges—are continually in danger of being subject to them. In a spirit of high adventure, the plays dramatize the dangers of travel and travail, and of being subject to others' trade restrictions *and* freedoms, their knives as well as their seductive bribes.

In Shakespeare's more familiar fiction of transglobal exchange, *The Merchant of Venice*, Belmont and Venice host or, in the case of the Jews and slaves, serve as a hostile or partial "home" to the various cultural others encountered in the play. Morocco and Aragon come to woo Portia, and other "strangers" come to engage in trade. The only movements abroad on the part of the play's principal transactors are carried out by Antonio's ships, which range over the globe, including Mexico, India, and Barbary. Unlike Egeon in *Errors*, Antonio remains squarely in Venice. While Salerio and Solanio personify Antonio's ships in their opening description of them (1.1.9–14, 27–29), Shylock's later claim that "ships are but boards, sailors but men" (1.3.21–22) deflates this characterization. In addition to deflating the heroic conception of merchandizing encountered elsewhere in the play and in Roberts's *Mappe*, Shylock's reference to sailors as "but men" is the *only* mention of the persons on Antonio's ships actually exchanging with Mexicans, Indians, or Moors.[17] *The Fair Maid of the West*, on the other hand, dramatizes the English's foreign travels and extended encounters and exchanges with cultural others.[18] In the course of their travels, the English become much more entangled with those others as they explore and experiment with their boundaries as transactors—what exchange-generated bonds they are willing, or not willing, to forge and maintain.

Barely submerged tensions *within* the economic nation prompt Heywood's Englishmen to go abroad and become entangled in exchanges with cultural others. Their travel-adventures are catalyzed by a tavern scuffle in which the nobleman Spencer accidentally kills a roaring gallant against whose defamation he defends Bess Bridges. Forced into exile to avoid the "compass / Of the law's severe censure" (1.1.2.152–53), Spencer must abandon loftier motives for joining the Azores expedition—"'tis for honor and the brave society / Of all these shining gallants" 91.2.9–10). Goodlack, Spencer's friend who was "born to no other fortunes but my sword," acknowledges that the gallants "seek abroad for pillage" (1.2.7–8).

Prompted by false rumors of Spencer's death after his departure from England, Bess Bridges leads a crew of Englishmen to Barbary on her ship, the *Negro*, a name that, according to Jean Howard, "suggests that the construction of Englishness depends on the simultaneous construction of what is non-English." Bess masters the ship and its crew just as she will later triumph over Moorish King's desire for her.[19] Bess's ostensible motive for the voyage is to retrieve Spencer's body in order to erect a monument to him, allowing her to offer her "constancy in love" as a model for "all maids hereafter" (I.3.4.93–94). Spencer leaves Fayal, one of the Azores islands, on a London merchant's ship routed to return to England by way of Fez, the exotic locale in Barbary where they all eventually reunite. In both plays, pirates, storms, intrigue, and transactions proliferate, suggesting that the union and multiple reunions of Bess and Spencer are contingent on their successful weathering of various exchanges with the cultural others they encounter during their voyages. Bess and Spencer cannot "enjoy" each other (a repeated term to characterize their coming together: 1.2.1.149, 2.3.2.89, 140) until the English find ways to dispel or absorb the threats to which they are exposed by transacting with cultural others. They must face the threat of various forms of erotic contact and sexual danger—kisses, seduction, castration, cuckoldry—and they must overcome the threat of themselves becoming corrupted transactors, resisting the temptation to accept bribes and "golden promises" (2.1.1.280).

Because the English find themselves hosted by these cultural others in Fez, they are forced to enact, or act out in fantasy, a number of the threats which in *The Merchant of Venice* are presented in a muted form. Like the "aliens" and "strangers" in Shakespeare's Venice, and like Egeon in *Errors*, the "Christian merchants" (I.4.3.16) of *The Fair Maid of the West* find themselves governed by the host country's trade regulations. Mullisheg, the king of the newly victorious Moors, spells out these regulations when he first appears in the play: "all such Christian merchants as have traffic / And freedom in our country, that conceal / The least part of our custom due to us, / Shall forfeit ship and goods" (I.4.3.12–19). Like *Merchant*, *Fair Maid of the West* dramatizes a trial in which this "cunning quiddit in the law" (I.5.2.3) is brought to bear, but it is the Moorish king who will "supply our judgment seat" and "sentence causes" (5.1.104–5) and the Christian Europeans who will be on trial.[20]

Before setting out for Barbary, Bess Bridges, like Portia, is figured in part as a sought-after commodity that drives men to voyage in pursuit of her—not overseas, in Bess's case, but across England.[21] At the opening of *Part I*, she is figured as the tavern sign that attracts customers and is associated with the commodity that they come to buy. When Spencer asks to see Bess rather than accept a cup of "the neatest wine in Plymouth" (1.1.34), the wine-drawer exclaims, "there's nothing in the mouths of these gallants but 'Bess, Bess'" (36). Just as Portia likens herself to a commodity before Bassanio "ventures" for her, Bess associates herself with the wine she serves when Spencer asks her to bring him some: "I know your taste, and I / Shall please your palate" (1.2.49–50). Bess's beauty, says one captain, "draws to [her tavern] more gallant customers / Than all the signs i'th' town else" (1.1.21–22). Wine is "drawn" by the drawers, customers are "drawn" to the tavern by Bess, and as Spencer and Goodlack's discussion of what "drew" (1.2.11) them to Plymouth reveals, the "shining gallants" populating the streets and taverns of Plymouth are "drawn" to foreign adventures, such as the "doubtful voyage" (6) to the Azores Islands. The elaborate pun on "draw" running through the two opening scenes sets up a parallel between being drawn by sexual desire and being drawn by the hope of "gain," "honor," or "pillage," motives which remain closely intertwined throughout both plays.

These linked eroto-commercial urges and their tendency toward violence or denigration unfold in the trial scene that closes *Part I*. Mullisheg sentences a French merchant "for dealing in commodities forbid" (5.2.55), an Italian merchant's men "for outrage and contempt" (67), and a Christian preacher for converting Moors.[22] Enamored of and anxious to please Bess, whom he hopes to have "bosom with a Moor" (I.5.1.9), Mullisheg discharges the merchants when her words pay their "ransom" (5.2.71). He pardons the preacher, condemned to death, when Bess agrees to grant a kiss. Rendering the value of his life equivalent to the erotic attentions of Bess, Mullisheg says that her "kiss was worth the ransom of a king" (86). Inspired by desire for Bess, Mullisheg's bounty comes to preside over the trial. Just as she earlier transforms Englishmen's antagonisms into alliances before setting out for Fez, Bess transforms Mullisheg's desire for her into noble generosity, staving off these initial dangers. Although Bess has already forced Mullisheg to agree to her terms before she will have any "commerce" with him—"Keep off; for till thou swear'st to my demands, I will have no commerce with Mullisheg, / But leave thee as I came" (FMWI 5.1.46–48)—the series of exchanges in this scene eroticizes the legal and commercial exchanges between the "Christian merchants" and the Moors, projecting all erotic desire onto Moorish bounty.[23] Bess's final prohibition against commerce with Mullisheg in fact invites it. She forces him to agree "to offer no further violence to her person than what he seeks by kindly usage and free entreaty" (I.5.1.57–58).

The threat of sexual danger becomes even more overt in the interchange following Bess's plea to Mullisheg to "do [Spencer] some grace for my sake" (89):

> *Mull.* For thy sake what would not I perform?
> He shall have grace and honor. —Joffer, go
> And see him gelded to attend on us.
> He shall be our chief eunuch.
>
> (5.2.90–93)

Instead of the knife-wielding usurer whose castrating potential is only figurative—Shylock demands "an equal pound / Of your fair flesh, to be cut off and taken / In what part of your body pleaseth me" (1.3.148–50)—*Fair Maid* presents the Moorish King who is a literal castrator.[24] Offering a lesson in the cultural relativity of value—a lesson even more striking than the spirits guarding the "three great round Globes of pure gold" on the Moroccan temple—Mullisheg presents castration as an honor-amassing gift. Just as Portia intervenes to save Antonio from Shylock's knife, Bess intervenes to spare Spencer. Bess implicitly positions his sexuality as a portion of her property that she wishes to preserve, and hints that she herself might fill in as the object of violent attention:

> *Bess.* Not for ten worlds! Behold, great King, I stand
> Betwixt him and all danger. —Have I found thee?—
> Seize what I have, take both my ship and goods,
> Leave naught that's mine unrifled; spare me him.
>
> (5.2.94–97)

Immediately following Bess's plea, Clem, Bess's servant and former tavern drawer, shows his understanding that a courtly "honor" has been offered. Oafishly ignorant of the meaning of "gelding" and oblivious to the dangers of cross-cultural exchange, Clem stands "betwixt [Bess] and all danger" by accepting the threatened gift: "Please your majesty, I see all men are not capable of honor. / What he refuseth, may it please you to bestow on me" (99–100). After leaving the stage to face the razor, Clem realizes what this "gift" entails and reenters "running": "No more of your honor, if you love me! Is this your Moorish preferment, to rob a man of his best jewels? . . . I am sure he hath tickled my current commodity" (126–30). Although Clem's absorption of the castration threat is comical, it is nonetheless successful in avoiding the dishonor that accrues by refusing a gift; the nervous laughter at Clem's jokes about the "barbers of Barbary" (II.1.1.50) continues throughout *Part II*. His pun on commodity brings to the surface the associations implicitly drawn between commercial and sexual danger, and uncomfortably reveals that in Barbary, men's bodies are potentially as commodifiable and woundable as those of women. Moreover, the chaste tavern maid proves to be dangerously complicit in the erotic overtones of exchange in Barbary.

The literal castration-gift safely deflected, Spencer asks Mullisheg to continue his exercise of cross-cultural generosity, positioning Bess rather than himself as an object of exchange: "Bestow this maid on me; / 'Tis such a gift as kingdoms cannot buy" (108–9). Mullisheg bestows Bess as a gift to Spencer, inspired by the pleas of Goodlack and Roughman, who appeal to the power of constant love, cross-cultural compassion, and the lure of fame among "foreign nations" (116). Their appeals inspire Mullisheg to graciously preside over the union of Bess and Spencer. The scene overlays the efforts to avoid punishments for violating trade regulations with efforts to avoid sexual pollution and castration, themselves presented as dangerous gifts. The successful dodging of these dangers is expressed by means of a gift transaction, as the formerly castrating father figure gives away the bride. The sheer violence of the threat attests to the monstrosity associated with the geographical other; the link between Moorish exchange practices and sexual pollution or mutilation is part of the process of violently differentiating them from the plain-dealing English. Intimations of erotic content in the English transactions surface as well, however, if only by means of their insistent denial.[25]

The reformed Moorish bounty that closes *Part I* immediately lapses back into lust and corrupt transacting in *Part II*, a play that intensifies the efforts to demonize the Moors by representing them as corrupt transactors. As Mullisheg comes to lament having given Bess away—"oh, what did I bestow / When I gave her away?" (II.1.1.197–98)—the multiple threats that accompany transacting with these cultural others resurface with a vengeance. Mullisheg's requests for kisses become more urgent attempts at seduction, and the castration threat returns in the form of narrowly escaped decapitations and the evasion of Mullisheg's bloodthirsty vows to "have his flesh cut small as winter's snow /

Or summer's atoms" (II.1.1.344–45). Mullisheg will have to be reconverted to bounty midway through the play, and it will be up to the English as supposedly honor-driven gift-givers to do so. By reforming the Moors as transactors, the English avoid the threats that transacting with them poses.

The success of Bess Bridges as a chaste but active transactor are central to this process of reformation. She displays exemplary bounty in England and in Barbary where she inspires the release of the merchants and preacher from penalties and in *Part II* when she offers herself and her crew to appease the reinvigorated wrath of Mullisheg, who is about to decapitate Spencer. Her virtuous giving earns her an international reputation. Later, shipwrecked on the shores of Florence, Bess encounters the Florentine merchant who received her aid at the end of *Part I*. His requital of her gift completes an exchange that unites the two plays: "She did me a great courtesy, and I am proud / Fortune, however enemy to her, / Has given me opportunity to make / A just requital (II.4.1.90–94). Offering her a return gift of a thousand crowns, the Florentine merchant attests to her famous liberality and virtue:

> that miracle of constancy,
> She who reliev'd so many Christian captives,
> Redeem'd so many of the merchants' goods,
> Begg'd of the king so many forfeitures,
> Kept from the galleys some, and some from slaughter;
> She whom the King of Fez never denied,
> But she denied him love.
>
> (II.4.1.107–13)

Antonio-like, Bess spares merchants from their forfeitures, and her active giving of gifts is continually linked to her chastity.

However chaste and idealized Bess's powers of giving and active exchanging might be figured—and however tenuous that figuration eventually proves—she continues to face the corrupt transacting and seductive offers of cultural others, including European others, well into *Part II*. The Duke of Florence's bounty is explicitly set in competition with—and hence is likened to—that of the Moors. For example, when the Duke points out that he "gave" Bess her "almost forfeit chastity" (II.4.1.147) by saving her from bandits intent on raping her, Bess calls it "a gift above the wealth of Barbary" (148). Like Mullisheg, Florence becomes a desire-driven dispenser of bounty in order to win the affections of Bess. Bess staves off the scheming gift-engendered advances of the Duke who "forc'd on her [his] bounty" (II.4.4.3–10), just as she had staved off those of Mullisheg. When Goodlack and Spencer are about to offer their services to the dukes of Mantua and Ferrara, Goodlack warns Spencer to "Beware of these Italians" (4.6.76), with claims about their "natural" vengefulness that are akin to the frequent jibes against "natural" Moorish treachery.

Although the English must carefully contend with the corrupt transacting of *European* others in these plays, these efforts are overshadowed in *Part II* by the play's central figure of sexual danger and denigrated transacting. The occluded Moorish woman mentioned by Gobbo in *The Merchant of Venice* becomes in Heywood's play the Moorish queen, Tota, whose vengefulness, lust, and corrupt transacting opens *Part II*. Although presented, in part, as Bess's rival, Tota functions as the horrific dark Moorish double of the chaste, honorably transacting, and very English Bess Bridges.[26] In fact, Tota plays out in an exaggerated, almost caricaturing manner the fears lurking behind the representations of actively desiring and transacting women, such as Bess (or even Portia). Lustful, vengeful, pollutive, *and* seductive, Tota employs corrupt transacting—bribery, tricks, seductive offers—as a means for quenching her jealousy and satisfying her desires. As we will see, the Moorish queen is disturbingly akin to Bess Bridges of *Part II*, but as a *black Moor* and as a Moorish *woman*, she serves the crucial function of purging the English economic nation of the anxieties that accompany the image of an actively transacting woman like Bess.[27]

The soliloquy by Tota that opens *Part II* establishes her, on the surface, as the opposite of what we have so far seen of capable, chaste, generous, idealized Bess:

> It must not, may not, shall not be endur'd.
> Left we for this our country? To be made
> A mere neglected lady here in Fez,
> A slave to others, but a scorn to all?
> Can womanish ambition, heat of blood,
> Or height of birth brook this and not revenge?
> Revenge? On whom? On mighty Mullisheg?
> We are not safe then. On the English stranger?
> And why on her when there's no apprehension
> That can in thought pollute her innocence?
> Yet something I must do. What? Nothing yet?
> Nor must we live neglected. I should doubt

> I were a perfect woman, but degenerate
> From mine own sex, if I should suffer this.
>
> (II.1.1.1–14)

Tota's introduction into the play at this point bespeaks and renders overt the covert anxieties about our upwardly and geographically mobile tavern wench. Tota's focus on "womanish ambition" and the pride of "mine own sex" implicitly recall Bess, the upwardly mobile tavern maiden. The speech not only links the two by virtue of the fact that both are women, but anticipates similarities between them that develop over the course of Bess's continued experiences as a foreign traveler, commonalities that include dissatisfaction with "neglectful husbands" and vows for revenge. For example, Tota's question, "Left we for this our country?"[28] sounds like Bess's response to the news of Spencer's counter-bond to Bashaw Joffer, a noble Moor: "Is this the just reward of all my travels?" (3.2.130). Bess's aside after Spencer rebuffs her in Florence likewise echoes Tota's opening soliloquy:

> I'll be so reveng'd
> As never woman was. I'll be a precedent
> To all wives hereafter how to pay home
> Their proud, neglectful husbands. 'Tis in my way;
> I've power and I'll do it.
>
> (II.5.2.78–82)

Bess's original desire at the opening of *Part I* to set out on her international voyage to serve as a model of constancy for "all maids hereafter" has clearly been refashioned over the course of her experience with transglobal commerce. She will now be a revenger and a "precedent / To all wives hereafter." The discursive space for Bess to frankly express her anger and acknowledge her power, as she does here, has been created by her "dark" double, Tota. At the same time, the likeness between the Moorish and the Englishwoman's efforts to transact their way to revenge, to "pay home / Their proud, neglectful husbands" threatens to collapse the cultural differences that uphold the integrity of the English economic nation.

Tota continues her role as Bess's double when she serves as her surrogate in a bedtrick, during which Tota believes she is lying with Spencer and Mullisheg believes he is sleeping with Bess. In fact, thanks to the ingenious scheming of the resourceful Englishmen, the Moorish king and queen are embracing each other. In order to preserve Bess's honor and to extricate themselves from corrupt gift-forged relations with the Moors, Goodlack and Boughman engineer a double bedtrick in which Tota stands in for Bess, and Mullisheg stands in for Spencer. The bedtrick and its aftermath creates a profusion of imagined cross-cultural sexual couplings. In addition to that between Mullisheg and Bess, and Tota and Spencer, Tota later thinks she slept with Roughman when the English plot is partly uncovered (3.3.113). Further, during his attempted escape, Spencer tells Alcade, a servant to Mullisheg, that he plans to "bosom" the "common'st courtesan in Fez," (2.5.33–34) in order to "be reveng'd" (32) on Bess for the supposed tryst with Mullisheg on the wedding night. In addition to this fantasy, Goodlack tells Mullisheg, who thinks he is about to sleep with Bess, "I have shifted in her place a certain Moor / Whom I have hir'd for money, which, poor soul, / [Spencer] entertains for Bess" (2.3.14–16). Although the bedtrick is meant to keep the English from erotic exchanges with the Moors, its protracted planning and execution virtually revels in the fantasy cross-cultural flirtations and couplings that it entails. We have come a long way from the muted threats of intercultural sexual commerce that the casket riddle in *The Merchant of Venice* invites. Like Shakespeare's bedtricks in *Measure* and *All's Well*, however, that in *The Fair Maid of the West, Part II* threatens to expose the commensurability, and hence commoditylike status, of all women.[29] It is doubly threatening in raising the possibility that Moorish and English women are interchangeable. (Mullisheg certainly cannot tell the difference.) If this bedtrick is doubly threatening, it is also doubly preservative; it prevents Bess's sexual despoliation by a Moor, and it keeps Spencer from coupling with Tota.

In her revenge-driven pursuit of sex with Spencer before the bedtrick, Tota disidentifies from her own "countrymen," hinting at her alignment with Bess who likewise finds herself among foreigners. Tota seeks an English accomplice, because as she asserts, "The Moors are treacherous, / And them we dare not trust" (II.1.1.29–30). She promises Clem, the first Englishman whose assistance she seeks, "more grace and honor . . . then e'er thou didst receive from Mullisheg" (II.1.1.94). "Grace and honor?" Clem replies, "His grace and honor was to take away some part, and she would honor me to take away all. I'll see you damn'd as deep as the black father of your generation, the devil, first!" (2.1.1.96–99) having had "some part" sliced off the last time he accepted an offer of Moorish bounty (the gelding at the end of

Part I), Clem runs away from these "golden promises," fearing that the "grace and honor" Tota offers will remove his remaining genitalia as well.[30] Clem warns Roughman, the next Englishman in line to receive Tota's offers: "if you will have any grace and honor, you may pay for't as dear as I have done. 'Sfoot! I have little enough left; I would fain carry home something into my own country" (107–9). Clem comically reveals the interlocking nexus of threats encountered in commerce outside of one's "own country": corrupt exchanges and castration, both associated with Tota's devilish blackness. His desire to "carry home something" points to the fear of sexual depletion that accompanies overseas ventures (not to mention hinting at the threat of venereal disease). No wonder, then, that the consumers of these texts are so grateful to stay in their own chairs, chambers, and warm and pleasant houses, without toil, "spending of substaunce," nor "werines of body," without "labor lost" (*MV* 2.7.74) as Morocco in *The Merchant of Venice* experiences.

* * *

By 1630–31, the years when the two plays comprising *The Fair Maid of the West* were performed in sequence before the king and queen of England, Lewis Roberts had completed the bulk of the globe-encircling travels and observations that culminated in the *Merchant's Mappe*. The carving up of the "massy Ball and all its traffique" was an increasingly pressing national and international issue.[31] Because *The Fair Maid of the West* dramatizes exchange with transactors who are explicitly positioned—geographically and imaginatively—beyond the boundaries of the economic nation, they reveal the centrality of exchange in embodying and enacting social and cultural identity. They likewise register the conceptual proximity between commercial and social or erotic practices, practices which were only coming to be seen in this period as isolated domains. By linking cultural and geographic others to corrupt exchange practices, these plays demonize those others, thus purging the economic nation of its unsavory features. The demonization of bribe-offering, castrating Moors is likewise an attempt to assert cultural differences, to counter the discourse of commensurability ushered in by the cross-global expansion of England's commercial enterprises. The plays provide their audiences with an imaginative strategy for countering the difference-eradicating processes that Roberts's *Mappe* registers and enacts. Despite their absence from the merchant brotherhood constructed in a text such as

Roberts's *Merchant's Mappe of Commerce*, women play a crucial role in the cultural imagination of a nation embarking on transglobal ventures. These plays reveal the central role of transacting women—including nonwhite women—in forming and severing the entanglements that are imagined to accompany international trade.

Notes

1. All quotations from Shakespeare are from David Bevington, Ed., *The Complete Works*, 4th ed. (New York: HarperCollins, 1992). Thanks to Ginger Mason Vaughan and Alden Vaughan who chaired the SAA seminar that prompted this collection; to Garrett Sullivan, John Gillies and Ginger Vaughan for their insightful comments on the earlier version of this essay; and to Carol Neely, Michael Shapiro, Richard Wheeler for their comments on the earliest incarnations of some of the ideas offered here. Portions of the material on Lewis Roberts were first presented at the "New Economic Criticism" conference sponsored by the Society for Critical Exchange, Cleveland, Ohio, October 1994.

2. Sandra Fischer notes that a "salute" is a kind of coin, *Econolingua: A Glossary of Coins and Economic Language in Renaissance Drama* (Newark: University of Delaware Press, 1985), 117. On salutes as an international, rather than an interpersonal, gesture of recognition, see note 17.

3. My understanding of the importance of exchange in constituting and symbolizing social relations has been shaped by the "classic" account of the gift economy in Marcel Mauss, *The Gift: Forms and Functions of Exchange in Archaic Societies*, trans. Ian Cunnison (Glencoe, Ill.: The Free Press, 1954), its extension in Claude Levi-Strauss, *Elementary Structures of Kinship*, trans. Bell et al. (Boston: Beacon Press, 1969), and reformulations and revisions of the gift economy by recent anthropological exchange theorists, particularly Christopher Gregory, *Gifts and Commodities*, (London: Academic Press, 1982); Nicholas Thomas, *Entangled Objects: Exchange, Material Culture, and Colonialism in the Pacific* (Cambridge, Mass.: Harvard University Press, 1991); Annette Weiner, *Inalienable Possession: The Paradox of Keeping-While-Giving* (Berkeley and Los Angeles: University of California Press, 1992); Keith Hart, "On Commoditization," in *From Craft to Industry: the Ethnography of Proto-Industrial Cloth Production*, ed. Esther N. Goody (Cambridge: Cambridge University Press, 1982), 38–49; and especially Arjun Appadurai, ed., *The Social Life of Things: Commodities in Cultural Perspective* (Cambridge: Cambridge University Press, 1986). See note 31 on feminist uses and critiques of the structuralist "exchange of women" paradigm that Levi-Strauss establishes.

In "'Stigmatical in Making': The Material Character of *The Comedy of Errors*," *English Literary Renaissance* 23 (1993), Douglas Lanier discusses how *Errors* takes as its focus "The discontinuity between identities and the external marks that display, support, and confirm them," 90. What he calls "external marks" are more properly speaking *acts of exchange*.

Arthur Golding's translation of Seneca's *De Beneficiis* can be seen as the paradigmatic sixteenth-century effort to privilege an idealized ethos of gift exchange—the giving, receiving, and requiting of "benefits"—over and against ordinary "merchandising": "The estimation of so noble a thing should perish, if we make a merchandise of benefits." Seneca, Lucius. *The woorke of the excellent Philosopher Lucius Annaeus Seneca concerning Benefyting, that is too say the dooing, receyving, and requyting of good Turnes*, trans. Arthur Golding (London: John Day, 1578.) Facsimile rpt. *The English Experience*, 694. (Amsterdam: Walter J. Jonson, 1974), sig. I2ᵛ. Those who wish to engage in benefiting must "tread profit underfoot" (sig. M2ᵛ).

4. The phrase "maiden isle" comes from the Moorish King Mullisheg in *The Fair Maid of the West, II* (5.1.90). Thomas Heywood, *The Fair Maid of the West, Parts I and II*, ed. Robert K. Turner (Lincoln: University of Nebraska Press, 1967). Richard Helgerson argues that the nation constructed in voyage writings "would of necessity be an England defined by its relation to those other more or less similar entities, an England reconstituted in response to a new global system of differences" *Forms of Nationhood: The Elizabethan Writing of England* (Chicago: University of Chicago Press, 1992), 153. John Gillies's discussion of the indebtedness of the Renaissance (and Shakespearean) geographic imagination to the ancient "poetic geography" puts some pressure on the "Newness" that Helgerson posits here. I am greatly indebted to Gillies's *Shakespeare and the Geography of Difference* (Cambridge: Cambridge University Press, 1994).

5. T. S. Willan, *Studies in Elizabethan Foreign Trade* (New York: Augustus M. Kelley Publishers, 1968). Willan is quoting John Wheeler, *A Treatise of Commerce*. Middelburgh, 1601. Facsimile Rpt. ed. George Burton Hotchkiss (New York: New York University Press, 1931).

6. This mastery of vision will later in the seventeenth century be accorded to the surveying, envious Satan in *Paradise Lost* who "Looks down with wonder at the sudden view / Of all this world at once" (III.542–43) as he makes his way out of the infernal regions. Milton explicitly likens Satan's cosmic travels to spice merchants' navigations on the "trading flood" (II.636–43). *John Milton*, ed. Stephen Orgel and Jonathan Goldberg (Oxford: Oxford University Press, 1991).

7. Thanks to Ginger Vaughan for helping me articulate this connection. John Gillies surveys the poetic project by which "uninhabited geographical entities" were "imaginatively possessed, which is to say moralised and mythologised" (36), a project in which Roberts and Heywood are engaged. On the notion of the "mental map," both a "signifying process" and a "mental entity," see esp. 54–59. Chapter 3 traces the conceptual links between maps, the world, and the theater. Also see Richard Helgerson, who points out that overseas voyage writing gave Europeans "conceptual possession of a world outside Europe they had hardly known" (151). See esp. chapter 4. Stephen Mullaney, *The Place of the Stage: License, Play, and Power in Renaissance England* (Chicago: University of Chicago Press, 1988), addresses the implications of the spatial location of the theater on the city's outskirts. For an astute discussion of the reconceptualization of land, social relations, and changing surveying technologies, see Garrett A. Sullivan Jr. "'Arden Lay Murdered in that plot of ground': Surveying, Land, and 'Arden of Faversham'" *ELH* 61 (1994): 231–52.

My sense of the connection between commerce and drama owes much to Muriel Bradbrook, *The Rise of the Common Player* (London: Chatto & Windus, 1962). She surveys how drama moves from being conceived primarily as an offering to a guild, university, local community, or aristocratic patron, to a commercial transaction between playgoers, actors, and theater-owners in the public theaters. Economic modes of analysis, broadly defined, inform a number of recent studies of drama in early modern England: Jean-Christophe Agnew's *Worlds Apart: The Market and the Theater in Anglo-American Thought, 1550–1750* (Cambridge: Cambridge University Press, 1986); Walter Cohen's *Drama of a Nation: Public Theater in Renaissance England and Spain* (Ithaca, N.Y.: Cornell University Press, 1985); Douglas Bruster's *Drama and Market in the Age of Shakespeare* (Cambridge: Cambridge University Press, 1992); and Lars Engle's *Shakespearean Pragmatism: Market of His Time* (Chicago: University of Chicago Press, 1993). The "poetics of culture" that Stephen Greenblatt models in the introduction to *Shakespearean Negotiations* (Berkeley and Los Angeles: University of California Press, 1988) is saturated with economic metaphors. A movement toward materialist analysis in literary and cultural criticism, particularly among feminists, brings with it an implicit interest in economic forms of organization, production, and exchange. See, for example, Valeris Wayne, ed., *The Matter of Difference* (Ithaca, N.Y.: Cornell University Press, 1991).

8. *The Merchant's Mappe of Commerce* (London, 1638). Roberts, born in 1596, sought service with the East India Company in 1617, was employed by it and the Levant Company, and later became a director of both. The *Dictionary of National Biography* calls *The Merchant's Mappe* "one of the earliest systematic treatises on its subject in English." The first edition appeared in 1638 (STC 21094) followed by four others, in 1677, 1690, 1700, and 1719. A facsimile reprint of the original edition is available in "The English Experience" series. A very short excerpt of the work appears in *Seventeenth-Century Economic Documents*, eds. Joan Thirsk and J. P. Cooper (Oxford, Clarendon Press, 1972), 491–94.

9. I borrow the latter phrase from John Gillies.

10. Such apologies persist well into the seventeenth century. On attitudes towards merchants and profit, see Helgerson chapter 4. He discusses Thomas Mun's work in reestimating merchants and in proffering a purely economic understanding of national interest, page 188. Joyce Oldham Appleby discusses the paradigm shift that Mun's work brings to economic thought, *Economic Thought and Ideology in Seventeenth-Century England* (Princeton: Princeton University Press, 1978), 37–41. Cf. Theodore Leinwand on Mun's construction of the merchant as the perfect "renaissance man," *The City Staged: Jacobean Comedy, 1603–13* (Madison: University of Wisconsin Press, 1986), 34–35. His second chapter treats Jacobean attitudes towards merchants, exempting merchants who engage in "large-scale overseas commerce" (22) from the castigated group. Appleby similarly points out that the newness and relative invisibility of certain forms of long distance or colonial trade exempted these practices from the kind of condemnation heaped on usury, enclosure, and abuses of the grain trade, pages 53–72. Appleby situates Roberts among the "old guard" of economic thinkers because, unlike more radical advocates of "free trade," he staunchly supports trading companies' monopolies over particular markets in *The Treasure of Traffik* (1641), 106–7. On monopolies as royal gifts, see David Harris Sacks, "The Countervailing of Benefits: Monopoly, Liberty, and Benevolence in Elizabethan England," in *Tudor Political Culture*, ed. Dale Hoak (Cambridge: Cambridge University Press), 272–91.

11. Philip Sidney, *Sir Philip Sidney's Defense of Poesy*, ed. Lewis Soens (Lincoln: University of Nebraska Press, 1970), 9.

12. *The Odyssey* sets the goals of maritime trade against those of epic heroism. Menelaos could not intervene to prevent the murder of Agamemnon, for

example, because he was off in Egypt making "a fortune / in sea-traffic among those distant races" (3.102–3). Homer, *The Odyssey*, trans. Robert Fitzgerald (New York: Doubleday, 1961).

13. Isaac Walton's commendatory verse, in fact, pits Roberts against Ortelius: "If though would'st be a States-man, and survey / Kingdomes for information; heres a way / Made plaine, and easie: fitter far for thee / Then great Ortelius his Geographie" (sig. a6).

14. Igor Kopytoff, "The Cultural Biography of Things," in *The Social Life of Things: Commodities in Cultural Perspective* (Cambridge: Cambridge University Press, 1986) ed. Arjun Appadurai, 71.

15. Here, as in the larger structure of his atlas, Roberts mimics what Charles V does to Mexican and Peruvian artifacts. See Hugh Honour, *The New Golden Land: European Image of America from the Discoveries to the Present Time* (New York: Pantheon, 1975), chap. 2. Despite focusing on its commodity cosmography, I hope to have conveyed my conviction that a commercial atlas like *The Merchant's Mappe of Commerce* is indeed a *cultural* production. Implicit in my reading is a sense of the dual status of this text as both "cultural production" and "economic document."

16. Kim Hall articulates the problem astutely, pointing to the "multivalent anxieties over cross-cultural interactions that permeate English fictions of international trade. . . . The exchange of goods (or even the circulation of money) across cultural borders always contains the possibility of other forms of exchange between different cultures. Associations between marriage, kinship, property, and economics become increasingly anxiety-ridden as traditional social structures (such as marriage) are extended when England develops commercial ties across the globe," "Guess Who's Coming to Dinner: Miscegenation in *The Merchant of Venice*," *Renaissance Drama* n.s. 23 (1992): 88. See also Kim Hall, *Things of Darkness: Economies of Race and Gender in Early Modern England* (Ithaca: Cornell University Press, 1995).

17. Likewise, except for Salerio's brief mention of spices and silks (1.1.33–34), there is little attention paid to the actual commodities on Antonio's ships. Given Antonio's constant presence in Venice, he seems a "sedentary" merchant who employs factors rather than a voyager like Roberts. See Willan, p. 4, on the rise of the "sedentary" merchant. Jay Halio notes in the Oxford edition of the play that Venice's worldwide trade had been curtailed by Shakespeare's time and, in fact, did not extend to Mexico (Oxford: Oxford University Press, 1993), 177n. Lewis Roberts rather gloats over the decline in Venetian world-trade status (sigs. Gg1–3). Salerio's elaborate metaphor personifying Antonio's ships as "rich burghers on the flood" who "overpeer the petty traffickers / That cursy to them, do them reverence" (1.1.10–13) figures international trading ships as personified practitioners of courtly manners. The lines might also refer to the practice of naval salutes between ships of different nations. According to Simon Schama, all foreign ships found in waters that were designated as British seas were required to offer a deferential salute to British vessels. He describes the deep conflict over maritime sovereignty that lay behind the mid-seventeenth-century debate between the English and Dutch over naval salutes in *The Embarrassment of Riches: An Interpretation of Dutch Culture in the Golden Age* (Berkeley and Los Angeles: University of California Press, 1988), 232–33.

18. Much of my argument treats the two plays as if they were one, following Rosalind Knutson's suggestion that, in addition to a successful response to the

first part of a play, some multiple part dramas were conceived as sequels, *The Repertory of Shakespeare's Company, 1594–1613* (Fayetteville: University of Arkansas Press, 1991), 53. Given the ample references it makes to the Cadiz and Azores expeditions, *Part I* is fairly easy to date between 1596–98, the same date as Shakespeare's *Merchant. Part II* is less reliably dated.

19. Jean Howard, "An English Lass Amid the Moors: Gender, race, sexuality, and national identity in Heywood's *The Fair Maid of the West*," in *Women, "Race," and Writing in the Early Modern Period*, eds. Margo Hendricks and Patricia Parker (London: Routledge, 1994), 110. Howard offers an excellent reading of the play as a "case study" in the construction of English national identity.

20. Mullisheg might be loosely fashioned after Ahmad El-Mansour, "the Golden," whose reign began after the battle of Alcazar in 1578. The most longstanding and successful ruler of the Saadian dynasty, El-Mansour's reign saw relative respite from the general political instability and lack of centralization that marked Moroccan history in our period. See William Spencer, *Historical Dictionary of Morocco* (London: Scarecrow Press, 1980). *Part I* seems to be set at the beginning of Mansour's reign, after "bloody and intestine broils." Like Heywood's *If You Know Not Me* in which Gresham deals with a Barbary merchant, *Fair Maid* shows some awareness of recent Morocco-England trade relations. This trade, which persisted until the deaths of El-Mansour and Elizabeth in 1603, culminated in a Moroccan embassy to England in 1600. On the embassy and the rumors, secrecy, and speculation surrounding it, see Bernard Harris, "A Portrait of a Moor," *Shakespeare Survey* (1958): 89–97; Willan 303–8, and Jack D'Amico, *The Moor in English Renaissance Drama* (Tampa: University of South Florida Press, 1991), 33–38. Like Bess Bridges and Spencer, who refuse Mullisheg's bounty, Elizabeth returned gifts to Mansour with the Moroccan emissaries (D'Amico, 37). Elizabeth had many diplomatic interchanges and exchanges with El-Mansour, including an illicit trade in arms, saltpeter, and gold, which circumvented the official sugar-cloth trade. Nevill Barbour explains that other European nations resented this unholy alliance, which in part represented anti-Spanish maneuvering, *Morocco* (London: Thames & Hudson, 1965), 107. Willan details the diplomatic exchanges between Elizabeth and El-Mansour, pages 172, 233–38, 293–94, 303–8. Often, Elizabeth appealed to the Moroccan ruler to intervene on behalf of English traders who were in conflict with one another. Willan's extensive survey reveals that it was usually English merchants who were in bad faith—circumventing the Moroccan king's monopolies, passing bad cloth to the Jewish middlemen and the Moors, or cheating each other. D'Amico offers a helpful overview of these dealings, pages 7–40. Lewis Roberts's account in the *Merchant's Mappe* largely postdates the period of sustained English-Moroccan trade; hence, his reference to the "late civil wars" which caused traffic's decline in the region.

21. See Gillies, pages 66–67, on Morocco's and Bassanio's account of Portia's voyage-inspiring focus of universal desire. Howard comments on the regional implications of the "West" in Heywood's title.

22. The juxtaposition of Roberts's *Mappe*, *Merchant of Venice*, and *Fair Maid* brings into relief the imaginative links between religious and more strictly "economic" senses of conversion. Both act 4 of *Merchant* and the final act of *Fair Maid Part II* end with an alien's religious conversion. Shylock's forced conversion at the trial supposedly draws him into the "brotherhood" of Christians, but this punishment combines with the others to complete the scape-

goating process, ensuring that Shylock is kept at bay by the Venetians themselves. Unlike Shylock—and true to the comic design of Heywood's travel-adventure—Bashaw Joffer, the "rare black swan" (II.2.6.104) with whom Spencer becomes entangled, converts willingly and eagerly.

The bond between Joffer and Spencer is an example of the play's presentation of affective, exchange-generated, homosocial bonds that cut across national lines and that threaten to be valued over affective bonds between Englishmen and Englishwomen. Upon hearing that Spencer has left her to remain faithful to his vow of allegiance to Joffer, Bess scans the affective accounts: "Prize you my love to rate it / Beneath the friendship of a barbarous Moor? / Is this the just reward of all my travels?" (II.3.2.127–30). Later in *Part II*, Spencer again forges an exchange-generated bond across national lines; his allegiance to an Italian Duke temporarily threatens to prevent his reunion with Bess.

23. Citing Heywood's *Gunaikeion*, the OED offers a tertiary definition of "commerce" as "intercourse of the sexes, esp. of a bad sense."

24. Howard argues that castrating Mullisheg replaces Bess as the chief figure of sexual danger in the play. While I agree with Howard's reading of Bess as an eroticized virgin whose chastity is obsessively scrutinized, we will see that it is the Moorish queen Tota, not Mullisheg, who diverts attention from Bess's sexuality. Bess's nickname and the subtitle of *The Fair Maid of the West*—"a Girl Worth Gold"—tantalizingly echoes the English translation of El-Mansour—"the Golden"—the Saadian king after whom I believe Mullisheg to be patterned.

25. My discussion here draws heavily on Gillies's excellent explication of the near collapse of the "laboriously constructed antitheses" of *The Merchant of Venice*—between Antonio as gift-giver and Shylock as usurer, between "pure" and "tainted" forms of commercial activity, between Venice as the promiscuous marketplace of the world and as the Aristotelian ideal of the integral *polis*, pages 125–37. My reading of the complicity of the English in the pollutive energies projected onto the Moors differs from Jack D'Amico's general sense of *Fair Maid* as a travel-morality adventure that reconfirms existing patterns of idealized English virtue, pages 85–86.

26. Carol Neely's discussion of the maid Barbary as Desdemona's double in *Othello* was crucial to my understanding of the relationship between the representations of Tota and Bess. "Circumscriptions and Unhousedness: Othello in the Borderlands," in *Shakespeare and Gender: A History*, Eds. Ivo Kamps and Deborah Baker. (London: Verso, 1995). Robert Turner's characterization of Tota's rivalry with Bess as "italianate jealousy" (xvii) rings rather funny, given the national identities constructed and juxtaposed in the play.

27. Focusing attention on Tota's blackness is crucial to the process of setting her apart from Bess so that she can become a repository of the denigrated features that are the inverse of Bess's idealized transacting. An interchange with Clem in the opening scene of *Part II* points to Tota's blackness and makes manifest its usefulness as a marker in distinguishing Englishwomen from cultural others. The play is thus a crucial contribution to the period's newly emerging discourses of race as a color-bound category. See Margo Hendricks and Patricia Parker, eds., *Women, "Race," and Writing in the Early Modern Period* (London: Routledge, 1994); Karen Newman, "'And wash the Ethiop white': Femininity and the Monstrous in Othello," chap. 5 of *Fashioning Femininity and English Renaissance Drama* (Chicago: University of Chicago Press, 1991), and Richmond Barbour's essay in this collection. The rhetorical and ideological

procedure at work in the latent alliance between Bess and Tota can be seen at work as well in Golding's Seneca's opposition between "benefits" and ordinary "merchandising." He purges the coercive, interested, and potentially exploitative features of "benefits" by locating them solely in the sphere of ordinary merchandising.

28. When he first appears in the earlier play, Mullisheg has just "conquer'd, aw'd and sway'd" all Barbary (I.4.3.7–8) after "bloody and intestine broils" (1). In addition to establishing trade regulations, he orders Alcade and Joffer to "Find us concubines, / The fairest Christian damsels you can hire or buy for gold, the loveliest of the Moors / We can command, and Negroes everywhere. / Italians, French, and Dutch, choice Turkish girls . . ." (28–32). As we have seen, Bess resists membership in this proposed harem by refusing Mullisheg's gold and by establishing her own terms for any "commerce" (I.5.1.47) with him. Tota is listed in the dramatis personae of *Part II* as "Queen of Fez and wife of Mullisheg." Although clearly not conceived when *Part I* was written, Tota is presented here as queen of one of the kingdoms of Barbary that Mullisheg recently conquered, explaining her claim to have left her home country. See note 20.

29. We begin to see the slippery status of women in the symbolic economies being traced here. In addition to being positioned as objects of exchange, Bess and Tota are active transactors and desiring subjects. On women as contradictory property, see Eve Sedgwick, *Between Men: English Literature and Male Homosocial Desire* (New York: Columbia University Press, 1985), especially chapter 3. Peter Stallybrass discusses the construction of "normative woman" as a property category in "Patriarchal Territories: the Body Enclosed" in *Rewriting the Renaissance: The Discourses of Sexual Difference in Early Modern Europe*, eds. Margaret Ferguson, Maureen Quilligan, and Nancy J. Vickers (Chicago: University of Chicago Press, 1986), 123–42. Gayle Rubin's influential essay, "The Traffic in Women: Notes on the 'Political Economy' of Sex," is an important starting point for understanding the exchange of women paradigm as Levi-Strauss formulates it, in *Toward an Anthropology of Women*, ed. Rayna Reiter (New York: Monthly Review, 1975), pp. 157–210. Gayle Greene and Coppelia Kahn provide a clear overview of the exchange of women paradigm and some feminist critiques of it in "Feminist scholarship and the social construction of woman" in *Making a Difference: Feminist Literary Criticism* (London: Methuen, 1985), pp. 1–36. See also Karen Newman, "Directing Traffic: Subjects, Objects, and the Politics of Exchange," *differences*, 212 (1990): 41–54. Feminist anthropological revisions include Henrietta Moore, *Feminism and Anthropology* (Minneapolis: University of Minnesota Press, 1988) and Annette Weiner, *Inalienable Possessions*. Marilyn Strathern offers some excellent clarification of the categories of analysis deployed in discussions of women and property relations in "Subject or Object? Women and the Circulation of Valuables in Highlands New Guinea," *Women and Property, Women as Property*, ed. Renee Hirschon (New York: St. Martins Press, 1984). If, following Arjun Appadurai and Igor Kopytoff, we view commoditization as a *process*, as a phase in the "social life of things," the problems with the structuralist paradigm on which the "traffic in women" construct rests emerge clearly.

Roberts briefly raises then eliminates the possibility of the commodification of English women. He opens his chapter on England and its cities by citing an anonymous commentator on the ornaments to be found there:

The Ornaments of this Country hath in times past beene expressed unto us by this verse,

> Anglia, Mons, Pons, Fons, Ecclesia, Famina, Lana.
> England is stor'd with Mountains, Bridges, Woll,
> With Churches, Rivers, Women beautifull.

But these are not the commodities that Merchants Looke after, therefore I will shew you in his proper place, those commodities which England doth naturally afford for merchandise. (sig. Ss6)

Roberts lists women among the ornamental features of the English landscape, but he sacralizes them, pointedly excluding them from the category of marketable commodities. The treatment of English women here parallels that of the golden globes atop the college in Marrakesh previously discussed. Thanks to Robbie Boerth for noting this parallel. Roberts's figuration of land as ornament—not commodity—points to the extent to which overseas merchant interests can be in line with those of the landed aristocracy.

30. Both Jack D'Amico, *Moor in Renaissance Drama*, and Anthony Barthelemy, *Black Face Maligned Race: the Representation of Blacks in English Drama from Shakespeare to Southerne* (Baton Rouge: Louisiana State University Press, 1987), 164, agree with my sense that Clem's castration is an anatomical reality in this scene. Jean Howard notes ambiguity, given that Clem enters running on the stage after the event has supposedly occurred, page 323n.

31. Beginning in the first quarter of the century, for example, an international trade rivalry with the Netherlands, England's former ally against the Spanish, intensified as each nation jockeyed to establish a commercial empire. On British-Dutch relations and economic rivalries in the early seventeenth century, see Schama pages 229–36. See Appleby, chapter 5, on the Dutch as a commercial model as well as a rival. Roberts depicts in detail an episode of Anglo-Dutch conflict off the shores of Negrita in which the native Africans simultaneously serve as the backdrop, the pawns, and perhaps, the beneficiaries of inter-European rivalries (sigs. H6–H6^v).

Marlowe, the *Timur* Myth, and the Motives of Geography

JOHN GILLIES

It is no accident that we always remember the effect of Marlowe's resounding geography.... To be a world conqueror in the various senses which the play gives to the term is the essence of Marlowe's Herculean hero.[1]

THOUGH Tamburlaine's unique power is celebrated in many types of image—apocalyptic, cosmological, volcanic, tempestuous, mythological, even Lucretian (when he embodies the "restless" jarring of the elements)—there seem good grounds for supposing that the imagery of geographical conquest is indeed its essence. Thus, Tamburlaine poses before a world map at the conclusion of Tamburlaine Part 2, and a speech of specifically geographical (as distinct from cosmological or other) aspiration is inserted at the crux of Part 1:

> I will confute those blind geographers
> That make a triple region in the world,
> Excluding regions that I mean to trace,
> And with this pen reduce them to a map,
> Calling the provinces, cities, and towns,
> After my name and thine, Zenocrate.
> Here at Damascus will I make the point
> That shall begin the perpendicular:
> And wouldst thou have me buy thy father's love
> With such a loss? Tell me, Zenocrate.[2]
>
> (I: 4.4.81–90)

In a sequence of defining moments in Part 1—the declaration of his world-conquering mission, the seduction of Theridamas, the defeats of Cosroe and Bajazeth—this seems most crucial, because most *hubris* laden. Where earlier moments and defined Tamburlaine against external adversaries and their conventional expectations, this one defines him against his wife-to-be and intimate pieties that can hardly be dismissed as conventional. For the first time in the play, our sympathies are seriously divided. We wonder why world conquest should absolutely require the destruction of Damascus, a city which Zenocrate begs Tamburlaine to spare and to which she is emblematically linked. This moment is exactly where Tamburlaine is most himself. It is utterly (if almost absurdly) characteristic that he should refuse to "circumscribe" his territorial ambitions on any account. This is a Mars unfettered by Venus, a Coriolanus fully prepared to trample his mother's womb.[3]

The moment is equally remarkable for defining Tamburlaine against the "Tamerlane" or "Tamberlaine" of European legend. In George Whetstone's *The English Myrror* (1586)—a parochial and topical version of the generic *Vita Tamerlains* from which Marlowe certainly worked—the seige of Damascus defines "Tamberlaine" in a different light. Almost as in Marlowe, the Damascans resist beyond the allotted period of mercy, at which point an untimely embassy of "Their wives and children cloathed all in white" is dispatched to the ominously blackened tents.[4] Again, much as in Marlowe, "Tamberlaine . . . caused his squadrons of horsemen to tread them under their feete, and not to leave a mothers child a live."[5] This, however, is where the accounts diverge. In place of Zenocrate (who is entirely Marlowe's invention), "a marchaunt of Genowa, somewhat favored of Tamberlaine" is so bold as to question this genocidal procedure:

> whom Tamberlaine (with a countenance fiered with fury) answered: thou supposest that I am a man, but thou art deceived, for I am no other than the ire of God, and the destruction of the world: and therefore see thou come no more in my sight, least I chasten thy over proud boldnes. The marchaunt made speed away, and was never afterwards seen in the campe.[6]

Where Marlowe, then, uses the Damascus episode to establish the primacy of the hero's global imperialism over his boyish romanticism, Whetstone (following the generic narrative) uses the episode to underline the hero's inscrutably apocalyptic malignity. How do we explain so radical a departure? One answer might emphasize context. Eric Voegelin has described "Tamerlane" as the creation of fifteenth-century Italian humanists traumatized by the wholesale collapse of the medieval political dispensation in their country.[7] Like Collucio Salutati's portrait of Julius Caesar, or Machiavelli's portrait of Castruccio Castracane,

"Tamerlane" represents the bleakest of power myths, the so-called "monarchioptantist" narrative, in which pure ruthlessness is celebrated as the only alternative to complete chaos. Though Whetstone's (1586) Elizabethan context is far removed from that of these Italian humanists, his vision is similarly bleak (though not so clear) and may be similarly explained. Whetstone, too, is traumatized: his "Tamberlaine" being conceived in fetishized opposition to a paranoid vision of the Turkish menace and the looming Spanish invasion.[8]

In this argument, Marlowe's radical intrusion of the imperial/geographic theme and his no less radical substitution of exuberance for bleakness, global megalomania for isolated desperation, might to some extent be explained by the *chutzpah* of Drake's raid on Cadiz in 1587 or the euphoria of the Armada Victory in 1588 (the years of writing). Francis Yates and Roy Strong have described the appropriation of Spanish imperial devises by English poets and painters after the Armada.[9] *Tamburlaine* participates in this exuberant *translatio*. Thus, Tamburlaine's posturing before a world map towards the end of Part 2 (5.3.146–61), might well suggest Elizabeth's fondling of a geographic globe in the *Armada* portrait of 1588; both "performances" virtually advertising their appropriation of the global icon in portraits of Charles V and Phillip II. The final exhortation to his sons (and arguably the English audience) to conquer the New World and the Antipodes can be read as one more Elizabethan appropriation of "the proudest device of the sixteenth century": the Pillars of Hercules and the motto *Plus Ultre*, or "Ever Further," which spectacularly flouted the warning Non Plus Ultra ("No Further") that Hercules was supposed to have set over his Pillars at the Strait of Gibraltar.[10] (It is significant that where Part 2 ends with a vision of going "ever further," Part 1 should have ended with Tamburlaine's agreement to stop at "Alcides posts".) Again, Tamburlaine's projected circumnavigation of the globe "from East unto the furthest West . . . along the oriental sea . . . about the Indian continent,/ Even from Persepolis to Mexico / And thence unto the straits of Jubalter" (I: 3.3.246–56) chimes with Andronica's prophecy of the Renaissance discoveries and the oceanic empire of Charles V in *Orlando Furioso* (15.17–22).[11] In both cases, the circumnavigation of the globe (pointedly Anglified in Harington's translation of 1591) is visualised from an Eastern rather than a Western perspective—in reverse as it were.

Certainly, the mood of 1588 helps explain the presence of

The frontispiece to *Purchas His Pilgrimes* (London, 1624). By permission of the Folger Shakespeare Library.

A detail of Tamburlaine's head from the frontispiece to *Purchas His Pilgrimes* (London, 1624). By permission of the Folger Shakespeare Library.

geographic wish-dreaming in *Tamburlaine*. What explains Marlowe's decision to combine the imperial theme with the Tamerlane myth specifically? Why is his imperialist a barbarian—and such a barbarian—and the "Wrath of God" to boot? Stephen Greenblatt has suggestively juxtaposed the hyperbolic violence of Tamburlaine with prosaic instances from the voyagers, which shock us almost more by their tonal banality.[12] Similar shocks of recognition can be had by comparing Tamburlaine with adventurers, such as Raleigh (who calmly reports massacring a Spanish garrison in Trinidad immediately after professing peace to them),[13] or a conquistador, such as Bernardo de Vargas Machua, whose portrait is underlined by his own workaday version of the imperial motto:

> *Ala espada y el compas*
> *Mas y mas y mas y mas*
> (By the sword and the compass
> More and more and more and more).[14]

"More" here can easily suggest "more bodies" as well as more space: the genocidal labours of conquest (an Indian head set into the frame of Bernardo's portrait rather suggests a souvenir). Another compelling analogy with Marlowe's Scythian can be found in the feral conquistador, Lope De Aguirre: a self-styled "Wrath of God," who bloodily usurped command of an expedition in search of *El Dorado*, navigated the Amazon from its source in the Andes to the Atlantic, formally and ritually "denaturalized" himself from Spain (compare Tamburlaine's ritual denaturalization and reconsecration, I: 1.2), proclaimed himself founder of a new world order founded solely on merit, and formally "possessed" himself of extravagantly Marlovian geographic vistas: Tierra Firme, Chile, and all South America from the Isthmus of Panama to the Strait of Magellan, "where ... the wide North Sea ... joins that other Sea which men call Southern".[15] (Werner Herzog—whose Aguirre boasts that he "will produce history as others produce plays"—seems to have read the Aguirre story through Marlowe.)[16] If Aguirre suggests Tamburlaine in his more rabid moments, Cortes—whom Charles V was careful to remove from Mexico once the conquest was secure—might suggest his dangerous independence of all save *fortuna* and *virtú*. Again, Cortes and Aguirre (like Tamburlaine) were "self-made" men, who did not stoop to conquer but audaciously seized their opportunities and then took (or were seen to take) them to Kurtzian lengths.

While attractive, however, such a reading is overstrained. It probably supposes too much about Marlowe's knowledge of Iberian voyage literature and even more about his ability—or desire—to formulate a post-Conradian (perhaps postcolonial) critique. More importantly, it fails to tell us anything about the weird disjunctiveness *within* Marlowe's conjunction of Renaissance imperialism and the Tamerlane myth. In one sense, this is a failure of aesthetic form: specifically, a disjunction between his emotionally primitive overinvestment in the hero and his tentative (but distinct) suggestions of moral judgement, rejection, and downfall—a kind of aesthetic dyslexia. In tragic terms, there is no true *agon* (encounter of opposing principles) no "recognition" and no *catharsis* (resolution). The plays are neither ironic nor disenchanted in the Euripidean sense. We simply don't know what to make of them. They are "uncanny." Stephen Greenblatt has some inspired things to say about this: Tamburlaine is predictable within his unpredictability, living out a "repetition compulsion" within his very inversions of the ordained; the spaces he conquers are meaninglessly abstract; his time is that of the clock, mechanically removed from the natural and ritual order, never (despite the promises) growing to "sweet fruition" (I: 2.7.29).[17]

Here, I want to suggest that the plays are uncanny in the Freudian sense of a dream-image, which is at once intimately known and yet estranged, hence horrific. The Tamerlane of European legend was already uncanny in this way: a *traum*-figure cathecting a waking trauma. Whetstone, Perondinus, and other retailers of the legend seem stupefied by Tamerlane. They never quite know whether to praise him for his military prowess (superior to that of any ancient commander), be grateful to him for defeating a contemporary other (the Turk), reverence him as the living sign of God's displeasure, or shudder at his appalling ferocity. "Normal" moral judgments are suspended in a kind of dazed admiration. We can speculate that this is precisely what attracted Marlowe to the legend. "Tamerlane" already invited the headier Marlovian *admiratio*, which creates both a literally more "attractive" figure (not just through the relatively conventional love interest of Zenocrate, but also through the virtually erotic responses of other male characters, and a figure whose imperialistic urge is itself eroticised in sixteenth-century European terms. The drive to eroticise and idealise, however, actually increases Tamburlaine's uncanniness for the reason that Marlowe shows little corresponding interest in sanitizing him, in downplaying his ferocity. This contradiction—not itself a feature of the generic *Vita*—begets the "aesthetic dyslexia" mentioned earler.

What, then, lies behind the heightened uncanniness of Marlowe's treatment of the Tamerlane myth? The answer may have less to do with Tamerlane as such than with Marlowe's unconscious dread of what most infatuates and enthralls him—of what is the very stuff of Tamburlaine's charisma as distinct from Tamerlane's mere grimness—the Renaissance wish-dream of global empire. Insofar as the global dream can be represented by the imperial devices mentioned earlier, its principle lies in repudiating ancient prohibitions on imperial ambition and ancient ignorance of the extent of the earth. Thus, *Plus Ultre* rejects Hercules's dictum—at once a moral axiom and a statement of geographic fact—*Non Plus Ultra*. Ariosto's praise of circumnavigators who "passe about the earth as doth the Sunne" inverts an ancient commonplace on the futility of boundless ambition (men have no business following the sun).[18] The "prophetic" status accorded in the Renaissance to the myth of "the golden fleece"—

in which the fleece might represent Eastern spices or American treasure and the navigational achievement of Tiphys (helmsman of the Argo) anticipates that of Columbus—inverts the Euripidean and Senecan readings of the myth, which are respectively about the folly of miscegenation and the *hubris* of voyaging. As a classicist, Marlowe would have recognized these inversions, especially as the imperial devices require only a crude knowledge of their classical origins to function as "devices." As an accomplished classicist, he should, indeed, have recognized rather more about their classical derivation; namely, its illegitimacy, and superficiality. All the above mentioned inversions tend to be partial—crude misprision rather than artful *emblème renversé*. In this cultural negotiation, the ancient discourse is money laundered. Specifically, its wider moral dimension is shortchanged, fiddled, concealed, and repressed. This process is most apparent in the second and third of my examples. In Cicero, "follow the sun" is about ambition, not geography. The true force of these utterances cannot be negated by the geographic feats of a Magellan or a Drake (as Ben Jonson appears to appreciate by his wholehearted return to them in his *Catiline*).[19] More tellingly, imperialist rehearsals of the golden fleece legend in the Renaissance tend to omit Medea and, consequently, idealize Jason, while the ubiquitously cited "prophecy" of Columbus in the second chorus of Seneca's *Medea* is read quite against the grain of what is a ringing denunciation of the evils of voyaging.[20] To generalize, the Renaissance inversions tend to miss the essentially moral character of the ancient "boundary" discourse, in which the crossing of geographic bounds (*termini, fines*) is prohibited more out of a concern for the integrity of social bonds (*mores, modum*) than a concern for geography as such.[21] Though the ancients generally felt themselves to be dealing with simple geographic fact, this discourse tends to operate as a moralized geography in which the primary role of the geography is to vehiculate the moral.

If for no other reason, Marlowe's familiarity with the ancient boundary discourse may be assumed on the basis of his translation of the first book of Lucan's *Pharsalia*. Here, as in all the key classical narratives of boundary violation, two complementary movements can be discerned: an outward, aggressive and exploratory movement, on the one hand, and an intimately invasive or entropic movement on the other (usually represented as a violation of the mother, the family, the self, or the homeland). Thus, Caesar is imagined as turning from his conquests at the northernmost extremities of the earth to invade Rome with all the ferocity of the wilderness he has been sent to subdue. Before crossing the Rubicon (geographic boundary between Cisalpine Gaul and Italy) he dreams of incestuously violating the maternal body of Vesta—the ultimate barbarism. A follower vows simultaneously to follow him to the ends of the earth and plunge his sword into the most forfended sites: "brother's bowels, / Or father's throat, or women's groaning womb" (377–78).[22] Marlowe, of course, likes this kind of talk and alludes admiringly to Lucan's Caesar in *Tamburlaine*. One may indeed speculate that he was attracted to the first book of the *Pharsalia* for the same reason that he was attracted to the Tamerlane story. It too is uncanny and disjunctive. Nostalgic as he was for the vanished republic, Lucan's main intention had been to attack Julian imperialism—opposing Cato's conservatism (*servare modum finemque tenere*, or "follow the rules and hold the line") to Caesar's unprincipled overreaching—yet his addiction to hyperbole and his tendency to revel in scenes of apocalyptic carnage are strikingly at odds with his purpose.[23] Marlowe, it can be said, reads Lucan not for the moral but for the style and the vision, which then become the style and vision of Tamburlaine. The point to be made of this is that Marlowe was actually too aware of—perhaps too deeply struck by—the entropism of Lucan's Caesar and other ancient exemplars of overreaching to easily disinvest himself of it, even when prompted by the Renaissance imperial vision of "more and more and more and more," and by his own hypertrophic libido. This brings us back to the uncanniness of Tamburlaine, in which the dream of ceaseless conquest is indulged to the full, yet haunted by the ancient *traum* of incest, pollutiveness, entropy, systems-collapse, and identity loss.

I now want to unpack three symbolic and/or ritual structures in which the imperial-geographic motive exemplified by the "blind geographers" speech (with which we began) is "haunted" by phantoms of the ancient moral-geographic conscience. The first of these is found in the reiterated stage spectacle of the triumph, an inherited ancient ritual of geographic mastery. This, I want to suggest, has a paradoxically double (or divided) aspect. For the most part, Tamburlaine's triumphs are a megalomanic perversion of the Roman institution that is their source. At certain key moments, however, Tamburlaine is pathetically dutiful in his observance of triumphal emblems, with the result that the demonstration of spatial mastery strikes us as hollow—because it is so transparently ritualistic. The second structure I wish to unpack is that of the "banquet," another ancient ritual expression of spatial mastery. Here, I want to focus mainly on the banquet scene in the first play (4.4) which, I suggest, is at once a celebration of spatial mastery and a half-expressed and half-suppressed condemnation of it. The third structure in which I am interested is confined to the second of the two plays. This might be described as a mutation of what is a key symbolic feature of the first play: the juxtaposition of Tamburlaine's imagery of dynamic expansiveness with an imagery of entropy and decay associated with enemies, such as Cosroe and Bajazeth. Here, I argue that the juxtaposition "mutates" in the second play to the degree that both its poles—expansive and entropic—converge on Tamburlaine alone. What prompts my use of the metaphor of haunting in the case of all three of these textual formations is the curious way they are divided against themselves. It is as if Marlowe were at cross-purposes in both plays without acknowledging or coming to terms with it, possibly without even knowing it. All three structures are like palimpsests in which a shadowy outline—a painter's cartoon perhaps—is discerned behind the finished textual product while being at utter variance with it. I don't believe that we have an adequate model for conceptualizing this state of affairs. The division is partly aesthetic (it is never properly declared or resolved at the textual level). It is possibly editorial. (Is Marlowe conflating earlier versions of the play-text at the level of printing, suppressing an older and more conventionally moral version of the play from his printed version just as—we are told—he had repressed certain "fond and frivolous jestures" of the staged version?)[24] Again, the division may be between conscious and unconscious textual structures. Alternatively, we might apply the textual/subtextual paradigm of Stanislavski (though this is plainly inadequate as it stands for the reason that all plays have subtexts). However we account for it—and we will probably never do better than speculate—the division is there, and is perhaps better described than explained.

1. Triumph

The *Tamburlaine* plays are full of triumphs. Tamburlaine enters in triumph with captured or dying, or ritually abased enemies. His armies "progress" through countries and traverse continents, their even pace never delayed beyond a set period of three days (with each day marked by an emblematic color, first white, then red, and finally black). So irresistible is he that warfare becomes identical with conquest, which immediately seeks a triumphal form. (Interestingly, this sequence seems a mirror-inversion of the "progress" of eighteenth-century Moroccan rulers described by Clifford Geertz. In this loose nomadic confederation, the "progress" ritual was unstable—often resulting in a real, as distinct from "ritual", assertion of territorial power that verged on warfare.)[25]

Compared to the Roman triumph, however, the Marlovian triumph is unsettlingly dysfunctional. Whereas the former—not unlike the Renaissance entry pageant and/or masque of "exotic" character—typically acted as a ritual means of domesticating geographic otherness (or barbarism)—of bringing it safely within the orbit of the eternal city, offering it to the tutelary gods, disarming it, subordinating it, and assimilating it—Tamburlaine's triumphs represent the victory of barbarism over civilization. Marlowe's common themes are the destruction of cities and empires, the rape of women, the slaughter of families, the humiliation of magistrates, and the mockery of gods. The perversion extends beyond the ritual end to the ritual form. In the ancient triumph, captive kings were at least distinct from the exotic beasts that often accompanied them. In Marlowe's triumphs, however, captives (especially kings) are invariably treated as animals; thus, kings of various nationality are harnessed to his chariot, and Bajazeth is drawn about in a cage—not by horses—but by "two Moors" (I: 4.2.). Tamburlaine's triumphs are without spatial or temporal limit:

> There, while he lives, shall Bajazeth be kept,
> And, where I go, be thus in triumph drawn;
> . . . .
> These Moors, that drew him from Bithynia
> To fair Damascus, where we now remain,
> Shall lead him with us whereso'er we go.
> (I: 4.3.85–100)

Similarly, they are without civic focus or religious piety; their sole purpose is to feed the hero's megalomania and sadism:

> And see, my lord, a sight of strange import,—
> Emperors and kings lie breathless at my feet. . . .
> All sights of power to grace my victory.
> (I: 5.2.407–9)

This contrasts sharply with the Roman practice of ensuring that the *Triumphator* was accompanied by a minder whose sole task was to whisper in his ear: "Remember you are only a man."[26]

The most auspicious account of a triumph in ancient literature is perhaps Virgil's accounts of Augustus Caesar's victory over Cleopatra in the "shield of Aeneas" passage of the *Aeneid*:

> ... Caesar has entered the walls of Rome in triumphal procession,
> Three times a victor; he dedicates now a thanks-offering immortal
> To Italy's gods—three hundred great shrines all over the city.
> Caesar, enthroned in the marble-white temple of dazzling Apollo,
> Inspects the gifts from the nations and hangs them up on the splendid
> Portals: subjected tribes pass by in a long procession—
> A diversity of tongues, of national dress and equipment.
> Here Vulcan had represented the Nomads, the flowing robes of
> Africans, here the Leleges, Carians, Gelonian bowmen;
> Some carry a picture of Euphrates, its waters pacified;
> There go the Morini, furthest of men, the branching Rhine,
> The Scythians untamed, the Araxes fretting about its bridge.[27]
> (8.714–28)

While Virgil is not so officious as to remind Caesar he is only a man, this literary triumph, nevertheless, retains its religious and civic character. Marlowe's habit of enumerating diverse nations (often in terms of appropriate ethnic, geographic, and climatic detail) is possibly indebted to what Virgil plainly saw as the ultimate triumph, yet Marlowe was perhaps even more impressed by the accounts in Plutarch and Lucan of Julius Caesar's triumph over Pompey's sons, by reason of its patent *hubris*.[28] In triumphing over other Romans, Caesar virtually turned the ritual on its head because the essence of the triumph was Rome's subordination of barbarism. (Antony too was a Roman, but Virgil had taken care to represent him as a renegade and the leader of barbarians, not Romans).

The dysfunctionality of the Marlovian triumph is strikingly apparent in Marlowe's use of the river imagery. In the Roman triumph, images of rivers—the Euphrates and the Araxes in the previous passage—would be borne along in the procession in conventional representation of the now subordinated geographic entity. In literary examples, these very images—like other manifestations of defeated otherness (animate or inanimate, animal or human) in real triumphs—implicitly acknowledge the Roman yoke. Thus, in Virgil, the Euphrates is "pacified" and the Araxes "frets." In this respect, the triumph is remarkable in the Roman literary tradition for the reason that river-violation as such is generally depicted as impious and transgressive. Thus, in the second chrous of Seneca's *Medea*, the mischief of racial intermingling is conveyed in an image of distant peoples promiscuously drinking from rivers of other distant peoples ("Indians quench their / thirst in cold Araxes,/ Persians now drink from / Elbe and Rhine routinely").[29] Herodotus describes how the host of Xerxes drank a river dry.[30] In Juvenal, the Syrian river Orontes pollutes the Tiber (with "its babble and brawl, its dissonant harps and timbrels").[31] In Lucan, Alexander is described as fouling the waters of distant rivers with the gore of local inhabitants:

> ... he drove his sword home
> in the breast of every nation; he defiled distant
> rivers, the Euphrates and the Ganges, with Persian
> and Indian blood; he was a pestilence to earth, a
> thunderbolt that struck all people alike, a comet of
> disaster to mankind.
>
> (10.33–38 ff.)

As we shall see in greater detail shortly, this last form of river violation is most suggestive of Tamburlaine (particularly in the second play). There, lakes "swell above the banks" with carcasses of the slain, fish "fleet aloft and gasp for air" (II: 5.2.202–7). Because "the hosts of Xerxes" which drank "the mighty Parthian Araris ... was but a handful to that we will have," the armies of Tamburlaine will drain bigger rivers still (I: 2.3.13–17). Finally, grotesque Disneyland rivers ("as vast and deep as Euphrates or Nile" I: 5.2.378) will be created out of blood.

Paradoxically, however, while Marlowe systematically perverts the ancient triumphal idiom in his efforts to supercharge it, his triumphs are haunted by a peculiar pathos. Zenocrate's funeral is also a kind of triumph. The scene begins with a procession "four attendants bearing the hearse of Zenocrate, and the drums sounding a doleful march; the town burning" II: 3.2) and then takes the form of a ritual "placing" of monuments. First, a pillar is set with an inscription in Arabian, Hebrew, and Greek: "This town, being burnt by Tamburlaine the Great / Forbids the world to build it up again" (II: 3.2.17–18). Then, a streamer is hung: "wrought with the Persian and Egyptian arms, / To signify she was a princess born, / And wife unto the monarch of the East" (II: 3.2.19–22). Then, a tablet is laid registering "her virtues and perfections" (II: 3.2.23–4) and finally Zenocrate's picture.

Strangely, Zenocrate's funeral is actually more evocative of ancient triumphal ritual than Tamburlaine's victories are. It has the military, geographic, and ethnographic features of the victories, but it also has a Roman emphasis on place, the need to memorialize and monumental emblems. Far from expressing spatial mastery, however, this ritual starkly advertizes the futility, the evanescence, of Tamburlaine's conquests. As Zenocrate's death has emptied them of meaning, so Tamburlaine's attempts to inscribe her permanently into the landscape appear merely emblematic, ritualistic, and utterly static compared with the cosmographic dynamism of the "blind geographers" speech, which privileges its particular place (Damascus) in an aggressively counter-ritualistic fashion.

2. Banquet

Banquets—mostly imaginary and linked to an imagery of feeding, "glutting", and drinking—are also ubiquitous in the *Tamburlaine* plays. Their "spatial" character is derived from the conscious use of a classical trope in which the ends of the earth are ransacked for the sake of gluttony.[32] Thus, in the second play, Tamburlaine promises to feast his troops before fighting Orcanes:

> Then will we triumph, banquet and carouse;
> Cooks shall have pensions to provide us cates,
> And glut us with the dainties of the world;
> Lachryma Christi and Calabrian wines
> Shall common soldiers drink in quaffing bowls,
> Ay, liquid gold, when we have conquer'd him,
> Mingled with coral and with orient pearl.
> (II: 1.6.91–98)

The similarity of this passage to the most famous use of the trope in Renaissance England—the gluttonous fantasies of Sir Epicure Mammon in *The Alchemist* (2.2.69–87)—is clear.[33] Again, as with Mammon, the imagery of geographic extremity and ethnic variety is linked to other forms of consumption besides eating:

> A hundred Tartars shall attend on thee,
> Mounted on steeds swifter than Pegasus;
> Thy garments shall be made of Median silk,
> Enchas'd with precious jewels of mine own
> . . . .

> With milk-white harts upon an ivory sled
> Thou shalt be drawn amidst the frozen pools,
> And scale the icy mountains' lofty tops,
> . . . .
> My martial prizes, with five hundred men,
> Won on the fifty-headed Volga's waves,
> Shall we all offer to Zenocrate . . .
>
> (I: 1.2.93–104)

In both types of passage, however, the consumption is conspicuous precisely because of the exotic/geographic element, and consumption is, therefore, an expression of spatial mastery.

This banquet theme finds full dramatic expression in the "banquet scene" of the first play (I: 4.4)—immediate dramatic context of the "blind geographers" speech and of Tamburlaine's refusal to spare Damascus. Ostensibly, Zenocrate's plea signals a change of mood. Her only words up to this point in the scene have indicated gleeful approval of the brutal humiliation of Bajazeth and Zabina ("My lord, how can you suffer these / Outrageous curses by these slaves of yours?" I: 4.4.26–7), yet an actor of the part would have good reason to suspect that her subtext is less than gleeful. Zenocrate has been very quiet (perhaps unresponsive) amid the party atmosphere generated by Bajazeth's tantrums in response to Tramburlaine's attempts to force-feed him. She has, moreover, already made an appeal for Damascus and already been refused in the first "cage" scene (I: 4.2.123–24). However it is paced, then, it is clear that Zenocrate emotionally withdraws from her group during the banquet scene. The simple explanation for this is that she is downcast at the impending ruin of Damascus. I want to argue, however, that something more complex is involved: something within the deep emblematic structure of the banquet scene itself. This is because we need an explanation not just for the grief that Zenocrate shows at the rape of Damascus two scenes later (I: 5.2), but also for her grief at the suicides of Bajazeth and Zabina, whose degradation is the focus of the banquet scene.

A close reading of the banquet scene reveals the presence of other tropes besides the geographic. Superficially, the scene proposes a contrast between the success ("sweet fruition" I: 2.7.29) of Tamburlaine's party and the abjection of Bajazeth and Zabina. When Zenocrate withdraws, of course, this contrast is potentially subverted (depending on how pointedly the withdrawal is signaled in the acting), yet subversion is already present in a less visible emblematic theme that I will call "the death of the family." This is clearly signaled at the beginning of the scene by a pair of classical allusions. In the first, Tamburlaine promises his lieutenants "to make Damascus" spoils as rich to you / As was to Jason Colchos' golden fleece" (I: 4.4.8–9). In the second, Zabina prays:

> ... may this banquet prove as ominous
> As Progne's to th'adulterous Thracian king
> That fed upon the substance of his child!
>
> (I: 4.4.23–25)

Superficially, these allusions are counterpointed; the "golden fleece" being auspicious and the cannibal banquet ominous. Indirectly, however, they are linked in that each refers to a master myth of the death of the family. In both these myths, an outraged wife revenges herself on her husband by butchering her offspring (striking out "through her own bowels" as George Sandys was to put it in his commentary on the Procne story in Ovid).[34] This is obvious in the case of the "Progne" myth, rather less so in the case of the "golden fleece" myth. In its ancient mythic form, the prize of the "fleece" image is clearly implicated in a death of the family theme—in Jason's marital betrayal and Medea's murder of children (and of her own brother, earlier in the story). In its Renaissance imperial form (in which the "fleece" represents the wealth of the Indies), the image is auspicious. Medea and her bad karma are suppressed.[35] Superficially, then, Tamburlaine's use of the "golden fleece" image to inspire his troops might be no more controversial than were propagandistic eulogies in praise of the conquistadors or Rubens's use of "fleece" imagery in a pageant of 1616 to promote Antwerp's role as an entrepot of the Indies trade.[36]

This, however, would be to read the allusions independently of their dramatic and theatrical context. The opening stage direction tells us that Tamburlaine enters "all in scarlet," ordering his attendants to "hang our bloody colours by Damascus, / Reflexing hues of blood upon their heads, / while they walk quivering on their city walls, / Half-dead for fear before they feel my wrath" (I: 4.4.1–4). In terms of staging, then, the banquet is framed by red flags, hosted by a figure dressed in red, and held for the express purpose of terrifying the Damascans (regardless of whether they are visible on an upper stage area). What I want to suggest here is that Marlowe's use of the color red is focused and subtle, as well as emphatic. The force of Zabina's reference to the cannibal banquet is far more resonant if directed at a figure clad "all in scarlet" and more focused if we remember that this figure is the only figure so accoutred.[37] My point is that these powerful theatrical signals ensure that the topos of the cannibal banquet acts to frame our response to the numerous cannibal images (mostly jokes) that follow. Tamburlaine offers Bajazeth food to eat. Bajazeth replies he would rather feed on Tamburlaine's "blood-raw heart" (I: 4.4.12), The response is "thine own is easier to come by; pluck out that, and twill serve thee and thy wife" (13–14). At this point the theater of cruelty becomes positively sadistic: "Sirrah, why fall you not to? Are you so / daintily brought up, you cannot eat your own flesh?" (36–37). Tamburlaine bullies Bajazeth into eating a morsel from the point of his sword. A stage direction tells us that Bajazeth "takes the food and stamps upon it" (between 42 and 43). Tamburlaine tells him to pick it up and eat it, or "I will make thee slice the brawn of thy arms into carbonadoes and eat them" (46–47). A henchman then suggests that Zabina herself would last Bajazeth for a whole month. Tamburlaine offers his dagger to the henchman, saying "Despatch her while she is fat" (I: 4.4.51–52).[38] In such a context, Tamburlaine's blood-red costume must clearly identify him with the ill-omen of the cannibal banquet. Here, then, is a powerful theatrical rationale for Zenocrate's withdrawal. As the banquet and its tasteless interlude are staged for the benefit of the citizens of Damascus, Zenocrate (herself Damascan) would make the connection between the cannibal banquet and the fate of her country, her city, and her family. Her withdrawal from the fun helps establish that connection for the audience.

In the long concluding scene of the play (I: 5.2) dealing with the rape of Damascus, the structural antagonism between Zenocrate and Tamburlaine, and the corresponding structural homologies between Zenocrate and Tamburlaine's victims are more clearly stated. Aside from Bajazeth and Capolin, the victims are female and a "disshevell'd" Zenocrate bewails them all. Herself a virgin, Zenocrate is identified with "the sun-bright troop / Of heavenly virgins and unspotted maids" (I: 5.2.263–64) who are slaughtered offstage after their futile embassy. The likelihood here that the virgins were dressed in white rather suggests that Zenocrate is too (in contrast to Tamburlaine's black). She is consistently described in images of purity and is likely to have been in white during the banquet scene, also in contrast to Tamburlaine's red (white is the token of mercy). She enters in act 5 scene 2 to describe a scene of carnage:

> Damascus' walls dy'd with Egyptian blood,
> Thy father's subjects and thy countrymen;
> The streets strow'd with dissever'd joints of men,
> And wounded bodies gasping yet for life;
> But most accurs'd, to see the sun-bright troop
> Of heavenly virgins and unspotted maids . . .
> Guiltlessly endure a cruel death.
>
> (I: 5.2.259–68)

Whether or not some attempt was made to stage this spectacle—perhaps by hanging "our bloody colours" from the tiring-house wall—is unclear. It is plausible in view of Techelles's earlier claim to have "hoisted up their slaughtered carcasses" on "Damascus' walls" (I: 5.2.67–68) and in view of how Zenocrate signals her awareness of the bodies of Bajazeth and Zabina: "But see, another bloody spectacle" (278). As these two bodies are physically present onstage, the rape of Damascus may have literally been *the other* "bloody spectacle." In any case, subtle and surprising emblematic linkages are made. While Zenocrate is plainly linked to the virgins (by sentiment, sex, nationality, and probably costume), her "dishevell'd" (76) hair (a theatrical sign of female madness, as well as grief) links her to Zabina who goes mad for grief by switching from verse into babbling prose (247–57)—another stage convention for female madness. The babble, indeed, hints at further links between the two women that echo the banquet scene. In her ravings, Zabina seems to imagine herself as a mother feeding an infant who is simultaneously threatened ("Go to my child; away, away, away! Ah, save that infant! Save him!" 250–51) yet cannibalistic ("Bring milk and fire, and my blood I bring him again" 247–48). Images of Damascus ("The sun was down—streamers white, red, black" 252–53) intrude into her recollection of Bajazeth's humiliation in the banquet scene ("Here, here, here!—Fling the meat in his face" 253–54). What seems to have happened is that the joke in the banquet scene about Bajazeth eating his wife has turned into this grotesque parody of nurturance, which has then fused with the imagery of infant murder imagined by the virgins.[39] Zabina appears to address all this to another woman ("I, even I, speak to her" 252). Who else could this be if not Zenocrate? It seems likely, then, that Zabina "calls" to Zenocrate before being "answered" by Zenocrate's lament over her.

As a ritual of geographic mastery, then, the banquet scene is schizophrenic. Tamburlaine treats the whole world as consumable—witness the "course . . . of crowns" (stage direction, I: 4.4.113–14) in which crowns are offered to his followers literally on a plate. The very abundance of his feasting requires the self-consumption of Bajazeth and Zabina—and finally of Zenocrate, too, who is offered abundance at the price of home, family, city, and the female principle she represents. Having constructed this powerful emblematic design, however, Marlowe fails to carry it through.[40] The play has been building towards a tragic ending of the Greek or Senecan type (an implosion into incestuous/cannibalistic carnage) but is sidetracked into a banal, tragi-comic conclusion as if in bad imitation of a Restoration epic of love, war, and contrived divisions of loyalty.

3. Entropy

The final instance in which the imperial-geographic motive is "haunted" by a moralizing phantom of the ancient geography, takes the form of a breakdown of the key juxtaposition between the signature imagery of cosmographic expansiveness and the imagery of entropy or systems-collapse. The most memorable early statement of this juxtaposition would have to be the stage tableau centered on Tamburlaine's vaunts over the defeated Cosroe:

> Nature, that fram'd us of the four elements
> Warring within our breasts for regiment,
> Doth teach us all to have aspiring minds.
> Our souls, whose faculties can comprehend
> The wondrous architecture of the world,
> And measure every wandering planet's course,
> Still climbing after knowledge infinite,
> And always moving as the restless spheres,
> Wills us to wear ourselves and never rest,
> Until we reach the ripest fruit of all,
> That perfect bliss and sole felicity,
> The sweet fruition of an earthly crown.
>
> (I: 2.7.18-29)

Dynamic and purposive verbs—"warring," "aspiring," "comprehend," "measure," "climbing," "always moving"—activate, control, and subtend a space which is at once Lucretian and cosmic.

They make that space what it is: a cartographized extension of the human body, an expression of Faustian will. Its architectural and tensile qualities are thrown into sharp relief by the complementary words of Cosroe:

> My bloodless body waxeth chill and cold,
> And with my blood my life slides through my wound;
> My soul begins to take her flight to hell,
> And summons all my senses to depart.
> The heat and moisture, which did feed each other,
> For want of nourishment to feed them both,
> Is dry and cold: and now doth ghastly Death
> With greedy talents gripe my bleeding heart,
> And like a harpy tires on my life.
>
> [I: 2.7.42–50]

Death here is imagined as entropy, a comprehensive systems-collapse, in which the body—now defined by images of denial (cold, hunger, thirst, dessication)—incontinently transfers its appetites to the elements which had once constituted it.

Bajazeth, too, is defined against Tamburlaine in terms of this expansion/entropy juxtaposition but in another way. The Turk is entropic not merely in defeat and decline, but at the very height of his power:

> As many circumcised Turks we have,
> And warlike bands of Christians renied
> As hath the ocean or the Terrene sea
> Small drops of water when the moon begins
> To join in one her semicircle horns.
>
> (I: 3.1.8–12)

The body here is subject to a double "en-tropy" or encirclement: both by the act of circumcision and by the "semicircled" moon. Paradoxically, this is a form of power which is acted upon—called forth by an external power (the moon)—rather than acting. More paradoxically, Bajazeth's power is entropic in the patently distempered sense of the dying Cosroe:

> The spring is hinder'd by your smothering host,
> For neither rain can fall upon the earth,
> Nor sun reflex his virtuous beams thereon,
> The ground is mantled with such multitudes . . . .
> And all the trees are blasted with our breaths.
>
> (I: 3.1.50–53)

Bajazeth's only strategy for opposing Tamburlaine's spatial mastery—his drive to commensurate, to "comprehend"—is to exhaust it with matter, to extend it beyond its pre-Cartesian powers of "extension":

> I have of Turks, Arabians, Moors, and Jews,
> Enough to cover all Bithynia.
> Let thousands die: their slaughter'd carcasses
> Shall serve for walls and bulwarks to the rest;
> And as the heads of Hydra, so my power,
> Subdu'd shall stand as mighty as before . . . .
> Thou know'st not, foolish-hardy Tamburlaine,
> What tis to meet me in the open field,
> That leave no ground for thee to march upon.
> (I: 3.3.136–47)

It is a futile hope. Perhaps because for Marlowe space is humanly extensive and Ortelian (inherently mappable, commensurable, and comprehensible), Bajazeth's strategy of befuddling Tamburlaine with sheer matter is bound to fail. It is as impossible for Tamburlaine to be overwhelmed by numbers as it is for numbers to be unnumberable or space to be unextendable.

This is why it is all the more odd that the Tamburlaine of the sequel play, in turn, should exemplify yet another version of "entropy," behaving more like the slave of space than its master. One oddity of the later play is that, while more obviously indebted to Ortelius than the earlier play—in the sense that Ortelius is the direct source of a major itinerary, the probable model of the world map introduced in the final scene, and the probable authority for the later play's more confident use of geographical detail and cartographic terminology—the later play remains relatively lacking in cosmographically *inspired* passages, such as the "blind geographers" speech: passages in which geography "sings" and cartography functions ontologically as a master-image of human perceiving, desiring, willing, and acting (as in the "aspiring minds" speech). By my count, the later play offers only two of the symphonic geographic compositions with which the earlier play abounds: Orcanes's description of the extent of Tamburlaine's forces ("He brings a world of people to the field . . . ," 1.1.67–76) and Tamburlaine's own use of the world map (5.3.146–61) to evoke the "world of ground" in the west and south that yet remain to be conquered. Other geographic passages—vistas, lists and itineraries—tend to be either perfunctory (for all their extra detail) or positively grotesque and oppressive in a way that is reminiscent of Bajazeth. In this second type of passage, mapscapes (cartographer's-eye-views of land, seas, and rivers) function as vast receptacles for the slain, thus, landscapes are smothered or obliterated—seas and/or rivers are clogged, "glutted," discolored, and polluted—with bodies and bloody effluent:

> Our Turkey blades shall glide through all their throats
> And make this champion mead a bloody fen;
> Danubius' stream, that runs to Trebizon,
> Shall carry, wrapt within his scarlet waves . . .
> The slaughtered bodies of these Christians;
> The Terrene main, wherein Danubius falls,
> Shall by this battle be the bloody sea . . .
>
> (II: 1.2.31–38)

Not all such visions are Tamburlaine's (this is Orcanes, the Turkish commander who takes over from Bajazeth), but Tamburlaine is their prime exponent and focus. Thus, Tamburlaine is "the monster that hath drunk a sea of blood / And yet gapes still for more to quench his thirst" (5.2.13–14). At the destruction of Babylon:

> Thousands of men, drown'd in Asphaltis' lake,
> Have made the water swell above the banks,
> And fishes, fed by human carcasses,
> Amaz'd swim up and down upon the waves,
> As when they swallow assafoetida,
> Which makes them fleet aloft and gasp for air.
>
> (II: 5.2.202–7)

Where the first *Tamburlaine* play is energized by geography, it is as if the second play is exhausted by it. Geography here is no longer the measure of human aspiration. It is merely a grist to the mill of appetite, a consumable, or rather a site of conspicuous consumption, a rubbish tip, a bespattered and clogged vomitorium. Tamburlaine's geographic impulse here is less beholding to Ortelius than to Lucan, specifically to Lucan's portrait of Alexander who is condemned for defiling distant rivers with the bodies of distant peoples. (It is perhaps significant that Marlowe has Tamburlaine die unhistorically like Alexander of a distemper near the city of Babylon.)

For all this, of course, Marlowe has it both ways by ending the second play with one of the most tub-thumpingly "New Geographic" moments of either play when a world map is introduced to the stage for the dual purpose of the hero elaborating his triumphal itinerary and exhorting his auditors to conquer the "world of ground" that remains. Strangely, for a fourteenth century Mongol or a classical "Scythian" (and he is both), Tamburlaine appears totally uninterested in Europe and indicates instead the New World in the west and the unknown continent in the southeast (specifically a region corresponding the northwest coast of what is now called Australia, which Ortelius labels as the regions of "Beach," "Lucach," and "Maletur"). At the start of the second play, Tamburlaine's domains are described as extending to:

> ... the oriental plage
> Of India, where ranging Landtchidol
> Beats on the regions with his boisterous blows,
> That never seaman yet discovered.
>
> (II: 1.2.68–71)

Now, doubtless inspired by Marco Polo's accounts of the fabulous wealth of these regions, he exhorts his followers to cross the Timor Sea (*Mare Landtchidol* in Ortelius), invade "Beach," and conquer the Antipodes ("the people underneath our feet"). What would the audience have made of this division of geographic motive? Some, I suggest, swaggered off like Walter Raleigh "to seek new worlds, for golde, for prayse, for glory".[41] Others may have trudged away as from a theater of God's judgments. Those thoughtful enough to grasp the utter contradiction were perhaps as puzzled as I am today. One thing is clear. Having stated the contradiction, Marlowe was unable to resolve it.

Conclusion

Unpacking these three textual structures—triumph, banquet, and entropy—does not really give us a single key (whether psychoanalytic, cultural-theoretical, textual-compositional, or Stanislavskian) to the enigma of these plays. What it may do, however, is problematize our own cultural and scholarly practices in respect of Elizabethan classic drama: whether that is the "traditional" reflex of "privileging" the aesthetic object over other cultural objects, or the cultural-materialist orthodoxy which makes a point of "de-privileging" the classic relative to other cultural objects. On the one hand, it is perhaps true that we expect too much of such works if we want them to explore deep cultural contradictions and yet achieve aesthetic unity. On the other hand, I (at least) would want to suggest that a play like *Tamburlaine* manifests—with a power unsurpassed by any other Renaissance geographic or "poetic geographic" text—the schizophrenia of the Renaissance geographic imagination caught (as it is) between the amoralism of the New Geography and the moralism of the old. Marlowe sets forth this contradiction without perhaps even stopping to reflect that it is a contradiction, but that is already much.

If my proposition in respect of the geographic agonism of these plays is accepted, then the question —Why did Marlowe fuse the Renaissance wish-dream of global empire with the Timur myth? —answers itself. Tamburlaine was a truly inspired choice for such a vision. He is a conquistador like Aguirre and Cortes, a voyager like Drake and Raleigh, and yet is a "pestilence to mankind" like Lucan's Caesar and his Alexander, but he is no mere amalgam. In Tamburlaine, Marlowe created a figure unforeseen in either the ancient or the Renaissance imagination of empire. For the Renaissance—rather as for Conrad's Marlowe at the beginning of his story—the empire builder was a bringer of light into darkness. For the ancients, the empire builder was also an enlightener of darkness, so long as he had the moral fiber to stop before being swallowed by it. In Tamburlaine, Marlowe gives us a figure whose imperialism is actually coeval with his darkness and otherness. This isn't some sort of cryptopostcolonial critique. It is dreamwork, but—to apply a Renaissance distinction—it is more *somnium* than *phantasma*.

Notes

1. Eugene Waith, *The Herculean Hero in Marlowe, Chapman. Shakespeare and Dryden* (London: Chatto & Windus, 1962), 63.

2. *Christopher Marlowe: The Complete Plays*, ed. J. B. Steane (Harmondsworth: Penguin, 1969).

3. See the discussion of this and other 'incestuous-invader' myths in my *Shakespeare and the Geography of Difference*, (Cambridge: Cambridge University Press 1994), 195, note 67.

4. Cited in J. S. Cunningham, ed., *Tamburlaine The Great* (Manchester: Manchester University Press, 1981), 323. Further references to Whetstone are in the text.

5. Ibid, 323.

6. Ibid, 323.

7. Eric Voehelin Macchiavelli's Prince: Background and Formation, *Review of Politics* 13 (1951): 142–68.

8. *The English Myrror* has two parts, a history of the world and an idealized contemporary portrait of England. The former proves that world history has been blighted by a succession of "empires," unnatural political entities which are the expression of "envy." The worst of these are the Turkish and Spanish empires. Tamberlaine is thus celebrated both for smashing one of the two biggest threats to proper Christian order and for serving as a kind of charm against the other.

9. Frances Yates, *Astraea: The Imperia Theme In The Sixteenth Century* (Harmondsworth: Penguin, 1977); Roy Strong, *Glorinana: The Portraits of Queen Elizabeth I* (Thames & Hudson, 1987).

10. For the English appropriation of Spanish Imperialism, see Strong's discussion of the Armada portrait in *Gloriana*. For "the proudest device," see Earl Rosenthal, '*Plus Ultre, Non Plus Ultra*, And the Columnar Device Of The Emperor Charles V,' *JWCI* 34 (1971): 204–28.

11. The citation is from, *Orlando Furioso, Part One*, Barbara Reynolds (Harmondsworth: Penguin, 1975).

12. See Stephen Greenblatt "Marlowe and the Will to Absolute Play" in *Renaissance Self Fashioning: From More to Shakespeare* (Chicago: University of Chicago Press, 1980), 193–221.

13. See V. S. Naipaul, *The Loss of El Dorado: A History* (London: Andre Deutsch, 1969). Naipaul describes Raleigh's attack on St. Joseph as follows: "At sunrise English and Indians came to St. Joseph. 'After a fewe shot' the fight was over. They entered the plaza, the English crying, 'Paz! Paz! Peace!' They found about a dozen Spaniards and killed all except Berrio and the old man who had been Berrio's deputy . . . The Spanish women who had been left behind had run to the forest. Ralegh said of these Spaniards that they 'had escaped killing'. He aimed at the extermination of the Spaniards in this part of the world, and he wrote of the massacre as he felt a man of action should. 'To leve a garrison in my backe interested in the same enterprize, who also dayly expected supplies out of Spaine, I should have savoured very much of the asse.'" (46)

14. Portrait and motto are cited facing the title page in J. H. Elliot, *The Old World and the New, 1492–1650* (Cambridge: Cambridge University Press, 1970). *Mas alla* is the Spanish vernacular version of *Plus Ultre*, perhaps suggesting that in Spain, the cultural reach of the new global imperialism extended well beyond the sphere of royal propaganda.

15. Stephen Minta, *Aguirre: The Re-creation of a Sixteenth Century Journey Across South America* (New York: Henry Holt & Co, 1994), 180. See also, *The Expedition Of Pedro De Ursua & Lope De Aguirre In Search Of El Dorado And Omagua In 1560–1*, Translated from Fray Pedro Simon's "Sixth Historical Notice Of The Conquest Of Tierra Fierme" by William Bollaert, introduction by Clements R. Markham, (New York: Burt Franklin, 1971).

16. Werner Herzog, *Aguirre: der Zorn Gottes* (New York: New York Video, 1991).

17. See note 9.

18. For the citation from Ariosto, see, *Orlando Furioso In English Heroical Verse By Sr. John Harington* (London: G. Miller, 1634), Book 15 verse 14, line 7. For an ancient commonplace on the futility of following the sun, see "What inhabitants of those distant lands of the rising or setting sun . . . will ever hear

your name", in "Scipio's Dream" in *De Republica De Legibus*, ed. C. W. Keyes, The Loeb Classical Library, (Cambridge, Mass: Harvard University Press; London: Heinemann, 1948) 260–83, 276. See also, "Follow the sun and find not their ambition" (4.2.219) in Ben Jonson's rendering of Cicero's first oration against Catiline, *Catiline*, eds. W. F. Bolton and Jane F. Gardner (Great Britain: Edward Arnold, 1972). Jonson's play abounds in ancient terminal imagery read sympathetically with (not antipathetically against) its native grain.

19. See note 18.
20. See the discussion of voyaging and the Medea myth in *Shakespeare and the Geography Of Difference*, 19–25, 134–37.
21. See the discussion of *termini* in *Shakespeare and the Geography Of Difference*, 7–12.
22. Ibid, 22–23. See also "Lucan's First Book Translated Line for Line", in *Christopher Marlowe: The Complete Poems and Translations*, ed. Stephen Orgel (Harmondsworth: Penguin, 1971).
23. The latin citation is from Lucan, *Pharsalia* 2.381, in ed. And trans. J. D. Duff, Lucan: *The Civil War, Books I-X*, The Loeb Classical Library, (New York: Putnam; London: Heinemann, 1928), 84–85.
24. Cited in, J. S. Cunningham, ed., *Tamburlaine The Great: Christopher Marlowe* (Manchester: Manchester University Press; Baltimore: Johns Hopkins University Press, 1981), 21.
25. See, "Centers, Kings, and Charisma: Reflections on the Symbolics of Power", in *Local Knowledge: Further Essays in Interpretive Anthropology*, ed. Clifford Geertz (New York: Basic Books, 1983), 121–46.
26. For this detail, as for an excellent discussion of triumphs generally, I am indebted to Anthony Miller's essay in this volume, "Domains of Victory: Staging and Contesting the Roman Triumph in Renaissance England."
27. *The Eclogues, Georgics And Aeneid Of Virgil*, trans. C. Day Lewis (London: Oxford University Press, 1966), 375.
28. See T. J. B. Spencer, ed., *Shakespeare's Plutarch* (Harmondsworth: Penguin 1964), 76. Sir Thomas North's translation of the relevant passage reads as follows:

> This was the last war that Caesar made. But the Triumph he made into Rome for the same did as much offend the Romans, and more, than anything that ever he had done before; because he had not overcome captains that were strangers, nor barbarous kings, but had destroyed the sons of the noblest man in Rome, whome fortune had overthrown.

In the opening scene of *Julius Caesar*, Shakespeare collapses this occasion into the earlier victory over Pompey.

29. Michael Townshend, trans., *Medea*, in *Classical Tragedy Greek And Roman*, ed. Robert Corrigan (New York: Applause, 1990), 512. See the discussion of this passage in *Shakespeare and the Geography of Difference*, 24.
30. Source: Herodotus 7.21 "While they were encamped here, all the rivers I have mentioned supplied enough water for their needs except the Echeidorus, which was drunk dry". Cunningham cites the passage in his edition of *Tamburlaine*, p. 588 (see note 3).
31. From the third satire, see *The Satires of Juvenal*, trans. Rolfe Humphries (Bloomington: Indiana University press, 1958), 35.
32. See Juvenal's eleventh satire, in *Satires*, 135–43; especially p. 140. See also Sallust's description of the vicious character of Catiline and his cocon-

spirators, "to gratify their palates they scoured land and sea," in J. C. Rolfe, ed., *Sallust*, The Loeb Classical Library (London: Heinemann; Cambridge, Harvard University Press, 1960), 23.

33. Ian Donaldson, ed., *Ben Jonson* (Oxford and New York: Oxford University Press, 1985).

34. George Sandys, *Ovid's Metamorphoses Englished* (Oxford, 1632) New York & London: Garland, 1976), 228.

35. See the discussion of this myth in *Shakespeare and the Geography Of Difference*, 16–19.

36. See, Elizabeth McGrath, "Rubens's Arch of the Mint," *JWCI*, 37 (1974): 191-217.

37. The opening stage direction of the banquet scene reads: "A banquet set out; and to it come Tamburlaine all in scarlet, Zenocrate, Theridamas, Techelles, Usumcasane, Bajazeth drawn in his cage, Zabina, and others." (I: 4.4).

38. These two jokes at the expense of Zabina's size are not the first. Zenocrate has already taunted her as a "Disdainful Turkess, and unreverend boss" (I: 3.3.168), where "boss" has the sense of "fat woman." The suggestion is certainly in line with Bajazeth's praise of Zabina as mother of three super-Herculean sons, with "limbs more large ... than all the brats y-sprung from Typhon's loins" (I: 3.3.103–9). Zabina may well have been played by a mature male with a strong hint of drag.

39. Some eighteen lines of the First Virgin's speech (I: 5.2.17–36) focus on the death of the family: husbands, wives, the elderly, and infants:

> O, then, for these, and such as we ourselves,
> For us, for infants, and for all our bloods,
> That never nourish'd thought against thy rule,
> Pity ...
>
> (I: 5.3.33–35).

40. This is in spite of the fact that the death of the family theme takes up where it left off in the second play, where we witness the death of Olympia's family and, arguably, of Tamburlaine's own.

41. See, "The 11th: and last booke of the Ocean to Scinthia," in *A Choice Of Sir Walter Ralegh's Verse*, ed. Robert Nye (London: Faber, 1972), 43. In addition to "Virginia," Elizabethan imperialists had ambitions in the southern continent. E. G. R. Taylor ("John Dee and the map of North-East Asia," *Imago Mundi*, 12 [1955; reprints 1970]: 103–6) describes no less than two abortive Elizabethan attempts—one by Pet and Jackman, the other by the promoters of Drake's circumnavigation—to explore the southern continent. Both emanated from John Dee, who was himself inspired by Marco Polo's account of fabulous wealth in these regions.

The "Strange" Geographies of *Cymbeline*
GLENN CLARK

AT his accession to the English throne, and for years afterward, King James was determined to unify Scotland and England. This interest frequently led him to commentary on the status and meaning of the borders and border dwellers of his kingdoms, as in his "Proclamation for the Uniting of England and Scotland" issued in May, 1603. James expressed his desire "utterlie to extinguishe as well the name as substance of the bordouris, I mean the difference between them and other parts of the kingdome. For doing quhairof it is necessarie that all querrellis amoungst thaim be reconcyled and all straingenes between the nations quyte removed."[1] For James here, the existence of borders and border dwellers results from the "straingenes" between his kingdoms; to do away with such borders, he felt that the English and Scottish should be reconciled in "ane universall unanimitie of hartis."[2] Despite, or perhaps in recognition of, the difference that his Scottish accent and spelling imply, James finds no value in the perpetuation of "straingenes" or borders between the English and the Scots. Some supporters of the Union echoed their sovereign on this score, arguing in religiously oriented, pro-Union pamphlets that division inherently contradicted "the unity of God himself, of His universe, and of God with man before the Fall and after the Redemption."[3] The king seemed willing to push the valorization of human unity relatively far; he instituted a policy of tolerance toward Catholics and promised to maintain peace.[4]

If James was interested in the geopolitical restructuring of Britain and in altering the mentalities of its inhabitants, Shakespeare's *Cymbeline* dissects and dramatically highlights the relation between geography and a subjective sense of identity and of otherness. From one point of view, the play shares the king's goal of denaturalizing the mutually self-perpetuating rhetorics of hostile alterity and geopolitical artifice. Shakespeare accomplishes this task by emphasizing rhetorics of mapping, measuring, and profitability as the motive forces of geographies and cosmographies that estrange the British from their land and create rivalries over the land. To these forces of alienation, Shakespeare contrasts a rhetoric of geopolitical naturalism in which social order is determined by a natural spatial order. This rhetoric resonates with its associated ritual and pastoral ethos, and promises a new social foundation in which rivalries are ultimately neutralized. I will argue that every reference to a spatial order in the play is rhetorical, and that each geographical rhetoric is explicitly available to appropriation by alternative polemics. Shakespeare will imply that the theater itself can reinforce the king's preferred construction of British geography, thus giving it an advantage over pernicious alternative interests.

Under the impetus of new historicism, several critics have recently (re)discovered a Stuart, and even a pro-Union, *Cymbeline*.[5] No one has explicitly documented the spatial and geographical poetics that accompany this Jacobean polemic. Shakespeare's Renaissance geography responds to the shifting nature of spatial relationships, both cosmographical and geographical, by representing two different kinds of spatial practice. By spatial practice, I mean both the ways in which characters allow their understanding of the physical space surrounding them to constitute their sociopolitical identities: and at the same time, the way in which their actions and beliefs are designed to construct the spaces around them. One form of spatial practice is characterized by the application of a rhetoric of commensurability and commodification to lands and people, and the subsequent mobilization of their value by means of maps and discourses of both exploration and colonialism. A very different practice is rooted in a conservative perception of divinely ordered space that is deeply meaningful on its own and which produces a faith in the paradigmatic qualities of the natural landscape.

At this point I should distinguish my terms from those of Henri Lefebvre, who uses the idea of spatial practice in an ambiguous sense. He is concerned with the production of social space as an embodiment of relations of production and power, and as a substitute for an immaterial notion of ideology.[6] His spatial practice, in one sense, simultaneously presupposes and "secretes" social space. It is composed of spatial "competence" and "performance" which perpetuate spatial organization, yet it is discernible within and by the subject only as a perception or a bodily *habitus*. As such, spatial practice is distinguished from *representations of space*, which are the dominant and regulating conceptions that describe a particular aspect or mode of social space, such as maps of transportation networks or the Ptolemaic universe. It is also distinguished from *representational spaces,* which are the traces of earlier forms of social space remaining within a new form of social space. Such traces are experienced intuitively or emotionally by subjects and are "lived" reminders of an antiquated structure of spatial meaning. Spatial practice, however, is also the sum of each of these spatial experiences, as each contributes to the historical generation of space. This larger definition of spatial practice is close to my own use of the phrase. Shakespeare's characters deploy certain conceptualizations of space, as well as memories of a formerly meaningful cosmic space, to fashion their own competing geographies. These geographies are social spaces, in Lefebvre's sense, in that they organize the social relations of power and production in society. The spatial practices of Shakespeare's characters, however, are not quite the same as Lefebvre's spatial practice in that these subjects are at least partly conscious of the social spaces or geographies they wish to create. Their manipulations aim at the production of particular modes of space whose significance is quite clear to the characters. In *Cymbeline,* shifts in the dominant spatial practice depend more on rhetorical forcefulness than on the social relations of production.

King James intended his pro-Union rhetoric to generate a spatial practice in which British geopolitics would be determined by the natural, unmodified landscape of the island. In his speech to Parliament in March 1603, James articulates his sense of the way the borders of political geography do not correspond at present to a border-free natural geography:

> Yea, hath hee not made us all in one Iland, compassed with one Sea, and of itselfe by nature so indivisible, as almost those that were borderers themselves on the late Borders, cannot distinguish, nor know, or discerne their owne limits? These two countries being separated neither by sea, nor great River, Mountaine, nor other strength of nature, but only by little small Brookes, or demolished little walls, so as rather they were divided in apprehension, then in effect ... whereby it is now become like a litle World within it selfe, being intrenched and fortified round about with a naturall, and yet admirable strong pond or ditch, whereby all the former feares of this Nation are now quite cut off ... [7]

James argues that divisions are made on the British landscape by subjective "apprehension" and not in response to objective geographical "effect." Through "apprehension" he implies what he will make explicit in his "Proclamation" two months later: that is, that the animosity and fear perpetuated between the Scots and English are responsible for the perception of a meaningful border between the two countries, rather than any aspect of the natural landscape.[8] The "Brookes" along which the borders run are too small to be meaningful, and the ancient Roman walls no longer carry significance. In fact, James believes that the borderers themselves have no objective, land-based way of determining the limits of their country. The king emphasizes the natural integrity of the island as a whole, suggesting that the only meaningful border is the "admirable strong pond" provided by God.[9] Britons, James implies, should live in harmony with their natural surroundings and learn how to interact with each other in response to the natural signs of the landscape in which they live. For James, natural space should determine the political space in which social relations occur. The political must flow out of the natural and not vice versa.

The king's allies also frequently assert an analogical relationship between natural and political geography. Francis Bacon, as a member of the King's Learned Council, expresses his disdain for the separation of the two countries in an essay written explicitly for James: "And yet there be no mountains nor races of hills, there be no seas nor great rivers, there is no diversity of tongue or language, that hath invited or provoked this ancient separation or divorce."[10] Sir William Cornwallis similarly chooses the metaphor of a geographical marriage to support the king's position:

> Against outward invasions nature hath cared; we are environed by the sea, and so knit together both by religion, language, disposition, and whatever else can take away difference; as unlesse we breed disagreeing affections, we are indissoluble. Neither can we nourish these unlesse we will contradict Heaven it selfe. Behold how we are joyned, God, Nature, & Time have brought us together, and so miraculously if we observe the revolutions of time, as me thinketh the very words after the consummation of a marriage, shall not be unproperly used, *Those whom God hath joyned together, let no man seperate.*[11]

The association of marriage and geography within the discourse of this perpetually delayed Union leads us—and perhaps led Shakespeare—to the delayed gratifications of *Cymbeline's* romance.

Until *Cymbeline's* plotlines converge on Wales, the play cannot represent the king's privileged spatial practice. There is simply no natural, nonsocialized geography with which to start. Geographies seem always already dangerously subjective. This may have much to do with the fact that during the sixteenth and early-seventeenth centuries, the "new geography"—a product of the rediscovery of Ptolemy's *Geographia* in 1400 and information collected by Renaissance explorers and voyagers—was bringing all things worldly into the realm of European representation.[12] The human agency behind geographical representation suggests the possibility of flux within those representations. Consequently, the threat that another people might take control of the process of representing made the politics of exploration a site of deep anxiety. Throughout Shakespeare, voyaging brings danger; specifically, the threat of the infusion of the other, the exotic, within the homeland. John Gillies has recently written that "the voyager controls the boundaries. It is the voyager's function to manage the exotic . . . Shakespeare's voyagers tend to form deeply compromising relationships with the exotic, to the point where the two types sometimes merge in the same character.[13] Posthumus, having arrived in the Italy demonized in sixteenth-century English xenophobic discourse, does not manage "the exotic" successfully. The result is that he is drawn into a complex spatial practice by a master of rhetoric whose intent is not simply to penetrate Britain's boundaries, but to draw rivalries and "apprehensive" social relations out of an unnatural geography invested with an economic significance which actually increases the impact of boundary violations.

Though Posthumus journeys to Rome under compulsion, Shakespeare endows him with a biography that associates him with the freedom of movement and expanding horizons characteristic of the Renaissance. The group awaiting Posthumus's arrival with Philario in Rome discusses his travels in a way that emphasizes his progression from place to place. Iachimo has "seen him in Britain," while the Frenchman has "seen him in France."[14] Posthumus himself excuses his previous quarrel with a Frenchman by saying that he was then "a young traveller." More importantly, however, this scene allows the destabilization—though not the neutralization—of strangeness and even exoticism. The appellation "stranger" shifts unpredictably between Posthumus and Iachimo. Philario first asks his companions to treat Posthumus well as "a stranger of his quality." Then, as the "country ladies" debate takes on energy and Iachimo begins to manipulate the somewhat over-proud Posthumus, the wily Italian calls himself a "strange fowl." Posthumus eagerly takes up this hint and notes that Iachimo "makes no stranger of me: we are familiar at first" (1.4.101–2).

Iachimo is not innocently trying to make Posthumus feel "at home." He is cannily unsettling the differences between himself and the Briton in order to perpetuate the "commercial" venture that has already begun, in hopes of reaping a very large profit. In the sources of *Cymbeline*—Boccaccio's ninth novella of the Second Day in the *Decameron* and its German variant, *Frederyke of Jennen*—the "country mistresses" debate takes place among merchants meeting at an inn. This scene's irrepressible commercial language—seemingly odd among a group of courtiers—is one of Shakespeare's thematic expansions on his sources. Iachimo requires Posthumus to feel "at home" in order to facilitate his willingness to deal, to give the Italian an opportunity to profit. Iachimo initiates the transaction by comparing Imogen to Posthumus's diamond, a comparison Posthumus at first accepts by acknowledging that he "rated her" as he does his diamond. When Iachimo pushes his metaphor farther, however, claiming that Imogen must be "outpriz'd by a trifle," Posthumus immediately denies the grounds of comparison. Of the diamond ring and Imogen, he states that "the one may be sold or given. . . . the other is not a thing for sale, and only the gift of the gods" (1.4.84–85). Posthumus does not precisely reject the objectification of Imogen—she may be a "thing" to him, but not a thing for sale—but he does deny her commodification. He relies here on a notion of the gift unsullied by commercial exchange or profit.

Gift language held a particular valence in the early seventeenth century. Patricia Fumerton has argued that it was deployed to compensate for developing international trading ventures, such as the immensely complex schemes of the East India Company, which were beginning to alert the English to the porousness of English economic and cultural boundaries. Strangers contacted overseas were perceived to be the source of a frightening "strangeness" in England. Complex overseas transactions even began to be viewed as a potential source of internalized barbarity, particularly after the massacre at Hormuz in 1623, which generated fears of English cannibalism. The apparent incorporation of barbarity, Fumerton argues, was accompanied by fears of the disincorporation or dismemberment of the polity. To counteract this fear, or at least to clear himself of any taint of profiting from barbaric trade practices, King James disingenuously continued to emphasize an Elizabethan view of England as a gift-culture united by reciprocal obligations. Such a culture was promoted in court entertainments. Fumerton notes that James deployed gift-discourse in negotiations surrounding the Great Contract in 1610, in which he argued that he ought to receive the deal he desired as a gift owed to him by his subjects. In return, of course, he would continue to reciprocate with his royal blessings.[15] Posthumus uses the gift-notion like the king does, as a hedge against threatening commercialism. The gift-ethos constitutes a serious threat to Iachimo's plan, and he cannot let Posthumus define Imogen as a gift. As Marcel Mauss has shown, the gift obligates the beneficiary to reciprocation. Gift-reciprocation, unlike a strictly economic market, does not demand immediate exchange or the negotiation of the values of the gifts themselves.[16] Thus, Imogen cannot be given an exchange value, and she is owed, in essence, only to the gods. Iachimo, however, wants to use Imogen as a commodity. It should be no surprise that Posthumus's attempt to retrieve a gift-culture by claiming that Imogen is a "gift of the gods" is overwhelmed by Iachimo's manipulations.

The Italian needs to shift Posthumus's thoughts back toward exchange and profit, and he does so by associating alterity with profit. Iachimo has already interpellated both himself and Posthumus as "strange" subjects, and he now fashions an argument in which profit is an inevitable consequence of the meeting of strangers. Iachimo tells his rival that "You may wear [Imogen] in title yours; but you know strange fowl light upon neighboring ponds. Your ring may be stol'n too . . . A cunning thief, or a (that way) accomplish'd courtier, would hazard the winning both of first and last" (1.4.88–93). The "neighboring pond" alludes to both the "country" and the "mistress" at stake in the debate. Iachimo threatens to cross both the geographic borders of Britain and the physical borders of Imogen's body. Imogen will soon confirm her poetic identification with Britain when she fears that Posthumus has been unfaithful and thus "Has forgot Britain" (1.6.113). Though he may be "strange fowl" on Posthumus's British pond, Iachimo admits, their ponds are neighboring, and Iachimo can alight on one or the other. Part of Iachimo's challenge lies in his implication that "strangers" are not separated by insurmountable distances, and Posthumus should not put so much stock in the security of borders between near neighbors. Having already lost a secure sense of just who is "strange" here in Rome, Posthumus is in a position to doubt just how "strange" Iachimo might seem in Britain. If exchanges occur across identity boundaries, then they can occur across geographic boundaries, too.

Across such borders, Iachimo suggests, many risky but potentially profitable transactions do occur. As such, they entail the possibility of profit. Thus, a border-crosser may "hazard the winning" and take a risk in order to gain a profit. If Iachimo loses what he has "hazarded," as his gambling metaphor suggests, the gain must default to Posthumus. Iachimo tells Posthumus what the Jacobeans already knew, that the meetings of English with foreigners are both risky and profitable. He simply emphasizes that such meetings, and the risk and profit that they entail for one side or the other, are unavoidable. This complex tactic proves successful, for Posthumus promptly recommodifies Imogen in his comment "I fear not my ring." In its genital symbolism, the "ring" metonymically represents Imogen, so the figure implicates her in the exchange value of the ring itself. Thus, Posthumus implicitly agrees that his wife, like the ring, can be risked for profit. Iachimo can now move easily onto his explicit challenge, in which he wagers his estate against Posthumus's ring that he can "get ground" of Imogen. After Posthumus accepts the wager, Iachimo seals it with something of a commercial insult:

> You are a friend, and therein the wiser. If you buy ladies flesh at a million a dram, you cannot preserve it from tainting. But I see you have some religion in you, that you fear. (1.4.134–37)

Here, perhaps, is a trace of the deep fear of barbarous contagion—perhaps even cannibalism—supposedly carried by English traders that Fumerton describes. Iachimo represents Imogen not merely as a commodity, but as meat that may not be stored or transported without the danger of becoming tainted. Posthumus's sense of his wife as a gift has entirely faded. He may be shocked by this crude description of her commodification, yet he is not frightened away. He too has something to gain in this deal, and he immediately asks that "covenants" be drawn between himself and Iachimo. Twice more, in fact, the two men ask that "articles" or a covenant be drawn up (1.4.143, 156, 164). Iachimo's "voyage" will certainly be as much "venture" as adventure.

In this scene, the dangers of voyaging and traveling have combined with the anxieties surrounding commercialism and commodification in the early modern period. Both present threats to boundaries, but both offer the possibility of profit. Jean-Christophe Agnew has argued that during the early-modern period in England, the topographically situated rituals that regulated commercial markets during previous centuries slowly evaporated, leaving an increasingly placeless market in which the liquidity of commodities came to characterize a self-hood that was no longer "authorized within the traditional religious, familial or class frame."[17] All places became potential markets, not just the church porch or market cross, and market-goers were beginning to treat each other instrumentally, as indifferent sites of risk and profit. Consequently, Agnew argues, the emotional boundaries necessary between competing individuals found their counterparts in emotional boundaries or thresholds within the self. Multiple selves, a kind of internal otherness, developed in response to the pervasiveness of objectifying market relations.[18] The debate between Iachimo and Posthumus sketches this process, but only Iachimo knows how to employ it. He rhetorically diminishes the boundaries between Italy and Britain, and subjects both himself and his rival to a powerful discourse of strangeness. This allows him to induct Posthumus into a competition for the commodified Imogen with surprising ease and simultaneously prepares the Italian for his own self-estrangement in Britain.

When Iachimo reaches Britain, he comes as a surrogate for Posthumus. He is, if only initially, "a noble gentleman of Rome" (1.6.10). Such a designation gives him the opportunity he needs to make his "voyage," while his self-affirmation as "the Parthian," who remains dangerous even while on the defensive, gives him the confidence to carry on with a difficult task.[19] Iachimo's self-fashioning by means of this manipulation of space and time indicates the ease with which he can improvise the spatial or geographical components of subjectivity. For Iachimo, spatial structures are rhetorical tools, rather than descriptions of objective phenomena. His "use" of space, though as we will see inconsistent, is always in his interest.

When Iachimo meets Imogen, he immediately tries to make Posthumus seem mad and incomprehensible in order to appropriate his intimacy with the British princess. He begins a subtle slander of Posthumus by invoking the spatial distinctions of hierarchical cosmology:

> What, are men mad? Hath nature given them eyes
> To see this vaulted arch and the rich crop
> Of sea and land, which can distinguish 'twixt
> The fiery orbs above and the twinn'd stones
> Upon the number'd beach, and can we not

> Partition make with spectacles so precious
> 'Twixt fair and foul?
>
> 1.6.31–38

Iachimo's cosmological metaphors imply what he would like to be seen to believe. He leads up to the thoroughly dishonest hint that Posthumus has known "two ... shes" by emphasizing the orthodox and absolute hierarchical distinction between the celestial and the terrestrial. In the metaphor, the celestial "fiery orbs above" represent Imogen, while the terrestrial stones on the beach suggest the base Roman woman with whom Posthumus is supposedly involved. Imogen is to believe that Posthumus's defiance of this cosmic hierarchy is madness, because such a distinction is plainly available to natural sight. Iachimo also seems to call upon another kind of distinction, allegedly ignored by Posthumus even though it too is naturally obvious. This is the difference between commonness and incommensurable uniqueness. The "Roman woman" is one of many, basely commensurable or "number'd" stones on a beach, while Imogen is a unique and ungraspable heavenly object. Iachimo will later call her "the radiant sun." Posthumus, according to Iachimo, ignores the astonishingly obvious fact that Imogen is one of a kind, and instead surfeits on a woman who is interchangeable with any number of others. In effect, Iachimo describes the celestial as unique and unapproachable, while the terrestrial is common and available to human measurement. At this point, we may doubt that Iachimo is sincerely invested in this idea, because it is so obviously in his interest. We cannot yet be certain of the degree to which he conceives of orthodox cosmology as a source of useful rhetoric rather than an objectively accurate description of the universe.

Iachimo's description of the orthodox structure of the cosmos, redolent as it is with moral consequence, should prohibit the spatial practice in which he promptly engages, but it does not. The contradiction between Iachimo's implied belief and his practice indicates his rhetorical appropriation of a seemingly inflexible ideology. His specular violation of Imogen and her bedchamber represents a disturbing tactical reversal of the orthodox and morally laden spatial system he had earlier articulated. Its goal is proprietorship of Imogen's body:

> . . . . The flame o' th' taper
> Bows toward her, and would under-peep her lids,

> To see th' enclosed lights, now canopied
> Under these windows, white and azure-lac'd
> With Blue of heaven's own tinct. But my design!
> To note the chamber, I will write all down:
>   [Takes out his tables.]
> Such and such pictures; there the window; such
> Th' adornment of her bed; the arras, figures,
> Why, such and such; and the contents o' th' story.
> Ah, but some natural notes about her body,
> Above ten thousand meaner moveables
> Would testify, t'enrich mine inventory.
>
>   2.2.19–30

Iachimo finds the "natural notes" in the mole under Imogen's breast. The implicit comparison he invokes between the natural parts of Imogen's body and the artificial objects or "meaner moveables" in her room accentuates the purpose of his rhetoric. Imogen's body and the objects in her room are not absolutely different in Iachimo's view, but rather differ in the degree to which they can "enrich" this "inventory." Imogen's body is simply composed of more valuable "moveables" than her room. In order to make his gaze functional and profitable, he fragments and objectifies Imogen's body and bedchamber. As Nancy Vickers has pointed out, such fragmentation is "in some senses inherent to any descriptive project" but was not, for Shakespeare, a sufficient or even morally neutral form of description.[20] In several sonnets, particularly 21 and 106, poetic praise and blazoning are figured as either incapable of grasping true worthiness, or as a banal kind of selling or commodification. Patricia Parker has expanded the critique of the blazon to include the inventory found in the literatures of exploration and colonialism. Iachimo explicitly describes his memorialization as the taking of an "enriched" inventory. Parker argues that both blazon and inventory are rhetorical forms intended to invoke "natural plenitude, copia, wealth or increase." At the same time, this rhetoric functions to control and take possession of the objects catalogued by naming them and accounting for them.[21] Iachimo's rhetoric has several purposes. He hopes that his itemization of Imogen and her room will allow him to take possession of her just as taking inventory was often preliminary to the colonizing of a new land. At the same time, he hopes that the process of fragmentation will increase Imogen's value to him by making her, in a sense, copious. His "voyage" will be most profitable only if it gains as much "land" as possible.

In the process of making Imogen copious and value-laden, however, Iachimo maintains only partial consistency with his rhetoric of orthodox cosmology and value. Earlier, he had assigned value to the celestial and the singular or incommensurable. Here, he maintains the value of the celestial by emphasizing Imogen's heavenly-blue eyes in which the sparkling stars stand out. Imogen, however, is no longer singular and incommensurable. In fact, the process of fragmentation multiplies her and makes her available to valuation through the accounting procedure of the inventory. While earlier, to be "number'd" was to have little value, at this point a form of counting or numbering increases value. Iachimo must recognize the purpose of this enumeration. In his opening lines, he throws doubt on the value of such a method for measuring the true worth of a person, saying that when he first came across Posthumus's reputation, he "could then have looked on him without the help of admiration, though the catalogue of his endowments had been tabled by his side, and I to peruse him by items" (1.4.4–7). The catalogue would be intended not only to provide evidence for its subject's reputation but to enhance it, to lead to "admiration." Iachimo, however, is too conscious of the effect to be fooled. Moreover, now that Posthumus's "endowments" include Imogen herself, and since "he must be weigh'd rather by her value than his own," his reputation, Iachimo believes, is blown far out of proportion. Iachimo's resentful sense of the incongruity between Posthumus's real worth and his "worded" value when "weighed" with Imogen is perhaps the deepest motivation for his treachery. In response, he will make Posthumus's weighty "catalogue of endowments" his own.

I suspect that Iachimo momentarily suppresses the meaning of his inventory by deploying the celestial language. This language connotes the marvelous nature of Imogen's body, which elicits a reaction not unlike wonder on Iachimo's part. Stephen Greenblatt argues that wonder functions, at least in part, to distract a speaker's or reader's attention from an act of possession by suggesting the unpossessability of the marvelous object.[22] Shakespeare himself alerts us to the dubiousness of "heavenly" descriptions in sonnet 21, in which those "Who heaven itself for ornament doth use" are complicit in the "selling" of the praised woman. For Iachimo, as for the poor sonneteers lambasted by Shakespeare, "heavenly praise" is a hollow rhetoric but not uninterested rhetoric. Its goal is the fragmentation and commodification of the praised object, both of which enable the praiser to profit. Iachimo does not entirely distract himself from his act of commodification. For like a tragi-comic version of Marlowe's Augustinian Mephistopheles, he briefly acknowledges his evil actions when he says "hell is here" as he shuts himself back in his trunk.

The echo of *Dr. Faustus* at this point is telling. For if we may find some explanation for Faustus's tragedy in his recognition of the hollowness of received orthodoxies, we may think something similar about Iachimo. The Italian voyager uses the metaphor of cosmic categories contingently. He can easily take hold of the universal hierarchy and change it into functional rhetoric. Thus, he can state the cosmic theory as a moral orthodoxy in which the celestial is available to humans only through veneration, or he can "number" and appropriate the celestial, making it basely commensurable, while allowing a now clearly hollow veneration to obscure the act of possession. Such rhetoricization may be possible in part because of the contemporary deterioration of the conception of the hierarchical universe itself, and the substitution for it of a voidlike, homogenized space.[23] This may have drained spatial distinctions of their absolute moral value and transformed the ancient paradigm into a nostalgic rhetoric. At least one other writer perceived the social effect of decay within the traditional ordering of space. Within a very few years of Shakespeare's creation of *Cymbeline* (ca. 1609–10), John Donne wrote "An Anatomy of the World: The First Anniversary." In this poem, a lament for the death of an innocent girl, Donne expresses anxiety about the social effects of the "new philosophy." For Donne, the homogenization of space is best represented as a fracturing of spatial relationships:

> And new philosophy calls all in doubt,
> The element of fire is quite put out;
> The sun is lost, and th'earth, and no man's wit
> Can well direct him where to look for it.
> . . . .
> 'Tis all in pieces, all coherence gone;
> All just supply and all relation:
>
> (205–8, 213)[24]

The "new philosophy" leaves "all in pieces." Ancient relations, both social and spatial, have broken down. Donne's nostalgia for the ancient cosmic order captures his mourning for the innocence of the dead girl. As her innocence has departed with her body, so spatial innocence has also disappeared. The representation of space is no longer a given; homogenized space is a human construction:

> For of meridians, and parallels,
> Man hath weaved out a net, and this net thrown
> Upon the heavens, and now they are his own.
> Loth to go up the hill, or labour thus
> To go to heaven, we make heaven come to us.
>
> (278–82)

Humans put spatial representations to work for themselves, Donne argues. The very act of representing homogenized space is like throwing a maplike "net" of meridians and parallels over the heavens and then drawing that captured space down to earth. In Lefebvre's terms, Donne describes a moment in the production of space, specifically, the production of a new representation of space. Such production is "an activity which involves the economic and technical realms but which extends well beyond them, for these are also political products and strategic spaces."[25] For Lefebvre, maps are political and strategic because they represent and perpetuate social relations in space. As space fragments under competing strategies of representation, maps multiply. Cosmic homogenization in the sixteenth century was accompanied by massive European exploration of the new world and the rapid evolution and spread of maps. While Donne uses an image from the new geography—"meridians, and parallels"—to figure the human appropriation of the universe, Iachimo takes that human appropriation as a precedent for the creation of his own "new geography." This is not to say that geography and cosmography are identical. William Cunningham's *Cosmographicall Glasse* (1559), for example, carefully distinguishes cosmography, geography, and chorography. Rather, I suggest that for Iachimo both celestial and geographical space are available to enumeration and measurement—and become produced, social spaces—at the same time. Iachimo clearly uses a homogenized, morally-neutral geography strategically, and a map is incipient within that geography.

Iachimo's memorial inventory of Imogen's bedchamber and body does not take long to become a map. In this regard, the intertextual relation between Iachimo's soliloquy and *The Rape of Lucrece* is significant. Iachimo associates himself with Tarquin—claiming national identity with "Our Tarquin"—who looks on Lucrece's breasts as "ivory globes" and "maiden worlds unconquered."[26] Interestingly, Lucrece's beauty puts Tarquin in mind of maps, for he sees in her sleep "the map of death." Shakespeare thus associates some maps, at least, with the conquest or colonization of new lands. Patricia Parker argues that colonizers and explorers organize and control newly partitioned territory through maps. She claims that Renaissance maps represent part of the institution of private property, initially justified by the characterization of partition as an increase in wealth.[27] In the scene in Imogen's bedchamber, Iachimo fragments Imogen's body and room, and re-organizes the fragmented information in a form most profitable to him. In essence, Iachimo's map is a form of rhetorical copia in which fragments of information are juxtaposed to persuade Posthumus of the wealth he has lost.

Iachimo returns to Rome like a voyager clutching a new map. Posthumus greets him with a comment on the speed of his journey, saying that "winds of all the corners kiss'd your sails, / To make your vessel nimble" (2.4.28–29). The four winds were commonly represented iconographically on the frames of Renaissance maps and in older geographies and were explicitly associated with the "four corners of the world" and with wide-ranging world travel.[28] Posthumus's choice of metaphor is prophetic, because Iachimo has come with evidence of the boundaries he has crossed. He would, he says, "make a journey twice as far, t'enjoy / A second night of such sweet shortness which / Was mine in Britain" (2.4.43–45). Iachimo's Britain is well within the frame of his world map. Apparently, it entered that frame with even more ease than the Britain Posthumus had lauded only moments earlier, the Britain that bravely resisted the incursion of Julius Caesar.

The "imperial" power of Iachimo's map lies in its ability to appropriate and transfer copious amounts of valuable information from one location to another. William Cunningham blissfully describes the map's power to bring into "a warm & pleasaunt house . . . The diversitie of countries: natures of people, and innumerable forms of Beastes, Foules, Fishes, Trees, Frutes, Stremes, and Meatalles.[29] Iachimo is equally pleased with his map. Detailing the interior of the bedroom, he easily recounts the spatial fragments he had noted to himself while Imogen slept. He emphasizes the tapestry illustrating the meeting of Antony and Cleopatra, by which he cruelly flaunts his apparent success at crossing cultural boundaries and, like Antony, gaining the intensely charged love of a very erotic woman. The tapestry illustrates

> Proud Cleopatra, when she met her Roman,
> And Cydnus swell'd above the banks, or for
> The press of boats or pride. A piece of work
> So bravely done, so rich, that it did strive
> In workmanship and value, which I wonder'd
> Could be so rarely and exactly wrought,
> Since the true life on't was—
>
> 2.4.70–76

By insinuating that he has claimed the position of Antony, Iachimo suggests how completely he has replaced Posthumus. Both Antony and Cleopatra take risks in loving across cultural boundaries, and Iachimo implies that his own risk has payed off grandly. Nature, or culture, or both—Cydnus swelling with boats or pride—celebrate this love. Through the erotic power of his description, the "bravery" and "riches" of the tapestry seem to accrue to him. Iachimo is shielded from echoes of Antony's ultimate defeat by the very fact that he is about to prove just how much "territory" he has gained. If there are any connotations of loss of power and influence, they fall to Posthumus. Turning the knife in Posthumus's back even farther, he says of the tapestry that "the true life on it was," thus estranging the Briton, once again, from his own land.

Iachimo then offers the still-unconvinced Briton "More particulars." In a phrase confirming his production of a "mental map," he recalls that "The chimney / Is south the chamber" before giving further sensuous details about the room and Imogen's body (2.4.80–81). He has used the cardinal directions to sustain the memory of his visual perception of the room. A mental map, in John Gillies's succinct formulation of the idea, "represents a fusion of both 'conceptual' and 'visual' processes."[30] The conceptual aspect of Iachimo's mapping can be inferred from his choice of explicitly sensual objects to memorize and recall. That is, Iachimo's map is shaped by the fictional image of Imogen's adulterous sexuality that he wishes to represent to Posthumus. Iachimo's practice also accords with the view of J. B. Harley and David Woodward that "The significance of maps . . . Derives from the fact that people make them to tell other people about the places or space they have experienced."[31] Iachimo has visually experienced Imogen's place all too intimately and has described the "particulars" inside boundaries Posthumus thought inviolable. Earlier, when Iachimo had alluded to Imogen as "ladies flesh," he had refused to take back his words, claiming to be "master of [his] speeches" (1.4.140). Here, Iachimo is master of both speech and map, and both enable him to reap a profit.

In order to neutralize Iachimo's profit, Posthumus himself resorts to the kind of rhetoric in which maps are incipient. Harley and Woodward remind us that during the sixteenth and seventeenth centuries maps were used as historical and legal documents "to establish national precedents in discovery . . . or rival territorial claims."[32] At the very least, Posthumus imagines a map of some "particulars" of Britain that will allow him to rival Iachimo's claim to his sexual and geographic property. We hear little about the specifics of the letter Posthumus sends to Pisanio; it is not even clear whether it contains a map in the conventional sense or is simply a set of directions. The letters Pisanio and Imogen read in scenes 2 and 4 of act 3 suggest directions (or even a general command to set out for Milford Haven). Cloten, however, claims to have appropriated "mapp'd" information from Pisanio, and admits that the information provides "the very description of their meeting place" (4.1.2,24). According to the text, Pisanio gives Cloten only the letter he had received from Posthumus, though it is possible that we are meant to assume that Cloten receives more specific directions from Pisanio. This seems very unlikely, given Pisanio's hostility to Cloten. Whether or not a conventionally drawn map has passed from Posthumus to Pisanio to Cloten, it seems reasonable to assume that Posthumus begins with a mental map. While Posthumus, unlike Iachimo, does not design his map to gain profit from Imogen, he does intend it to neutralize Iachimo's appropriation of British "ground." This map originates in what King James would call an "apprehension"—an unfounded fear—of the fictional geography created by Iachimo. Posthumus hopes to reestablish his own control of Britain and its boundaries by effecting complete control over Imogen. Though he is not as alienated from "Britain" as he believes, his map takes its origin from his inaccurate impression nevertheless.

The geographies built out of maps and measures in the play are associated with social unrest and disorder. They do contribute to the deferral of reunification—and indirectly to the intensification of fulfillment—that structures romance as a genre. Despite the fact that Posthumus's map is romantically felicitous in that it begins the process leading to reunification, none of that positive energy is garnered by Posthumus in Italy. His motives are clearly misguided, and he can take no credit for the unintended consequences of his spatial practice. Shakespeare works hard to evoke a very different kind of geographical usage in "Cambria." This is not a geography built from human machinations and desires for profit, but one in which the landscape itself enables a faith in natural harmony and social unity. Indeed, spatial practice here depends on faith in the meaningfulness of the landscape. The rhetoric of that faith, in turn, energizes the landscape, making it seem fully and dramatically present as Belarius and the princes live vibrantly in the woods or as Imogen directs all her emotional energy into her search across the hills for Milford Haven. This dramatic presence accentuates the strong symbolic resonance of Wales, as does the presence of Milford, toward which the major plots and characters converge.[33] Milford Haven was dear to James as the landing-place of his great-grandfather Henry VII, who united England after the Wars of the Roses. James hoped to eliminate harmful internal divisions just as Henry had done. The Tudors, as well, had celebrated Wales as the country of their origin and as the birthplace of their mythical progenitor Arthur.[34] Wales was a virtually sacred geography.

In the play, Wales immediately promises unity. When Imogen first imagines traveling to Milford Haven, she seems to believe that Welsh geography will actively facilitate her reunion with Posthumus. She asks Pisanio to judge from his master's letter how far away Milford lies, but before he can answer, she claims that quantitative distances have no relevance in Wales:

> Read, and tell me
> How far 'tis thither. If one of mean affairs
> May plod it in a week, why may not I
> Glide thither in a day? Then, true Pisanio,
> Who long'st like me to see thy lord; who long'st
> . . . .
> . . . . say, and speak thick
> (Love's counsellor should fill the bores of hearing,
> To th' smothering of the sense), how far it is
> To this same blessed Milford. And by th' way
> Tell me how Wales was made so happy as
> T'inherit such a haven. But first of all,
> How we may steal from hence; and for the gap
> That we shall make in time, from our hence-going
> And our return, to excuse.
>
> 3.2.49–64

While Imogen twice asks the distance to Milford and then how many miles they can ride in a day, such measures do not capture the spirit of the geography she imagines before her. She sees herself "gliding" across the country in a mere day, as if the landscape itself will respond to her desire by shrinking. A trip through Wales will produce a "gap" in time not simply in the sense that she and Pisanio will be missed for some time at court, but such a gap will be in the fabric of time itself, as though the two travelers will leave conventionally measured time for a Welsh space-time harmonized with Imogen's desire. Milford becomes the focal point of a privileged mystical or sacred geography that cannot be mapped in the same way as other geographies. "Blessed Milford" dominates Imogen's mental map of Wales in a way similar to that in which Jerusalem dominated and gave meaning to medieval "T-O" maps.[35] Thus, Imogen is attracted to Milford "as though by magnetic force."[36] The Romans are pulled by the same force, for they, like Henry VII, land their troops at Milford. As Imogen says, "Accessible is none but Milford way" (3.2.82).

Imogen never finds Posthumus in Wales, of course, but even so the land still generates the mystical aura she imagines. This atmosphere originates in the rituals that seem to highlight the presence of the land itself. The land dictates the form of its celebratory ritual, as Belarius and the two princes practice it. Unlike Iachimo, Belarius brings to life his devotion to cosmic order:

> . . . . [Stoop,] boys, this gate
> Instructs you how t' adore the heavens, and bows you
> To a morning's holy office. The gates of monarchs
> Are arch'd so high that giants may jet through
> And keep their impious turbands on without
> Good morrow to the sun. Hail, thou fair heaven!
> We house i'th' rock, yet use thee not so hardly
> As prouder livers do.
>
> 3.3.2–9

Despite their "uncivilized" existence, Belarius says, they do not take the heavens for granted. Here, the cave itself suggests a ritual which reifies universal order.[37] It encourages the boys to see themselves in perspective, to avoid the *hubris* of impious "giants" and to cast their thoughts outside of themselves. Inscribed within ritual, cosmic order becomes far less manipulable than the homogeneous space upon which Iachimo's improvisations depend. For Belarius, this ritual maintains cosmic order and hierarchy, without demanding political submission to Cymbeline.[38]

Belarius's interpretation of the landscape does maintain a political register, however. In this prized landscape, Belarius presses the two changeling princes to engage in

> "our mountain sport: up to yond hill,
> Your legs are young; I'll tread these flats.
> Consider, when you above perceive me like a crow,
> That it is place which lessens and sets off,
> And you may then revolve what tales I have told you
> Of courts, of princes, of the tricks in war"
>
> (3.3.10–15)

Belarius tells his "sons" that their distance from the court affects their view of it. As the hills and flats create perspective, Belarius says, so the boys ought to understand that the court looks better than it is from their distant, naive viewpoint. Belarius uses the physical space of hills and flatland to perpetuate a contemplative, pastoral ethic, or perhaps more precisely a pastoral modulated by a didactic and venatorial georgic ethic.[39] James himself, who often required an escape from court via the hunt, would likely have been moved by this scene of young men being taught an appreciation for nature, as well as encouraged to hunt. While this is not quite the absolutist pastoral of the later-Stuart masque, which celebrates the king as god of nature, it is nevertheless ideologically sympathetic to the king.[40] Belarius asks the young men to be true to their geography, to care about it, and to let it influence their thoughts. Careful contemplation of the landscape and its perspectives justifies Belarius's authoritative knowledge of court and country. Though Belarius intends to perpetuate a division between the country and the court, his employment of a nature-based politics recalls King James. James had also asked his subjects to let their natural geography direct them to political obedience when he reminded them that God had made Britain "all in one Iland" and that he hoped to have "all straingenes between the nations quyte removed." For both James and Belarius, the political is prefigured in the natural landscape.

Notoriously, the queen and Cloten also base their politics on geographic fact. In order to persuade Cymbeline to forego the tribute demanded by Rome, they claim that the natural contours of the island suggest the appropriate political and military strategy. Both echo James's own pronouncements about the integrity of the British island and emphasize its natural defenses. "Britain's a world / By itself," Cloten asserts, recalling James's "litle

World within it selfe" from the 1603 speech to Parliament. His mother distinguishes her island in even more memorable terms:

> . . . . That opportunity
> Which then they had to take from's, to resume
> We have again. Remember, sir, my liege,
> The kings your ancestors, together with
> The natural bravery of your isle, which stands
> As Neptune's park, ribb'd and pal'd in
> With oaks unscalable and roaring waters,
> With sands that will not bear your enemies' boats,
> But suck them up to the topmast.
>
> 3.1.14–22

The wicked queen depends for her rhetoric on Britain's natural defenses as an island. Surrounded by a deadly sea, Britain really is a world by itself. The similarity between her language and King James's speech is shocking. Intention, however, makes a difference. James's rhetoric was motivated by a desire to neutralize the national distinctions within Britain, while the queen and Cloten are much more interested in justifying British defiance of Rome. James searches for an Augustan peace, while Cymbeline's queen attempts to justify war. In effect, her politics refuse ritual harmony and partake of none of the hospitable and regenerative energies of the landscape.[41] Belarius's geopolitics, by contrast, carry a way of life, or an ethic of living.

If, as Imogen complained just before meeting Belarius and the two princes, "Foundations fly the wretched," then the Welsh inhabitants cannot be wretched (3.6.7). Their faith is founded—literally—on rock.[42] Their outward-looking, antiegocentric morning ritual at the cave secures traditional social responsibility and values of charity. Wales itself becomes something like a hospital or a church in the play, regenerating healthy social energies by means of ritual. Belarius directs a near-Christian "burial" of Imogen and Cloten, emphasizing both natural cycles and rank hierarchy. The sacredness of direction in Wales—rather than the rhetorical utility of direction—is confirmed when Guiderius and Arviragus remember the importance of laying the seemingly dead Fidele's head to the east, traditionally the most sacred direction in Christian churches and on the "T-O" maps.[43]

The real importance of Welsh geography to the play's polemic of unification becomes clear when Imogen actually loses her way to Milford, which she had seen from the top of a mountain, and comes upon a "savage hold" where she quickly realizes that her sense of the land developed at court is inaccurate. She realizes that her new companions give more generously than "Great men" whose interest is merely "That nothing-gift of differing multitudes" (3.6.85). The notion of the gift, rejected earlier in the play by Iachimo, is reintroduced in Wales. After benefitting from the generous hospitality of Belarius and his boys, Imogen reevaluates a geography limited by a prejudiced "London" perspective:

> Our courtiers say all's savage but at court.
> Experience, O, thou disprov'st report!
> Th'imperious seas breeds monsters; for the dish
> Poor tributary rivers as sweet fish"
> (4.2.33–36)

This is a rich geopolitical metaphor, looking forward prophetically to the play's reunification of Britain and Rome and optimistically to history's union of England and Scotland. The disguised princess implies that while the "imperious seas" of Cymbeline and his queen have bred the monster Cloten, the meager "tributary river" Wales has bred "sweet Fish" in the forms of Guiderius and Arviragus. "Imperious" here connotes Henry VIII's tactical definition of empire as a fully-autonomous kingdom.[44] Autonomy is rejected in favor of a "tributary" relationship, which promises the successful mixing of cultural streams and creates a gift-inspired bond of generosity and goodwill between kingdoms. The geographically and culturally marginal or "poor" culture gains the status of a respected gift-giver, neutralizing court or London-centrism. The frightening "savages" on the margins of Britain vanish in a geography inflected by generosity. "Tribute" is a sign of charitable acceptance and goodwill rather than an enforced penalty. It creates reciprocal bonds that benefit everyone involved. In a 1608 speech to the House of Commons, Francis Bacon rejected the idea that the union with Scotland was a threat to England because of the poverty of the Scots:

> For indeed, it must needs be confessed, that for the Goods of the Mind and Body, they are Alteri Nos, Other our selves. For, to do them but right, we know in their capacity and understanding, they are a People ingenious; in Labour industrious; in Courage valiant; in Body hard, active and comely. More might be said, but in commending them, we do but in effect commend ourselves: for they are of one piece and continent with us; and the truth is, we are participant both of their Virtues and Vices.[45]

Like Imogen, Bacon rejects the idea of significant cultural marginality in Britain. The English and Scottish, Bacon suggests, are so closely bound that they participate in each other's subjectivities. They are "Alteri Nos" to each other. Generous "commendation" of the Scots must inevitably reflect on England. Such is the effect of gift-giving, for as Mauss argues, to give is to give some part of oneself, of one's spiritual essence. From this transfer is born the requirement of reciprocity and the bond of generosity.[46] Where the process begins is not as important as what it creates.

Imogen's choice of metaphor is also important because her words, like those of Belarius, recall the language of King James. In his March 1603 speech to Parliament, James also used the metaphor of rivers running into the sea. While arguing that historical unions between kingdoms have not led to the overbearing dominance of one region, the king says that "even as little brookes lose their names by their running and fall into great Rivers, and the very name and memory of the great rivers swallowed up in the Ocean: so by the conjunction of divers little Kingdomes in one, are all these private differences and questions swallowed up."[47] Once again, James uses geographic order as a sign of proper political order. Imogen's rhetoric, similarly, emphasizes a political geography. By bonding imperial center and margins, she neutralizes the "dishonor" of tribute that prompted Cymbeline's refusal to pay, while James erases the threat of regional dominance by privileging the entire fluid system over its constituent parts. In these geographies, the court does not produce better people than the country, while the central ocean of empire carries no more value than its tributary rivers. In the play, then, there can be no disgrace when outlying lands pay tribute to the imperial center, for doing so is part of the natural order, an order that appears in the patterns of the landscape. In this way, Imogen's words foreshadow the play's pacific conclusion and justify the reinstitution of tribute as the natural gift of outlying Britain to central Rome.

The conclusion of the play is also about the reinstitution of a "natural"—and political—order: the royal family. The characters' articulation of this order repudiates Iachimo's rhetorical exploitation of cosmic hierarchy and affirms spatial orthodoxy. When Cymbeline thankfully acknowledges the return of his two lost sons and his daughter, he does so in terms of a celestial reordering: "Blest pray you be, / That after this strange starting from your orbs / You may reign in them now!" (5.5.370–72). The vehicle and tenor of the spatiopolitical metaphor are fully compatible. Nor can there be any loss in this re-ordered universe for those who value it in its own terms. The return of Guiderius and Arvirargus, Cymbeline tells Imogen, means that she "hast lost by this a kingdom." Imogen disagrees, explaining that she has "got two worlds by it" (5.5.374). In Imogen's place, Iachimo might well have felt keenly the loss of a kingdom as the loss of profit, but Imogen has learned to value the natural order in its cosmographic or geographic configurations above all else.

A reinstitution of the priority of the natural to the political, however, does not fully describe the final geopolitical effect of *Cymbeline*. The play never ties up several loose ends. Not every character who appears in the fifth act has been "reoriented" by a Welsh experience like Imogen. Iachimo, for example, exhibits shame for his deeds, but his reformation is suspicious. Even in his confession, he continues to employ a kind of copious expansion of circumstances, reminiscent of his earlier fragmentation of Imogen:

> Upon a time—unhappy was the clock
> That strook the hour!—it was in Rome—accurs'd
> The mansion where!—twas at a feast—O would
> Our viands had been poison'd, or at least
> Those which I heav'd to head!
>
> (5.5.153–57)

This itemization of time and place gains Iachimo only rhetorical profit, yet his epistemological stasis is unnerving within the larger structure of romance regeneration. More important, perhaps, are the attitudes of Guiderius and Arvirargus. The two princes are not fully satisfied with their life in the Welsh countryside. They claim a sense of imprisonment and lost opportunities after Belarius tells them of the superiority of their way of life. For them, Wales is "a cell of ignorance, travelling a-bed / A prison, or a debtor that not dares / To stride a limit" (3.3.33–35). These "sparks of nature," as Belarius calls the princes' ambitions, are reminiscent of Julius Caesar, whose geopolitical ambition "swell'd so much that it did almost stretch / The sides o' th' world"(3.1.49–50). While Cymbeline's criticism of Caesar may be suppressed by his final gift of tribute, geographical striving still presents the ominous threat of war. Caesar's legend had been darkened in antiquity by the fear that he had polluted Rome when he transgressed the bounds of the Roman world.[48] The two princes are caught up in the regenerative energies of the play's conclusion, but their futures remain unclear. Their only comments pertain to the justifiability of the execution of Cloten, which, though a felicitous act within the play itself, does not necessarily portend a continuation of Cymbeline's peace.

The play even suggests that natural signs themselves do not necessarily promise peace or unity. The bellicose natural politics of the queen and Cloten make this clear enough. Natural order cannot do all the work of politics by itself. It can be ignored, as by the young princes, or misused, as it is by the queen, and it can be held in contempt, as it is by Iachimo. Even the ritual performed by Belarius to reify universal order is determined by his need to keep the princes away from the court and thus to perpetuate his punishment of Cymbeline. The queen's ill use of British geographical integrity is only the most obvious allusion to the weakness of James's natural politics of space. Each version of the right ordering of the relationship between the contours of nature and the contours of political order is built out of motivated rhetoric. The rhetoric of political naturalism can be appropriated and used persuasively for ends diametrically opposed to those of the king. Shakespeare, however, seems to suggest a method of giving the right order between geography and politics a defense against hostile appropriations. The theater itself may be able to replicate the function of Welsh ritual in its perpetuation of spatial order. The most privileged space in the play is also a space of theater. Welsh ritual is dramatic in its gesture and speech, while the Welsh landscape is suggestively coterminous with the stage. Here, Imogen acts her part as a boy and Belarius acts his part as a father. Both cases of "acting" further the final restoration of harmony. Even more importantly, the playwright apparently emphasizes the stage itself as the site of Welsh ritual. When Belarius says "[Stoop,] boys, this gate / Instructs you how t' adore the heavens" he speaks not just of the mouth of the cave, but probably also of the arch of one of the tiring-house doors. This self-referential hint indicates the role of the theater in uniting the British subject to its space. Kent van den Berg has argued that the playhouse, which was not uncommonly construed as a cosmic emblem (as in the *Globe* theater), becomes an extension of subjective space by virtue of its concave shape and allows the spectator to participate in the transformations that occur on stage.[49] The cave on stage is like a concave theater allowing its spectators and players—Imogen, Belarius, and the princes—to be transformed and realigned by the physical qualities of the place itself. Shakespeare represents a space of theater coterminous with the space of lived experience—that is, theater is implied to be an inherent part of pious, patriotic British life—and thus makes his own place within a Jacobean vision of Britain.[50]

Such realignment would certainly be King James's goal as well, who hoped that the disappearance of the borders would allow a realignment of his subjects' very hearts. *Cymbeline* provides a grounded alternative to the disorder and manipulations enabled by homogenized space and the methods of the new geography. *Cymbeline* does not wholly condemn the new technologies of exploration and human ingenuity, but it does want them to be subject to a ritualized and theatricalized spatial order. Perhaps, the play suggests, Jupiter's descent—if read as the perpetuation of traditional hierarchies within ritual and belief—can defend a unifying physical space from those whose interests do not lie in unity. The theater itself may act as a privileged locus for the ritual reorientation of spectators within a politically meet geography. Though James never saw the real union of England and Scotland he desired, the play at least reminds him that his ideal geography has the King's Men to stand up for it. In "th' world's volume," as Imogen describes the wonderous Britain, the theater may be "of it, but not in't."

Notes

I am grateful to Doug Bruster, John Gillies, Laurie Shannon, and Richard Strier for their careful consideration of earlier versions of this essay. Stephanie Friedman and members of the University of Chicago's Renaissance Workshop helped clarify my thinking about many of the issues involved in this paper.

1. *The Jacobean Union: Six tracts of 1604*, eds. Bruce Galloway and Brian Levack (Edinburgh and London: Scottish Historical Society, 1985), xii.
2. Ibid., xii. Evidence for English opposition to the Union is explicit in the *Journals of the House of Commons*, vol. 1 (1547–1628). See, for example, 20–23 April 1604.
3. Ibid., xxix.
4. Linda Woodbridge, "Palisading the Elizabethan Body Politic," *Texas Studies in Literature and Language* 33 (1991): 342.
5. These critics include Patricia Parker, "Romance and Empire: Anachronistic *Cymbeline*," in *Unfolded Tales: Essays on Renaissance Romance*, eds. George Logan and Gordon Teskey (Ithaca and London: Cornell University Press, 1989); Leah Marcus, *Puzzling Shakespeare: Local Reading and Its Discontents* (Berkeley, Los Angeles, and London: University of California Press, 1988); and Woodbridge. Each of these critics owes much to Emrys Jones's seminal essay "Stuart *Cymbeline*" in *Shakespeare's Later Comedies*, ed. D. J. Palmer (Harmondsworth: Penguin, 1971).

6. Henri Lefebvre, *The Production of Space*, trans. Donald Nicholson-Smith (Oxford: Blackwell, 1991), 10–12, 32–46, 229–291.

7. King James 1, *The King's Majesties Speech in Parliament* (London, 1603), sig. B2r.

8. Among the OED definitions of "apprehension" are "The action of 'feeling' anything emotionally; sensitiveness or sensibility to; sympathetic perception;" and "Fear as to what may happen; dread." A degree of fear among border dwellers was surely the result of centuries of cross-border hostilities between Scotland and England.

9. Claire McEachern notes these lines by James as an example of his recognition and use of "the integrity of British geography." *The Poetics of English Nationhood, 1590–1612* (Cambridge: Cambridge University Press, 1996), 143.

10. Francis Bacon, "A Brief Discourse Touching the Happy Union of the Kingdoms of England and Scotland," in *The Letters and the Life of Francis Bacon*, ed. James Spedding (London: Longmans, Green, Reader, and Dyer, 1868), 3:92.

11. Sir William Cornwallis, "The Miraculous and Happy Union of England and Scotland" (London, 1604), sig. D1r.

12. John Gillies writes that the *Geographia* "with its geometric grid (allowing a *scientific* sense of orientation, distance and proportion) and its modern refusal to privilege a sacred omphalos, defined the very possibility of a new geography.... [Ptolemy's] true significance is to have broken the imaginative hold of the 'Christian topogaphy' of Cosmas and Isidore in the fifteenth century," *Shakespeare and the Geography of Difference* (Cambridge: Cambridge University Press, 1994), 172.

13. Ibid., 101.

14. William Shakespeare, *Cymbeline*, in *The Riverside Shakespeare* (Boston: Houghton Mifflin, 1974), 1.4.1, 11. All further references to the play will be to this edition and will be cited parenthetically within the text.

15. Patricia Fumerton, *Cultural Aesthetics: Renaissance Literature and the Practice of Social Ornament* (Chicago and London: University of Chicago Press, 1991), 187–204.

16. Marcel Mauss, *The Gift: The Form and Reason for Exchange in Archaic Societies*, trans. W. D. Halls, (New York, London: Norton: 1990), especially 10, 17–18, 35–37; Fumerton, *Cultural Aesthetics*, 31–34; Richard Strier has suggested to me that the language of the "gift" in the play echoes Reformation theology. In Iachimo, we may detect the reprobate who is unable to accept the notion of the free gift of grace from God.

17. Jean-Christophe Agnew, *Worlds Apart: The Market and the Theater in Anglo-American Thought, 1550–1750* (Cambridge: Cambridge University Press, 1986), 10. See also 28–53, 65–97.

18. Ibid., 79–85.

19. Classical sources evince hostility to the Parthians, who delivered the Romans a devastating defeat at the Battle of Carrhae. Plutarch classes the Parthians among the Barbarians and compares their appearance to the long-haired Scythians. That the Roman Iachimo should, even for a moment, claim identity with the people most associated with the danger to Rome of its own imperial adventures is testimony to his ability to incorporate alterity within himself for utilitarian purposes. The allusion may also suggest a degree of sexual deviancy on Iachimo's part, since classical sources also make much of the Parthian Queen Musa's incestuous marriage to her son Phratacees during the reign of

Augustus. See Neilson C. Debevoise, *A Political History of Parthia* (Chicago: University of Chicago Press, 1938); Plutarch, *Life of Crassus*, 16–33.

20. Nancy Vickers, "'The blazon of' sweet beauty's best': Shakespeare's Lucrece," in *Shakespeare and the Question of Theory*, eds. Pat Parker and Geoffrey Hartmann (New York and London: Methuen, 1985), 95–101.

21. Patricia Parker, *Literary Fat Ladies: Rhetoric, Gender, Property* (London and New York: Methuen, 1987), 131–35.

22. Stephen Greenblatt, *Marvellous Possessions: The Wonder of the New World* (Chicago: University of Chicago Press, 1991), 80.

23. Many philosophers and scientists from the late middle ages until the late seventeenth century are responsible for this transformation. Perhaps the most important of these natural philosophers for Shakespeare's era was Giordano Bruno (1548–1600). Bruno published *De L'infinito universo e mondi* and other works in England in 1583. According to Alexander Koyre, "Bruno's space, the space of an infinite universe and at the same time the (somewhat misunderstood) infinite 'void' of Lucretius, is perfectly homogeneous and similar to itself everywhere: indeed, how could the 'void' of space be anything but uniform—or vice versa, how could the uniform 'void' be anything but unlimited and infinite?" *From the Closed World to the Infinite Universe* (Baltimore: John Hopkins Press, 1957), 46.

24. John Donne, *The Complete English Poems*, ed. A. J. Smith (Harmondsworth: Penguin, 1971).

25. Lefebvre, *Production of Space*, 84–85.

26. *The Rape of Lucrece*, in *The Riverside Shakespeare*, 402, 407, 408. This complex of associations is examined further in Georgianna Ziegler, "My Lady's Chamber: Female Space, Female Chastity in Shakespeare," *Textual-Practice* 4 (1990): 81–83; Robert Miola, "Cymbeline: Shakespeare's Valediction to Rome," in *Roman Images: Selected Papers from the English Institute, 1982*, ed. Annabel Patterson (Baltimore and London: Johns Hopkins University Press, 1984), 52–53.

27. Parker, *Literary Fat Ladies*, 150.

28. Gillies, *Geography of Difference*, 67, 160–61.

29. William Cunningham, *The Cosmographicall Glasse*, The English Experience, no. 44 (New York and London: Da Capo Press, 1968), fol. 120.

30. Gillies, *Geography of Difference*, 59.

31. J. B. Harley and David Woodward, *The History of Cartography, Vol. I: Cartography in Prehistoric, Ancient and Medieval Europe and the Mediterranean* (Chicago and London: University of Chicago Press, 1987), 2.

32. Ibid., 10.

33. By "dramatic presence," I mean that the Welsh scenes exhibit a life of their own—a distinct spatial practice—which distinguishes them from the rest of the play and allows them to take particular hold of the audience. I will describe Welsh rhetorics of natural harmony and gift giving, which make these scenes central to an understanding of the play's orthodox spatial poetics. In this sense, I disagree with Jodi Mikalachki, who argues that the Welsh space of "unmitigated Britishness" must in the end be forgotten in the civilizing union of Britain and Rome. "The Masculine Romance of Roman Britain: *Cymbeline* and Early Modern English Nationalism," *Shakespeare Quarterly* 46 (Fall 1995): 301–22.

34. Jones, "Stuart *Cymbeline*," 257–58.

35. John Gillies, "Posed Spaces: Framing in the Age of the World Picture,"

forthcoming in *The Rhetoric of the Frame*, ed. Paul Duro (Cambridge: Cambridge University Press), 4.

36. Marcus, *Puzzling Shakespeare*, 120.

37. Robert Miola believes that in Wales "daily business accords harmoniously with divine order." *Shakespeare's Rome* (Cambridge: Cambridge University Press, 1983), 219. Despite its obvious sources in the greenwoods of comedy, I am arguing that Wales is precisely not to be compared to C. L. Barber's place of Saturnalian holiday (*Shakespeare's Festive Comedy* [Princeton: Princeton University Press, 1959], 3–15, 222–39) or to the "second place" that Alvin Kernan finds throughout Shakespeare, a place usually in "nature" that allows the breakdown of legal and rational restraints found in the city. "Place and Plot in Shakespeare," *Yale Review* 67 (1977): 52.

38. Patricia Parker demonstrates that these lines echo those of Evander in the *Aeneid* as he shows Aeneas into his home on the future site of Rome. This is a moment of poetic geography confirming the Western translation of Empire from Rome to Britain, as it had earlier been translated from Troy to Rome. "Romance and Empire," 203. I believe Shakespeare also uses these lines to evoke Jacobean political naturalism.

39. Alastair Fowler argues that *As You Like It*, a play surely on Shakespeare's mind when he wrote the Welsh scenes in *Cymbeline*, regularly combines the otium of pastoral with the didacticism of georgic. *Kinds of Literature: An Introduction to the Theory of Genres and Modes* (Cambridge: Harvard University Press, 1982), 253–54. Elsewhere, Fowler notes that Renaissance georgic digressions often include precepts, instruction, meditations on the good life, and landscape description. These elements loosely characterize Belarius's speeches, while Arvirargus's brief evocation of a cold December echoes Hesiod's winter scene in *Works and Days*. "The Beginnings of English Georgic," in *Renaissance Genres: Essays on Theory, History and Interpretation*, ed. Barbara K. Lewalski (Cambridge, Mass. and London: Harvard University Press, 1986), 111.

40. Stephen Orgel, *The Illusion of Power: Political Theater in the English Renaissance* (Berkeley, Los Angeles and London: University of California Press, 1975), 49–58.

41. As Mikalachki explains, the queen is the play's primary representative of the savage British woman who must be displaced in order for a civil, masculine Britain to come into being through union with Rome. "Masculine Romance," 312–14.

42. Like the wise man of Jesus' parable. Matthew 7:24–27.

43. Gillies, "Posed Spaces," 4. See also B. L. Gordon, "Sacred Directions, Orientation and the Top of the Map," *History of Religions* 10, no. 3 (1971): 212–16.

44. Jenny Wormald, "The Creation of Britain: Multiple Kingdoms or Core and Colonies?" in *Transactions of the Royal Historical Society*, 6th ser., no. 2 (1992): 190.

45. Francis Bacon, "The Union of the Two Kingdoms" (Edinburgh, 1670), sig C2v.

46. Mauss, *The Gift*, 12.

47. King James, *Speech in Parliament*, sig. B3r.

48. Gillies, *Geography of Difference*, 21–23.

49. Kent T. van den Berg, *Playhouse and Cosmos: Shakespearian Theatre as Metaphor* (Newark: University of Delaware Press; London and Toronto: Asso-

ciated University Presses, 1985), 50. Van den Berg also suggests that Shakespeare's theatrical space gives the spectator the confidence to "stand outside of the entire macrocosm and comprehend the totality of existence as the reflection of subjective wholeness and self-sufficiency." A pro-Union and Augustan *Cymbeline* would certainly wish its spectators to see the very rocks and caves of Britain as stages representing their own "subjective wholeness."

50. Leah Marcus argues that while Shakespeare does call for subjective transformation in the interests of Union, the theatrical "proteanism" of the play partially subverts the King's authority. *Puzzling Shakespeare*, 140. I would argue that the play's theatricality, while self-interested, finally serves the purposes of an order that is not at all subversive.

Domains of Victory: Staging and Contesting the Roman Triumph in Renaissance England

Anthony Miller

A ritual display of the far-flung lands, peoples, and riches conquered by Rome's military power; an equilibration of her internal political forces; a religious solemnity: the Roman triumph incorporated multiple signifying potentials that were long appropriated and reappropriated by the ancients for contending political purposes. This process recurs in the ceremonial, literary, and theatrical imitations of the Roman triumph in Renaissance England. Victory festivities like those after the Armada, royal entries and progresses, and civic events like London's Lord Mayoral shows all aggrandized their participants by reviving or reinterpreting the triumphal custom of epitomizing the geography of conquest. They vaunted the defeat of foreign foes, claimed a pacific conquest over the land of England, or displayed the spoils of foreign trade. Many were recorded in books, giving the fugitive festivity a continuing existence and creating a new domain of print in which writers and illustrators might exercise their power of perpetuation.[1] This domain displayed also imaginary triumphs, bestowing prestige on actual heroes by hailing them as triumphators or directing implicit rebuke at actual rulers who had failed to merit the honor. The Renaissance theater delighted in an event that itself turned a city into a theater. By representing the triumphs of historical conquerors from Coriolanus to Tamburlaine, the London stage displayed its own version of remote histories and exotic geographies. Dramatic texts thus implicate themselves in the contentions over dominion that are encoded in the staging of any triumph.

Three related sites disclose the ideological tensions in English revivals and representations of the Roman triumph. One is the appropriation by the Renaissance monarch of the role of triumphator, with its associations of a political authority based on conquest. This appropriation may be countered when oppositional forces attempt to call the monarch to account in the military aspect of the role, through strategies of appeal, admonition, or challenge. A second site is the translation by the monarch of the ideal of conquest through war and strenuous *virtus* into an ideal of conquest through peace and easeful supremacy. This translation is challenged especially by the proponents of militant Protestantism, who recuperate for their cause the martial origin of triumph. A third site is the contest between court and city, in which the London authorities initiate their own triumphs of a mercantile imperialism that masters geographical space through trade. These triumphs seek to reappropriate for the city of London the status of successor to the *urbs Roma*.

This essay studies the political and ideological encoding of the Roman triumph at these three sites in the period of Shakespeare's career and suggests how the representation of the triumph in Shakespeare's major Roman plays is implicated in contemporary contestations.[2] Triumphs play a crucial part in each of these plays. As in Roman lore, they yield tragic demonstrations of the turn of fortune's wheel. At the same time, Shakespeare is attentive to their diverse political functions. *Julius Caesar* begins with a triumph and various attempts to discredit, appropriate, or rival Caesar's triumph, focus the play's political conflicts. The variety of triumphs in *Antony and Cleopatra* enact even more richly the contention over the semiotics of the event. From her first entry, a mock-triumph of Eros, to her triumphal garbing for death, Cleopatra subverts or reappropriates the Roman military ethos. Where the triumph displayed foreign captives and spoils on the stage of the Roman city, Cleopatra strives to invert the model by displaying a captive Rome on the stage of Egypt. The crisis of *Coriolanus* turns on the hero's triumph after the Volscian war, which is appropriated by the patricians as a legitimization of their power and resisted by the tribunes as a threat to theirs. In all these texts, Roman issues translate also into English issues, and I attempt to recuperate aspects of the elusive "local" Shakespeare, operating in the discursive space defined by Leah Marcus, "between the evanescent interpretation which fascinated Renaissance audiences . . . and the broader kinds of interpretation facilitated by our own more general explanatory models."[3]

I

In ancient Rome, a triumph was the procession of a victorious consul from the Campus Martius, outside the city walls, around one or more of the Circuses, and along the Via Sacra through the Forum, where an encomiastic oration was delivered, to the temple of Jupiter Capitolinus, where the consul offered sacrifices. The procession comprised the Senate, a display of spoils and eminent captives, paintings and models representing conquered lands and peoples, animals decked for sacrifice, the triumphator, and his army. The triumphator stood in a chariot drawn, like the chariots of Jupiter and Apollo, by four white horses. His face was painted red, and he was dressed in robes of purple and gold from the treasury of Jupiter Capitolinus. An attendant held a crown over his head, symbolizing his status as a god-king. The danger that this status might corrupt its holder and the state always haunted Romans; hence, the attendant whispered the apotropaic words "Remember that you are only a man," to avert the enmity of the fates toward the triumphator's success and to remind him that victory and life itself were passing gifts of fortune. The triumph had a carnivalesque aspect, under privilege of which the soldiers sang bawdy and satirical verses. It also had a dreadful aspect, which despatched the principal captives to execution as the procession passed the prison of the Tullianum. All this ritualized the geographical reach of Roman power. Pompey's triumphs displayed Rome's hegemony over the three continents known to the Romans: "For others before him had celebrated three triumphs; but he celebrated his first over Libya, his second over Europe, and this his last over Asia, so that he seemed to have included the whole world in his three triumphs." Caesar's triumphs compress onto the stage of Rome and into an even briefer span of time an even more impressive geographic span: "he celebrated five triumphs, four in a single month, but at intervals of a few days, after vanquishing Scipio; and another on defeating Pompey's sons. The first and most splendid was the Gallic triumph, the next the Alexandrian, then the Pontic, after that the African, and finally the Spanish, each differing from the rest in its equipment and display of spoils."[4]

Gilbert Highet acutely distinguishes some of the social energies manifested in the triumph: "That was Rome: power, efficiency, cruelty, frank humanity, frequent gaiety, and grave reverence for the gods."[5] He suggests, however, an equilibrium that they rarely attained, since he omits the rapacious accumulation of foreign wealth and the fierce political contentions that emerge in historical accounts of triumphs. Livy and Plutarch report the constant allegations, often politically motivated, that triumphators were guilty of excessive exactions of tribute or inadequate donatives, of political overreaching or faulty generalship.[6] Modified to include these features, Highet's synecdoche holds for Rome—and for Rome's self-declared inheritors.

Renaissance studies, reenactments, and representations of the Roman triumph also staked rival political claims. The status of the triumphator as god-king had meant that the Roman republic jealously circumscribed triumphal celebrations, while the emperors detached them from their strictly martial origin in order to exploit their legitimating and aggrandizing potential. The classical authors who instructed the Renaissance about the triumph align themselves variously along this ideological divide, from Livy the Pompeyan republican, through Suetonius the disabused insider, to Plutarch the admiring imperialist. Likewise with the studies of the triumph produced by the indefatigable industry of the Renaissance humanists. One of these, the *Pandectae triumphales* of François Modius (Frankfurt, 1586) merits particular attention for its relevance to England. Modius views Roman history from the vantage of a north European Catholic who was capable of taking a broad historical view of religious and political issues. Ben Jonson owned and annotated a copy of his book.[7] Modius' impressive volume of a thousand folio pages prints a table of triumphs from Romulus to Tiberius and narrates in detail twenty ancient triumphs. It describes surviving triumphal arches, columns, and pyramids, and transcribes their inscriptions. Complementing his antiquarian zeal are Modius's records of contemporary events. Broadening the term *triumph*, in the Renaissance manner, to include a variety of public festivities, he documents the ceremonial entries, coronations, weddings, and funerals of modern emperors, kings, popes, and archbishops. The book climaxes with forty-six pages on the election and coronation of Modius's emperor, Maximilian II, twenty years earlier. A second part of the *Pandectae triumphales* catalogues aristocratic jousts, mostly in Germany, with lists of participants and engravings of their insignia.

Modius's scholarship encodes a political ideology. For the German subject of the Holy Roman Empire, *Romanitas* has migrated from Rome to Germany. Modius claims for his nation and for his book the right to display Roman virtues and the customs of far-flung nations. The virtues of a renewed Rome are embodied less in the monarchy than in the nobility of Germany. It is this nobility, not the Emperor, to whom Modius dedicates the *Pandectae triumphales*. Though it includes monarchic solemnities, the book gives more attention to aristocratic *virtus*. In doing so, it aligns itself in general with Roman republicanism and in particular with the ideology of elective monarchy. Modius's treatment of monarchy confirms this alignment. In describing the institutions and customs of monarchies from Charlemagne to Maximilian and from England to Muscovy, he reveals their great diversity. Not all monarchs are hereditary; some are elected, and some must be confirmed by election. Modius includes in their company the doges of Venice, who were servants of a republic and rigidly limited in power. He even includes a triumph of the "emperor of the Turks" and generously presents the infidel as a model of royal graciousness, greeting with kindly nods his Greek and Hebrew no less than his Turkish subjects (sig. cc3^v). Modius's humanistic scholarship historicizes and demystifies royalty.

Even when celebrating a signal victory in war, a royal triumph might occasion equivocation, if not challenge. After the destruction of the Armada, Elizabeth bore trophies of the vanquished in procession to St. Paul's, as Henry VII had done after Bosworth and as the Roman triumphators had borne trophies to the Temple of Jupiter.[8] Elizabeth's triumph was memorialized in a Latin collection, *Triumphalia de victoriis Elisabethæ . . . contra classem instructissimam Philippi* (1589).[9] Its longest poem, "Aretophila," is a narrative in epic hexameters. With its praise of an Elizabeth unmoved by peril and of her valiant admirals, the poem functions like the speech in praise of the triumphator and her army. An ode proclaims Elizabeth the antitype of the biblical types of female heroism, Deborah, Jael, Judith, and Esther, making the Christian God England's patron as Jupiter Capitolinus was Rome's. Other poems exult in the fall of the Spaniards or prophesy the fall of the French Catholics and of the Pope himself, parading in imagination these vanquished nations at the head of Elizabeth's triumph. The writers who bestow a literary triumph on Elizabeth modulate their celebration, however, into a strenuous call to renew her *virtus* in further battle. The authors of the *Triumphalia* are aware that they are commemorating defensive victory, not imperial conquest. The book is a triumph mounted by Protestant militarism at the auspicious historical moment that saw not only the defeat of Spain but the accession of the Protestant Henri IV in France. The authors or addressees of poems include the Elector Palatine Frederick V, Prince Joannes Casimir, and Daniel Rogers, all proponents of English intervention on the continent. The duty, allure, and opportunity of a Protestant English imperialism are urged on Elizabeth in terms that rebuke her reluctance to play the part of a militant *fidei defensor*. "Aretophila" envisages the geographical progress of a Protestant English empire that will challenge the vast Catholic successor to the Roman Empire:

> Perge agedum iustis patriam tutarier armis,
> Belgarumque urbes, venerándaque templa piorum.
> Perge tuis alias acquirere finibus oras,
> Et Lusitanos sceptris adiungere portûs,
> Numine tam dextro. Te defensore, repugnax
> Relligio falsæ solidis stet firma columnis,
> Perpetuum florens.
>
> (sigs. c3–c3ᵛ)

[Come! proceed to protect with righteous arms your native land, and the cities of the Belgians, and the revered temples of the pious. Proceed to add other shores to your dominions, and to put Portuguese harbors under your scepter, since divine power is so favorable to you. With you as defender, may stout religion stand on solid pillars, resistant to the false and flourishing perpetually.]

Elizabeth is the recipient of similar admonition and rebuke in a literary triumph three years later. Joshua Silvester's *Triumph of Faith* (1592) is a translation of Guillaume Du Bartas' *Triomfe de la Foi* (Paris, 1572).[10] This triumph is descended from the much reprinted Christianized and moralized literary versions, Petrarch's *Trionfi* and Savonarola's *Triumphus Crucis*, but it conflates this inheritance with memories of Roman militarism. "Faith sits triumphant on a coache of golde," like a victorious Roman consul, but the coach is biblical gold "Of *Tubals* worke," its wheels "like / The holy wheeles, the great Ezechiel saw" (sig. B1ᵛ). In a similar bifurcation, the troops marching in Faith's triumph are allegorical figures like Constancie, Pacience, and Charitie, and her principal captive is Reason, but the other captives in her triumph are historical enemies of faith from Cain and Pharaoh to Mahomet and his Turkish champions, culminating in the contemporary figure of "Solyman," i.e., Suleiman the Magnificent (d. 1566; sigs. B2ᵛ–B4⁴). The "First Song" of the triumph ends with a call for Christian kings to join forces against "*Faith's* foes" to recapture the cities of the Levant lost to the Turks, especially "*Famagosta* lost a yeare ago" (i.e., in 1571; sig. C1). Du Bartas's religious allegory is at the same time a political manifesto, in all likelihood directed by the Protestant poet against the controversial alliance between the Catholic monarchy of France and the infidel Porte, which had been renewed in 1569. For its part, Silvester's translation celebrates the recent victory of the Protestant faith over the papist Armada and envisages England bearing the standards of godly war into the Mediterranean, whose geography will no longer be contested merely between infidels and papists.[11]

The accession of James I occasioned the most self-consciously Roman of English triumphs.[12] Here too, issues of current politico-religious policy are woven into the humanist text. In the spirit of James's triumphal entry to London in 1604, Cambridge University dutifully published a collection of Latin poems called *Threnothriambeuticon*, or "Dirge-Triumph."[13] Ponderously diplomatic, the book combines, "with a defeated joy, / With a dropping and an auspicious eye," complaint at the death of Elizabeth and rejoicing at the accession of James. It also combines festive praise of James with political admonition. Samuel Hawarden of King's College contributed the poem that adopts most fully the discourse of triumph. James accedes like the most illustrious of Roman triumphators,

> Qualis Scipiades, post Libyam iugo
> Subiectam Latio, cùm capitolia
> Cinctus nobilium flore cohortium,
> Scandit victor in aurea.

(sig. C2)

[As when Scipio, after subjecting North Africa to the Latin yoke, ascends to the golden Capitol as a victor, surrounded by the flower of his noble troops.]

As in the *Triumphalia* for the destruction of the Armada, jubilation at James's accession is countered by the grim realization that the papist foe remains powerful and dangerous. Despite his Roman pretensions, James does not qualify as a true triumphator, because he has won no decisive victory. Instead of displaying pacified realms, this triumph views with dread a world full of dangers. The appurtenances of papistry, which ought to be displayed as trophies in the triumph of the Protestant victor, are still at large. They will be captured and the foe vanquished only by the exercise of James's "warlike spirit." Hawarden's poem itself breathes the warlike spirit of an older Cambridge, the progenitor of Spenser and his Redcrosse knight. The James to whom it awards a triumph is not the new monarch with his policy of peace through accommodation with the Catholic powers:

> Horrendam rabidâ fauce tonans Papa
> Quàm diram in miseros nos strueret luem?
> Nostri quàm citò lux, per scelus, & nefas,
> Esset nubila sæculi?
> Quæ pestes premerent? quæ mala nos? fratres,
> Idola, impia reclusio pectoris,
> Execratio, crux, sancta aqua, monstràq;
> Quotquot styx habet impia?
> Nec quæ præsidij spes superest, nisi
> Tu morum radio, tu iubare inclytæ
> Vitæ, hæc discutias, vimq; Papæ tuo
> Frangas Marte Draconicam.
>
> (ibid.)

[What a dreadful and terrifying affliction might the Pope be contriving for our suffering people, thundering with raving voice! How quickly might the light of our age be clouded over by villainy and sacrilege! What plagues might weigh upon us, what woes! Friars, images, the impious laying bare of the breast, curses, crosses, holy water, prodigies: however many impieties hell contains! Neither does any hope of defense remain unless, by the radiance of your character, by the brightness of your renowned life, you dash all these things to pieces and shatter the dragonish power of the Pope by your warlike spirit.]

Comparable claims and challenges to the status of triumphator are inscribed in Shakespeare's Roman plays. *Julius Caesar* opens with Caesar's triumph for his victory over "Pompey's blood." The first phase of the play's action is defined by civic dissension over this triumph and a series of attempts to appropriate its symbolic language or to create alternatives to it. Caesar and the commoners take a carnival pleasure in the triumph and in the games of Lupercalia, two events that Shakespeare conflates. Shakespeare's comic cobbler plays the part of the λύδος who marks some ancient accounts of the triumph,[14] while Caesar shows a genial approval of plays and feasting. However, Caesar also seeks to turn the social harmony of his triumph to political advantage by making his triumph a vehicle for a new political order based on personal charisma and popular will. He directs his political appeal over the heads of the "nobles" to the "commoners," replacing the triumphator's claim to the Senate with his pageant of the offering of the crown. Such populism was always a risk posed by triumphs; hence, their careful circumscription under the republic and the importance of triumphal symbolism in the process by which Augustus and his successors refashioned the republican constitution.[15] Nevertheless, the people do not succumb as Caesar hopes. Their off-stage shouts encode two possibilities of triumph, in Brutus's fear that "the people do choose Caesar for their king" and in Casca's revelation that they have thwarted his royal aspirations. The public manifestation through which Caesar seeks to establish monarchy also provides a means for the people to assert their political will—as Shakespeare's London would welcome James but in doing so would affirm its own status.

Julius Caesar also stages more direct opposition to Caesar's attempted appropriation. Like the failures of English monarchs to make conquests, Caesar's triumph for a victory in civil war focuses opposition. The tribunes seek to restrict triumphal honors according to austere republican precedent, which required victory in a foreign war with enemies put to rout. Cassius displays the jealous emulation of the republican era. Brutus devises his own ill-judged triumph for the overthrow of Caesar, which paradoxically replicates Caesar's improper triumph for a victory over fellow Romans. The weapons Brutus seeks to display are not rendered harmless and decorative as in triumphs, and they are red not with festive or godlike gilding but with blood:

> Then walk we forth, even to the, market-place,
> And waving our red weapons o'er our heads,
> Let's all cry, "Peace, freedom, and liberty."
> (3.1.108–10)

In *Julius Caesar*, the contention over the semiotics of the triumph is centered on the single event of Caesar's triumph. In *Antony and Cleopatra*, it expresses itself in a variety of triumphs. The play opens with a mock-triumph, the unthinkable spectacle of a barbarian woman leading captive a Roman triumvir before a stage audience of dismayed, not exultant, Romans. Its most vividly represented triumph occurs in Enobarbus's description of Cleopatra's *navalis triumphus* on the river Cydnus. This event manifests the actual power that could be exerted by triumphal symbolism, for Cleopatra's magnificence effects the erotic and political conquest that it simultaneously celebrates. In this play, subversive appropriations displace and win out over the traditional military ethos of triumph.[16] A victor, Ventidius, declines a triumph because of its political dangers, and Octavius's ambition to display the captive Cleopatra is thwarted. The play ends with the victor not mounting a triumph but overseeing a funeral procession, while Cleopatra's death is endowed with triumphal qualities. The struggle for the signifying power of the triumph thus continues, while Octavius's disappointment in victory and Cleopatra's victory in death also enact the tragic proximity of victory and defeat that was always a lesson of triumphs.[17] Shakespeare, too, enters the struggle to appropriate triumph. His play encodes dramatically the festive aspect of triumph, exuberant in its vast subject and sprawling form, juxtaposing the majestic, the ruthless, and the clownish. Cleopatra's imagining of Caesar's triumph, with its audience of mechanic slaves and its cast of quick comedians and squeaking boys, finally draws together—indeed equates—Caesar's triumph and Shakespeare's play. Enacting its own cultural dominion over both Rome and Egypt, the play itself constitutes the triumph that (as Shakespeare makes it seem) eludes Caesar.

Coriolanus encodes the solemn and hieratic aspect of triumph. The turbulence of the action is controlled by the knowledge that Rome's "course will on" with the splendid ease of a triumph; Coriolanus himself prevails with similar ease in battle and in revenge. Nevertheless, there is nothing easy in the city's political struggles; the play lays open the contestation that underlies triumphal ease. It is the hero's triumph (more correctly, *ovatio*) after his victory over Corioles that marks at once the crucial dramatic crisis for the play and the crucial political crisis for Rome. The triumph is rendered at length and with historical accuracy: formal oration of praise, reception at the city gates, carnival enthusiasm, procession to the Capitol, and crowning with oak. This triumph, however, does not fulfil its politically integrative function. As godlike triumphator, Coriolanus personates a threatening Mars, not a benevolent Jupiter. He imports the military ethos into the city, whereas the triumph left it outside or admitted it under strictly controlled conditions. The civic celebration tellingly conjoins ceremony and power, as both patricians and tribunes recognize the opportunity or the threat of Coriolanus's assuming the consulate:

> *Volumnia.* only
> There's one thing wanting, which I doubt not but

Our Rome will cast upon thee. . . .
Sicinius. On the sudden,
I warrant him consul.

(2.1.200–2, 221–22)

II

Long before the Renaissance, military triumph had metamorphosed into the *adventus* or royal entry. The metamorphosis begins with Augustus, whose triumph after Actium is rendered pseudoprophetically in the *Aeneid* as a manifestation less of martial prowess than of benevolent and uncontested empire. The fruits of his victory are not the monetary distributions greedily disputed in republican times, but three hundred temples. The spoils of war become the free gifts of Caesar's peoples: "*Ipse . . . dona recognoscit populorum.*" The procession of the conquered meets respectful wonder, not humiliation or vengeance.[18] A peaceful world now willingly presents itself to the Roman gaze. The metamorphosis was advanced by an emperor like Nero, who triumphed disgracefully for victory not as a warrior but a musician.[19] The metamorphosis was completed by Christianity. As Christian artists translated the pagan iconography of "The Emperor Triumphing over His Enemies" into "The Triumph of Christ," or borrowed the form of narrative bas-reliefs on triumphal arches for narrative mosaics in churches, so late Roman emperors and medieval kings entered their cities like Christ entering Jerusalem.[20]

Renaissance royal entries inherit these characteristics. At a typical Elizabethan entry, to Norwich in 1578, the queen spoke in terms of the triumphator's conquest and spoils, but she translated them into the moralized terms of reciprocal duties: "We come not therefore, but for that whiche in right is our owne, the heartes and true allegeance of our Subjects, whiche are the greatest riches of a Kingdome: whereof as we assure our selves in you so do you assure youre selves in us of a lovyng and gratious soveraigne."[21] A reception at the city gates corresponded to the triumphator's seeking and gaining admission to Rome. A speech by the city Recorder corresponded to the encomium before Senate or people. Pageants, which might include representations of confounded adversaries, corresponded to the displays of spoils and of defeated enemies. The monarch's godlike splendor—Elizabeth in her coronation entry to London, for example, "dressed in a royal robe of very rich cloth of gold. . . . and on her head over a coif of cloth of gold . . . a plain gold crown"—corresponded to the Roman triumphator clad in the splendid robes of Jupiter Capitolinus.[22]

Renaissance royal entries thus combined antique triumph with medieval *adventus*.[23] The forms of antique triumph celebrate not foreign conquest but domestic harmony. They cast the monarch as hero, even when he or she had won no victory. The monarch enters to take possession of his or her own, not as the recipient of a privilege from a jealously free city. The triumph attempts to eliminate the contention of rival political interests; what is celebrated is unquestioned and unquestionable dominion. Such a claim is, however, apt to produce new kinds of contention, and there are indications in English royal entries of tensions beneath the triumphal surface. These tensions emerge in the entry's double function of applauding and instructing the monarch. Admonition, which takes up and extends the warnings about *hubris* and mortality offered to the Roman triumphator, necessarily entails a degree of challenge, if only in claiming the right to instruct. In their coronation entries to London and Edinburgh, Elizabeth and Mary Queen of Scots were presented with symbols of Protestantism designed to teach and test their fidelity to the reformed faith.[24] In his triumphal entry to London in 1604, James was greeted with symbols of the city's own identity and power.

In accordance with James's proclivities, Jonson's Londinium arch gives formal primacy to allegorical figures of "Monarchia Britannica" and "Theosophia." Those figures are overshadowed, however, from above by the model of the city itself in its towered splendor and variety, and they are dwarfed from below by the *Genius Urbis,* in the living shape of the heroic actor Edward Alleyn, lodged in a more impressive niche and flanked by personifications of the city's counsel and warlike force. These powers, lodged in the broad central base of the arch, literally and metaphorically support the regal power above; "with those armes of councel and strength, the *Genius* was able to extinguish the kings enemies, and preserve his citizens."[25] Again, on the eve of James's entry, the Cinque Ports staged on the Thames a mock water battle, doubtless intended to school the *rex pacificus* in the importance of England's naval power, which had been cultivated by Elizabeth, in the latter part of her reign at least, and vindicated by the defeat of the Armada. The king's reaction is highly revealing, as he attempts to render the power of the Cinque Ports and the navy reassuring but with a simile that expresses simultaneously discomposure at their potential menace: "Their love was like the wildfire unquenchable."[26]

A cognate development to the royal entry is the triumph of peace. The Elizabethan courtier, Lodowick Lloyd, published *The Triplicitie of Triumphes* (1591),[27] a small compendium of ceremonials for royal birthdays, elections, coronations, and funerals. Lloyd's bias, in conformity with Elizabethan policy, is to redirect triumphal energies from war to peace. "But all these triumphes of Alexander, of Caesar, and of others were gotten with blood, and after lost with blood: therfore sing we of Eliza, the prince of peace" (sig. c4). For Thomas Dekker, "*Tryumphs*, are the most choice and daintiest fruit that spring from *Peace* and *Abundance*; *Love* begets them; and *Much Cost* brings them forth."[28] At Rome, triumphs were awarded only for an irreversibly secure victory; thus, in a sense, they celebrated peace but peace based in war and conquest. Even allowing for the expansion of the term *triumph* in the Renaissance, Lloyd and Dekker's usages are strikingly at variance with the militaristic Roman ethos. In Renaissance England, the appurtenances of military conquest are used to extol a policy of nonmilitarism.

Like the royal entry, the triumph of peace originates in the Christianization of Roman custom; in England, it subserves in particular the Tudor claim to have healed the wounds of civil war. Both origins are evident in Elizabeth's London entry of 1559, an exercise in Protestant biblical typology and an anxious appeal for a peaceful transition between reigns. Elizabeth is saluted as a Deborah, esteemed for peaceful no less than warlike feats. "In war she, through gods aide, did put her foes to flight, / ... In peace she, through gods aide, did alway mainteine right." She is a queen—almost a goddess—of peace. "So now that jarre shall stint, and quietnes encrease, / We trust, O noble Queene, thou wilt be cause alone."[29] Elizabeth's frequent progresses are all triumphs of peace, with the paradoxical attributes implied by that term. They display a woman conqueror who marches splendidly and unthreatened through her peaceable kingdom, entertained by harmless mock-combats and conquering hearts that are already compliant. The symbolism of victory over a formidable enemy is paradoxically applied to a political situation from which the very idea of an enemy—or resistance, or dissent—has been eliminated. Instead of displaying models of conquered lands, the Queen displays herself as loving conqueror and, in turn, views her own land on obedient display.

James's London entry of 1604 sought to transform even more

radically the militarist ethos of triumph. Its proclamation of a golden age of peace reversed the Ovidian myth of war expelling peaceful justice. Jonson's climactic triumphal arch displayed Peace victorious over Mars and the *Genius Urbis* expelling a *Flamen Martialis* by the power of James and his "Sweet peace."[30] The studiously classical iconography of James's entry and the precedent of the *pax augustana* claim peace no less than war as a Roman virtue. However, even the display of a world made peaceful by James's virtues and arts could not exclude national contentions. The entry occasioned an inauspicious quarrel over precedence between the French and Spanish ambassadors.[31] Triumphal arches were erected by the Italian and Dutch merchants of London, ostensibly a peaceable gesture but inevitably introducing rivalries. Did the arches signify their donors' abasement, like the tribute of conquered peoples, or their superiority, as in the verdict that the Italians had built the handsomest arch?[32] The Dutch arch challenged James's policy of peace with Spain, the occupying power of the low countries. Though incorporating figures of Peace, this arch also displayed figures of armed justice and scenes of battle. Perhaps overstating the commitment of Elizabeth to the Dutch cause, the speech addressed to James at this arch solicited him to grant his fellow Protestants the same protection. The pacific and nurturing imagery in which this protection is described does not conceal the fact that it must in practice be martial "intreating wee may be sheltred under your winges now, as then under hers."[33]

James's pacifism is both confirmed and challenged by the uses of triumph in books published later in his reign. *The Triumphs of King James the First . . . Published upon his Maiesties advertisement to all the Kings, Princes and Potentates of Christendome, and confirmed by the wonderfull Workes of God. declared in his life* (1610) is a skirmish in the pamphlet war between James and the papacy over the king's oath of allegiance for recusants.[34] Its author, George Marcellin, pronounces James's triumph over the French controversialists Coeffeteau and Pelletier. "Let the Laurell wreaths be wrung out of their hands, to impale the victorious head of our IAMES, truely *Triumphant*, over *Pagan idolatrie*, and *Popish Heresie*" (sig. B3^v). This is a victory both won and celebrated by writing. James's weaponry is his book and the learning it displays; he requires no display of conquered lands because he rules a dominion of the mind. "The very written book it selfe doth furnish us with strength sufficient, to vanquish and convince all the answerers of the worlde, and their answers" (sig. B4). James's power is expressed in majestic repose; his sphere of action contracts from continents and battlefields to the royal seat. "And therefore we see him, not running, like *Aratus*, with a drawne sword in his hand, upon the Wals of Rome, and to the Tyrants gate, to take revenge in his iust displeasure, but seated. Seated in signe of Royall power and Soveraignty of his owne right & Iustice. Sitting on his Throne, in signe that . . . *The King that is seated upon his Throne, chaseth all evill out of his sight*" (sig. D2ᵛ). The *Triumphs of King Iames* urges the princes of Europe to meet in a council of religious reconciliation, to be presided over by James as Constantine had presided over the council of Nicaea. James's triumph of peace thus endows him with imperial stature and issues in a call to action, but again it is action expressed in the form not of warfare but of speech.[35]

It is war in the low countries that again challenges James's pacifism in a triumph book published at the historical juncture that found James on his closest terms with the United Provinces. In 1612–13, James brokered an alliance between the States and the German Protestant Union, married Princess Elizabeth to Frederick V the Elector Palatine, and joined with France to block the Spanish candidate from succeeding the Emperor Rudolph II.[36] Seizing this moment to encourage still more active measures, there appeared *The triumphs of Nassau; or a description and representation of all the Victories both by Land and Sea, granted by God to the noble, high, and mightie Lords, the Estates generall of the united Netherland Provinces. Under the conduct and command of his Excellencie, Prince Maurice of Nassau* (1613).[37] This book narrates the history of Dutch resistance to Spain from 1588 to 1609. It is replete with epic battlefield episodes. Twenty-eight folio pages are given to the siege of Bergen, twenty-one to "the horrible, bloudie, and unheard of siege" at Ostend. The book memorializes heroic feats and displays the cities that were conquered or defended, like the tableaux incorporated in Roman triumphs. Indeed, the book is the triumph that was denied to Nassau by jealous fates and indolent allies. It implicitly challenges James's cultivation of triumphs of peace, hinting that England failed in her duty by the low countries, both under Elizabeth, even when ostensibly aiding them (sigs. D2–D2ᵛ, Aa3ᵛ), and under James, when he entered into an ignoble peace with Spain. The pairing of James's exaggerated claims about his royal status and his lack of active virtue could well be alluded to in the dedication: "That which slender iudgements call greatnesse . . . is not so, but a bumbast of titles and other shreds of fortune ... But a mind well grown then best shewes it owne hight when it sends downe, and puts off the slippers of fortune." (sig. p4). One Englishman to achieve such greatness, the book teaches, is Sidney's brother, Robert Viscount Lisle. *The Triumphs of Nassau* is dedicated to Lisle's nephews the Earls of Pembroke and Montgomery, a gesture toward reviving the faded hope of a Sidney-Dudley gathering point for Protestant militarism.

Shakespeare's Roman tragedies participate in the Elizabethan and Jacobean discourse that revives and interrogates the triumphal royal entry or the triumph of peace. The civil war triumph that opens *Julius Caesar* encodes as well the Renaissance triumph of peace. The holiday rejoicing of the people dramatizes the Romans' conviction (according to Plutarch) that "to be ruled by one man alone, it would be a good mean for them to take breath a little after so many troubles and miseries as they had abidden in these civil wars."[38] This hope corresponds to the Tudor claim to have restored peace to England after the "troubles and miseries" of civil war. It was a claim open to question in both Rome and England. The tribunes object to Caesar's triumphing despite not having won a foreign victory:

> What conquest brings he home?
> What tributaries follow him to Rome,
> To grace in captive bonds his chariot wheels?
>
> (1.1.32–34)

Protestant militarists likewise objected to Elizabeth's failure to pursue foreign conquest. As the tribunes recall Pompey's triumphs in order to discredit Caesar's, so Leicester's triumphs in the low countries and (later) the triumphs of Nassau discredit the Elizabethan and Jacobean triumphs of peace. Caesar's triumph also has the marks of a royal entry. He displays none of the humble consciousness of his own mortality and none of the subjection to the state that were part of the triumphator's role. Caesar speaks the language of overweening Renaissance absolutism:

> The cause is in my will, I will not come:
> That is enough to satisfy the Senate.
>
> (2.2.71–72)

If in its detail Caesar's language is proleptically Jacobean, the general contrast between his vaunting and his mortality also encodes the situation of Elizabeth in 1599. Like Elizabeth's, Caesar's personal powers are in decline, and he is childless; like hers, his triumphs splendidly mask problematic political tensions.[39]

At the end of *Antony and Cleopatra*, Octavius pronounces that "The time of universal peace is come," doubtless in compliment to James's Augustan pacifism. Like English monarchs, Shakespeare's Octavius thus paradoxically uses the martial symbolism and function of triumph to promulgate peace and presents martial activity as peaceable. However, the triumph by which Octavius means to inaugurate peace is compromised by his concealed intent to lead Cleopatra captive, an intent that negates his generous protestations. The translation of triumph from war to peace is problematized in England by comparable contradictions. In Ireland, James presided over the consolidation of Elizabeth's conquests through limited but significant warfare, though for the most part James, like Octavius, eschewed war but practiced or benefited from legal subterfuge. The peace policy of both was to a degree a high-sounding rationalization of such practices, dictated also in Augustus's case by political caution and in James's by economic weakness.[40] As has been noted by earlier writers, there is also a resemblance between James's lackluster character as a triumphal performer and Shakespeare's dour Octavius. After the éclat of his 1604 entry, James participated in few public triumphs. As Octavius's triumph is dramatically upstaged by Cleopatra's spectacular performances in life and death, so James's subjects rejoiced nostalgically in the splendor of Elizabeth's reign.[41]

The most heavily compromised of Shakespeare's triumphs of peace occurs at the end of *Coriolanus*. After she has saved Rome from the avenging Coriolanus, Volumnia is greeted with the marks of a triumphator—public rejoicing and senatorial recognition (5.4.47–51, 5.5.1–3). For a Jacobean audience of about 1608, the threat posed by the exiled Coriolanus might have translated into Roman terms English anxiety about its own exiles, whether treasonous papists or, potentially, the puritans whom James had threatened to "harry . . . out of the land."[42] Volumnia's triumph marks a bloodless victory of the kind cherished by James and memorialized in the *Triumphs of King Iames the First*. But the political reality of Volumnia's victory is discomfiting. Having engineered the rise of Coriolanus by inculcating in him the ethos of Roman militarism, Volumnia brings him down with guileful speech, a weapon that he has never learned to wield. The ideal of peaceable victory is represented by Volumnia's sacrifice of her son to the interests of the city.[43]

III

Renaissance triumphs were not an exclusively royal prerogative. The annual pageants celebrating the inauguration of the Lord Mayor of London staked the city's claims to a political dignity commensurate with its economic power. These civic triumphs corresponded in form to ancient and royal triumphs. They could thus fulfill corresponding but rival functions, especially as they came to fill the vacuum created by James's aversion to public festivities.[44] The Lord Mayor's show consisted of his journey to Westminster, where he took his oath of office, and his return to the City, where his guild mounted processional tableaux.[45] An excursion to the center of royal power was thus followed by a triumphal return to the center of civic power, an itinerary symbolic of the uneasy relationship between the two centers. Like royal entries and triumphs of peace, the event was not strictly triumphal. The Lord Mayor had performed no martial feats, nor, at the beginning of his term, could he claim analogous feats of civil rule. What his guild and his city celebrated were their trades or mysteries, their history, and their autonomy. Their models in doing so were the mercantile cities of Renaissance Europe and the city of Rome, founded by Trojan Aeneas as London was founded by Trojan Brutus. London proudly translated its Lord Mayors into Consuls and its aldermen into Senators.[46] London's merchant class, tightly knit through trade, marriage, and friendship, might plausibly claim to constitute the new patriciate of its civil republic. It possessed its own *cursus honorum*, through which, as at Rome, candidates progressed toward the highest office. Like the consulate, that office was rotated annually. Like Roman *fasti*, London triumphs record the names of previous Lord Mayors who were free of the same guild as the new incumbent.[47] They enumerate the kings and lords who have been admitted to the guild, and whose names dignify the London shows as distinguished tributaries dignified the Roman.[48] London triumphs elaborate their own myths of the antiquity of the city guilds, and their own repertoire of mayoral heroes. Sir William Walworth, who in 1381 cut down the rebel Wat Tyler for contumely against the king, is manufactured into as exemplary a hero in London lore as Cincinattus in Roman.[49]

The *Romanitas* cultivated by Jacobean London, nevertheless, differs sharply from its original. The Lord Mayors' shows valorize and romanticize a mercantile, not a martial, heroism. Roman Senators were forbidden to engage in commerce, but commerce underpins the status of London and its Senators. Where plundered riches were displayed in the Roman triumph, it is riches created by trade and industry that are vaunted in London. Classical writers catalogue at length captured arms and booty, but Anthony Munday's *Triumphes of Re-united Britannia*, announcing the arrival of "The Shippe called the Royal Exchange," catalogues the spoils of the even wider world that can be conquered through peaceful trade in the form of "spices, silkes, and indico," of pepper, cloves, and mace (ll.107–33). Munday's *Chrusothriambos* catalogues and displays the industrious art of the goldsmith and allied trades, from "Pioners, Miners, and Delvers" to the "industrious Finer" and "the Mint-Maister, Coyners, Gold-Smithes, Jeweller, Lapidarie, Pearle-Driller, Plate-Seller, and such like, all lively acting their sondry professions" (ll.57–65).[50] Their consumption of far-flung and exotic materials and their role in sustaining the commonwealth endow these mysteries with a dignity that challenges comparison with the Roman mystique of war and the mysteries of state celebrated in James's triumphs and masques. Valorizing the mercantile implies a rewriting of James's historical mythography. For James, his advent turned an iron age back to a golden: "*Redeunt Saturnia regna.*" For the city fathers, such marks of the iron age as sailing the seas and digging in the bowels of the earth—though not the warfare traditionally associated with them—signify an epoch of useful industry.[51] Likewise, in *The Triumphs of Re-united Britannia*, Munday puns on the name of the new Lord Mayor, Sir Leonard Holiday, as initiator of a novel kind of industrious holiday. As in the revived Golden Age, Astraean justice is restored, but in the person of the Lord Mayor, not the king, and to a cityscape of *negotium*, not a landscape of *otium*. Munday implicitly contrasts mayoral rectitude with courtly idleness and profiteering, and he plays off his welcome to Sir Leonard Holiday against Dekker's welcome to the king in the previous year, which declared that "*Brittaine* till now nere kept a Holiday":

> When good provision for the poore is made,
> Sloth set to labour, vice curbd every where,
> When through the Citty every honest trade,
> Stands not of might or insolence in feare,

> But Justice in their goodnesse does them beare:
> Then, as before, in safety I may saie:
> All that yeare long, each daie is *Holliday*.⁵²

A combination of lavishness and sobriety characterizes the Lord Mayors' shows. In boasting the wealth and benefactions of city and guilds, London triumphs announce the city's global dominion and vie with the donatives of the Roman triumph, the lavish displays at James's court, and the tradition of aristocratic bounty. A mercantile prudence, however, also prevails. The companies of London display the gains of their peaceful conquests, but they are even more concerned to conserve and invest their gains. *Chruso-thriambos* acknowledges a fraternal bond between the companies of Goldsmiths and Fishmongers, but the text is careful to specify who pays the bill:

> No, 'tis the Gold-Smiths sole Society
> That in this Triumph beares the Pursse for all:
> As theirs the like, when like their lot doth fall.
>
> (ll.373–75)

In this as in other respects, the civic triumphs are the product of intricate social negotiations and contradictions. On the one hand, they distinguish themselves from courtly idleness by teaching the virtue of industriousness and from the improvidence of James's masquing by their scrupulous account-keeping. On the other hand, they align themselves with James by adventuring across the globe in order to bring home the trophies of peaceful triumphs.⁵³ Similarly, as earlier writers have pointed out, the city authorities who obstructed dramatic performances employed dramatists to create their triumphs, just as dramatists who might ridicule merchants on stage glorified them in triumphs.⁵⁴ Thus, the city of London now condemns shows and now utilizes them; in those shows, it places itself now at odds with the monarch and now in accord with him. Shakespeare reads similar negotiations and contradictions back into the triumphs of the city of Rome in his Elizabethan *Julius Caesar* and his Jacobean *Coriolanus*.

The republican oligarchy of *Julius Caesar*, like London's merchant oligarchy, jealously protects its power from monarchy on one side and from the common people on the other. In doing so, this oligarchy too exhibits a double standard. It stigmatizes shows as idle things, but it attempts to use shows to win political prestige. On the one hand, Brutus is not gamesome, Cassius loves no plays, Casca scorns the tag-rag people who clap and hiss Caesar "as they use to do the players in the theatre." Brutus's forum speech is a businesslike accounting to the people, in contrast to Antony's spectacular presentation of himself and of Caesar's slain body and bloody garment. Brutus, however, marks Caesar's overthrow by mounting a quasi-triumphal procession, with a display of weapons and victorious cries. The distinctively bourgeois voice of the London authorities and their allies, the puritan divines, is heard rather in the tribunes of *Julius Caesar*. Exhorting men to industriousness, identifying them with their trades, and insisting on the wearing of workaday garb, they exhibit a stay-at-home prudence and a mistrust of the "holiday" customs of Caesar's triumph. In order to impugn Caesar more effectively, however, the tribunes are willing to invoke memories of Pompey's equally splendid triumphs—as the London guilds were willing to participate in aristocratic values and myth making, boasting of their antiquity, their royal and noble patronage, and their mayoral heroes. Shakespeare's Rome, like his England, strikes an uneasy balance between domestic caution and imperial boldness.

In *Coriolanus*, even more than in *Julius Caesar*, the triumph is also a site of political tension and an occasion of political disruption. As in Jacobean London, this site constitutes a meeting point between traditional power and new claims of economic power. The right and the power to rule Rome are disputed between the aristocratic warrior order of nobles and the popular and mercantile order represented by the tribunes. The nobles owe their political preeminence to their success in war. One of the means by which they exploit their military prestige into political power is the triumph. Coriolanus's victories, their celebration in a form of triumph, and his ascent to the consulate, are all related events. The tribunes and the people for whom they speak, on the other hand, thrive in a time of peace. After the exile of Coriolanus, they view with satisfaction a mercantile Utopia, reminiscent of Munday's London in the mayoralty of Sir Leonard Holiday:

> Our tradesmen singing in their shops and going
> About their functions friendly . . .
> This is a happier and more comely time
> Than when these fellows ran about the streets,
> Crying confusion.
>
> (4.6.8–9, 27–29)

Haughtily or furiously, the nobles resist mercantile values. Volumnia curses Rome's "trades" and "occupations." Menenius scorns its "apron-men," its "crafts," its "pair of tribunes that have wrack'd for Rome / To make coals cheap" (4.1.13–14; 4.6.96, 118; 5.1.16–17).

However, there are surprising points of contact between the two sides. If the Tribunes laud the blessings of peace, their office also owes its existence to conflict. In order to speak *for* the commons, they must define an authority to speak *against*. Coriolanus is only too ready to cast himself in this role, and it is on the occasion of his triumph that the Tribunes discern his threat to their position and combatively challenge his rise to civic power. Conversely, the element of display in the triumph and in the ritual of consular elections partakes of the marketplace. Coriolanus condemns the traditional means of claiming a triumph, a message or speech to the Senate, as a devaluation of his *virtus*. Shakespeare's Jacobean vantage point endows the politics of the Roman triumph with the attributes of a bidding war. The summing-up of the spoils of conquest is performed in the manner of merchants marketing their wares and keeping their accounts, as Cominius computes Coriolanus's opponents and his "seventeen battles" (II.ii.100), and Volumnia and Menenius compute the number of his wounds:

Vol. He receiv'd in the repulse of Tarquin seven hurts i' th' body.
Men. One i' th' neck, and two i' th' thigh—there's nine that I know.
Vol. He had, before this last expedition, twenty-five wounds upon him.
Men. Now it's twenty-seven.
(2.1.149–55)

Coriolanus despises this marketing activity as work fit for the "commons," "Well then, I pray, your price a' th' consulship.?" (2.3.73–74). The text, however, represents a republican Rome where, as in Jacobean London, the "nobles" cannot remain uncontaminated by the powerful new model of social relations created by the mercantile city.[55]

The intricate negotiations thus generated both correspond to and differ from the negotiations between crown and city that mark the Jacobean Lord Mayors' shows. James the peacemaker does not resemble the bellicose ruling élite of *Coriolanus*; in fact, his pacifism aligns him with the Tribunes. On the other hand, the charge against Coriolanus of "affecting one sole throne, / Without assistance" (4.6.32–33) and the maneuvring for supremacy between him and the "commons" encode, as has long been recognized, the Jacobean tensions between crown and parliament.[56] This issue also bears upon the conventions of the triumph. The Roman triumphator personated both a god and a king, but his powers and status were strictly delimited. He was required to appeal to the Senate for the privilege of a triumph, to wait outside the walls of the city until the appointed day, and to relinquish his imperium on the next day. When Marius entered the Senate wearing the *toga palmata* of the triumphator, he was forced to withdraw. The harsh disposition of Coriolanus is at odds with the courtesy of the triumphator, and unhappily in accordance with the peremptoriness of King James. Aufidius diagnoses (*mutatis mutandis*) the inflexibility of both:

> Not to be other than one thing, not moving
> From th' casque to th' cushion, but commanding peace
> Even with the same austerity and garb
> As he controll'd the war.
> (4.7.42–45)

Shakespeare thus touches on an issue that also arises in the Lord Mayors' shows. The commemoration of the favors done by James's predecessors to the Merchant Taylors' company in Munday's *Triumphes of Re-United Britannia* (1605) instructs James, tactfully but unmistakably, in the courtesy that he notoriously lacked:

> *Henrie* the fourth . . .
>   Thought it no disgrace to his high state,
>   To weare the Clothing of the Companie,
>   A most Majestike royall courtesie. . . .
>   Of my sixt *Henry* they as freely gainde. . . .
>   He wore their clothing, milde and graciously:
>   For Princes loose no part of dignity,
>   In being affable, it addes to Majesty.
>   (ll.375, 378–80, 383, 385–87)

The multiple significances of the Roman triumph comprehend a range of contending political forces in Renaissance England. The monarchy imitates and modifies the triumph in accordance with a prudent pacifism, domesticating its mythology of imperial mastery. Aristocratic Protestant warriors revive the triumph as a monument to thwarted *virtus* and a bellicose call to a warfare that will display Catholic Europe on the stage of Protestant London. Metropolitan merchants stage triumphs to dignify the city and its accumulation of peaceful spoils through trade. The forms in which these negotiations are carried on display a corresponding convolution. The conquering ethos of the Roman triumph is reshaped first by the emperors and then by Christianity. Christian monarchs of the Renaissance turn the process back on itself, utilizing the triumph to translate their political claims into Roman terms. Shakespeare seems to travel in both directions in his representations of the triumph, as in his representation of Roman history in general. He acculturates the celebration of Roman conquest and its political stresses in terms of Renaissance England; his Rome is English. He also seizes on the Roman triumph as a way of writing about English imperial ventures; his England is Roman.

Notes

1. On triumph books, see Roy Strong, *Art and Power: Renaissance Festivals 1450–1630* (Woodbridge, Suffolk: Boydell & Brewer, 1985), 175–79, and Wendy Wall, *The Imprint of Gender: Authorship and Publication in the English Renaissance* (Ithaca, N.Y.: Cornell University Press, 1993), 111–27.

2. Shakespeare's earlier Ovidian writings also introduce triumphs. *Titus Andronicus* begins with Titus' fortune at its height, manifested in his triumphal entry to Rome. The fact that the triumph encompasses also the funeral of his dead sons and the play's wildly destructive action thereafter, exemplify the warnings of the triumphator's attendant about infirm glory. The villain, Aaron, counters military triumph with the subversive Ovidian triumph of love: 2.1.12, in *The Riverside Shakespeare*, ed. G. Blakemore Evans (Boston: Houghton Mifflin, 1974). After the rape in Lucrece, Tarquin departs in an antitriumph, where captor is confounded with captives and cannot exhibit his shameful spoils: "A captive victor that hath lost in gain; . . . Leaving his spoil perplexed in greater pain" (ll.730, 733).

3. *Puzzling Shakespeare; Local Reading and Its Discontents* (Berkeley and Los Angeles: University of California Press, 1988), 37.

4. Plutarch, *Life of Pompey*, 45 (Loeb trs.); Suetonius, *Julius Caesar*, 37 (Loeb trs.). For ancient sources, see C. Daremberg and E. Saglio, *Dictionnaire des antiquités grecques et romaines* (Paris: Hachette, 1877–99), s.v. "Triumphus." The definitive modern study is Hendrick Versnel, *Triumphus* (Leiden: E. J. Brill, 1970); see also Ernst Künzl, *Der römische Triumph* (Munich: C. H. Beck, 1988). On Roman triumphs and geography, see Claude Nicolet, *Space, Geography, and Politics in the Early Roman Empire*, Jerome Lectures, 19 (Ann Arbor: University of Michigan Press, 1991), ch. 2. For a wide-ranging bibliography, see Robert Baldwin, "A Bibliography of the Literature on Triumph," in *"All the world's a stage . . .": Art and Pageantry in the Renaissance and Baroque*, eds. Barbara Wisch and Susan Scott Munshower, Part 1, *Papers in Art History from The Pennsylvania State University* 6 (1990): 359–85.

5. *Poets in a Landscape* (Harmondsworth: Penguin, 1957), 239.
6. Livy, 45.35, 38.44–46; Plutarch, *Aemilius Paulus*, 30–31.
7. For Jonson's copy of Modius, see David McPherson, *Ben Jonson's Library and Marginalia*, Studies in Philology 81, no. 5 (1974): 71–72, and, for selected transcriptions of his annotations, *Ben Jonson*, eds. C. H. Herford and Percy and Evelyn Simpson (Oxford: Clarendon Press, 1925–52), 11, 594–96. For other humanist writings, see W. Milgate, "Donne and the Roman Triumph," *Parergon* 1 (1971): 18–23.
8. M. J. Rodríguez–Salgado et. al., *Armada 1588–1988* (London: Penguin/National Maritime Museum, 1988), 274; Gordon Kipling, "Triumphal Drama: Form in English Civic Pageantry," *Renaissance Drama* n.s. 8 (1977): 40.
9. Ed. "N. Eleutherius," STC 7570. The book does not show a place of publication. The second edition of STC speculates that it was published in Germany.
10. STC 21672.
11. The Franco-Turkish alliance dated from 1536. Its revival in 1569 made possible the Turkish capture of Cyprus. See Stanford Shaw, *History of the Ottoman Empire and Modern Turkey* (Cambridge: Cambridge University Press, 1976–77), 1, 177. For an earlier English example of the use of Petrarch's *Trionfi* to support a political program, see Kenneth R. Bartlett, "The Occasion of Lord Morley's Translation of the *Trionfi*: The Triumph of Chastity over Politics," in *Petrarch's "Triumphs"; Allegory and Spectacle*, ed. Konrad Eisenbichler and Amilcare A. Iannucci, University of Toronto Italian Studies, 4 (Ottawa: Dovehouse, 1990), 325–34.
12. Among many modern accounts, see David M. Bergeron, *English Civic Pageantry 1558–1642* (Columbia: University of South Carolina Press, 1971), 71–89, and Graham Parry, *The Golden Age Restor'd: The Culture of the Stuart Court, 1603–42* (Manchester: Manchester University Press, 1981), ch. 1. Both books reproduce illustrations of the triumphal arches discussed below.
13. (Cambridge, 1603), STC 4493. There was a parallel volume containing poems in English, *Sorrowes Joy* (Cambridge, 1603), STC 7598.
14. For example, Appian, *Punica*, 66.
15. See Jean Gagé, "Les clientèles triomphales de la république romaine: A propos d'un aspect du 'principat' d'Auguste" *Revue historique* 218 (1957): 1–31.
16. Parodic triumphs occur in Latin literature as early as Plautus in the golden age of Roman conquest (*Amphitruo*, 185–262; *Bacchides*, 1068–75). Parodic triumphs become a convention of the love elegy (Propertius, 2.8, 14, 4.8; Ovid, *Amores*, 1.2, 7, 2.12): see Karl Galinsky, "The Triumph Theme in Augustan Elegy," *Wiener Studien* 82 (1969): 75–107. On the appropriateness of Shakespeare's parody and burlesque triumphs to court events, see H. Neville Davies, "Jacobean *Antony and Cleopatra*," *Shakespeare Studies* 17 (1985): 123–58.
17. See the treatment of the tragic reversals that befell Aemilius Paullus (Livy, 45.1; Plutarch, *Aemilius Paullus*, 34–35), Scipio (Petrarch, *Africa*, 9.410–20), and Germanicus (Tacitus, *Annals* 2.41).
18. *Aeneid*, 8.714–28.
19. Suetonius *Nero*, 25.
20. Transformations of triumph are traced in Michael McCormick, *Eternal Victory: Triumphal rulership in late antiquity, Byzantium, and the early medieval West* (Cambridge: Cambridge University Press, and Paris: Editions de la Maison de Sciences de l'homme, 1986). See also E. H. Kantorowicz, "The King's

Advent," *Art Bulletin* 26 (1944): 207–31; Michael Greenhalgh, *The Classical Tradition in Art* (New York: Harper and Row, 1978), 21–22; Strong, 42–97; Loren Partridge and Randolph Starn, *Arts of Power: Three Italian Halls of State 1300–1600* (Berkeley and Los Angeles: University of California Press, 1992), 149–256.

21. David Galloway, ed., *Records of Early English Drama: Norwich 1540–1642* (Toronto: University of Toronto Press, 1984), 252.

22. Bergeron, *English Civic Pageantry*, 14, 23–25.

23. Strong, *Art and Power*, 42.

24. On the general issue, see Sabine MacCormack, "Change and Continuity in Late Antiquity: The Ceremony of Adventus," *Historia* 21 (1972): 721–22. On the queens' entries, see Bergeron, *English Civic Pageantry*, 20, 24; Kipling, "Triumphal Drama," 53; Wall, *The Imprint of Gender*, 117–20.

25. Jonson, *Part of the Kings Entertainment in Passing to His Coronation* (1604; reprinted, 1616), ll. 93–95, in Herford and Simpson, vol. 7. On Alleyn's role, see Andrew Gurr, *The Shakespearean Stage 1574–1642*, 3d ed. (Cambridge: Cambridge University Press, 1992), 10. I take James's entry as an instance of triumphal contestation rather than of unproblematized royal dominance: cf. Gail Kern Paster, "The Idea of London in Masque and Pageant," in *Pageantry in the Shakespearean Theater*, ed. David M. Bergeron (Athens: University of Georgia Press, 1985), 52–63. For contrary readings, see Jonathan Goldberg, *James I and the Politics of Literature* (Baltimore: Johns Hopkins University Press, 1983), 30–33, 54; Leah Marcus, *The Politics of Mirth* (Chicago: University of Chicago Press, 1986), 64–65, and *Puzzling Shakespeare*, 163, 168, 184.

26. David M. Bergeron, "Gilbert Dugdale and the Royal Entry of James I," *Journal of Medieval and Renaissance Studies* 13 (1983): 115.

27. STC 16632.

28. *Troia-Nova Triumphans* (1612), ll.1–3, in *The Dramatic Works of Thomas Dekker*, ed. Fredson Bowers (Cambridge: Cambridge University Press, 1953–61), vol. 3.

29. *The Quenes Majesties Passage through the Citie of London to Westminster the Day before her Coronacion* (1559), in Arthur F. Kinney, *Elizabethan Backgrounds* (Hamden, Conn.: Archon, 1975), 32, 20. On the continuing impact of Elizabeth's entry, see Bergeron, "Middleton's *No Wit, No Help* and Civic Pageantry," in *Pageantry in the Shakespearean Theater*, 65–66, and Curtis Perry, "The Citizen Politics of Nostalgia: Queen Elizabeth in Early Jacobean London," *Journal of Medieval and Renaissance Studies* 23 (1993): 94.

30. *The Kings Entertainment*, ll.533–644.

31. Bergeron, *English Civic Pageantry*, 74.

32. As expressed by the Venetian ambassador Nicolo Molin and implied by the English spectator Gilbert Dugdale: Bergeron, *English Civic Pageantry*, 78, and "Gilbert Dugdale and the Royal Entry," 119.

33. Dekker, *The Magnificent Entertainment: Given to King James*, ll.698–99, in Bowers, vol. 2. In 1619, the English merchants of Lisbon erected a triumphal arch that asserted English prestige to Iberia, as the Italians and Dutch had asserted their prestige to England in 1604. At a time when popular opposition to James's Spanish alliance was intensified by the outbreak of the Thirty Years' War and the abandonment to the Hapsburgs of Bohemia (the kingdom of the Protestant Frederick Count Palatine and James's daughter Elizabeth), the merchants' arch also deployed the official Jacobean rhetoric of peace to encode a

threat of war, on behalf of the "English nation" as distinct from the crown. This arch displayed "a Lyon, and a Leopard, one bearing the Sheild of Spaine, the other that of England, with sharpe pointed swords goaring and thrusting one at an other, yet in the midst ... two Olive branches were drawne, being the symboles of peace ... the English nation did hereby intimate to the King [of Spain], their noble demerit in the Conquest of *Portingall,* by their ancient descent, and the inviolable amitie they have retained with the Kings of this Kingdome, implying further, their desire of love and peace betweene the Kings of Great Britaine and Spaine" (*The triumphant and sumptuous Arch erected by the Company of English Merchants residing at Lisbone, upon the Spanish Kings entry made thereinto* [1619], STC 19843, sigs. B2ᵛ–B3).

34. STC 17309.

35. For the issues of the controversy, see *The Political Works of James I,* ed. Charles Howard McIlwain, Harvard Political Classics, 1 (Cambridge, Mass.: Harvard University Press, 1918), 55–80. The obscure Marcellin is not mentioned in this study or in David Harris Willson, "James I and His Literary Assistants," *Huntington Library Quarterly* 8 (1944): 35–57. On speech as manifestation of Jacobean power see Goldberg, *James I and the Politics of Literature* 47–50.

36. Samuel R. Gardiner, *History of England from the Accession of Iames I ... 1603–1642* (London: Longmans Green, 1883–84), 2, 161–63; Parry, *The Golden Age Restor'd,* ch. 4.

37. STC 17676.

38. *Caesar,* [57], in Geoffrey Bullough, ed., *Narrative and Dramatic Sources of Shakespeare* (London: Routledge and Kegan Paul, 1958–75), 5, 78.

39. See Mark Rose, "Conjuring Caesar: Ceremony, History, and Authority in 1599," *English Literary Renaissance* 19 (1989): 291–304.

40. On the Anglicisation of Ireland under James, see J. C. Beckett, *The Making of Modern Ireland 1603–1923* (London: Faber, 1966), 40–48; *A New History of Ireland,* ed. T. W. Moody et al., vol. 3 (Oxford: Clarendon Press, 1976), 187–210. On Augustus' methods, see Ronald Syme, *The Roman Revolution,* corrected ed. (Oxford: Clarendon Press, 1952), 2–4, 154–57, 303–4, 521–24. On the financial embarrassments inherited and compounded by James, see Frederick C. Dietz, *English Public Finance 1558–1641* (New York: Century, 1932), 86–133.

41. Compare the various contemporary criticisms of James's public persona, cited in Davies, "Jacobean *Antony and Cleopatra,"* 128, and Shannon Miller, "Topicality and Subversion in William Shakespeare's *Coriolanus," Studies in English Literature 1500–1900* 32 (1992): 292. The phenomenon of Elizabethan nostalgia and its historiography are judiciously reviewed in Perry, "The Citizen Politics of Nostalgia."

42. Gardiner, *History of England,* 1, 157.

43. For a contrary treatment, see Steven Marx, "Shakespeare's Pacifism," *Renaissance Quarterly* 45 (1992): 85–86. For Marx, Volumnia's triumph enacts unproblematically "James's emblem: the triumph of Eirene over Mars."

44. Glynne Wickham, *Early English Stages* (London: Routledge and Kegan Paul, 1959–72), 2(1), 237–38.

45. See Bergeron, *English Civic Pageantry,* Part 2, passim; Theodore B. Leinwand, "London Triumphing: The Jacobean Lord Mayor's Show," *Clio* 11 (1982): 138–39. My discussion of the political claims of the civic triumphs is anticipated by Paster, "The Idea of London."

46. Anthony Munday, Chruso-thriambos. The Triumphes Of Golde (1611) ll.1–7, 145–50, in Pageants and Entertainments of Anthony Munday, ed. David M. Bergeron, The Renaissance Imagination, 11 (New York: Garland, 1985); Dekker, Britannia's Honor (1628), ll.23–25, in Bowers, vol. 4. The Lord Mayors' shows, with their chariots and floats, resemble the ancient triumph more closely than do the royal entries, where the emphasis fell more on arches and stationary tableaux: Kipling, "Triumphal Drama," 37, n. 1.

47. For example, Munday, Chrysanaleia: The Golden Fishing (1616), ll.273–92.

48. For example, Munday, The Triumphes of Re-united Britannia (1605), ll.407–34; Dekker, Troia-Nova Triumphans, ll.364–407.

49. Walworth was memorialized in the Lord Mayor's show of 1590 (Bergeron, English Civic Pageantry, 133–34) and in Munday's Chrysanaleia (ll.179–236); Walworth also figures as one of Richard Johnson's Nine Worthies of London (1592), STC 14685.7. Walworth's feat encodes at once the assertiveness of the civic oligarchy vis-à-vis the crown and its anxiety vis-à-vis the populace.

50. Elizabeth's entry to Norwich in 1578 had educed a provincial instance of this mercantile self-assertion, a tableau demonstrating and boasting the skill of the city's weavers. See Galloway, Records, 254–55. For typical Roman catalogues of booty, where art yields to military prowess, see Livy, 26.21, 33.23, 34.52.

51. On the topical issues encoded in Munday's show, see Leah Marcus, "City Metal and Country Mettle: The Occasion of Ben Jonson s Golden Age Restored," in Pageantry in the Shakespearean Theatre, ed. Bergeron, 26–47.

52. Lines 482–95. For Dekker, see 1. 308, n.

53. This alignment was apt to be unstable. In 1606, there were already complaints at court by "divers Merchants and Merchant's wives . . . of much Injustice and Oppression done [in Spain] to our Nation" (Davies, 126); compare this with the implications of the triumphal arch of the English merchants at Lisbon in 1619 (n. 33, above). For detail of the relations between court and city, see Robert G. Ashton, The City and the Court 1603–1643 (Cambridge: Cambridge University Press, 1979), ch. 1–3; R. Malcolm Smuts, Court Culture and the Origins of a Royalist Tradition in Early Stuart England (Philadelphia: University of Pennsylvania Press, 1987).

54. Leinwand, "London Triumphing," 138. Munday epitomizes these negotiations, as an actor and playwright who also declares himself (on the title pages of a number of his shows) "Citizen and Draper of London."

55. The relation between Shakespeare's play and the emerging market economy and its political consequences are admirably analyzed, with particular reference to conditions in Warwickshire, in Richard Wilson, "Against the Grain: Representing the Market in Coriolanus," Seventeenth Century 6 (1991): 111–48.

56. The seminal study is W. Gordon Zeeveld, "'Coriolanus' and Jacobean Politics," Modern Language Review 57 (1962), 321–24; the most extensive is Clifford Chalmers Huffman, Coriolanus in Context (Lewisburg, Pa.: Bucknell University Press, 1972).

Contributors

JOHN MICHAEL ARCHER, Associate Professor of English at the University of New Hampshire, Durham, is the author of *Sovereignty and Intelligence: Spying and Court Culture in the English Renaissance.*

BRUCE AVERY is Assistant Professor of English at San Francisco State University and is currently working on a book about maps and their relationship to Renaissance literature.

RICHMOND BARBOUR is Assistant Professor of English at Oregon State University and the author of "The Elizabethan Jonson in Print," "Jonson and the Motives of Print," and "'When I acted Young Antinous': Boy-Actors and the Erotics of Jonsonian Theaters."

GLENN CLARK is a Ph.D. candidate in English at the University of Chicago, working on a dissertation exploring representations of hospitality in English Renaissance literature.

JOHN GILLIES is Senior Lecturer in the Drama Division at Latrobe University, Australia, and the author of *Shakespeare and the Geography of Difference.*

SARA HANNA, Associate Professor of Engish at New Mexico Highlands University, has published articles on Shakespeare's classicism and iconography.

LINDA MCJANNET, Professor of English at Bentley College, is the compiler of the Garland Bibliography of *Henry VIII* and the author of several essays on Shakespeare, Renaissance drama, and dramatic theory. Her study of the voice of English stage directions from medieval times to the closing of the theaters is forthcoming from the University of Delaware Press.

ANTHONY MILLER is Senior Lecturer in English at the University of Sydney, Australia. He has edited Shakespeare's *Richard III* and *Julius Caesar* and is working on a study of ceremonial reenactments and literary representations of the Roman triumph in Renaissance England.

RHONDA LEMKE SANFORD, University of Colorado at Boulder, is writing her dissertation on "Maps and their Representation in English Renaissance Literature."

BARBARA SEBEK is Assistant Professor of English at Colorado State University. Her current project is a book about the discourses of exchange in early modern representations of social and sexual relations.

VIRGINIA MASON VAUGHAN, Professor of English at Clark University, is the author of *Othello: A Contextual History* and the co-author (with Alden T. Vaughan) of *Shakespeare's Caliban: A Cultural History*.

Index

Africa, 132–37; Barbary region of, 177, 185–90, 191–95
Africanus, Leo, 132–34, 141, 145, 149–50 n. 12, 152 n. 33
Agnew, Jean-Christophe, 197 n. 7, 237–38
Aguirre, Lope de, 208, 226
Alexander VI, 35–36
Alexander the Great, 109, 116
Alleyn, Edward, 271
All's Well That Ends Well, 193
Angelou, Maya, 82–83 n. 9
Anne, Queen (of England), 130, 131, 139–40
Antioch, 88, 103 n. 3, 113
Antony and Cleopatra, 105 n. 27, 113, 122, 128 n. 34, 129; Cleopatra as Egypt, 73, 74–76, 77, 84 n. 21; and Roman triumph, 261, 268–69; and royal entry, 276; setting of, 87, 107, 114, 119
Appadurai, Arjun, 195 n. 3, 201 n. 29
Appleby, Joyce Oldham, 197 n. 10, 202 n. 31
Ariosto, Ludovico, 205, 209
Aristophanes, 46, 60
Athens, 113, 117, 118, 124
atlases, 8–11, 22–24, 34

Bacon, Sir Francis, 233, 251–52
Baker, Sir Richard, 24
Barber, C. L., 258 n. 37
Barber, Peter, 83 n. 12
Barbour, Nevill, 199 n. 20
Barthelemy, Anthony Gerard, 16 n. 9, 152 nn. 31 and 33, 202 n. 30
Bartlett, Kenneth R., 284 n. 11
Beaumont, Francis, 148 n. 2
Berger, Harry, 55, 61–62 n. 17
Bergeron, David M., 284 n. 12
Best, George, 145, 152 n. 34
Bloch, Maurice, 49, 53, 62 n. 19

Boemus, Johannes, 23
Boerth, Robbie, 202 n. 29
Bolgar, R. R., 126 n. 2
Boose, Lynda E., 140, 145, 149 n. 4, 151 n. 30, 152 n. 39
Bowes, Jerome, 175 n. 36
Bradbrook Muriel, 196 n. 7
Braudel, Fernand, 163
Bray, Alan, 174 n. 19
Brooke, Ralph, 70
Bruno, Giordano, 257 n. 23
Bruster, Douglas, 197 n. 7

Caesar, Julius, 204, 210–11, 214, 244, 253, 262
Camden, William, 9, 70, 138, 143–44, 146–48, 150 nn. 19 and 21, 153 n. 46
Campion, Thomas, 130
Carey, Lucius (Viscount Falkland), 102
Carleton, Dudley, 139–41, 143, 145, 146, 148, 152 n. 39
Cartwright, John, 102
Case, John, 64–65, 67
Casimir, Prince Joannes, 265
Castle of Perseverance, The, 24
Cato, 112, 211
Cecil, William (Lord Burghley), 48, 161
Certeau, Michel de, 44 n. 38, 63
Chancellor, Richard, 156–58, 165
Charles V (king of Spain), 205, 208
Cicero, 112, 113, 117, 123, 124, 128 n. 31, 210
Cnidus, 104 n. 12
Cohen, Walter, 197 n. 7
Columbus, Christopher, 63, 69, 74, 153 n. 41, 210
Comedy of Errors, 103 n. 1, 107, 114, 121, 172 n. 2, 186; Christian elements in, 94; and commerce, 176–77, 178, 195 n. 3; geography of, 88–

290

INDEX

94, 99, 113, 116, 127 n. 19; Hellenistic elements in, 13, 83 n. 11, 92; pre-Christian elements in, 86–87; sources, 87, 92–93
commodity exchange, 14, 177–95
Conrad, Joseph, 226
Coote, C. H., 20–21, 42 n. 9, 44 n. 37
Corinth, 93
Coriolanus, 107, 119, 128 n. 31; and civic pageantry, 280–82; and Roman triumph, 261, 269–70; and royal entry, 276–77
Cornwallis, William, 233
Cortes, Hernan, 208, 226
Cunningham, J. S., 228 n. 30
Cunningham, William, 36, 38, 243, 244
Cymbeline: and cartography, 32–33, 41, 70–75, 77–79, 230–31, 234, 244–55; and Imogen's body, 12–13, 70–75, 81, 239–41, 243–45; and national identity, 14, 230–31; Posthumus' wager in, 69–75, 236–41; sources of 80, 235; and travel literature, 74–81

D'Amico, Jack, 199 n. 20, 200 n. 25, 202 n. 30
Daniel, Samuel, 62 n. 20
Davies, John, 65, 68, 82 n. 8
Dee, John, 9
Dekker, Thomas, 272, 278–79
Delphos, 113
Descartes, René, 25
Devi, Mahasweta, 79–80
Donne, John, 68, 69, 70, 72, 242–43
Drake, Sir Francis, 205, 210, 226
Drayton, Michael, 22, 25, 34, 38, 102
Drummond, William (of Hawthornden), 20, 131
Du Bartas, Guillaume, 265–66
Durkheim, Émile, 183

Eden, Richard, 155
Edward VI (king of England), 156, 157–58
Edwards, Paul, 153 n. 46
Elizabeth I (queen of England), 15, 48, 56, 64, 143, 149 n. 4, 172 n. 2, 264; as Astrea, 65; Armada portrait of, 205; death of, 83 n. 10; Ditchley portrait of, 22, 64, 66, 80, 85 n. 25; as Europa, 64, 65; in royal processions, 264–66, 270–71, 272, 287 n. 50; and Russia, 161, 164
Engle, Lars, 197 n. 7
Ephesus, 88, 92, 93–94, 102, 113, 116
Epidamnum, 91, 93, 127 n. 19
Euripides, 112, 115, 210

Fischer, Sandra, 195 n. 2
Fletcher, Giles, 155, 161, 162–65
Forman, Simon, 84 n. 24
four continents, 9, 12
Fowler, Alastair, 258 n. 39
Franks, Michael, 82 n. 9
Frederick V (king of Bohemia, Elector Palatine), 265, 274, 285 n. 33
Freedman, Barbara, 32, 47
Frey, Charles, 42 n. 7
Fumerton, Patricia, 235

Geertz, Clifford, 213
geography: classical concepts of, 210; literary, 21; "New," 27–31, 224–25, 234, 255; poetic, 8; relation to theater, 15, 22–24, 40–41. See also atlases; maps
Gillies, John, 47, 112, 153 n. 41, 179, 234, 245; *Shakespeare and the Geography of Difference*, 11, 16 n. 10, 43 n. 17. 83 n. 12, 86, 106 n. 34, 150 n. 16, 152 n. 36, 174 n. 25, 196 n. 4, 256 n. 12
Gilroy, Paul, 174 n. 33
Globe Theater, 23, 41, 49, 129, 254
Golding, Arthur, 195 n. 3, 201 n. 27
Gombrich, E. H., 33
Goss, John, 16 n. 3
Gower, John, 95, 98, 100–1, 103 n. 3, 104 n. 18
Greece: history of, 110–12, 123–25; as licentious, 108; literature of, 115–16; national character of, 108, 112–26; opposed to Rome, 13, 110–18, 124–26; Shakespeare's construction of, 107, 113–26
Greenblatt, Stephen, 84 n. 22, 197 n. 7, 207, 208–09, 241
Greene, Gayle, 201 n. 29
Gregory, Christopher, 195 n. 3

Hakluyt, Richard, 9, 11
Halio, Jay, 198 n. 17

Hall, Edward, 155
Hall, Kim F., 149 n. 4, 151 nn. 23, 28, and 30, 152 n. 31, 175 n. 40, 198 n. 16
Hamlet, 63
Harley, J. B., 27, 33–34, 35, 53, 60, 245, 246
Hart, Keith, 195 n. 3
Hartog, François, 75–76, 84 n. 22
Harvey, P. D. A., 20, 21
Hastings, Lady Mary, 168, 175 n. 36
Hawarden, Samuel, 266–67
Helgerson, Richard, 22, 23, 32, 40, 47, 48, 83 n. 12, 196 nn. 4 and 7 Henri IV (king of France), 168, 171, 264
1 Henry IV, 15, 19, 108; Hotspur's language, 56–57; map display, 12, 32, 44–45 n. 50, 53–60, 168; sources, 53, 62 n. 20
2 Henry IV, 108
Henry V, 139
2 Henry VI, 12
Henry VII (king of England), 247, 248, 264
Henry VIII (king of England), 140, 155, 175 n. 36, 251
Herodotus, 75, 108, 110, 116, 228 n. 30
Herzog, Werner, 208
Heywood, Thomas: *Fair Maid of the West*, 33, 177–78, 179, 184–95; *If You Know Not Me*, 199 n. 20
Highet, Gilbert, 126 n. 2, 262–63
Hoenselaars, A. J., 16 n. 8
Holiday, Leonard, 278–79, 280
Holinshed, Raphael, 53, 62 n. 20, 155
Homer, 110, 115, 116, 197–98 n. 12
Horsey, Jerome, 168
Horace, 123, 124
Howard, Jean, 185–86, 199 nn. 19 and 21, 200 n. 24, 202 n. 30

James I (king of England), 15, 139, 246, 247, 249, 278; accession of, 83 n. 10, 138; and civic pageantry, 278, 281–83; desire for unified Britain, 14, 138, 230, 232–34, 235–36, 250, 252, 254–55, 256 n. 9; and royal entry, 266, 271, 272–75; and Spanish alliance, 285–86 n. 33
Jenkinson, Anthony, 158–59, 165, 166, 169

Jones, Eldred D., 16 n. 9, 130, 152 n. 31
Jones, Emrys, 115, 255 n. 5
Jones, Inigo, 141, 142, 146
Jonson, Ben, 20, 26, 115, 128 n. 28, 130–48, 263, 271, 273; *The Alchemist*, 216–17; *Catiline*, 210, 228 n. 18; *Every Man Out of his Humour*, 131–32; *Masque of Beauty*, 139, 140, 148; *Masque of Blackness*, 130–48
Julius Caesar, 99, 107, 120, 228 n. 28; and civic pageantry, 279–80; and Roman triumph, 261, 267–68; and royal entry, 275–76
Juvenal, 109, 228 n. 32

Kahn, Coppelia, 201 n. 29
Karrow, Robert W. 8, 16 n. 3
Kernan, Alvin, 258 n. 37
King Lear, 15, 39, 41, 45 n. 55; love test in, 50–53; map display in, 12, 31–33, 34–35, 37–38, 49, 50–53, 168
Knapp, Jeffrey, 138, 151 n. 21
Knutson, Rosalind, 198–99 n. 18
Kolodny, Annette, 63, 75, 78
Kopytoff, Igor, 183, 201 n. 29
Koyre, Alexander, 257 n. 23

Landis, Joan Hutton, 104 nn. 9, 10, and 11
Lanier, Douglas, 195 n. 3
Leech, Clifford, 114, 126 n. 3
Lefebvre, Henri, 25–27, 33, 43 n. 27, 62 n. 18, 169, 231–32
Leinwand, Theodore, 197 n. 10
Levi-Strauss, Claude, 195 n. 3, 201 n. 29
Lithgow, William, 102
Livy, 263
Lloyd, Lodowick, 272
Lord Mayors' pageants 130
Love's Labors Lost, 14, 154–55, 166–72; and blackness, 166–72; Russian masque in, 154–55, 168–72; and slavery, 14, 155, 155–72
Lucan, 210–11, 214, 224, 226
Lynam, Edward, 35

Macbeth, 32
McCormick, Michael, 284 n. 20
McEachern, Claire, 256 n. 9

INDEX

Macedon, 103 n. 3
Machiavelli, Niccolo, 204
Magellan, Ferdinand, 210
maps, 46, 27; definition of, 11–12; as masculine, 64, 68; as political, 13, 69: relation to theater, 22–24, 28, 40, 47–48, 60–61; and space, 25–27; and symbolism, 34–36, 248, 250. See also atlases; geography
Marcus, Leah, 255 n. 5, 259 n. 50, 261
Marlowe, Christopher, 27, 105 n. 23, 137, 203–29, 242. See also Tamburlaine
Mary I (queen of England), 158
Mary (queen of Scots), 271
Masque of Blackness, 130–48; and blackness, 140–41, 146; and British racial anxiety, 13, 146–48; and geography, 131–37; staging of, 141–43
Mauss, Marcel, 184, 195 n. 3, 236, 252
Measure for Measure, 92, 193
Mercator, Gerhard, 8, 9
Merchant of Venice, 44 n. 35, 92, 114, 185–91, 198 n. 17, 199 nn. 18 and 22, 200 n. 25
merrygreeks, 108, 126
Merry Wives of Windsor, 83 n. 11
Middleton, Thomas, 130
Midsummer Night's Dream, 107, 113, 118, 122
Mikalachki, Jodi, 257 n. 33, 258 n. 41
Miola, Robert S., 117–18, 128 n. 32, 257 n. 26, 258 n. 37
Modius, François, 263–64
Montrose, Louis, 82 n. 3
Moore, Henrietta, 201 n. 29
Morgan, Victor, 32, 33
Much Ado About Nothing, 84 n. 24
Mullaney, Steven, 149 n. 9, 196 n. 7
Munday, Anthony, 131, 145, 153 n. 41, 278, 279, 280, 282, 287 nn. 49, 51, and 54
Münster, Sebastian, 134, 135, 136
Mytilene, 91, 101, 113

Naipaul, V. S., 227 n. 13
Neely, Carol, 200 n. 26
Newman, Karen, 201 n. 29
New World, 63, 74, 77, 78, 138, 153 n. 41
Nicolls, Thomas, 111

Norden, John, 48
Nosworthy, J. M., 84 n. 24

Olds, Sharon, 83 n. 9
Ordinalia, 24
Orgel, Stephen, 149 n. 4, 150 n. 16
Ortelius, Abraham, 9, 40, 42 n. 9, 86, 104 nn. 12, 13, and 14, 156, 198 n. 13, 223, 225; "Descriptio Peregrinationis D. Pauli," 89–91; *Theatrum Orbis Terrarum*, 8, 9–11, 12, 21, 23, 47, 88, 101, 104 n. 10, 129
Othello, 30–31, 33
Ovid, 218

Parker, Patricia, 83 n. 10, 83–84 n. 16, 84 n. 23, 175 n. 37, 240, 255 n. 5, 258 n. 38
Parry, Graham, 284 n. 12
Paul, Saint, 88, 91, 102
Pentapolis, 91–92, 95–96, 97, 113, 122, 127 n. 20
Pericles, 107, 113, 114, 115, 120–22; authorship, 103 n. 5; geography of, 88–92, 94–97, 99–100; Hellenistic elements in, 13, 92, 97; pre-Christian elements in, 86–87, 98–99; sources, 87, 94, 96, 98, 100–1
Petrarch, 12, 70–71, 265
Philip II (king of Spain), 205
Plato, 139
Platter, Thomas, 23–24, 139
Plautus, 87, 104 n. 17
Pliny, 147
Plutarch: history of Greece, 116, 117, 118, 123–24, 128 n. 27; history of Rome, 118, 125, 263; as source, 109, 110, 115, 214; view of Scythians, 256 n. 19
Porter, Thomas, 83 n. 13
Pory, John. See Africanus, Leo
Ptolemy, 46, 134, 135, 234

Rabasa, Jose, 174 n. 25
Rackin, Phyllis, 32, 47, 61 n. 3, 62 n. 26
Raleigh, Sir Walter, 12, 63, 69, 207, 225, 226
Randolph, Thomas, 159
Rape of Lucrece: and cartography, 12, 28, 64; and *Cymbeline*, 243–44; de-

scriptions of Lucrece, 64, 68–69, 82 n. 5, 83 n. 10; Roman elements in, 107, 114, 119, 120, 283 n. 2
Relihan, Constance C., 106 n. 37
Richard II, 12, 32, 36, 37, 38
Richard III, 28, 30
Roberts, Lewes, 33, 197 n. 8; *Merchant's Mappe of Commerce*, 177–84, 185
Rogers, J. D., 11, 42 n. 9
Roman triumph, 15, 27, 40, 130, 211–16, 228 n. 28, 260–87; and Lord Mayors' shows, 277–83, 287 n. 46; monarch as triumphator, 261; Renaissance reenactments of, 263–67; and Shakespearean tragedy, 267–70, 275–77, 279–82
Rome, 138; national character of, 109, 112–13; opposed to Greece, 13, 109, 118–20, 124–26. *See also* Roman triumph
Rosenthal, Earl, 227 n. 10
Rubens, Peter Paul, 218
Rubin, Gayle, 201 n. 29
Russia, 154–67, 164; and Muscovy Company, 156–58, 161, 165, 166; and slavery, 164–67, 171, 174 n. 31

Sacks, David Harris, 197 n. 10
Sallust, 228–29 n. 32
Salutati, Collucio, 204
Sandys, George, 102, 218
Savonarola, Girolamo, 265
Saxton, Christopher, 16 n. 6, 21–22, 34–35, 38, 48, 85 n. 25
Schama, Simon, 198 n. 17, 202 n. 31
Seaton, Ethel, 21, 42 n. 9
Sedgwick, Eve, 201 n. 29
Seneca, 111–12, 122, 195 n. 3, 201 n. 27, 210, 215
Shakespeare, William, 108–9; sonnets, 28–30, 33, 240, 241. *See also* individual works
Shirley, Rodney W., 44 n. 37
Sidney, Henry, 156, 158, 165
Sidney, Sir Philip, 20, 26, 156, 164–67; *Astrophil and Stella*, 164–67, 174 n. 32; *Defense of Poesy*, 181
Sidney, Robert, 275
Silvester, Joshua, 265
Skelton, R. A., 16 n. 4
Smuts, R. Malcolm, 151 n. 23

Sophocles, 110
Sparta, 103 n. 3
Speed, John, 48, 60, 101–3
Spencer, T. J. B., 108
Spenser, Edmund, 40
Spevack, Marvin, 87
Spivak, Gayatri, 79–80
Stallybrass, Peter, 82 n. 7, 201 n. 29
Stapfer, Paul, 107
Stimpson, Catherine, 82 n. 5
Stone, Lawrence, 151 n. 24
Strabo, 46, 161
Strathern, Marilyn, 201 n. 29
Strier, Richard, 256 n. 16
Strong, Roy, 205, 227 n. 10
Suetonius, 263
Sullivan, Garrett A., 196 n. 7
Syracuse, 91, 93, 116
Syria, 95

Tamburlaine, Parts I and II, 14, 21, 40, 41, 129, 137, 203–29; banquet scene, 212, 216; and entropy, 221–25; geography of, 203–5, 221–25; map scene in, 27, 32, 39–40, 203, 205; and myth of Tamerlane, 204–9, 226; triumphs, 211, 212–16
Tamerlane, 204–7, 208–9, 226
Taming of the Shrew, The, 81
Tempest, The, 8, 15, 21, 78–79
Tharsus (Tarsus), 88, 96, 99, 102, 113
Thomas, Nicholas, 195 n. 3
Thucydides, 111, 116
Timon of Athens, 114, 115, 125; Greek elements in, 107, 113, 117–18, 119, 120, 121, 123, 125; pagan elements in, 99
Titus Andronicus, 82 n. 5, 83 n. 10, 107, 119–20, 122, 125, 283 n. 2
Tokson, Elliot H. 16 n. 9
Tomi (place name), 104 n. 12
Townshend, Aurelius, 130
Troilus and Cressida, 30–31, 83 n. 15, 107, 108, 113, 114, 115, 116–17, 118, 120
Troy, 113
Tuan, Yi-Fu, 39
Turberville, George, 159–60, 162
Turner, Robert, 200 n. 26
Turner, Victor, 45 n. 56
Twelfth Night, 21, 27, 29, 44 n. 37, 107, 108, 113, 114, 116, 121

Twine, Laurence, 95, 96–97, 98, 103 n. 3, 105 n. 21
Two Noble Kinsmen, 107, 114, 116, 118, 119, 120, 122
Tyacke, Sarah, 48
Tyre, 88, 96–97, 98, 113

Valois, Marguerite de, 168
Van den Berg, Kent, 254, 258–59 n. 49
Van der Straet, John, 30, 63, 83 n. 15
Vargas Machua, Bernardo de, 207–8
Vaughan, Alden T., 16 n. 2, 42 n. 7
Velz, John, 126 n. 3
Venus and Adonis, 107, 113, 114, 119, 120
Vermeer, Jan, 36–37
Vespucci, Americo, 63, 83 n. 15
Vickers, Nancy, 68–69, 77, 240
Vico, Giambattista, 8
Virgil, 214, 270
Voegolin, Eric, 204

Wales, 14, 247–51, 254, 257 n. 33
Wallerstein, Immanuel, 165–66

Walsingham, Francis, 149 n. 9
Walton, Isaac, 198 n. 13
Walworth, William, 277, 287 n. 49
Weiner, Annette, 195 n. 3, 201 n. 29
Wheeler, John, 180
Whetstone, George, 204, 205, 209, 227 n. 8
White, R. S. 174 n. 32
Wilford, John Noble, 22
Willan, T. S., 198 n. 17, 199 n. 20
Wilson, Richard, 287 n. 55
Winter's Tale, The, 15, 86, 107, 113, 114, 116, 118, 119, 120, 122, 131
Wolff, Larry, 173 n. 8
Wolffhardt, Elisabeth, 107–8
wonder cabinets, 8, 49
Woodbridge, Linda, 83 n. 10, 255 n. 5
Woodward, David, 245, 246
Wright, Edward, 21, 44 n. 37

Yates, Francis, 205
Young, David, 61 n. 14

Zeno, 109
Ziegler, Georgianna, 83 n. 16, 257 n. 26